MW01015601

STEPFAMILY
COURTSHIP

STEPFAMILY

COURTSHIP

How to Make Three *Right* Re/marriage Choices

PETER GERLACH, MSW

COPYRIGHT © 2001 BY PETER GERLACH.

LIBRARY OF CONGRESS NUMBER: 2001117556

ISBN #: HARDCOVER   1-4010-1694-4

SOFTCOVER   1-4010-1695-2

All rights reserved. No part of this book may be reproduced or transmitted in any form or by any means, electronic or mechanical, including photocopying, recording, or by any information storage and retrieval system, without permission in writing from the copyright owner.

This book was printed in the United States of America.

To order additional copies of this book, contact:
Xlibris Corporation
1-888-7-XLIBRIS
www.Xlibris.com
Orders@Xlibris.com
10826

CONTENTS

To our living and future children—specially my sister Gail's daughters, Brandie, Tabatha, and Deanna; and their present and unborn youngsters.

14 Courtship Danger Signs

It's currently estimated that well over half of typical U.S. re/marriers divorce pyschologically or legally, despite one or both partners divorcing before. This suggests that one or both mates chose the wrong *people* (plural) to re/wed, at the wrong *time*, for the wrong *reasons*. The "/" in re/wed and re/marriage notes that it may be a stepparent's first union.

I've spent 20 years working as a therapist with over 600 courting and troubled couples. Over 80% of the partners seemed to be significantly "split," (wounded) psychologically. Less than 5% knew this, and virtually none were aware of being often controlled by a protective, reactive "false self" (p. 139).

One of six common psychological wounds is *reality distortion*, like denial, minimization, exaggeration, projection, emotional numbing, repression, and delusion. These distortions, plus major unawarenesses, unconsciously promote the three wrong re/marriage decisions. If you and/or your partner have any of the inner wounds you'll learn about in Project 1, you probably won't know it. Your wounds and needs may cause you to ignore these 14 danger signs, or minimize them and what they mean to you and any dependent kids.

If you're seriously considering re/marriage involving prior kids, fill out this checklist honestly. Use your findings to decide whether to study and apply the seven protective projects in this book. They can effectively neutralize the 14 dangers below, and help you make three wise re/marriage decisions. Parenthesized items below point to sections in this book. Underlined references like ..**/***.htm point to Internet articles at this nonprofit educational site: http://sfhelp.org. Add the pointer to that base address to access the article, like this: http://sfhelp.org/**/***.htm.

If you fudge your answers here, you're putting yourself and any dependents at risk of great future heartache and loss.

14 Danger Signs

__ 1) **Persistent inner voices (thought streams):** *"Don't re/marry / this person* or *these people / now!"* If you have warning thoughts like these, and/or relationship doubts or worries when you let your mind get quiet, something's *wrong*. If you ignore such thoughts or avoid mental quiet times, I believe you risk future re/marital stress and possible re/divorce. Meditate, and invite your inner voice to tell you specifically why it's warning you. Then *listen*. Try journaling about these warnings, without editing for logic or "common sense." To learn more about your inner voices, read Project 1 in Part 2.

__ 2) **Feeling high urgency or *desperation* to re/marry and/or cohabit**. A related symptom is feeling intensely like "I can't live without you!" Such feelings in you or your partner are a brilliant *red light*. They suggest a false self is controlling one or both of you, and possible co-dependence. (pp. 139 and 413)

__ 3) A related symptom is **seriously discussing re/marriage in less than (roughly) 18 months since you met**, or less than about 18 months since any marital separation. *Stop* and explore, perhaps with qualified professional help, what the urgency is about. It's often excessive (unbalanced) neediness and fear. Read Project 7, and do at least the "right *reasons* to re/marry" worksheet on the Web at ..07/rt-reasons.htm. S-l-o-w d-o-w-n!

__ 4) If you or your partner say or think **"My kids come first, with me,"** STOP all re/marriage plans! In my experience, this is a major indicator of probable re/divorce. The biggest single conscious reason for the re/divorce epidemic in our country is bitter, disillusioned stepparents saying "I got too tired of coming in second (or fifth) with my mate." The flip side is bioparents saying "I got too tired of having to choose, and feeling guilty."

Typical re/married bioparents must choose between their kids and new mate *often*. These loyalty conflicts (p. 186) and related relationship "triangles" are common and divisive in normal multi-home stepfamilies. If you doubt this, *reality-check it with stepfamily* co-parents (bioparents and stepparents) who have been re/married at least five years. (Project 2)

__ **5) Reluctance to use and discuss the Project-7 worksheets** (p. 481). If you or your partner postpone or avoid reading and discussing this book, and/or filling out the right-re/marital-choice worksheets on the Web (..07/links07.htm), something's *wrong*.

__ **6) Ongoing ex-mate hostility, and/or "endless" hassles with them** over divorce settlements, parenting agreements, and/or child visitations, custody, and/or support. If an ex mate is ceaselessly angry, combative, uncooperative, dishonest, or secretive, s/he's probably controlled by a false self (p. 139). Often when one ex mate is psychologically wounded, so is their former partner. In my experience, verbal and legal threats to or by your ex, attempts to confront and reason with them, and/or financial or child-related punishments, usually make such hostile behavior *worse*. *Do not expect that if you or they re/marry, their attitude or indifference will change!* See the Web article at ..Rx/ex/split.htm.

A related courtship danger sign is . . .

__ **7) Ongoing or sporadic *legal action* between divorced ex mates**. If you and/or your partner are or were involved in one or more court suits over finances or co-parenting with an ex mate or a relative, *red light!* People hire lawyers when they can't negotiate successfully, and/or when they want to punish someone. Post-divorce legal battles probably mean that one or both divorced partners . . .

+ Are psychologically wounded and controlled by a protective false self (Project 1); and/or . . .
+ Don't know the seven effective communication skills yet
(Project 2); and/or . . .
+ Haven't *really* grieved and accepted their marriage ending (Project 5); and/or . . .
+ Haven't forgiven themselves or their ex for "what happened" (or didn't) between them. See ..Rx/ex/
forgive.htm.

__ **8) Fantasizing that your current partner, and/or
their kids, ex mate, or kin, will change** seriously unpleasant traits "somehow" after you re/marry. S/He or they probably *won't*, no matter how loving, patient, pious, reasonable, or persuasive you are. If they're not going to change,
do you still want you and any dependent kids to commit
"'Til death us do part"?

Another courtship danger sign:

__ **9) Many recent major life changes or traumas** in the
last three to six months, for you, your partner, and/or one or
more of your minor biokids. Examples: firings or new jobs,
changing homes, schools, or churches; separation and/or divorce; sudden great financial losses or gains; deaths or major
health impairments; pregnancies and births; graduations or
flunk-outs; legal suits or judgments; natural disasters, bankruptcy, home break-ins or muggings; rape or murder; sudden
family or home membership shifts . . .

Such major life-events all cause disorienting *losses* (broken emotional/spiritual bonds) that require time and solitude to
grieve well. When many losses come back-to-back, the combined grief emotions and forced changes can unbalance adults'
and kids' judgments, and skew their needs. If this danger sign
is true now, it's probably *not* a good time to make major long-
range life decisions like stepfamily re/marriage commitments!
Invest in your future by taking many months to sort everything
out, do some healthy grieving (Project 5), and rebalance your
lives first! *Take a long-range view!*

Another major courtship alert is . . .

__ **10) Suspected or sure active addiction/s to substances** (including sugar, fats, carbohydrates, nicotine, caffeine, and prescription or street drugs), **activities** (including overwork, gambling, and social causes), **moods** (like rage or excitement) **and/or relationships** (co-dependence.) If you or your partner suspects that either of you, any ex mate, key relatives, and/or any minor or grown child are now addicted: *orange light.*

Past or present addictions indicate psychological wounds and false-self dominance. Solid 12-step recovery from addiction is the gateway to *full* recovery from these wounds (Project 1). 12-step wisdom suggests avoiding any major life decision like cohabiting or re/marriage until achieving at least one year of sobriety. Longer is safer. Assessing this danger sign requires that you to understand what a true addiction is. Do you? See p. 496.

__ **11) Chronically ill or acting-out biokids.** Do you and/ or your alluring partner have a minor or grown child who has recurring . . .

_ Serious academic and/or social problems, including few or no friends, or preferring toxic (troubled) friends;

_ Trouble with truancy, gangs, cults, or the law;

_ Non-experimental drug use, or clear chemical dependence, including food;

_ Talk of or actual running away from home;

_ Excessive stealing, defiance, lying, or secrecy;

_ Excessively-emotional outbursts and/or mood swings;

_ Suspected or clinically-diagnosed ADD or AD/HD syndrome (attention-deficit / hyperactivity disorder);

_ talk about or gestures toward suicide or self-mutilation; and/or . . .

_ depression, or sleep, digestive, or eating problems like anorexia, bulimia, and obesity?

In kids and adults, these are symptoms of _ significant psychological wounding and _ a prior and/or present low-nurturance family (p. 48). Any chronic or periodic symptoms like these are re/marital *red lights.* Don't commit to form or join a stepfamily until you find the real causes for these symptoms, and the caregivers and kids make clear progress towards healing them. Re/marriage or cohabiting are *not* the medicines of choice!

__ **12)** If you and/or your courtship partner have **a history of "failed" or no intimate relationships**, *red light.* These symptoms suggest serious false-self dominance and related shame, fear, trust, and bonding disorders. The best response to these is education and personal recovery (Project 1), not stepfamily re/marriage!

__ **13) Keeping major personal or family secrets.** If you, your partner, or any of your prospective co-parenting partners (ex mates and their partners) regularly distort or withhold key truths, rethink any current re/wedding plans. In my experience, such behavior is a sure symptom of major personality-fragmenting and a legacy of hidden excessive shame, fear, and reality distortions. See Project 1 (p. 137).

A final courtship alert is . . .

__ **14) Repeated avoidances.** If you or your partner *consistently* avoids _ honest, intimate discussions of, and/or _ conflicts on, any of the issues in this chapter and book, or _ you deny your avoidances, *red re/marital light!* Avoiders and people who always want to "have *fun!*" or "focus on the bright side" fear or distrust something. They're unconsciously putting their suspicions and anxieties in charge of your relationship's growth. Here are some classic avoidances to watch for. See the referenced Web articles for more perspective and suggestions.

+ "We are not now, or *will not* be, a stepfamily." If you or your courtship partner have a living child from a prior relationship, yes you are. See Project 3 (p. 199).

+ "Stepparenting is basically no different than bioparenting." The intents to nurture, guide and protect are the same, but _ minor stepkids have *many* extra needs they need help with (p. 454), and _ the caregiving *environment* is different in ~40 ways: ..10/co-p-dfrnces.htm.

+ "We should handle our own problems," vs. using qualified outside help. Typical stepfamily problems require
special knowledge and skill to resolve. You'll probably
need an *informed* coach or guide to help you acquire
these. See ..11/counsel.htm.

+ "A family's just a family. Stepfamilies aren't all that different. I / we do *not* need to study what's normal and
real in a stepfamily now." Read Part 1, the comparison
on p. 423, and these Web articles: http://sfhelp.org/04/
myths.htm, and ..09/develop1.htm. Then see what you
think.

+ "We've all lived together (or dated) for ___ months without big problems, so *we're* not likely to re/divorce!"
Estimate: well over 50% of American couples *just like
you* don't make it. Would you board a plane with those
odds of it crashing? See p. 69.

+ "There's no point in doing this 'psychological-wound
evaluation' (Project 1). It's just psychobabble from some
shrink, and sure doesn't apply to us. We're not crazy,
and the past is over and done with." *Double red light!*

+ "Our (co-parenting) ex-mates are absolutely not, and never
will be, part of our new family!" This is a serious reality distortion (denial). see Projects 3 and 5 in Part 2.

+ "I / we don't need to read or discuss all this stepfamily
stuff. Our life experience as grown adults, spouses and
veteran parents is enough!" Then why do over half of
U.S. couples *just like you* ultimately re/divorce?

+ "I'll *never* have to choose my kids over my partner, after
re/marriage. You *all* come first with me!" This is a classic, toxic delusion. See p. 186 and ..09/triangles.htm.

+ + +

After 23 years' research, I believe the signs above are reliable predictors of major stepfamily re/marital stress and probable re/divorce. *The more of these factors that exist in your courtship situation, the higher your odds of future stepfamily heartache, frustration, and loss.*

Needy, scared, and/or shamed false selves will usually minimize, rationalize, or ignore courtship warning signs like these. Your minor kids depend on you to heed them! **If you have several or many of these symptoms,** I urge you to take *months* to study the five hazards and seven courtship projects outlined in this book *before* committing you and any dependent kids to a risky stepfamily re/marriage. If you partners and your ex mates seem to have few or none of these symptoms, that's a cautious green light to keep doing your pre-stepfamily research together!

Acknowledgements

This book's existence and content have been indelibly shaped
by . . .

+ My parents. They would never have dreamed that our 20
years of living together would have led to this series of books.

+ My mother's father, Frank McNair. Without his dedication to our family's financial security, I couldn't have taken this
journey. He was a stepfather and step-grandfather, and the son
of an alcoholic family as I am.

+ My former wife Liliana and her daughters Jenny and
Julie. We innocently tried to make our idealistic step-dream
come true, and taught each other our delusions along our fine
and foul years together. I look back with regret and compassion at how much Lana and I didn't know.

+ My stepmother Connie and my stepsisters Candy, Kate,
Chris, and Karen. They showed me the warmth and potential
that stepfamilies can create. So did Susan Kerwin and her be-
guiling daughter Jessica.

+ Many, many teachers and colleagues, including Drs. John
and Emily Visher; Dr. Esther Wald; Dr. Cliff Sager; Dr. Richard
Schwartz; Annette Hulefeld; Cathleen Rich; Claudia Black;
Rokelle Lerner; Robert Subby; Robert Ackerman; Charles
Whitfield; Janet Woititz; Sharon Wegshieder-Cruse; David
Wright; Dr. Milton Erickson; Dorothy and Bob Bolton, Drs.
Hal and Sidra Stone, Virginia Satir . . . These names represent

the scores of authors, presenters, and instructors I have learned from for decades about families, relationships, parenting, communication skills, addiction and trauma recovery, and human development.

+ Special thanks go to John and Sally Radka; Jeanette and Steve Bell; Shirley and Ralph Hutson; Lou and Bill Scanlon; Sr. Bettye Lechner; Sr. Cathy Trainer; Paulette Moha; Don and Lorrie Gramer; Jeanne and Joe McLennan; Joanne Webber; David Cohen and Jackie Needleman; and Dr. Robert Keim. Jeff W., Jane R., Ronnee C., and Danna and Sam E. gave me a family during my early recovery years.

I'm profoundly grateful to the many hundreds of stepfamily co-parents and kids with whom I've consulted in classrooms, over the phone and Internet, and in my office since 1981. These wonderfully normal, special, often troubled people taught me about the intricate kaleidoscope of daily stepfamily challenges, heartaches, and delights.

I'm thankful for the encouragement, wisdom, and spirit of authoress and stepmom Gloria Lintermans. She helped me draft the first version of what has developed into a series of books, and introduced me to the publishing world.

Over all, I'm grateful for the One who nurtures us all, and for my Self and inner family..

Part 1) Foundations

1) Introduction

2) Get the most from this book

3) What's a *high nurturance* family?

4) Why most U.S. re/marriages fail

5) A pre-re/marriage quiz

6) Stepfamily realities

7) One stepfamily's story

8) 12 long-term co-parent projects

1) Introduction

Should You Read This Book?

This chapter hilights:
+ A stepfamily perspective,
+ Why this stepfamily-courtship book exists,
+ Who should read it,
+ What's in it, and...
+ What's unique about it.

Perspective

Stepfamilies have existed as long as humans have lived in communal groups. They're characterized by adults co-nurturing kids from their mate's prior unions. Unlike most modern foster and adoptive parents, active *step*parents are emotionally, financially, and legally connected to a stepchild's divorced or widowed mother, father, and kin for decades.

A century ago about 90% of America's stepfamilies followed the death of a child's mother or father. Since World War II and the medical and sexual "revolutions," about 90% of U.S. stepfamilies now follow the *divorce* of a child's bioparents. If both bioparents eventually remarry, their minor biological kids may have four co-parenting adults in two homes telling them how to eat, talk, dress, act, brush their teeth, and do their homework. One implication of this swift change is that our warp-speed culture hasn't had time to form and integrate behavioral and role norms for people in post-divorce stepfamilies.

From one view, average stepfamilies are just like traditional intact biofamilies (p. 424). They are adult couples and one or more minor kids doing "family things" together. Stepfamily and biofamily co-parents all pay bills, go to work and school, and have holidays, cavities, vacations, pets, dreams, friends, colds, problems, and triumphs. In structure and dynamics, however, typical two or three-home nuclear stepfamilies differ from intact one-home biofamilies in over *70* ways (p. 425)! These combined differences cause most step-homes and relationships to act and *feel* as different from a "normal" biofamily as a poodle differs from a giraffe. Both are four-legged mammals, but they have *really* different lifestyles!

Because of these unexpected differences and four other hazards, typical newly-re/wedded mates soon feel startled and uncertain about what they've bought into. (The "/" notes that it may be a stepparent's first union.) Rosy romantic visions fade or shatter, as stepfamily realities like those in Chapter 6 implacably emerge. Partners' original shared expectations about stepfamily relationships and life often prove unrealistic. Resident and visiting stepkids face several dozen alien adjustment needs (p. 454), many of which their co-parents aren't aware of or can't empathize with. Relatives, unaware of stepfamily differences and realities, are often critical or unempathic. They automatically use inappropriate *bio*family "shoulds" and "musts."

From a welter of unexpected alien stressors, the romantic dreams of re/marrying couples often turn into mounting confusion, frustration, hurt, resentment, and anxieties. When these couples seek effective local and media help, they're often frustrated to discover that there is little or none. You'll glimpse the common results of this when we meet the McLean–Tilmon–Cohen stepfamily in Chapter 7.

Partners' psychological wounds and unawarenesses, stepfamily stresses, and social ignorances combine to wreck well over half of typical U.S. stepfamily re/marriages. Previously-divorced, middle-aged bioparents and their minor or grown kids experience the losses, agony, shame, and financial and social convulsions of family breakup and divorce *again*. The millions of hurting, bewildered, disillusioned survivors of stepfamily breakups form an invisible subculture in every state. The personal and social impacts of our unremarked American stepfamily re/divorce pandemic are tragic, incalculable, *and preventable*.

After researching full time since 1979 and living in two stepfamilies as a stepson, stepgrandson, stepbrother, and stepfather, I believe this scourge exists because of . . .

Five Re/marriage Hazards

They are . . .

1) Co-parents' mixes of psychological wounds from low-nurturance childhoods. Unseen and unhealed, these wounds pass unintentionally down the generations. The main wound, significant false-self dominance, seems to be our cultural "elephant in the living room." Few adults and no kids are aware of it, so far.

2) Blocked grief in adults and kids, over two or three major sets of losses (broken emotional-spiritual bonds). Frozen mourning is fostered by psychological wounding, personal and social inhibitions, and inherited ignorance. It inhibits forming high-nurturance stepfamily bonds, and promotes significant psychological, physical, and family-relationship problems.

3) Widespread unawareness of _ key communication, grieving, relationship, and co-parenting skills; and _ stepfamily norms, adjustment tasks, uniquenesses, and realities. You can gauge your knowledge of these in Chapters 5 and 6.

4) Neediness and romantic-love idealism, which inevitably distort fiancés' judgments. Happily, there seems to be no cure for this. The last hazard is . . .

5) Little practical, *informed* help available for stepfamily adults and kids in the media and in most civil and church communities. "Informed" means what you'll read in this series of books.

Chapter 4 provides more detail on each of these toxic hazards. Part 2 of this book outlines seven ways courting couples can protect themselves and their kids from them. Married couples, grandparents, and single men and women can benefit greatly from the first six of these projects.

Why This Book Exists

Roughly one sixth of Americans belong to a stepfamily. The Stepfamily Association of America estimates that 60% of U.S. stepfamily re/marriages fail legally. Millions of other adults and kids exist in *psychologically* divorced homes, because separation and/or legal re/divorce aren't practical. This suggests the urgent need for clear pre-re/marriage guidance. Since 1979, I've sought to understand *why* so many well-meaning partners can't make it. In that time, I've found no other book or resource that offers practical advice to courting co-parents on how to understand the five hazards (above) and their implications, and then soberly evaluate whether to form a high-risk stepfamily.

This book is the third in a planned series. I'm writing the series to help *prevent* the re/divorce trauma which is a silent scourge affecting millions of American adults and kids. I haven't studied re/marriage in other nations, and I suspect the hazards are the same. This book aims to empower courting co-parents to choose the right *persons* (plural) to re/wed, for the right *reasons*, at the right *time*.

My larger goal is to raise public awareness of what I see is a cultural menace far greater than AIDS: the toxic personal and social impacts of low-nurturance parenting. These impacts spring from two to six emotional-spiritual wounds resulting from the instinctual urge to *survive* (vs. thrive) in a toxic family environment. After 15 years' clinical study and experience with these wounds (and recovery from them), I strongly suspect they are key contributors to most of our major social problems. So far, few people know about the common development and harmful dominance of a protective "false self" (p. 139).

Should You Read This Book?

Yes, if you are any of these . . .

+ A custodial or noncustodial dad or mom considering separation or divorce, or adjusting to it. If it's your first, the odds are about 75% that you'll re/marry within seven years after legal divorce, forming a stepfamily.
+ A widowed parent who may re/marry.
+ A childless adult who wants to court or marry a bioparent with living minor or grown kids.
+ A concerned friend or relative of such women and men, specially a grandparent or sibling.

And you can benefit from this book if you're . . .

+ A human-service professional who wants to support troubled, divorced or widowed, and re/marrying couples and their kids. This includes clergy, counselors, therapists, educators, doctors, divorce mediators, case workers, and family-law legislators, attorneys, enforcement professionals, and judges. This book is also for the professionals who teach, fund, supervise, certify, and evaluate family-service providers. Most human-service professionals have no *informed* training in what you'll read here and in the related Web articles.

If you see yourself above, **you probably don't know what you don't know** about the five re/marriage hazards (Chapter 4) and some key relationship skills (Chapter 5). Longing for elusive happiness, comfort, love, security, and companionship, most re/marrying co-parents don't really *want* to believe these five hazards apply to them. The eventual cost of not knowing and believing is very high: expensive middle-aged re/divorce, shattered dreams, and seriously troubled kids.

If you're in a stepfamily now, or in a troubled first marriage, the ideas in this book may save your relationship. The first six of the seven projects outlined here are vital for your and your kids' long-term personal and family welfare.

What's In This Book?

Part 1 provides . . .
+ Suggestions on getting the most from this guidebook and the related resources (Chapter 2).
+ 28 Traits of a high-nurturance family, and what happens to adults who didn't get enough of them as kids (Chapter 3).
+ An outline of five factors that destroy well over half of American re/marriages (Chapter 4). I believe three of them cause most first-divorces and many other social problems.
+ A self-assessment quiz on life skills and knowledge that successful co-parents need (Chapter 5).
+ An overview of stepfamily realities, based on 23 years' research (Chapter 6).
+ A true vignette of a typical three-home nuclear stepfamily (Chapter 7). And . . .
+ A summary of 12 co-parent projects that I believe can help typical couples beat the gloomy re/divorce odds (Chapter 8).

Part 2 provides a chapter on each of the first seven of these projects. Courting co-parents can use them to evaluate whether they should re/marry or not. The last chapter in Part 2 sums everything up, and suggests next steps.

Part 3 offers nine supportive resources:
+ A checklist of behavioral traits of people with significant false-self dominance.
+ A checklist of traits common to people burdened by *co-dependence*: a form of relationship addiction that probably results from inner wounds and ignorance.
+ 72 structural and dynamic ways that typical stepfamilies differ from intact biofamilies.
+ A worksheet to help identify co-parents' recent priorities. This helps resolve stressful loyalty conflicts.
+ A summary of over *50* concurrent developmental and special adjustment needs that typical stepkids must fill.
+ A summary of key criteria defining the right *people* and

the right *reasons* to re/marry and form or join a stepfamily, and the right *time* to do so.

+ A glossary of useful stepfamily and relationship words and terms, from a false-self perspective.

+ Selected resources: Web links, recommended readings, newsletters, organizations, and games. And . . .

+ A thorough index.

What's Different about This Stepfamily Book?

Five things:
+ The intended audience (*not* just stepparents);
+ My life experience, training, and writing style;
+ The five remarital hazards and 12 projects;
+ The four-part theory underlying these; and . . .
+ An extensive non-profit Web site that backs up this series of books with hundreds of detailed articles and worksheets, and provides links to other resources.

In my research since 1979, I've read over 350 lay and professional books and articles about divorced families and stepfamilies. In preparing to write this, I scanned over 35 stepfamily books in print last year (2000). Most lay books for stepfamily adults are autobiographic, anecdotal, and superficial. Many of these are written by impassioned stepparents for other stepparents (usually stepmoms), excluding their bioparent-mates. While interesting and validating, *none* of these writings acknowledge the five hazards you'll read about here or offer protections against them. Only *Stepfamily Realities*, by Australian clinician Margaret Newman, explores the *inner* world of typical co-parents in any depth.

The guidelines that these well-meaning authors offer are largely focused on surface problems, not the underlying ones. For instance, most books counsel readers to "communicate openly and honestly," and "have realistic expectations." The authors don't describe what effective communication *is*, and why most co-parents can't do it. Virtually none of these books propose more than a handful of realistic stepfamily expectations. This book points to over 60. Not one of the books I've read explores stepfamily *grieving* in any depth, what to do if an adult or child is blocked in their mourning, or why acting on this is essential (Project 5).

This book is unique in major ways:

It is written specifically to adults considering re/marriage involving existing kids and ex mates, and the people who support them. It is *not* written just for stepparents.

My Unique Background

The content and design of this series of books comes from a wide range of learning and experience over 63 years . . .

A Stanford University bachelor's degree in Mechanical Engineering (BSME). That led to 17 years' work for GT&E and IBM in a range of engineering, marketing, teaching, and management roles. Followed by . . .

23 years' research on clinical and lay stepfamily literature, including a 180-page master's-degree thesis that took two years to compose. Stepfamily experts Lawrence Ganong and Marilyn Coleman judged it to be a Ph.D.-level effort. During these years, I've had . . .

Over 17,000 hours of clinical consultations with ~1,000 typical Midwestern divorced and stepfamily adults, and some of their kids; and **over 3,000 "warm-line" phone calls** to the nonprofit Stepfamily Association of Illinois since 1981. I've also spent . . .

20 months moderating the "Stepfamily Issues" forum at http://www.divorcenet.com; and . . .

I've given over 100 lay and clinical seminars on stepfamily-related issues, including classes at Governor's State and Northern Illinois Universities.

Seven years on the board of a large public community mental health center, including a term as President, taught me much. So did my years of personal experience as a **stepson, stepgrandson, stepbrother, and stepfather** of two minor girls. And . . .

I have been in personal recovery from growing up in a very low-nurturance (alcoholic) family since 1985. I have worked clinically with scores of adults doing similar personal-healing work. The insights and empathy gained from these 16 years, and from studying many clinicians who have gone before me, shape these pages. I know what stepfamily divorce feels like, too.

Unique Topics

This is the only book for courting and re/married co-parents which (1) proposes the **five interactive hazards** above as the reason that most American couples make three wrong re/marital decisions for themselves and their kids, despite life experience, love, desire, and "common sense;" and then (2) outlines **seven specific evaluation projects** that suitors can use to decide whether to remarry or not, in the face of these five hazards. The next volume, *Build a High-nurturance Stepfamily* (Xlibris.com), proposes five more vital projects, if you decide to re/marry.

Unique Web Resources

This series of books is augmented by **over 600 educational Web pages** at http://sfhelp.org. These articles, worksheets, and links to other resources provide a wealth of specific background and tools for courting and re/married co-parents. They're based on my professional study and clinical experience since 1979. These Web pages include over 80 articles proposing specific solutions to common stepfamily relationship problems (http://sfhelp.org/Rx/dx.htm). You'll find many pointers to these free Web articles throughout this book.

Unique Foundations

The ideas in this series of books and Web pages integrate **four related fields of knowledge.** I believe no co-parents and few or no family professionals have ever studied and combined these four in a divorce and stepfamily context:

An integrated model of wholistic personal, relationship, and family health. This includes a theory on how low psycho-spiritual nurturance promotes *false-self development* in kids. I believe this is probably the least understood, most potent cause of American divorce and other social ills. Project 1 (p. 137) proposes how to assess for psychological wounds, and offers options on how to reduce them and their impacts. The companion book "Who's *Really* Running Your Life?" (Xlibris.com, 2000), provides more detail and resources.

Proven family-systems and family therapy ideas, which have matured since their cultural introduction two generations ago. This is the first stepfamily book written by an engineer-therapist (BSME-MSW) to apply these ideas concurrently to our *inner* family of personality subselves, and our outer (step)family systems. Inner and outer family-system concepts allow understanding and resolving complex stepfamily relationship problems. I write this after 11 years' experience doing *inner* family therapy with hundreds of average clients. No other published lay or clinical stepfamily author has this knowledge and perspective so far.

Project 2 (p. 167) invites courting couples to evaluate their abilities to problem-solve effectively using **seven learnable communication skills.** They're described and illustrated in *"Satisfactions—*7 Relationship Skills You Need to Know" (Xlibris.com 2001), and at http://sfhelp.org/02/links02.htm. I write about these skills after 30 years' experience studying, practicing, and teaching them professionally. And . . .

Project 5 (p. 248) invites co-parents to learn healthy grieving basics, and then evaluate themselves and prospective stepfamily members for blocked grief. This project is based on **a three-level model of healthy and blocked grief.** My experience is that such blockage in adults and kids is a major unseen contributor to personal, relationship, and family distress. I've never found another stepfamily or parenting book that examines this in any detail, or suggests specific options to help co-parents _ assess for it and _ unblock it.

Bottom line: this stepfamily book is practical and unique in many ways. It defines five major hazards co-parent partners face, offers seven solutions and many resources, and aims to empower you to make *informed* re/marriage decisions for yourself and any dependent kids. **The book and series focuses on discovery, recovery, and *prevention* of further family trauma.**

The length of this guidebook suggests how much information you'll find here. My goal has been to make this series a coherent progression of realistic, practical ideas. The book is modular, so you can refer to sections of the book as your saga unfolds. One price of modularity is some repetition of key ideas. If you *do* re/marry, the first six projects in Part 2 usually continue for some years.

The next chapter suggests ways you can harvest maximum long-term benefits from these pages.

2) Get the Most From This Book

This guidebook offers a *lot* to learn, tailor, and integrate! Whether you're a co-parent or a stepfamily supporter, reading this and the related Internet materials will probably challenge your patience, your commitment, and some cherished beliefs. Your motivation to make wise *long term* re/marriage and stepfamily choices will determine what you get from the ideas here. This chapter suggests how you can accumulate the most benefit from investing your time in reading this. Reminder: the "/" in "re/marriage" notes that it may be a stepparent's first union.

Prepare

First, read or scan the two prior volumes in this series: "Who's *Really* Running Your Life?", and "*Satisfactions*—7 Relationship Skills You Need to Know." These will help you learn whether a false self dominates you or your partner, and how to problem-solve effectively together. These are the "text books" for the first two of the seven essential courtship projects summarized in Part 2.

Access the Internet: You'll find many references in this book (..***/***.htm) to articles and worksheets in an extensive non-profit educational Web site. Append the references to http://sfhelp.org/ to get the full address like the one below.

To get the most from the books in this series, you'll need to access this site. If you don't have Internet access yet, your public library or a friend may be able to help you go online. Once there, you can download or print any of several hundred stepfamily articles at no cost. One part of the site lists Web and offline stepfamily resources: http://sfhelp.org/11/resources.htm. This is updated periodically, and connects you with a wide range of other sources of information and support. This includes stepfamily discussion forums.

Third, **if you have a partner**, I suggest that you **read this book with them**, ideally out loud. Take your time. If either of you find that emotions and/or questions arise, stop and discuss honestly what's going on. If either of you is psychologically wounded (hazard 1 and Project 1) your protective false selves may try to persuade you against this.

As you evaluate who, why, and when to re/marry, **help each other keep a long-range view**. It's inviting to just focus on your courtship, a commitment ceremony, kids' immediate needs, and/or a place to live. *Good courtship times and cohabiting are* not *reliable guides to re/wedded stepfamily life!*

Because one or both of you have a living child, _ **accept that you all are in a pre-legal** *step***family**. Then accept _ that your stepfamily is *far* more complex and alien than you partners may think; and _ that your (step)kids' "other parents" are and will be full members of your multi-home stepfamily, as long as your kid/s live. So will any new partners and stepkids of theirs. Then _ accept that without shared effort at the 12 projects summarized in Chapter 8, your odds of re/divorce are well over 50%. Would you board a plane knowing the odds of it crashing were that high? Your safety odds go up as you do the projects in this book together. Finally . . .

Build your motivation to *learn* **together** as co-parenting teammates vs. competitors or individuals. Many re/divorced co-parents I've met have said, "If I'd only known what it was going to be like!" Troubled co-parents add ". . . I wouldn't have re/married."

Here's perspective on some of these suggestions . . .

Read the Prior Two Volumes First

Because you're reading this, the odds are high that you, any courtship partner, and any ex mate/s, are psychologically wounded (not crazy). If so, you won't know it, because wounded feels *normal*. Your wounds and unawarenesses will probably block you from getting the most from this series of books. **The first volume**, "Who's *Really* Running Your Life?— Free Your Self from Custody, and Guard Your Kids," will help you decide whether you and any other key adults are controlled by a false self. If you are, the book offers a framework for how to recover from your wounds, and help your kids with any they may have. That's the "textbook" for Project 1 in this book. See the gist of it in the ~45 Web-page articles and worksheets at ..01/links01.htm.

The second book is "*Satisfactions*—7 Relationship Skills You Need to Know." It distills my 30 years' learnings about communicating and relating effectively with others. If you can't name and describe the seven mental/verbal communication skills, you, your partner, and ex mates probably aren't using them yet. Project 2 in this book will introduce them.

Together, these seven skills will empower you co-parents to effectively problem-solve the *many* concurrent conflicts you'll encounter if you choose to re/marry. Therapy offices and family-law dockets are full of couples who don't know how to communicate well, or who can't because of *inner*-family chaos. Helping each other develop these skills will make the other six re/marriage-evaluation projects in this book much easier for you partners. If you don't have *Satisfactions* yet, learn about these seven mental/verbal skills on p. 167 and on the Web at ..02/links02.htm.

Reality: if protective false selves (p. 139) control you and/ or your beloved, the seven skills can only be of limited help. Incidentally, these skills work just as well among your subselves as with other people! More about that in Project 1.

Read This Book Out Loud with Your Partner

If you do, I suspect you'll each have different emotional reactions to the many ideas and suggestions here. Experiencing each other's reactions will invite discussions, and increase your mutual awarenesses and learnings. If either of you feels resistant to reading this together, parts of your personality probably want to avoid facing some scary reality, like "We may discover that we shouldn't be together," or "To be with you, I'll have to face something really uncomfortable."

Take many weeks or months to read this book and the related materials together. Most of the seven projects here include self-discovery worksheets you can use to deepen your personal and shared awarenesses. "Getting through" this book is *not* the objective. Understanding and applying its ideas to your unique personal situation, and making three right re/marriage decisions for you and any kids is your true payoff.

Help Each Other Keep a Long-range View

You partners are evaluating an exceptionally complex, expensive, far-reaching life decision: stepfamily re/marriage and co-parenting. If you re/wed and ignore the 12 protective projects in Chapter 8, the odds are that you'll eventually re/divorce in middle age. Your desires, excitement, idealisms, and the complexity and high stakes here, can make impulsive decisions appealing ("C'mon, it'll all work out. Let's do it!"). This is specially true if one or both of you partners are feeling very lonely, lusty, overwhelmed, weary, and/or scared. Focusing short range is also appealing if you're feeling pressured to re/marry by needy kids, kin, or others.

Veteran co-parents and stepfamily researchers generally agree that it takes four to 12 years *after* re/wedding for a new multi-home stepfamily to merge and stabilize. Each time an ex mate re/marries, moves, has a baby, or a child moves in with their other parent, you all will have to re-do many of the *30+* adjustment tasks on p. 435. As you would if you were building a house by hand together, *take your time*. Patiently take small steps in your complex re/marriage-evaluation process. Some of your personality subselves will probably lobby against that.

Notice your self-talk (thought streams and images) now . . .

Accept Your *Step*family Identity and What It Means

Bookmark this page, and go to p. 423. Read how typical stepfamilies like yours differ from intact biofamilies in over *70* structural and dynamic ways. Then scan the stepfamily-reality summary on p. 91 and return here. Because of all these factors together, you and your partner are at *high* risk of having unrealistic stepfamily expectations (..04/myths.htm) despite your maturity and life experience. This is true even if you were raised in a stepfamily. If either of you minimizes or rejects that you're considering forming or joining a *step*family (vs. "just a family"), *yellow light.*

Also: even if your children are grown, **their other bioparents, stepparents, stepsiblings, and step-kin are full psychological, legal, and financial members of your stepfamily**. The needs, feelings, and life circumstances of all these people (e.g. money and wholistic health) will affect your lives for many years. Ignoring these people sharply increases your chance of making up to three costly *wrong* re/marriage decisions.

"Our nuclear (step)family" includes all the people living in your kids' two or more co-parenting homes. If either of you partners resists this reality, *yellow light!* Chapter 6 and Projects 3 and 4 in Part 2 will help you lovebirds and your ex mates and kin learn more about what your stepfamily identity means. One meaning is . . .

Typical stepkids must fill up to three sets of adjustment needs (p. 454), *on top of* their several dozen normal maturation needs. Kids and co-parents in intact biofamilies don't face most of these adjustment needs. These many extra concurrent tasks, and there being three or more caregivers, makes stepfamily co-parenting *much* more complex than in intact biofamilies. Courtship Project 6 invites you partners to learn about this as you evaluate whether to re/wed. If you do re/tie the knot, continue this with Project 10: build a co-parenting team.

Build Your Motivation to Learn

Evaluating whether to re/marry will require you partners to learn new things, and to change some cherished beliefs. A normal illusion is "We're mature, seasoned adults and caregivers. Our experience, wisdom, love, and determination are all we need to evaluate re/marriage." Re/divorce statistics imply that assumption is *wrong* for most stepfamily suitors like you.

You each need some new knowledge, just as you would if you were planning a globe-spanning sailboat trip. To strengthen your motivation to learn, experience these **two guided images**. Options: tape record this, or have someone read it slowly to you. Relax in an undistracted place, and close your eyes. Breathe comfortably. Put current thoughts and concerns aside for now. Vividly imagine all your dependent and grown biokids and stepkids meeting together in a comfortable, safe place. See them enter one at a time. Now invite all your kids' living relatives to appear one at a time. Take your time . . .

Now imagine a set of unborn grandchildren and great grandchildren. These are the expanding fan of future people whose lives will be greatly affected by the stepfamily decisions you partners make in the coming months.

Now imagine you, your mate, and each of your kids' other parents joining the assembly. Include any who are dead, distant, or "uninvolved." All of you co-parents stand or sit together in front of the others. Finally, expand your inner image to include the generations of your ancestors that have passed on key beliefs, identity, genes, and some enduring rituals, values, wounds, and life scripts. Start with your parents' grandparents. Assemble them behind you, sitting or standing. Imagine introducing them to the throng one at a time.

Focus on this large group of related people before and behind you. See them all looking steadily at you co-parenting partners. Experience all the future kids and adults saying together from their hearts, "We're depending on each of you co-parents and all of you as a team, to guide and protect us!" Slowly look at the faces of each of your present and future kids. Now turn and look into the eyes of each of your related co-parents. Respectfully acknowledge your chosen responsibilities to your Selves, to each other, and to the whole group of born and unborn people before you. Say anything you wish to anyone or everyone in the group, including your ancestors. When you're ready, thank all of these people and serenely let them go. Notice how you *feel*. Take care of any needs you have, and . . .

Let the scene shift. Imagine you and your partner as very old people, sitting together peacefully in a comfortable place. You're reviewing your lives and what you have accomplished personally and together. Vividly imagine the words you'd like to think, speak, and hear. Take your time. Use these as guides:

"I'm so proud and thankful that I (we) . . ."

"I deeply regret that I (we) . . ."

"I wish . . ."

"I hope . . ."

Now imagine your grown children and their kids joining you, and describing what you two and their other co-parents gave them all, in detail. Again, imagine vividly what you and your partner would most want to hear and see. Tell or ask them anything you wish to. Hold this vision until it feels done. Then take a comfortable breath or two, and return to focused awareness in the present. If it's helpful, write down any feelings, thoughts, or insights you experienced.

If your re/marriage-evaluation patience wears thin, get quiet and undistracted, and refocus on your version of this imagery. Notice your feelings, thoughts, and priorities without judgment. Listen to your quiet inner voice. Read this guided image or your own out loud to each other periodically, to recharge your shared commitment to *learning* together, along the way.

It's hard for people who haven't *experienced* building a

dynamic multi-home, multi-generational stepfamily over many years to really understand the size and complexity of this overall learning project. To appreciate what I'm trying to guide you toward . . .

Imagine that you and your partner have been given a large plot of hillside land studded with trees and rocks. See yourselves standing together on this plot with your minor or grown kids and their other co-parents. Your shared wish is to design and build two or three functional, safe, attractive homes for you all to live in, *by hand*. You have a half-formed dream, paper and pencils, a calculator, and basic tools. Your only prior experience is building a garden shed or a kid's playhouse. You have no local architects, consultants, or contractors to help you. Your parents and other relatives have built garages (i.e. biofamilies) by hand, but never a full, multi-level home. They're willing to help, but are as new to this complex, shared dream as you are.

Review the specific steps you co-parents would have to take together to fulfill this vision over many years:

+ For each of your two or more homes, evolve and agree on a blueprint and specifications.
+ Decide on a budget and a financial plan, and agree on who will manage it.
+ Clarify and negotiate short and long-term responsibilities.
+ Evolve an effective way of handling unexpected situations together.
+ Acquire tools, clear and grade the land, and design and pour strong foundations.
+ Put up walls, add roofs, and then install plumbing, electricity, gas, climate controls, insulation, locks, and windows.
+ Do some of you want fireplaces? A sauna or hot tub? A workshop or studio? Skylights? Porches or decks? Balconies?
+ Agree on the décors, and help each other install them.
+ Spend time evaluating and picking the furnishings.

+ Plan and create the landscaping, including gardens, foun-
tains, trees, and other features. Finally . . .

Imagine the rich satisfaction of sitting in your living room
or on your deck, relaxing and basking in the glow of what
you've all built together by hand, and all the obstacles you've
overcome.

To decide wisely if you want to commit to this long, complex multi-stage stepfamily-merger process, you partners will
each have to learn some new skills and ideas via the seven
projects. Your co-parents will have to learn to learn, work, and
problem-solve as an effective team together. Who will lead you?

This book offers a framework to help you understand what
to expect if you mates decide to commit to this building project
with your kids, ex mates, and other relatives. It's a *big*, complicated, long-term project with potentially priceless payoffs!

Notice how you feel now and where your thoughts go, without judgment. Are you motivated to learn? Read this out loud,
and notice your reactions:

*"I clearly understand that to make three right long-term
choices about re/marriage, I'll have to learn things about me
as a person, and about grieving, communicating, and raising
kids. I'm ready to revise some things I already know and believe, and I accept that my past family and relationship experience is* not *an adequate or reliable guide for my deciding if I
should re/marry."*

Reality check: If you think this focus on courtship learn-
ing is overblown, see if you know any co-parents who have
been re/married over five years. They may be re/divorced or
not. If so, ask each one whether they think that learning about
stepfamilies before deciding to re/marry is useful. Ask if they'll
describe what they didn't know before making their nuptial
vows.

So **to get the most from this book** . . .

+ Read it with your partner, ideally out loud. Take months
to process what you'll discover.

+ Accept your identity as a pre-legal *step*family. Accept
that it differs from intact biofamilies in up to *70* ways,

while appearing similar (p. 424). These differences can combine to breed toxic, unrealistic expectations. To avoid that and make three *informed* re/marriage decisions . . .

+ As you read and discuss, help each other keep a long-range (e.g. next 10 years), wide-angle view. Include the needs and adjustment tasks of related co-parents and stepkids, vs. just focusing on your courtship.

+ Raise and keep your interest in learning new information and relationship skills until (and after) you make your re/marriage decisions. Help each other keep "the (open, curious) mind of a student." Stepfamily research and experience guarantees you partners ongoing "personal growth"!

Another factor that will affect how useful you find this book is how you feel about . . .

Your (Complex!) Re/marriage Decision

If you're divorced or widowed, recall how you decided to wed. If you're unmarried, you have impressions of how people decide to say, "I do" or "I don't." The decision to re/marry and form or expand a stepfamily is *far* more complicated than a first-marriage decision, for many reasons. If you partners are clearly aware of them, you're apt to make wiser decisions together. What reasons?

If you re/marry, the feelings, needs, priorities, and opinions of one or more kids, and one or more ex mates and their relatives (and any new partners) will affect you for decades. Australian stepfamily author Joy Connolly's book title will apply to you: "I Married a Family," not just an alluring person. In a re/wedding ceremony, you're really pledging yourself and any kids to your partner + his or her kids + ex mates + relatives + their conflicts + any future children or partners they choose. If you both have prior kids, you're co-committing to work at the long-range merger of four to six or more multi-generational families webbed together by genes, legal contracts, memories, bonds, needs, laws, and hopes.

If you're a bioparent, your decision to re/marry will affect each living minor and grown child emotionally and financially for many years. Stepfamily re/marriage is a personal and (grand)parenting decision.

Financial aspects of a re/marriage decision are far more complicated than typical first marriages. Pre-nuptial agreements, wills, insurance coverages, child support, childcare and living expenses; and clashing values about balancing, budgeting, saving, and spending are combined complexities that typical first-marriers don't face. Not discussing each of these thoroughly and honestly during your courtship makes re/divorce anguish and regrets more likely.

Unlike the first time around, **the degree to which divorced or widowed family members have grieved** their losses and adjusted to post-death or divorce life is a vital re/marriage decision factor. Unresolved hostility, disrespect, and distrust between divorced co-parents are highly corrosive to re/marriages and kids' securities, health, and growth. I believe undiagnosed blocked grief in adults and/or kids is one of the five reasons for our U.S. re/divorce epidemic.

Assessing **your and your prospective partner's abilities to solve problems (conflicts) effectively** as teammates is more crucial here than in a first-marriage decision. Typical stepfamilies have more concurrent inner and mutual conflicts, among more people, over more topics, than average first marriers. Assessing how well you prospective mates can resolve clashes over values, roles, priorities, loyalties, preferences, and physical assets is vital.

Courtship politeness, idealisms, and tolerances can hide powerful disagreements you'll discover between you, your kids, and any other co-parents. If you partners can't name the seven communication skills now (p. 173), *you probably don't know how to problem-solve effectively.* That's a primary cause of the toxic U.S. divorce scourge, and many parent-child problems. If you say proudly "My partner and I never fight!", *red light!*

You'll help each other learn how to problem-solve effectively in Project 2.

For these and other reasons, comparing your re/marriage-decision process to a first-marriage decision is like comparing driving an 18-wheel tractor-trailer to a go-cart. If you think this is an exaggeration, check it out with several veteran stepfamily co-parents!

Another way to optimize your investment in using this book is to . . .

Check Your Basic Attitudes

As you partners begin to appreciate the complexity, challenge, and risks of stepfamily life, you'll each have one of four initial attitudes about making your three re/marriage decisions:

+ Idealism and high confidence,
+ Cautious optimism,
+ Anxiety and self-doubt, or . . .
+ "No attitude."

The best of these is a shared attitude of "cautious optimism" about making a re/marriage decision you'll relish in your old age.

Whether you've married and raised kids before or not, your accumulated life experience and wisdom really are major assets. Oddly, divorce is an asset too. Most courting co-parents *never* want to experience that again, and want to protect their kids from its trauma. Unlike first-marriers, divorced co-parents know from painful experience that their romantic idealism and confidence can prove to be tragic illusions.

Are you aware of what your *real* attitude is about deciding whether to re/marry? Do you know clearly what your partner's *real* attitude is? Are your present attitudes based on stepfamily myths or realities? How do you know? Recall the premise that "Most courting co-parents don't know what they don't know." Are you co-parents effective learners?

Once you've taken these preparation steps and optimized your attitude, how else can you get the most from this book and the related resources?

View the time and energy you spend absorbing and applying these ideas **as an investment** vs. a chore. The implication is that you're going to get something valuable back. The priceless "something" is improved wholistic health + a solid, flourishing re/marriage + a high-nurturance multi-home stepfamily + giving your dependent kids and their unborn kids their best shot at healthy, satisfying, productive lives. Would you two like to savor these together as old people?

Recall a rich reward you've already experienced in your life after a long, sustained effort, like earning a higher-education degree. Use that patient, sustained effort and hard-earned payoff as a guide and inspiration for your long-term stepfamily investments.

Scan this whole book first before reading for meaning. Get to know the three sections, the seven projects, the worksheets, the resources, and the index. Grow your initial wide-angle vision of all the ideas here and how they fit together. **Then re-read for meaning**, seeing each project as a key part of the whole mosaic. The ideas and projects here develop in order. If you skip around, you're likely to be confused or build a fragmented awareness. Projects 1 and 2 are foundations for the other 10 co-parent projects in Chapter 8. See this visually on p. 129.

Discuss, clarify, edit, and tailor the basics in Part 1 and seven courtship projects in Part 2 with your partners and key supporters as you go. Edit the key ideas to fit your language, your experience, and your family cultures. Make these ideas *yours*: they'll work better for you all!

Do the extra readings and related worksheets as you read each of the seven projects, vs. skipping or postponing them. Invite your co-parenting partners to do the same. When you do the worksheets, read the directions and options, and take your time! Edit or change the worksheets if that's useful. The more effort and honesty you put into these explorations, the more you and your kids will harvest from your investments long term.

Notice your emotions and body, as you read, specially if you're male. Anxiety (worry) or *unease* are signals that something needs attention. If you read a section and think, "I can't remember what I just read," that's a signal too. Use your reactions as valuable pointers toward possibly uncomfortable personal or joint projects. For example, anxiety over accepting that "I'll have to choose between my child and my mate over and over!" is a clear sign that you need to do some important internal work . . .

Reality-check the opinions and suggestions you read here with veteran stepfamily co-parents, and/or *stepfamily-trained* professionals. They probably won't know the five hazards, the seven projects, or inner-family therapy, unless they've read this book.

Share this book and related Web pages with your co-parenting partners, supportive relatives, and older kids. Share them also with any professionals you consult along the way. Accept that most people greatly underestimate how *different* average multi-home stepfamilies are (p. 423). They'll offer heartfelt but often inapplicable advice based on their *bio*family experience and values.

If you discover inner wounds or experience relationship crises, please **don't substitute this book for qualified professional counseling**. This is a re/marriage-evaluation guidebook, not a do-it-yourself first-aid kit!

Authorize yourself to **mark the pages up** as you go: highlight or underline sections or ideas, asterisk key ideas, and scribble notes and questions. Copy any key nuggets and put them somewhere visible in your home. Make these pages *work* for you!

And to maximize your learnings here . . .

Develop "the mind of a student." One reason for widespread American divorce is *unawareness*. This book is not the only source of stepfamily help, though the scope and mix of key concepts here is unique. I encourage you co-parenting partners to seek additional stepfamily and re/marriage education from your library, veteran co-parents, audio and video tapes, media reports, informed classes (rare!), and real or cyberspace support groups. Be patient fellow researchers!

Note the **free 8-module re/marriage-preparation course** on the Internet at http://sfhelp.org/07/bhsf/intro.htm. It's based on the seven projects here, and my 15 years' experience at leading the course with over 50 groups of adult students. You can use it as a couple, though it's designed for groups of couples.

Expect to **use a bookmark** often, as you learn this rich mosaic of ideas. Many of the concepts and terms here are probably new to you, so I have provided cross-references throughout the pages to help you learn them. Use the Glossary (p. 493) in Part 3 to learn or clarify key stepfamily terms in these books.

Finally, as you partners read, process, and experiment, I encourage you to **keep your sense of humor, your curiosity, and your appreciation** of our universal human needs for *family*. Honestly and patiently done, these seven projects will produce a win-win out come: you'll either confirm your mutual guess that you have enough of the "right stuff" to try stepfamily re/marriage with initial confidence, or one or both of you will conclude "We're better off staying friends (or not)." The latter equates to saying "Our odds of being overwhelmed by the five hazards seem too high now."

Keep this light-hearted slogan in mind as you pilgrims research your alien stepfamily landscape:

"People who can laugh at themselves (uncritically)
will be richly entertained their whole life long."

Reality check: pause and reflect on what you just read. Breathe well, and notice your thoughts and feelings. How motivated are you partners to get the most from using this book and related resources now? Right now, I feel _ extremely motivated and interested; _ fairly motivated and interested, _ ambivalent: some motivated, and somewhat anxious and/or overwhelmed; _ pretty anxious and overwhelmed; _ *extremely* anxious and overwhelmed.

If you check either of the last two choices, give yourself time to digest and stabilize the ideas you've encountered so far. This series of books can empower you to succeed together *over time*.

The next two chapters lay a solid foundation for your re/ marriage evaluation. Would you agree that some families "work better" than others? To prepare for what you're about to read, get quiet and think of a family you've known who is "fully functional" or "wholistically-healthy." Then thoughtfully define ten or more specific traits that make it such a family. Then see how your traits compare to this:

3) What's a *High-nurturance* Family?

I propose that courting co-parents' *unawareness* is one of five hazards that promote wrong re/marriage decisions and eventual re/divorce. In my experience, many courting couples aren't aware _ what childhood *nurturance* really means, _ what high-nurturance relationships and families are, and _ how to merge three or more biofamilies to create a high-nurturance (wholistically healthy or "functional") stepfamily.

A psychological and/or legal divorce implies that the mates couldn't answer the first two of these well enough. If you and your partner aren't knowledgeable and clear on these three topics, and/or you disagree markedly on your answers, you and any minor kids risk major future stress and probable re/divorce. From 15 years' study of many researchers' opinions, this chapter offers perspective on the first two of the three questions above. If you opt to re/wed, Project 9 in the next volume of this series will propose an answer the third question. See http://sfhelp.org/09/merge.htm and ..09/project09.htm.

You can use this chapter as a resource for drafting your stepfamily mission statement and co-parent job descriptions in Project 6.

Let's start by defining a *family* as "an adult and one or more other people of any age who _ grow and maintain significant emotional and spiritual bonds, and _ consistently *want* to (vs. have to) help each other fill their respective daily needs."

Family members may or may not share common genes and ancestries. Why have families appeared across recorded history in all cultures?

Why Do Families Exist?

I've opened scores of relationship seminars and co-parenting classes with this seemingly brainless question. People sputter a little or look into space, then say something like "Well, *obviously* to have and/or raise kids, and uh, to be happy, healthy, and productive." I ask, "So do you have to have children involved to be a family?" Usually people respond "Uh, no, but . . ." After some discussion I ask: "What can a family (potentially) do better than any other human group?" I'm sobered by how vague typical co-parents are on this vital question. Many have never thought about it.

Premise: *"A family is the human environment where kids and adults can best help each other fill a set of universal human needs over time."* Each person in your life has three levels of needs: conscious, unconscious, and physical. The first two include some mix of these:

Core Spiritual/Emotional Needs

+ To give and receive love
+ Self awareness, acceptance, and respect
+ Spiritual faith, awareness, and communion
+ Personal and group identities
+ A viable life purpose, and resources to pursue it
+ Social acceptance, respect, and companionship
+ The chance to develop effective life skills
+ Comfort (support) with crises and losses
+ Knowledge of the world, and freedom to learn

+ Opportunity to conceive and nurture new life
+ Nurturing (vs. toxic) physical contact
+ Balanced work, play, and rest

+ Recognition, validation, and appreciation
+ Encouragements to grow and persevere
+ Emotional and physical *securities*
+ Sensory stimulation
+ Enough *hope*
+ Nurturing laughter

Mull this set of needs, and revise it to fit your beliefs and experience. Where else but in a family can you (ideally) get *all* of these met? You can fill subsets of these needs in good friendships, co-worker recognitions and career achievements, a kibbutz or commune, and church and social communities.

Do you agree that *"families exist to nurture (fill a set of core spiritual-emotional needs) each member over time, in a way that other human groups can't"*? We're concerned here with the subset of all families that include minor and grown children. Now let's refine this to propose . . .

"Families of procreation, re/marriage, foster care, and adoption exist to (1) produce wholistically-healthy, socially valuable, self-sufficient new adults, while (2) filling the core needs of *all* their members (above) well enough, as they and the Earth evolve."

Would you revise this? Would your parents, ancestors, and mentors agree with this definition? Your present and former mates? This two-part definition enables us to answer . . .

What is a Functional or *High-nurturance* family?

Depending on their leaders' knowledge and wholistic health, some families are more effective at filling their members' needs than others, over time. That is, every family can be judged somewhere between very low nurturance to very high nurturance. Let's say . . .

"A high-nurturance (functional or healthy) *family is one which (1) all members and (2) knowledgeable outsiders agree has met the above two conditions well enough."*

A dysfunctional, toxic, or unhealthy family is one that doesn't meet one or both of these conditions well enough, according to someone."

What does it take to produce a "wholistically-healthy, socially-valuable, self-sufficient adult"? A **basic premise here** is that to achieve this amazing feat, a child's nuclear family must have one or more adult co-parenting leaders, who consistently provide enough of a set of key traits well enough over time. Ideally the other adults in a young child's multi-generational (extended) biofamily provide these traits too. What are these key traits?

Traits of High-nurturance Families

Using our definition above, can you think of a past or present family you judge to be "high-nurturance"? What factors or traits cause you to award that judgment? See how many specific traits you can identify. Then compare your ideas to the items below. The goal here is for you to form your own clear, reality-based idea, not to assume my idea is "right." The 28 traits below come from my six decades of life experience, including 15 years' personal recovery from a low-nurturance childhood; 19 years' formal education; over 17,000 clinical hours with over 1,000 co-parents and (some) kids, and hundreds of hours of post-graduate professional study.

See if you think the combined traits below would probably help fill *all* family-members' sets of needs (above), not just those of minor kids. Like planning a global sailboat cruise or building several homes by hand, there are *lots* of "success" factors. Here's what they look like summarized together. If you use this as a checklist, check the main items in which you can confidently check all sub-items. Add the references in parentheses to http://sfhelp.org/ to get a Web-page address.

+ + +

___ 1) The family leaders consistently _ value, _ seek, and _ promote _ personal and _ family-relationship wholistic (mental + spiritual + physical + emotional) healths. The leader/s _ have few traits of false-self dominance (e.g. pp. 401 and 413); *or* if they do, _ they are well into true (vs. pseudo) personal recovery (p. 151 and ..01/recovery1.htm).

___ 2) All adult and young members _ are clear on who leads the family, and _ genuinely respect and follow their guidance often enough. Each leader is consistently effective at promoting _ teamwork (harmony), _ respect, and _ loyalty among all family members.

___ 3) The leaders _ hold clear, long-term family goals, and maintain clear _ priorities and _ effective plans to meet them. The leaders are consistently able to _ adapt and re-stabilize these in the face of significant family, social, and environmental changes and crises.

___ 4) All family members share strong *nurturing* spiritual (vs. religious) faiths. _ Individual spiritual preferences are respected and nurtured, rather than having to adopt someone's definition of "*the* one Way."

___ 5) All child conceptions and/or adoptions are well researched, discussed, and planned. There are no "oops" conceptions, abortions, or major ambivalences.

___ 6) All family members usually feel _ included, _ valued, and _ loved *unconditionally*. At times, that can manifest as _ respectful confrontations, and _ helping by not helping (not enabling).

___ 7) All members prize their _ personal dignity, _ self and mutual respect, and _ individuality. _ There are no c/overt gender biases.

___ 8) All family members generally _ trust each other, and _ exchange the truth _ promptly. There are _ no major family secrets or _ "no talk" rules implied or declared.

___ 9) All members consistently feel _ emotionally, _ spiritually, and _ physically safe *enough*.

___ 10) The family leaders consistently _ model and _ encourage _ feeling and _ expressing *all* emotions. Members _ usually distinguish between *feeling* emotions, and *acting* constructively or harmfully on them. _ No emotions are judged to be *bad* or *negative*.

___ 11) The family leaders are _ clear on the principles of healthy grieving (p. 248), _ usually model them spontaneously, and _ encourage other family members to _ learn and _ practice them. The family has _ a clear pro-grief policy (p. 297).

___ 12) _ Interpersonal communications and _ conflict resolution are usually _ prompt, _ mutually respectful, and _ effective: i.e. members usually get enough of their needs met, in a way that feels good enough to them all. _ Disagreements are seen as normal, not *bad* or *wrong*.

___ 13) All family members _ assert and _ respect _ each other's personal and _ their family's boundaries (limits) and _ related privacies. They _ equally respect the boundaries of guests and _ other households and _ families.

___ 14) All members grow real (vs. pseudo) emotional-spiritual bonds with _ each other and _ selected others (friends).

___ 15) The main family roles (responsibilities) are _ clear enough to all, _ appropriate in age and ability, _ negotiated respectfully, and _ firmly flexible (adaptable to change).

___ 16) Within age-appropriate norms, all family members usually accept personal accountability (responsibility) for their life choices and actions.

___ 17) Household and family rules are _ usually clear enough to all. The *consequences* of breaking the rules are _ enforced by the family leader/s, _ clear, _ respectful, and _ consistent *enough*. Leader/s are _ open to changing the rules as members and life conditions evolve.

___ 18) All members highly _ value and _ promote physical health, by balancing _ diets, and _ work, play, exercise, and rest.

___ 19) All family members _ get enough *nurturing* physical touching; and _ practice wholistically-healthy sexual _ values, _ limits, and _ behaviors.

___ 20) All members evolve clear _ personal, _ dyad (mate-mate, parent-child, sib-sib), and _ family identities.

___ **21)** Family members often take _ safe risks, within their limitations. *Mistakes* are _ accepted and _ *valued* as useful chances to learn, vs. sources of shame and ridicule.

___ **22)** All members feel *non-elitist* _ personal and _ family _ pride and _ loyalty.

___ **23)** Members are generally open to new _ people, _ ideas, and _ experiences.

___ **24)** Family members take _ local and _ global _ social welfare and _ ecology seriously, but not obsessively.

___ **25)** Spontaneous _ play and _ non-shaming laughter are common _ in and _ outside the family's home.

___ **26)** Family members often _ seek and _ enjoy time together, while _ respecting individual solitudes and privacies. Members usually _ *want* to congregate, vs. feeling obliged to.

___ **27)** Family members share consistent attitudes of _ realistic optimism and _ hope.

___ **28)** Each family leader _ can describe most of these traits spontaneously, and _ came from a childhood family which consistently had most of these traits.

This is not a complete or "absolute, true" compilation of high-nurturance family traits. I suggest it is "right *enough*." Shelves of books, reams of learned articles, and endless conferences debate these factors, and there are many viewpoints. **The basic premises here are:**

+ **Some** families are "healthier" (higher nurturance) and "more successful and productive" (more functional) than others.

+ **There** are specific factors that combine to shape any family's nurturance level, over time; and . . .

+ **Through** awareness and determined _ effort, informed, motivated leaders can increase their family's nurturance level over time.

How do you feel about each of these premises? They're the taproots of this book. They undergird Project 1, which is proposed as the antidote to the most toxic and common (re)divorce hazard: unseen psychological wounding. I believe that the high majority of U.S. divorced and stepfamily co-parents did *not* experience most of these traits consistently in their early childhoods. Neither did their ancestors. For perspective, see this sobering research summary: http://sfhelp.org/01/research.htm.

To grow your perspective, let's explore each of these 28 high-nurturance-family traits. They apply to any kind of family: bio-, step-, foster-parent, absent-parent, adoptive, homosexual, childless, and communal. You may find yourself evaluating your childhood family, your present family, and/or your partner's family, on these traits. Keep in mind that this is not about blame, it's about *awareness*. These factors are in rough order of importance, but aren't rigorously prioritized. Like parts of your car, each factor contributes to the functioning and stability of the whole (family) system. Use this as a checklist if you wish, and take your time. As you consider each trait, ponder "Could this factor be omitted and still have a stable, *high-nurturance* family, over time?" Refresh your mental definition of *family* as you read . . .

A Closer Look at the Traits

1) The **committed mates** who lead the family generally **value their relationship** *second* **only to their personal wholistic healths and integrity**, and their relationship with their Higher Power. They committed to each other out of conscious choice, rather than duty, impulse, fear, lust, or excessive need. Each partner was old enough at their wedding to have gained enough adult independence, clear identity, and accurate knowledge of themselves and the world.

Each leader _ has few false-self traits (e.g. Resources A and B), *or* _ is well along in effective personal recovery. The mates' _ clear, shared relationship goal was to be intentionally *inter*dependent, rather than unconsciously independent or co-dependent partners. Most or all relatives in their respective families _ genuinely supported and rejoiced at their marriage, and _ knew about it well in advance.

2) One or more adults are clearly and consistently in charge of the nuclear family's home/s, making useful policies and needed decisions as the family evolves in a dynamic world. Minor kids in the family _ don't feel significantly responsible for the welfare of younger children or disabled adults, or _ for making major household decisions. Dependent kids _ are truly free to be (responsible) children, vs. little adults, home-maintenance slaves, or Olympic superstars. They are _ steadily clear on this, vs. ambivalent or confused. The family's leaders _ steadily foster a sense of teamwork among family members, honoring each person's abilities to contribute, and respecting their current priorities and limitations.

3) The family leaders each have _ specific, realistic, harmonious *goals* for what they're trying to do as people, partners, **and** co-parents, long-term. **They also have _ viable, realistic *plans*** to reach their main family goals, and _ are working on their plans as co-operative teammates, not competitors or individuals. They _ *make* enough time to discuss their goals, plans, conflicts, and relish their achievements thoroughly, rather than fitting discussions in around other daily priorities and activities.

4) Each family member _ is genuinely (vs. dutifully or ambivalently) supported in developing her or his own spiritual quest, reverence for, and faith in, a benign Higher Power. Their **spiritual faith/s _ are based on unconditional love, compassion, trust, and hope**; vs. fear of "damnation," guilt and shame about "sinning," and/or duty or social approval. The family _ develops its own way of worshipping together, which strengthens and stabilizes their bonding, serenity, and group identity, over time. The family's spiritual faith _ is a significant personal, marital, and group resource in tough times. The family _ probably belongs to one or several high-nurturance spiritual communities by choice, rather than from social necessity or "pressure."

5) Each child conception is _ *chosen*, vs. accidental, and is _ fully deliberated and planned by both bioparents. Restated: each biological, foster, and/or adopted child is unambivalently *wanted* by each co-parent. _ Each parent felt genuinely pleased, optimistic, and ready and knowledgeable enough, about the responsibilities, stresses, and rewards of raising each (vs. the first) child, rather than feeling resigned and "we'll get through it somehow." _ Co-parents' extended families are generally warm, reliable sources of encouragement, stability, and helpful parenting advice and support, over time.

6) Each member of a high-nurturance family **consistently feels _ loved without conditions,** _ included, **and _ prized** by other members for who they are, vs. what they can do, contribute, or become. _ Each adult and child feels consistently known, appreciated, and accepted well enough by other members, and s/he _ spontaneously (vs. dutifully or anxiously) returns those blessings. _ No members have trouble forming healthy attachments to selected other living things.

7) All high-nurturance family adults and kids steadily **encourage themselves and each other to be** individuals: i.e. to fully develop and use their unique natural talents and gifts. They help each other to be **their true Selves**, not an ideal false self or someone's clone. Adults and kids consistently see each other as people of equal dignity and worth, regardless of age, knowledge, family role, and gender. **Each member feels fairly steady _ self and _ mutual respect** for and from other family members. No one is significantly wounded (psychologically)," so _ confusing mixed messages are rare.

8) Each member of a high nurturance family **is usually honest and direct** with themselves and all other members. This promotes high levels of shared trust and intimacy, with appropriate boundaries. There are _ few or no denials, repressions, evasions, lies, taboo subjects, hidden agendas, or family secrets in and among the family's homes. There is _ no spoken or implied "we don't talk about *that* here" rule. Adults and kids _ can disagree and confront each other safely, without significant fear of ridicule (shaming), attack, or rejection.

More proposed traits of high-nurturance, "functional" families:

9) Each adult and child in the extended (multi-generational) family **consistently feels** _ physically, emotionally, and spiritually **safe _enough_, short and long-range;** and each usually feels _ confident _enough_ of other members' safeties. All family members are generally comfortable _ requesting and _ receiving help from others. Based on history and experience, all the family's adults and kids _ share a solid trust that other members will _want_ to support them in times of need. This inner security shows in members' physical, mental, and emotional health: _ there is no significant history of psychosomatic illnesses or signs of "too much" personal worry, dread, fragmenting, or confusion.

10) High-nurturance **family members _ steadily encourage each other to feel**, name, and safely express all their current emotions, specially anger, sadness, confusion, despair (hopelessness), and anxiety (fear). This allows adults to _ steadily support each other in grieving their major life losses (broken bonds) promptly and well enough, over time. Adult "permissions" to _feel_ and _express_ emotions are _ modeled and _ taught consistently, allowing each minor child to grow their innate ability to grieve their losses naturally and effectively in their own way.

11) The family's leaders are _ clear on the principles of healthy three-level grieving, and _ encourage other family members to learn and practice them. The family _ has a clear pro-grief policy: i.e. the leader/s steadily _ model and _ promote values and behavior that encourage family members and visitors to _ feel and _ vent their grief feelings and _ describe their losses, without fear of ridicule, rejection, over-reaction, or indifference. Can you describe your personal, and childhood and current families' grief policies now? See p. 297, Project 5, and ..05/griefpol.htm.

12) Kids and adults in a high-nurturance family _ **usually communicate _effectively_.** Based on genuine (vs. pseudo) self and mutual respects, they each _ assert and get their current real needs met well enough, often enough. The co-parents _ often guide other members to stay focused, **and use** respectful assertion, *empathic* listening, and **win-win interpersonal problem-solving** skills to get their current key needs met. _ Internal and _ interpersonal conflicts are seen as normal, and potentially valuable, not "bad" or threatening. _ Arguing, fighting, and denying, ignoring, or deferring conflicts are unusual in the family, except among younger kids.

Kids and adults consistently exchange prompt, genuine, constructive _ affirmations and _ observations about each other's behavior, rather than manipulative, covert, or shaming feedback, or none at all. _ All adults and kids are usually comfortable and spontaneous in _ giving and _ receiving genuine praise and appreciations.

13) In a high-nurturance family, _ personal, mate-mate, adult-child, child-child, and family-outer world **boundaries are clear, appropriate, and consistent enough**. All family members _ are reasonably comfortable asserting needs and limits respectfully and directly to each other and other people, like *No, Not now, Yes,* and *Let's talk about your request.* _ Members set their inner and relationship boundaries this way without excessive guilt, confusion, shame, and/or anxiety. All family members _ are clear on the difference between a request and a demand (are you?). Generally, _ kids' and adults' needs for privacy are calmly asserted, heard clearly, and usually validated and respected by other members, without major resentments.

14) Because both biological parents truly wanted and loved them and showed that spontaneously and consistently, _ **each child and adult** in a high-nurturance family **can form true, vs. pretended or intellectual, emotional bonds** with _ each other and _ selected other people over time. This _ shows clearly in their spontaneous mutual enjoyment of being with each other; and in _ deep, real concern when any member or friend is "in trouble." Each family member _ is capable of genuine, unambivalent emotional/spiritual commitment to personal relationships with selected others, and _ can receive such commitment from these others. _ **Each family member has their own set of real friends,** vs. acquaintances. _ Opposite-gender friendships are accepted and valued.

_ Males and females can say in their own ways, and *mean*, "I really **love** you." _ No family members mistake pity, lust, dependency, or power for love.

15) All adults and kids in a high-nurturance home and family _ usually know "who's supposed to do what, among us?" **Family roles are _ clear, stable, and appropriate enough, and _ usually flex to meet local conditions.** Roles can be respectfully adjusted and renegotiated, as the family (and society) changes its needs, memberships, and resources. _ Kids don't parent their parents, balance the family checkbook, or call the plumber. Adults don't usurp their kids' responsibilities to learn how to study, socialize, be patient, and cope with success and failure. _ Caregivers don't live lost childhoods through minor kids. Younger people _ respect and at least consider the experience and knowledge of available grandparents, aunts, and uncles. It's _ steadily clear to everyone who the adults are and aren't (yet). Family roles _ shift and adjust effectively, as people mature and household memberships and the outer world change.

Family co-leaders _ confidently (vs. anxiously) delegate increasing responsibility and autonomy to dependent kids as their individual abilities grow. **Co-parents and adult kin _ are clear and co-operative on their core goals** of guiding their youngsters toward genuine self-confidence, self-respect, and healthy adult independence. Family adults _ usually practice what they preach, rather than giving mixed messages like "do as I say, not as I *do!*"

16) Leaders of high-nurturance families _ respectfully **encourage and confront each other and other members to take personal responsibility** for their choices and actions, rather than blaming others, deflecting, avoiding, manipulating, controlling, whining, analyzing, or hiding. This comes from _ adults and kids feeling consistently respected and valued, and usually not feeling shamed or ridiculed for making "mistakes." _ All family members are comfortable offering and receiving sin-

cere **apologies** where needed, and _ truly forgiving themselves
and each other for unintended or unavoidable hurts. _ No one
carries a "gunnysack" of old grudges or grievances, or needs
to get "revenge."

17) Family and household *rules* (shoulds, oughts, musts,
and have-to's) _ **are usually consistent, clear, appropriate
enough, and** _ **firmly flexible.** _ Consequences from breaking
the rules are clear enough to all, and are respectful, prompt,
and deemed "fair" and appropriate enough. Consequences are
_ respectfully described and enforced by the family's leaders
or their respected delegates. The consequences _ aim to teach
and guide, rather than punish and force obedience via fear,
guilt, pain, and/or shame. Was this your childhood experience?

18) _ **All family members respect, prize, and care for
their bodies and physical health.** Family leaders are _ informed
and proactive, not fanatic, about balanced nutrition and exercise. They _ ensure regular preventive health check-ups for
themselves and their dependents, and _ promptly get qualified
care for health problems.

Each family member is not excessively anxious or guilty
about, or ashamed of _ their physical endowments and lacks, _
their gender, and _ their gender-preferences. _ No one seriously criticizes another member's body shape, features, "looks,"
or self-care habits.

19) _ **Each member** in a high-nurturance family **gets enough
comfortable** *physical* **nurturing** (in their opinion). This includes
hugs, pats on the back, and appropriate caresses; vs. painful,
intrusive, shaming touch, or *no* physical contact. _ No one
ever feels physically threatened, unsafe, invaded, or used. _
Child discipline does not involve physical threat or pain. _ All
kids and adults, specially males, feel comfortable asking for
hugs, and hugging, caressing, and kissing other members non-
intrusively and non-sexually. Members and guests' individual
preferences about physical nurturing are acknowledged and
respected.

The family's leaders each _ have **healthy, well-informed
sexual attitudes, practices, and limits.** They model and en-

courage respectful understanding and enjoyment of all members' sensuality and sexuality, rather than fostering overt or covert anxiety, guilt, and/or shame. _ Adults and kids usually feel spontaneous and comfortable talking about sexual topics, questions, and (some) experiences, while keeping respectful privacies intact. Does this sound like the families you've belonged to?

20) All members of a high-nurturance family _ have **reasonably clear, undistorted ideas about their personal identity: "Who *am* I?"** Adults and kids can name their own, and each others,' current strengths, talents, key values, goals, preferences, and limitations, without major hesitation, doubt, judgment, or embarrassment (whew!). _ Their personal identity is based on who they *are*, not the roles they fill, what they do or don't, or physical traits. Does this sound like *you*?

Family members also _ share a sense of **group identity**: e.g. "We're the Greene-O'Connor family crew. We come from Irish, German, and English Protestant roots and traditions, and are proud to be Virginians and Americans. We observe most national holidays together, and love supporting each other at births, weddings, graduations, big anniversaries, and sometimes just for fun. We laugh and cry a lot together; (usually) listen to each other; get tough and blunt, at times; sometimes take expeditions together; and have plenty of love and warmth to go around for anyone who joins us." Household and family identity springs in part from all members participating in a shared set of adventures and rituals. These generate fond and painful **shared memories and mementos**, like photos, home videos, post cards, e-mails, and treasured heirlooms.

Pause here for a moment, and notice where your thoughts and feelings take you. Does this sound like the family you grew up in, so far? The family you help to manage now? Here's the last group of proposed high-nurturance traits . . .

21) Family members generally _ encourage each other to **risk** safe-enough new experiences. They _ **usually view "mistakes" as chances to learn,** rather than embarrassing evidence of personal badness or inadequacy. This reflects the family adults' _ **prizing life-long learning** about themselves, each other, and the past and present worlds and universe. High-nurturance family leaders _ help their kids to calmly handle self-doubts and peer criticisms and jeers, and to assert their own opinions, needs, and boundaries with balanced dignity and confidence. Members _ help each other to feel empathy and compassion, not responsibility for or smugness about, others' mistakes, shortcomings, fears, and "failures." Do you know what that feels like?

22) High-nurturance family **members _ openly share** and enjoy reasonable **pride, pleasure, and satisfaction in individual and group achievements and successes.** They're neither falsely humble nor arrogantly boastful. _ Non-elitist pride, balanced with real enjoyment of others' successes and recognitions, is regarded in the family's homes as a sign of personal and family health, rather than a "sin" or "weakness." As in a well-functioning athletic team, _ personal successes usually add to shared feelings of family success, satisfaction, pride, and bonding. Members are _ **spontaneous and genuine in praising** each other's achievements, and can receive praise graciously, without anxiety or false modesty.

23) All kids and adults in a high-nurturance family _ **feel free to experience and evaluate others' ideas, customs, and beliefs,** and to share their ideas and traditions with other people as co-equals. _ Kids are invited, not forced, to accept parental and ancestral traditions, rituals, and values. _ Visitors are usually welcomed into the family homes with real interest and courtesy, rather than suspicion, anxiety, pretense, or judgment. _ All members appreciate and accept the natural differences and sameness among each other, and among all other people, cultures, and nations. They have no need to feel part of a "special" ethnic, cultural, religious, or "class" that excludes some other "sub standard" people.

24) Adults and children _ spontaneously (vs. dutifully) share an appreciative **interest in, and proactive concern for, their community's well-being,** and at least local social and environmental health. In their own ways, _ they accept and act on their responsibilities to be thoughtful consumers, to conserve non-renewable Earth resources, and to be contributing citizens of our Global Village. Do the people in your home regularly turn off the lights in empty rooms and take short showers?

25) Adults and kids _ often **feel free to be spontaneous and playful, and to periodically relax enough**. Members all _ feel that real leisure and recreation (re-creation) is just as productive as "doing something." _ **Shared humor** is natural, spontaneous, and affirming, vs. forced, shaming, belittling, strategic, or demeaning. Kids and adults can often laugh *with* each other about their own foibles and "mess ups," as a normal and often productive part of life.

Typical people dominated by a false self reflexively use humor as a distraction or camouflage for guilt, pain, embarrassment, emptiness, and/or confusion. Do you know anyone who often grins or chuckles about painful experiences?

26) Adults and kids in a high-nurturance extended family _ **generally seek and enjoy time together**, while respecting individual solitudes and privacies. Members are _ usually invited, vs. *forced*, to participate in family events and gatherings.

I suspect that one reason my father moved our young family from Chicago to southern California was to escape his Teutonic father's *demand* that all three adult children and their partners and kids spend every Sunday afternoon with him and his compliant wife, regardless of the kids' needs or priorities. This made sense to my patriarchal grandfather (covertly nicknamed "the Iron Duke"), and split our extended family. Paradoxically, after enough alcohol, German songs and family *gemütlichkeit* (congeniality) would bloom, which really was fun. One result of our migration was that my younger sister and I rarely saw either set of relatives as we grew up: a *major* nurturance deprivation.

27) Members of a high-nurturance family _ **steadily encourage each other to feel** *realistic* **hope and optimism**, vs. unrealistic idealism, dread, pessimism, doubt, and/or fear. Adults and kids _ understand that being alive means having to adapt to constant change, risks, and losses. They _ work together to accept unplanned changes as opportunities, rather than dire crises or calamities. This does not prevent family adults and kids from feeling and expressing appropriate sadness, disappointment, and anger when prized things end.

28) In their own words, _ **each leader in a high-nurturance family can spontaneously and clearly describe many of these traits and values.** S/He can say clearly what a high nurturance or "functional" family _ is and _ aims for. Could each of your childhood caregivers do that? Could the people who raised *them*?

Notice your thoughts and feelings now. Would you like to belong to a family that had many of these characteristics? Does yours? Trying to grasp and integrate all 28 of these factors at once is hard! Recall the premises that high-nurturance families _ have many of the specific traits that you just read, and _ "work" (function) better than others. Do the premises seem more credible now? A typical reaction is "Yes, but this is a fairy tale! *No* family has most or all of these traits most of the time!"

Exactly. And almost half of America's first marriages self-destruct, and even more re/marriages do. Our TV screens and media headlines blare incessant reports of suicides, murders, legal suits, crime, and drug misery. See any connection? Muse: if most families had most of these 28 traits most of the time, would you guess that our media stories, and perhaps the cartoon industry, would have a different caste? Would the quality and productivity of your and your kids' lives improve if you and related co-parents committed to growing many of these high-nurturance family traits together?

Effects of Too Little Early Nurturance

What happens to the *millions* of young Earthlings who are unintentionally deprived of too many of these traits too often as they grow up? You'll meet Patty McLean and her stepfamily In Chapter 7. She had three families, and lost two of them in her first 13 years of life in America: her biofamily, her two-home absent-parent family, and her three-home stepfamily. Because her three main co-parents didn't know they were nurturance-deprived and psychologically wounded as kids, Patty got too few of these 28 nurturing traits *in all three* of her families. We can only guess how this will affect her choice of adult partner/s, her ability to nurture kids and grandkids, and her career choices.

How does all this relate to *your* re/marital and stepfamily choices and long-term success?

Six Psychological Wounds

People like Patty who get too few of these traits in their early years seem to adapt by developing a mix of up to six inner injuries. These occur gradually and *automatically* because of our primal human instinct to survive (vs. thrive):

1) Some degree of **personality fragmenting,** creating a protective "false self": a set of Vulnerable and Guardian personality subselves which disable the wise inner leadership of your developing true Self. This causes . . .

2) **Excessive shame and guilts**, and relentless "negative self talk": self criticism from a zealous, well-meaning *Inner Critic.*

3) **Major fears** of abandonment (aloneness), emotional overwhelm (conflict), loss, failure, and the unknown.

4) **Trust**ing others too easily or not trusting enough, including self-doubt and skepticism of a Higher Power.

5) **Reality distortions**, including denials, repressions, projections, idealizations, minimizations, and exaggerations.

These five wounds can combine to cause . . .

6) **Difficulty feeling and bonding**: forming solid emotional-spiritual attachments to your Self, other living things, and a benign Higher Power. This wound inhibits feeling and exchanging *love.*

I believe that the combined effect of these six wounds is probably the most powerful of five interactive reasons for widespread American personal misery and (re)divorce. We *all* have some of these wounds, and live "well enough" by our false self's standards. My experience is that most divorced and stepfamily adults (not just co-parents) have some or all of these wounds, and minimize or deny them and what they mean. *Because you're reading this, the odds are high that this applies to* you *and your present and past primary partners.* Notice your reaction. If it's "Not *me!*", could that be your false self protecting you?

In this book and related Web pages, a "significantly wounded" woman or man is (1) in partial or full denial of their set of these six psycho-spiritual wounds, (2) the *unintended* childhood nurturance deprivations that caused them, and (3) the *impact* of their combined wounds on the interpersonal relationships they prize the most.

Implications

Since 1981, I've seen a relentless pattern in hundreds of troubled stepfamily couples. Without identifying and recovering from their psychological wounds (Project 1), *courting co-parents seem to unconsciously pick each over and over again.* Adding ignorance of healthy grieving, effective parenting and communication skills, and stepfamily realities, promotes eventual re/divorce.

Co-parents' not foreseeing this in courtship starts a spiral of stepfamily stress and re/marital and co-parenting conflicts. This *replicates prior low family nurturance, and promotes deeper or new wounds for adults and kids alike.*

Project 1 provides you with an effective way to identify and heal your co-parents' inner wounds over time. This essential work breaks the toxic ancestral bequest of low nurturance and *inner*-family anarchy to the next generation. If you partners don't make significant progress on this foundation project *before* re/marriage, you're at high risk of minimizing the other six projects and choosing the wrong *people* to re/wed, for the wrong *reasons*, at the wrong *time*.

Reality check: this chapter proposes _ a set of universal human needs, _ why families exist, _ a definition of low and high-nurturance families, and _ 28 traits common to high-nurturance families and other groups. *The value of rest of this book to you depends substantially on your validating these four premises in your own life.* Therefore, I encourage you to reflect on how credible these premises are before reading further.

Think of "significantly troubled" adults and kids you know pretty well (including you?), one at a time. Compare what you know about their childhood family to the 28 traits outlined above. Do you suspect or know that the person grew up with relatively few of these family traits?

Think of adults and kids you've known whom you see as *healthy*, *successful*, *happy*, and *contented*. Compare what you know about their childhoods to your version of the 28 high-nurturance factors proposed above. Did they grow up with most of the traits?

As you do this, stay compassionately aware: typical (unrecovering) people in and from low-nurturance families are shame-based and fear based. They're masters at protective reality distortion: presenting a "healthy, happy" front to the world and themselves.

Do you need a break? When you're refreshed, we'll keep building your foundation for making three wise re/marriage choices.

The next chapter looks in more depth at the five re/marriage hazards that you, your kids, and their other co-parents face together. Naming and understanding the hazards can help you justify the seven courtship projects in Part 2, and raise your urge to *do* them.

If you know any (re)divorced co-parents, keep them in mind as you read . . .

4) Why Most U.S. Re/marriages Fail

Five Hazards That Successful Co-parents
Overcome

I've studied human behavior most of my 63 years. I've explored divorced-family and stepfamily relationships and dynamics professionally for over two decades. From these, I now believe there are five reasons that combine to cause well over half of average American stepfamily couples to split up, often within seven years of their vows and toasts. *Each of these hazards can be neutralized or avoided, once it's understood and accepted.* I suspect that the first four of these factors largely explain why almost half of American adults divorce the first time, and why many others remain single. Again, the factors are:

+ Co-parents' combined **psychological wounds**; plus . . .
+ Co-parents' **unawareness** of psychological, life-skill, and stepfamily realities (Chapters 5 and 6); plus . . .
+ **Blocked grief** in one or more stepfamily members; plus . . .
+ Needy, idealistic suitors choosing to re/wed in the **distorted mind state** of romantic love; plus . . .
+ **Lack of** *informed* recovery, re/marital, and co-parenting **support** in the media and co-parents' local communities, starting with officiating clergy.

Have you ever seen these ideas together? If you are or may be a courting co-parent, I propose that a mix of these five hazards will *definitely* affect you and those you care for. Their overall impact compounds, because the hazards interact with each other and other factors.

I expect you're feeling some skepticism and/or alarm. See if more perspective alters those. Keep in mind that Part 2 of this book proposes experience-tested ways you and any partner can overcome (vs. avoid) these stressors.

Hazard 1) Combined Psychological Wounds

I estimate that well over 80% of the hundreds of single and re/married co-parents that I've consulted with since 1981 were accidentally deprived of too many of the 28 high-nurturance family factors in the last chapter. They had many of the traits in Resources A and B in Part 3. Their childhood caregivers had done their best, in the face of their own psychological wounds, unawarenesses, and biases. These co-parents were living as well as they could in ignorance of these psychological injuries:

+ a disabled true Self,
+ excessive shame, guilts, and fears;
+ significant reality and trust distortions; and . . .
+ difficulty bonding and loving.

Imagine the relationship between two mates who aren't aware of their mixes of these wounds. Now imagine four to six such people in two or three related homes, trying to form a co-operative co-parenting team, without knowing how to negotiate and parent effectively. Could *you* and/or your fine partner be denying some mix of these six wounds? Most re/courting adults will discount the question, or confidently answer "No!" Many will add ". . . but my *ex mate* definitely has these wounds!"

Because parents aren't perfect, we *all* were neglected and wounded as kids, to some degree. **The key questions for you and your partner are . . .**

+ "How many of the six wounds do _ you and _ I and _ our
ex mates have, and _ how severe is each wound?"

+ "How can we identify and heal our inner wounds?"
And . . .
+ "_ How can we protect our kids from being dominated
   by a false self? _ Are they already significantly
   wounded? If so, _ what should we do?"

Seeing no wounds or options, moderately-wounded people
may judge their lives "OK enough" without personal healing.
Before true recovery, significantly wounded men and women
always have a tangle of ongoing health, relationship, money,
legal, and employment problems. They seem to die earlier than
adults from high-nurturance childhoods and peers in real vs.
pseudo recovery (p. 157). *Unrecovering people usually can't
begin to see their own wounds until they "hit (their personal)
bottom."* That often manifests as a(nother) divorce, bankruptcy,
depression, illness, job loss, arrest, or "breakdown."

Young kids adapt to low family nurturance by accepting
the symptoms of these inner wounds as *normal*. This is partly
because our caregivers had their own sets of injuries and ignored or mis-diagnosed them. Like kids with physical handi-
caps, nurturance-deprived children like Patty McLean (Chapter 7) learn instinctively to adapt and cope with life as best they
can. Until experiencing real recovery (usually) in midlife, most
wounded adults can't comprehend that there is a far healthier
and more satisfying way of living available to them and their
kids. Living with anxieties ("stress"), confusion, emotional
numbness or impulsiveness, loneliness, depression, and hidden shame becomes ho-hum and routine.

Common Effects of Psychological Wounds

I believe there are **four tragic, widespread personal and
social impacts** from co-parents' six inner wounds. They promote and are amplified by our society's current denials, despite massive evidence. Typical people like Jack, Ted, and Sarah (Chapter 7) who aren't aware they're often controlled by a
false self . . .

+ Unconsciously pick each other as primary partners, *over
   and over again*; and . . .
+ Unintentionally re-create the low-nurturance family they
   grew up in, which promotes some mix of the psychological wounds in their dependent kids; and the
   adults . . .
+ Often die early and unaware of who they *really* were, and
   what they could have achieved if they had recovered
   from false-self control; and the wounds . . .
+ Passively or actively contribute to an interactive web of
   social problems.

Notice where your thoughts go now. Can you repeat what
you just read? If not, your false self may be "driving your bus" at
the moment. Let's explore some perspective on these impacts:

1) Wounded Adults Pick Each Other Repeatedly

Co-parents controlled by false selves seem relentlessly attracted to other wounded partners. This may be because subliminally, shame "seeks its own level." Ex mate/s and alluring
new partners often have most or all of the six wounds, obviously or well-camouflaged. Needy and "in love" suitors (you?)
deny the wounds' origins and impacts, and their denials. This
means that several or all of a typical nuclear stepfamily's three
or more co-parents carry mixes of the psychological wounds
above, *and don't know it*. This combines with other major
unawarenesses (Chapters 5 and 6) to promote _ major stepfamily
conflict and stress, _ blocked grief, and _ ineffective communications. These and lack of informed social support cause accumulating personal and relationship stresses which eventually defeat love's newest dreams.

For many reasons, women and men who discover that their
second (or third) marriage has "failed" may resign themselves
to living in stable misery rather than experience the trauma,
expense, and risks of middle-aged redivorce. Millions of other
Americans feel the trauma is preferable to living in daily torment, specially if they're parenting minor kids.

Another inexorable result of false-self dominance and unawarenesses is that co-parents . . .

2) Unintentionally Wound Dependent Kids

Until troubled women and men achieve awareness and significant personal healing, they're very prone to re-create low-nurturance families. That *unconsciously* promotes adaptive false-self development in their dependent kids, just as the caregivers' (wounded) ancestors did. Until true (vs. pseudo) personal healing occurs, the silent bequest of ancestral "dysfunction" (inner wounding and ignorances) relentlessly passes down the generations and spreads in our society. Often, caregivers and professionals mistakenly designate their kids' wounds as personal *flaws*, character *defects*, personality *disorders,* or "adjustment problems." The real cause often stays in the shadows: adults' inherited psychological wounds, a chaotic *inner* family and disabled Self, ignorance, and a resulting low-nurturance environment.

Another common impact of the six inner wounds is to . . .

3) Live Below Your Personal Potential, and Die Early

In his lectures, recovery pioneer John Bradshaw uses a tombstone inscription metaphor to illustrate this third typical impact:

> *"Here lies Mary (John) Doe, who only lived half a life,*
> *and died never knowing who s/he really was."*

The paradox is that you can't know what you can dream and achieve until you break your (unseen) denials, and reorganize your inner family of subselves to trust the leadership of your true Self and Higher Power (Project 1). Believing you're capable of great things despite limiting childhoods and discouraging histories is an act of faith. Our ruling false selves protectively persuade us we're "average (or below)," and "shouldn't get our hopes up" about having a major impact on life on Earth. Baloney!

My badly wounded, addicted mother died just after her 50th birthday, in an era where average American women lived until their seventies. Genes, unawareness, and false-self dominance (wounds) cost her almost a third of her life. Her Christian Scientist mother died "of leukemia" at 47, when Mom was 15. Hospitals and hospices in your community are full of men and women like just them. From many stories like theirs and related research, I believe that unhealed false-self wounds weaken the immune system and promote psychosomatic *and* organic disorders. There are exceptions.

The last tragic impact of our interactive psychological wounds is cultural: they . . .

4) Contribute to an Interactive Web of Social Problems

As more unrecovering co-parents raise a widening fan of wounded kids, our society's finite resources are increasingly diverted to trying to counter (vs. heal) the *symptoms* of our wounded population: spiraling crime, addictions, poverty, abortions, welfare, divorce, "mental illnesses," suicide, obesity, homelessness, AIDS, and ill health.

We add more prisons, police, border guards, "miracle diets," and laws to control the symptoms, rather than focusing on what I see as our core problem: *Most American families are significantly low in emotional and spiritual nurturance. The (wounded) family leaders don't (want to) know it, or what to do about it.*

Led by our (wounded) legislators, policy makers, and media stars, we've all agreed to pretend otherwise (reality distortion) because the truth is too horrifying to face. Socially and religiously sanctioned low-nurturance (ineffective) parenting is the 600-pound gorilla in our national (global?) living room.

In 23 years' study and clinical practice, I have never seen any other stepfamily authors or speakers acknowledge some version of this inherited psychological wounding and its crippling effects. It's time to look at this sobering factor squarely and *do* something about it for our present and future kids. Project 1 here offers a viable scheme for safely bringing co-parents' inner wounds into awareness, and starting to *recover* from them.

I propose that if you partners avoid Project 1, you raise your odds of wrong re/marriage decisions toward 100%, despite your love, patience, dedication, experience, and hope. I have been recovering from *major* false-self dominance and related wounds for 15 years. I've been privileged to work clinically with scores of adults who are courageously reclaiming their lives from these wounds and related stressors. From my experience and theirs, I can report that true (vs. pseudo) recovery really improves life quality and productivity!

For many caregivers and human-service professionals, the impacts of denied psychological wounds are amplified by . . .

Hazard 2) Co-parent Unawarenesses

Co-parents like you are neither stupid nor shamefully ignorant. They're *unaware* because they weren't informed, and they don't know they *need* to be informed. Because few co-parents were raised in high-nurturance childhoods (extended family + schools + spiritual community + neighborhoods), they attempt marriage and child rearing with limited or no real understanding of the pre-re/marriage quiz items on p. 83, the stepfamily realities in Chapter 6, or the *60* common stepfamily misconceptions in ..04/myths.htm. In short, typical divorced and stepfamily co-parents *like you* are unaware of:

_ How to assess the nurturance level of key relationships and human groups. (Chapter 3 and http://sfhelp.org/01/health.htm)

_ The six common psychological wounds that can result from childhood nurturance deficits, their key symptoms and effects, how to spot significant false-self wounding, and how to restore true self leadership and inner-family harmony. Project 1 answers these.

_ How to use seven skills to think, communicate, and problem-solve effectively. The first of these is *awareness*. (Project 2 and ..02/links02.htm).

_ Common stepfamily traits, myths, realities, and adjust-ment tasks. This includes the special adjustment needs stepkids need to fill (p. 454).

_ How to assess for blocked grief and promote healthy mourning. (Project 5 and ..05/links05.htm).

_ High-nurturance self-care and childcare. And . . .

_ These five re/marital hazards, and the 12 protections out-lined on p. 122.

This book offers background and suggestions on each of these, and points to other sources of information and support. Partners' true-Self leadership, Self-motivated *education*, and risking second-order (core attitude) changes (p. 159) together can overcome this *unawareness* hazard!

In addition to _ unseen false-self dominance and _ toxic unawarenesses, typical divorced and courting co-parents like you, and your kids, face . . .

Hazard 3) Blocked Grief

Do you feel that the natural human healing process we call *mourning* can be blocked? We humans are born with the un-conscious ability to form strong emotional/spiritual attachments or bonds to other people, places, objects, freedoms, ideas, and activities. We learn to *care*. As our lives evolve in changing inner and outer environments, we inevitably must break these bonds by choice or uncontrollable circumstances. We call our broken emotional/spiritual bonds *losses*, so we're all *losers*.

We're endowed with a marvelous natural ability to recover stability after our losses via the three-level (mental + emotional + spiritual) process of grieving. The mental process moves from confusion to stable clarity. The emotional level moves through shock to distorted or "magic" thinking, to anger or rage, to sadness or despair, to stable *acceptance*. The spiritual level in-volves confusion and shaken (or no) spiritual faith, changing over time to initial, renewed, or even stronger faith in a benign Higher Power.

If allowed to complete over time, this natural three-level process frees adults and kids to resume a balanced life and form new bonds. However, our healing grief process can be slowed or blocked by a loser lacking inner and/or social permissions (shoulds, oughts, and musts) to go through these levels and phases at their own pace. Until experiencing credible inner and outer permissions to _ feel and _ express their grief questions and emotions as long as it takes, *blocked grievers often get physically and emotionally sick, and have relationship and other troubles.*

I believe that much of what is labeled "depression" is really being stuck in the sadness phase of normal grief. Our mega-billion-dollar psychiatric and pharmaceutical industries will strongly disagree. I also suspect that one major root of all addictions is the (fruitless) attempt to self-medicate the repressed and unexpressed rage and sorrow from major losses. This follows from the addict's not knowing they're _ being controlled by a misguided false self, _ unaware, and _ lacking inner and outer permissions to mourn.

Premise: low family-nurturance and co-parent unawareness promote blocked grief in their adults and kids. That may mean *you.* Notice your reactions . . .

(Re)marrying or not, typical women and men from low-nurturance childhoods have a special group of major childhood losses to mourn. Such people often accidentally inherit stern "shoulds" and "musts" that inhibit healthy grieving. Before true recovery, typical wounded adults aren't aware of this. They resist studying healthy grief and admitting that they may be protectively blocked.

Reality check: can you clearly describe _ the requisites for effective grieving now, and _ the signs of blocked grief? To assess your "grief IQ," take the good-grief quiz on p. 253. (Also at ..05/grief-quiz.htm).

Wounded adults and kids are often very uncomfortable around healthy grievers, because strong emotions in other people historically meant significant pain, guilt, and shame. So wounded, unaware co-parents give subtle or loud messages to active grievers, starting with kids: "Don't feel," and "Don't express your feelings around me or at all!" Sarah, Patty, and Jack in Chapter 7 all appeared to be blocked grievers. They seemed unaware of this, so the adults didn't see freeing blocked grief as a meaningful personal, marital, and stepfamily health issue.

Prior divorce or death causes a set of major losses for bioparents and their kids and close kin. Re/marriage and co-habiting causes *more* major losses for everyone, as well as wonderful gains for at least the new mates. Blocked grief promotes crippling addictions and illnesses, nourishes post-divorce hostilities, splits biological kids emotionally between their warring bioparents and family factions, and prevents even adult stepkids from accepting the kindest of stepparents.

Blocked mourning has clear symptoms, **and can be safely released** over time. Project 5 (p. 248) focuses on spotting and thawing frozen grief in co-parents and kids. As part of this project, you partners can learn to intentionally build *pro-grief* homes together, and to teach your kids the priceless ability to do "*good* grief." What did your caregivers teach you about grieving life losses *well*? Starting with yourself, could anyone dear to you currently lack solid inner and social permissions to *feel* and *express* their loss-related confusion, anger, and despair?

As if these three courtship pitfalls aren't enough, you face another. Fortunately for our species, it has no "cure:"

Hazard 4) Neediness and Romantic-love Distortions

We all have needs. Most wounded, unrecovering men and women are *extra*-needy. Many of their core needs (p. 49) aren't often or ever filled. They've usually learned to unconsciously camouflage this neediness from themselves (denial and repression) and others (pretending). Whether veteran spouses or never married, we wounded adults have high needs for affection, acceptance, empathy, affirmation, companionship, touching, sensual pleasure, safety, belonging, and hope: i.e. we need *love*!

Widowed and custodial "single" moms and dads also need at least situational help nurturing their minor kids and balancing many other responsibilities. Their minor and grown kids have special adjustment needs of their own, on top of the challenge of growing towards healthy independence. Human tradition and our hormones decree that adult pairing is normal, and most co-parents desperately need to be normal. (Do *you*?) So we court and decide to re/marry in a shared, wonderfully distorted mind-state: romantic love. Our normal idealistic dream is that co-committing and cohabiting will fill our and our kids' needs enough, and that life together will be significantly better than living alone.

False-self dominance, unawarenesses, neediness, and your primal urge to merge can combine to block you courting partners from wanting to learn what you're undertaking. You may not be motivated to learn what practical preparations you should make for long-term re/marital and stepfamily success. Does the illusion of "Our love will see us through" prevail? Sobering first-divorce (~47%) and re/divorce (over 60%) statistics imply that half or more of American adults *like you* currently make up to three wrong re/marriage decisions.

Typical men and women from low-nurturance childhoods who are "in (the benignly-deranged state of romantic) love" find that their minds (false selves) mysteriously "go elsewhere," when reading these stark statistics. I agree with veteran marriage counselor Dr. Harville Hendrix. He concludes that mate choice and commitment is far more an unconscious emotional process than a clear-headed rational one, though we try to convince ourselves otherwise. This is specially true in re/marriages involving prior kids and ex mates.

While there is (thankfully) no cure for romantic love, enlightened, recovering co-parents like you can learn to make more informed, balanced (spirit + head + heart + hormones) marriage decisions. You can help break the toxic (childhood wounding > divorce > stepfamily re/divorce) spiral that our wounded, unaware ancestors unintentionally pass on to us.

The last overarching hindrance to your re/marital and co-parental success is . . .

Hazard 5) Little Informed Support

Informed means "aware of the premises in this series of divorce-prevention books." Our media and most communities seem to offer little or no informed support for re/marrying partners and their kids and other co-parents. If suburban Chicago is typical, there are few or no *effective* _ pre-re/marriage and _ co-parenting classes, co-parent support groups, newsletters, or informed counselors in your community. Few clergypersons, teachers, therapists, divorce mediators, family law attorneys and judges, or medical professionals can describe the four re/divorce hazards you just read about. No one has trained them to see the whole mosaic of these five factors, and what impact they have on normal, well-meaning, needy people like the McLean-Tilmon-Cohen stepfamily you'll soon meet. *None* of them can name or describe the 12 safety measures in Chapter 8.

While competent in their specialties, many human-service professionals working with divorced families and step-people are like the five blind men exploring an elephant for the first time. Feeling the squirming trunk, one man says, "It is a snake!" A second man explores the elephant's ears, and says, "No, no, it is a palm frond." The third man runs his hands over the great belly and declares, "You're both mistaken. This is a boulder." Their fourth companion feels one of the mammoth legs and laughs: "you blind fools, this is clearly a tree!" The last blind man snaps, "How can you idiots not see that this is a rope!" He is holding the elephant's tail. All are making best-guess judgments of this new "thing," based on their prior experiences.

While typical co-parents like you can't educate the media or local community professionals on your stepfamily "elephant," you *can* intentionally educate yourself, and your kids, relatives, and friends via Projects 1 through 5. If you choose to re/wed, you can also start or contribute to a local co-parents' support (awareness-raising) group. See Project 11 and ..11/sg-intro.htm.

   # **Reality check:** see where you stand now: T = true, F = false, and "?" = "I'm not sure."

+ I can _ name and _ clearly describe the five hazards to successful stepfamily re/marriage (T F ?)

+ I can _ name and _ describe the six psychological wounds that come from too little early nurturance now (T F ?)

+ I accept that _ I and _ my partner may have mixes of these wounds, and not know it (T F ?)

+ I firmly believe all five hazards may significantly impact _ me and _ the people I care about now (T F ?)

+ I want to learn more about _ them, and _ the seven "antidote" projects in Part 2 now. (T F ?)

+ My partner is genuinely interested in learning about these now (T F ?)

+ I'm glad I'm reading this book now. (T F ?)

Recap

   This chapter outlines five hazards that I believe combine to cause most U.S. stepfamily re/marriages to fail, despite co-parents' love, maturity, and best efforts. If you're divorced, re/courting, or re/married, you adults and kids are at risk from:

   1) Adults' mixes of excessive shame, guilts, fears; trust and reality distortions, and bonding blocks from unseen false-self dominance; plus your . . .

   2) *Unawareness* (ignorance) of *inner*-family dynamics, communication skills, healthy grieving, and stepfamily and high-nurturance relationship concepts; plus . . .

   3) Frozen mourning in one or several of your kids and/or co-parents; plus . . .

   4) Your choosing to re/marry in a wonderful, ignorant, seriously-distorted mind state: romantic love; plus . . .

5) Lack of informed stepfamily and co-parenting classes, groups, and counsel in the media and your community.

Do you believe that these five factors could combine to cause you to (re)marry the wrong people, at the wrong time, for the wrong reasons? Can you think of any other reasons why so many Americans re/divorce? How many typical courting co-parents do you think could clearly name and discuss these five hazards? Could you, before reading this? If you and/or your partner have minor kids, they and any descendents silently depend on you to learn about and avoid these hazards!

Part 2 of this book offers seven specific protections against the combined power of these five toxic factors. The protections won't help if your false self persuades you that the hazards don't apply to you. You'll gain perspective on this when you meet the McLean-Tilmon-Cohen stepfamily in Chapter 7.

One proposed hazard is *unawareness*. The next two chapters give you a flavor of what typical courting co-parents like you need to know, in my seasoned opinion. Do you know what you don't know about key life skills and stepfamily realities? Notice your thoughts and feelings as you mull . . .

5) A Pre-re/marriage Quiz

45 Things Your Kids Need You to Know

Most lovestruck U.S. couples make wrong re/marital decisions because they're not aware of shared ignorances about _ themselves and each other, _ stepfamilies, and _ some key relationship skills. This quiz lets you gauge how much you and any partner know about key aspects of these three topics.

Pointers are given below to answers in this book, and on the Internet. Add the pointer (..**/***.htm) to http://sfhelp.org/ to form the whole Web address: http://sfhelp.org/**/***.htm. Another resource for Project-1 items below is "Who's *Really* Running Your Life?" (Xlibris.com, 2000).

Check each main item if you can confidently check all its sub-items ("_"). If you don't understand an item, see the chapters in Part 1, the projects in Part 2, and resources (Part 3), and/ or the referenced Web-pages.

+ + +

About Me and "Persons"

__ **1)** I can _ name and _ describe the subselves that comprise my *inner* family (personality); and I can _ say what each subself's main goal and talent is. (Project 1 and ..<u>01/ innerfam1.htm</u>).

___ **2)** I can _ clearly describe the difference between a "true Self" and a "false self," and _ I usually know when my *true* Self is making my key life decisions. (p. 139, Project 1, and ..<u>01/false-self.htm</u>). Is your Self taking this quiz now?

___ **3)** I can _ usually tell when a false self is controlling a child or another adult, and _ I'm often aware of my *inner* family's reactions when that's true. (Project 1, and p. 401)

___ **4)** I can name _ the six psychological wounds, and _ six or more of the behavioral symptoms of each of them. (pp. 66 and 401, Project 1, and ..<u>01/links01.htm</u>).

___ **5)** I can clearly describe to another person _ what the difference is between first-order human change and second-order change, _ how that difference relates to recovery from false-self dominance, and _ why that knowledge is vital to me and my loved ones in making major life decisions. (p. 159)

___ **6)** I know _ the difference between *shame* and *guilt*, _ where they each come from, and how to _ avoid and _ heal them over time. (Project 1, and ..<u>01/shame.htm</u>)

___ **7)** I know _ why *normal* anxiety is helpful, and _ how to reduce my anxieties and fears to an acceptable level. (Projects 1 and 2, and ..<u>01/fears.htm</u>)

___ **8)** I clearly know _ the difference between *spirituality* and *religion*, and _ how that relates to my and my kids' wholistic health. (Project 1)

___ **9)** I can _ name at least 25 of my rights as a unique, dignified human Being, and I _ usually live by them now. I _ respect and often _ encourage all others in my life to honor their identical rights, regardless of age, gender, culture, race, or role. (Projects 1 and 2, and ..<u>02/rights.htm</u>).

___ **10)** I'm usually clear on _ what my current *surface* needs are, and on _ my *true* needs "beneath" them. (p. 49, Project 2, and ..<u>02/dig-down.htm</u>).

___ **11)** I have _ soberly evaluated whether I was raised in a significantly low-nurturance family. If so, _ I am actively learning how that has been affecting my life choices so far. (pp. 48, 401, and 413, and Project 1)

__ 12) I can _ define what a *loss* is; and _ name the three levels of normal grieving and the _ key stages or phases of each of them, including _ when grieving is "done" well enough. (Project 5, and ..05/grief-intro.htm)

__ 13) I can describe _ the six key factors required for healthy three-level grieving, and _ how mourning can get blocked in a child or adult. (Project 5, and ..05/grief-6steps.htm).

__ 14) I know _ at least five of the symptoms of blocked grief, and _ how to support a mourner effectively. (p. 303, Project 5, and ..05/grief-symptoms.htm)

__ 15) I know _ the difference between active grieving and "depression," and _ how to react to each of these in _ myself and _ other people I care about. (Project 5)

__ 16) I can clearly describe _ what my *childhood* family's "grief policy" was, and _ how that affected my ability to mourn well. I can _ describe what my *current* family's grief policy is, and _ whether it promotes healthy or blocked grief. (p. 297, Project 5, and ..05/griefpol.htm)

About High-nurturance Relationships

__ 17) I can _ name the four groups of ingredients needed for a "healthy (high nurturance) relationship" between any two people, and _ at least 10 of the individual ingredients. See ..08/relationship.htm

__ 18) I can clearly describe at least six of the key differences between a *nurturing* relationship and a *toxic* relationship. See ..site/premises-pg.htm.

__ 19) I can now describe _ how the *inner* families of two people in a relationship interact, and I _ know how to talk about that interaction productively with my relationship partners. See ..01/ifs1-intro.htm and ..02/metatalk.htm.

__ 20) I can _ clearly describe each of the 34 relationship terms at ..02/terms.htm). I usually know _ when and _ how to apply them in my activities, and _ how to explain them clearly to kids in my life.

____ **21)** I can _ name at least seven or more of the common symptoms of "co-dependence" (relationship addiction), and _ I know whether *I* have the condition of co-dependence to a significant degree. If I do, _ I know my recovery options. (p. 413) or ..01/co-dep.htm, ..01/recovery1.htm, and Project 1.

____ **22)** I can clearly describe _ what a persecutor-victim-rescuer (PVR) "relationship triangle" is; _ why they can significantly stress our relationships (specially if minor kids are involved); and what responsible adults can do to _ avoid and _ dissolve these triangles. (..09/triangles.htm and Project 9).

____ **23)** I can _ describe what an "awareness bubble" is, and _ how partners' mutual awareness of such bubbles can help them avoid and resolve major communication and relationship conflicts. (Project 2, *Satisfactions,* and ..02/a-bubble.htm).

____ **24)** I can _ describe what *"effective* communication" is, _ the six needs all adults and kids try to fill by communicating, _ the four simultaneous messages we all decode *unconsciously* from each other, and _ at least 10 of the 25+ common dynamics that block communication. (Project 2, the book *"Satisfactions—*7 Relationship Skills You Need to Know" (Xlibris.com, 2001), and ..02/links02.htm).

____ **25** I can _ name the seven mental/verbal skills that promote effective communications, _ how to *do* each skill, and _ when to use each; and _ *I'm committed to helping the young people in my life learn to understand and use these skills effectively* (Ditto).

____ **26)** I can name at least 10 of the ~35 important *process* factors that I can be aware of as I communicate with other people. (Project 2, *Satisfactions,* ..02/awareness.htm, and ..02/metatalk.htm).

____ **27)** As I communicate, including with myself, I'm usually aware of the single core factor that determines whether my communication *may* be effective or not. (p. 170, Project 2, *Satisfactions,* and ..02/evc-intro.htm.

__ **28)** I can _ clearly describe what a *values* conflict is, _ why resolving it is different than a *resource* conflict or a *communication-need* conflict, and _ how partners can usually best resolve values conflicts. (Project 2, *Satisfactions*, and ..09/lc-intro.htm).

__ **29)** I can _ clearly describe the difference between *fighting* or *arguing,* and interpersonal *problem solving*; and I _ often apply that awareness effectively in resolving significant disputes in my inner and outer relationships. (Project 2, *Satisfactions*, and ..02/prblmslv.htm).

__ **30)** I can _ clearly distinguish between an *internal* conflict and an *interpersonal* conflict, and I _ know how to use that knowledge effectively in conducting my key relationships. (p. 501, Projects 1 and 2, and ..01/innerfam1.htm).

__ **31)** I can clearly describe _ the three kinds of assertion, and _ the difference between *assertion* and *aggression*; and I _ am often skilled at *asserting* respectfully to help others understand what I need from them. That includes _ giving assertive *praise.* (Project 2, *Satisfactions*, and ..02/assert.htm).

__ **32)** I know _ how to communicate effectively with a person who is "out of control," and I'm _ helping the young people in my life learn how to do that calmly and confidently. (Project 2, *Satisfactions*, and ..02/listen.htm).

__ **33)** I can describe _ "communication *mapping*", and _ when and _ how to use it effectively, to resolve major communication problems I have with key other people. (Project 2, *Satisfactions*, and ..02/evc-maps.htm).

__ **34)** I can clearly describe the key _ traits of, and the _ differences between *dependent, interdependent,* and *independent* relationships; and I can _ say how those ideas affect whom I choose for key relationships. (Project 7, and ..Rx/mates/love.htm).

__ **35)** I can name _ the three phases of a "divorce," _ the typical divorce-adjustment tasks kids and adults face, and _ how to judge when a divorce is "finished." (p. 503, ..pop/divorce.htm, and ..pop/divorce-adjust.htm).

About *Family* and *Parenting Basics* . . .

___ **36)** I can name at least 20 of the 28 traits of a high-nurturance ("functional") family. (p. 51 and ..01/health.htm).

___ **37)** I can describe _ what a family *mission* or *vision* statement is, _ how co-parents can evolve one over time, and _ why doing so is vital to prevent re/divorce trauma. (p. 325, Project 6, and ..06/mission1.htm).

___ **38)** I _ can define most of the terms in Resource G (p. 493), and _ I often use them effectively in conducting my family relationships. See also *Satisfactions* (Glossary) and ..02/terms.htm.

___ **39)** I can adequately diagram the *structure* of _ a healthy intact nuclear biofamily, and _ a multi-home stepfamily system; and _ I know how to use these diagrams effectively to help solve family structural problems. (..09/map-str1.htm).

___ **40)** I can clearly describe _ what *effective* parenting is, and _ at least 10 of typical kids' key developmental needs, as they grow toward adult independence. (p. 457, Project 6, and ..10/co-p-goals.htm).

___ **41)** I can clearly name _ the six psychological wounds that typical kids in or from significantly low-nurturance families often develop (p. 142 and Project 1), and _ at least 25 of the ~ 50 common behavioral traits that suggest these six wounds. (p. 401 and 413, or ..01/w1-gwctraits1.htm).

___ **42)** I can describe at least 10 of the several dozen typical concurrent adjustment needs that kids (and most co-parents) each have because of parental divorce or death and re/marriage. (p. 454 or ..10/kid-needs.htm).

___ **43)** I can clearly describe _ a family *role* conflict, _ a co-parent "job (role) description", and _ how such a description relates to a family's mission statement; and I can effectively help adults _ avoid and _ resolve family-caregiver role conflicts. (p. 340, Project 6, ..06/mission1.htm, ..10/job1.htm, and ..10/project10.htm).

___ **44)** I know _ how to draw a multi-generational family *map* or genogram, and _ how to use one to help understand and resolve significant family *role, membership,* and *relationship* conflicts. (p. 96 and ..03/geno1.htm).

__ **45)** I _ know and accept well over half of the stepfamily realities in Chapter 6 (p. 91) and _ the 44 items above, *or* I'm _ very motivated to learn, tailor, an apply them now. See also http://sfhelp.org/04/myths.htm.

I believe courting or re/married co-parents who can answer most of these items have the best chance for long-term health and relationship success. Anyone who can read can learn the answers!

Pause. Breathe well, close your eyes, and notice with interest what your "inner voices" (thoughts) are saying. What does that mean to you? Consider journaling about what's going on in your *inner* family, right now . . .

What Now?

How did you do? If you found these 45 questions overwhelming, easy does it. I've met few veteran co-parents who knew even a third of these personal, relationship, and family basics. Most of our parents and grandparents didn't know these things when they were raising us. Many human-service professionals weren't taught them either!

I hope this quiz experience will motivate you to learn more about your unique, amazing *inner* family via Project 1, and how you can significantly raise the nurturance levels in your internal and social relationships. If you want to share, discuss, or give a copy of this quiz to someone, see http://sfhelp.org/07/quiz.htm.

As you see, there's a *lot* to learn, apply, and teach your kids! Doing this patiently over time with "the mind of a student" is a priceless investment in raising the quality of your days, your health, and your life. Option: re-scan this quiz, hi-light or star the items that raise your anxiety or interest, and follow each of the references over some weeks to learn what's there. Another option is to find a learning partner to do this with, and assess and discuss as you go.

Reality check: See how your inner crew feels about what you just read:

1) I firmly agree that my partner and I would benefit from learning the topics above, over time (T F ?)

2) I'm sure my partner will agree on this with me now (T F ?)

3) I want to allocate time and energy to learning these concepts in the weeks ahead. (T F ?)

4) Learning about these topics with my partner is among my top five life priorities now. (T F ?)

5) I'm confident I can learn as much as I need to about these topics over time, in order to make wise stepfamily re/ marriage decisions in Project 7. (T F ?)

6) My Self is answering these questions now. (T F ?)

Recap: I believe that *unawareness* (lack of conceptual knowledge and current-environment consciousness, not stupidity) **is one of five causes of** widespread family unhappiness and **(re)divorce**. This quiz invites you to experience how much there is for you to learn and form your *own* opinions about, to _ co-parent effectively and _ make *informed* re/marriage decisions. Typical divorced and re/wedded co-parents and their lay and professional supporters couldn't name all the items in this quiz, let alone answer each of them in any depth.

To further shrink unawareness and prepare you to make three wise re/marriage choices, see how realistic your ideas about stepfamilies are. Study this summary of . . .

6) Stepfamily Realities

Typical courting co-parents like you aren't aware of some normal aspects of typical multi-home stepfamilies like those summarized below. This sharply raises the odds you and your partner will make complex re/marriage decisions based on ignorance and distorted (biofamily-based) expectations. See which of these factors are new to you, and note your reactions to them. Add the pointers below (..**/***.htm) to http:// sfhelp.org/ to get the Web address of supportive Web materials. For example, see a version of this chapter at http://sfhelp.org/ 03/facts.htm.

A *stepfamily* has at least one adult taking the role of stepmom or stepdad. S/He provides part-time or full-time nurturing, protection, and guidance to one or more of her or his partner's minor or grown biokids, who are expected to accept and learn the non-voluntary role of *stepchild*. Step, foster, and adoptive co-parents usually have no genetic link to the kids they nurture.

Stepfamilies are normal! They've been around as long as tribal members raised the children of dead or disabled bioparents. Stepfamilies have probably been the majority family type across centuries and cultures, until modern healthcare greatly reduced the human mortality rate in the past century.

Our current English prefix "step-" comes across a thousand years from the Middle English root "stoep." William the

Conqueror's subjects used that root to describe "orphaned" or "deprived" minor children, and any families that cared for them.

There are almost **100 structural types of multi-home stepfamily**, considering combinations of . . .

+ Child custody (sole, joint, physical, and legal);

+ Parenthood (no prior kids; one or more prior sons, and/ or daughters; one or more "ours" kids, or none; prior kids dead; kids dependent or grown; teenagers or none; stepparent adoption or not . . .);

+ Co-parents' prior marital status (divorced, widowed or never married); and . . .

+ Stepkids' other bioparent's status: _ living or dead; _ single and never remarried or re/divorced; or _ re/married with or without resident and/or visiting minor, teen, or grown stepkids).

This diversity means that unlike most intact-biofamily members, typical stepfamily adults and kids like you will never meet people in a similarly-structured stepfamily. This can foster vague or sharp feelings of social isolation and "weirdness."

Typical **stepfamilies differ from intact biofamilies in over 30 structural ways**, including more roles, homes, and members (p. 425). Typical extended (multi-generational) stepfamilies can have over 100 members related by genes, wills, contracts, and marriage licenses; from three or more previously-unrelated extended biofamilies, living in *many* widely-scattered homes.

Gee-whiz fact: The number of possible relationships among all your step-members ("R") is often incomprehensible. In any group of beings, R = [N (the number of members) x (N-1) / 2]. So a three-generational stepfamily with 87 adults and kids can have [(87 x 86) / 2] = 3,741 possible relationships! Similarly, a household of five kids and adults has [(5 x 4) / 2 = 10] possible relationships. Pets and "close family friends" add more.

A new six-co-parent, five-child nuclear stepfamily living in three homes has [(11 x 10) / 2] = 55 relationships to negotiate, stabilize, and prioritize. Most of these are people who have only recently just met. How many relationships are there in your home? In your whole family? How long does it take you to stabilize a new relationship? How can you tell when a group of relationships has *stabilized*?

More stepfamily realities:

Average **new** two or three-home nuclear **stepfamilies have up to 30 simultaneous adjustment tasks** to resolve which members of average intact biofamilies don't face (p. 435 and ..<u>09/ sf-task1.htm</u>). The tasks come from adults and kids needing to negotiate post-re/wedding mergers of over a dozen emotionally-charged topics and resources like family roles, rules, rituals, and traditions; family and ancestral values, priorities, and morals; physical assets and legal ownership; spiritual and religious beliefs and practices; communication styles; and balances of work, play and rest.

And typical new stepfamilies have to . . .

Evolve up to 15 alien new *roles*, usually with no personal experience or social norms. For example: step-uncle, stepson, half-sister, step-cousin, non-custodial biofather, step-great-grandmother, stepmother, step-niece . . . These evolve while members revise the 15 traditional extended-biofamily roles like son, daughter, aunt, grandfather, sister-in-law, brother, mother . . .

There are no socially accepted norms for these strange new step-roles yet. That means members of each stepfamily (you all) have to negotiate them and the rules about how to perform the roles well, over time. This is usually confusing, awkward, and frustrating for everyone at times, specially if the adults involved aren't effective thinkers or communicators. Also . . .

Typical stepparents and bioparents want to guide, nurture, protect, and enjoy their (step)kids. However, the personal, household, and social **environments in which stepparents try to achieve these goals differ in ~*40* ways** from average intact biofamilies. Also, typical minor stepkids need *informed* caregiver help with filling up to four sets of confusing developmental and adjustment needs. See ..<u>10/co-p-dfrnces.htm</u> and p. 454 or ..<u>10/kid-needs.htm</u>.

Combined, these differences and alien tasks inevitably yield confusion, doubt, misunderstandings, frustrations, "failures," and stresses for the adults and kids involved. This is one of the reasons that effective communication (Project 2) is so vital among your nuclear stepfamily's three or more co-parents, kids, and kin!

About 90% of U.S. stepfamilies form after the divorce of one or both new mates. A brief century ago, ~90% followed the death of one or both mates' prior partners. We've come a long way in the last two generations in reducing the shaming stigma of divorce, and there's more to go.

Still *more* stepfamily realities . . .

American **stepfamily couples are more apt to differ widely** in age, race, religion, ethnic ancestry, and educational level than typical biocouples. Stepfamily wives are more likely to be older than their husbands than in first marriages. Collectively, these differences may _ add to members feeling personally and socially *odd* or *unusual*, _ hinder biofamily mergers, and _ cause shifts in friendships and biofamily approval and allegiances.

As they mature, extended stepfamilies pass through **extra developmental stages** that intact biofamilies don't encounter. These stages may inhibit or alter the quality of adults' and kids' individual developmental growth. See ..09/develop1.htm.

A typical minor or grown stepchild may . . .

+ Have three or four co-parents (a divorced biomom and biodad, and a stepmom, a stepdad, or both), living in two different homes.

+ Have zero to eight living co-grandparents, and a proportionately large number of step-aunts, uncles, cousins, and other relatives.

+ Have biosiblings, stepsiblings, and/or half-siblings in the same home, in their other bioparent's home, in both homes, or neither.

+ May be legally adopted by their stepparent. Most U.S. stepparents don't adopt, so they have far fewer legal rights and responsibilities for their stepkids (..Rx/spsc/adopt.htm).

+ may have the same first name as a stepsibling and/or their same-sex stepparent, and may have a different last name than their re/married biomom.

+ may receive no bequest if a stepparent dies without a will, even if they were emotionally close for many years. And typical stepkids may . . .

+ feel sexually attracted (or attractive) to a resident or visiting stepsibling, and/or a stepparent, because the incest taboo is weaker in average stepfamilies. The odds of stepdaughter incest by a step-relative are significantly higher than daughters in biofamilies (..Rx/spsc/lust.htm).

+ change homes. In about 30% of typical U.S. stepfamilies, one or more minor children change primary residence to live with their other bioparent. This creates waves of unexpected emotional, financial, structural, legal, and lifestyle changes in and between both their homes (..Rx/spl/kid-moves1.htm). And . . .

+ face up ~35 concurrent adjustment tasks from childhood trauma, parental divorce and remarriage/s, and becoming a stepchild, on top of ~25 normal developmental tasks. Kids often face these confusing needs with little or no informed guidance from co-parents, teachers, relatives, or others. (p. 454 or ..10/kid-needs.htm).

To help these paragraphs become more real, study the *partial* diagram of a real stepfamily below. The names are false, but the people are real.

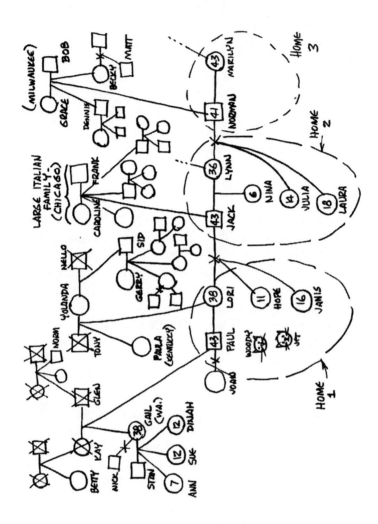

In other ways, average multi-home stepfamilies and intact nuclear biofamilies look just the same (p. 424). This can lull courting co-parents into a false sense of pre-re/wedding security ("A family's just a family. How different could our new family be?"). They (you?) have little motivation to learn or apply what you just read.

So What?

Unawareness of all these combined structural and dynamic differences, and their implications, causes up to 60 common misconceptions about stepfamily life for courting couples and supporters (..04/myths.htm). This puts you partners at risk of trying to build a complex multi-home, multi-task stepfamily with unrealistic (biofamily based) expectations—like expecting your lungs to work normally under water. Co-parents seeking help with the resulting confusions and conflicts may not discern that most clinicians, clergy, and self-help authors are equally prone to use bio-based myths vs. step-norms.

Reality check: imagine asking your counselor, minister or rabbi, and your kids' key teachers and relatives, to name over half of the stepfamily realities you just read. How do you think they would do?

These stepfamily unawarenesses add to those you read in the last chapter. Are you better appreciating the simple statement "most co-parents don't know what they don't know about typical stepfamily norms, dynamics, and stressors"? Does *unawareness* seem more credible and meaningful as a re/divorce hazard now?

Read about you and your courting peers and broaden your perspective at ..07/sf-scene.htm. To help that sketch and the stepfamily realities above come to life now, meet a real stepfamily: the McLean-Tilmon-Cohen clan . . .

7) One Stepfamily's Story
Meet the McLean-Tilmon-Cohen Clan

Though every stepfamily is as unique as a fingerprint, they all have common themes. This book springs from the themes of hundreds of unique stories that co-parents, kids, and authors have told me since 1979. This chapter illustrates the themes with a sketch of the McLean-Tilmon-Cohen stepfamily. Their five co-parents and five minor kids living in four related homes form one of almost 100 structural kinds of nuclear stepfamily. Four of the caregivers are dual-role co-parents: they each have bioparent and stepparent responsibilities and goals.

Their full story could easily fill a book. The vignette you're about to read hilights enough of their saga to illustrate the five stepfamily-re/divorce hazards (Chapter 4) at work. It also illustrates a typical couple's reaction to early-phase stepfamily education and therapy. The names here are false, but the people and their situation are real. These co-parents and kids represent *millions* of U.S. stepfamilies, probably including yours.

Sarah, Jack, and Patty's Story

Understanding "Who's who?" in a typical stepfamily can be confusing. To help place the people in this story, study the partial stepfamily map (genogram) below. For simplicity, all 12 co-grandparents, and dozens of the five minor kids' other relatives aren't shown. Neither is Ted McLean's 35-year old "girl-friend" Tanya, the divorced custodial mom of four-year-old Melissa.

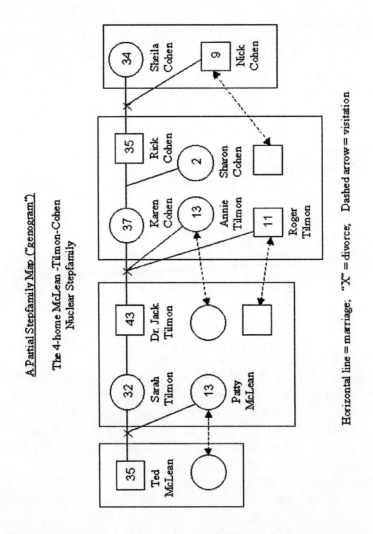

A Partial Stepfamily Map ("genogram")

The 4-home McLean-Tilmon-Cohen Nuclear Stepfamily

Horizontal line = marriage; "X" = divorce; Dashed arrow = visitation

Patty McLean came into my office with her Mother Sarah Tilmon on a Saturday morning. The slender, pretty 13-year-old had never worked with a counselor before, though she knew her mother had gone to several for "something." Patty had recently asked her Mom to "talk to somebody" about "something" to do with her live-in stepfather Jack.

Sarah was a vivacious, overweight, 30-something brunette. Months before, she met with me because of tensions in her one-year-old remarriage to a wonderful divorced father of two non-custodial kids Roger and Annie. Sarah was struggling with a web of personal, parental, and remarital "problems." She had a high school education, and worked as a beautician. Just before she brought Patty in, Sarah told me matter-of-factly that she (the Mom) had been sexually molested at 13. She'd had no professional help in coping with the massive psychological wounds that resulted.

Sarah sketched her stepfamily story. Eye contact seemed hard for her. It appeared that she had again chosen a strong-willed, take-charge partner like her first husband Ted, though Jack was not alcoholic as Ted was. Eventually Jack came in with Sarah to support her getting "parenting education." In his mid-forties, he was a dentist with a successful suburban practice. That was an initial clue to me, for many psychologically-wounded adults seem to choose a "helping profession," as I have.

Jack was compact, talkative, opinionated, and somewhat righteous. He felt he had given "his all" to his former wife Karen and his kids. He was still angry and "mystified" about Karen's divorcing him, and her "irrational" claim that he was "impossible to live with." With little emotion, this earnest dual-role dad said that his father had deserted him and his mother when Jack was about six. This suggested low childhood nurturance to me, as did Sarah's sexual abuse.

Sarah's second husband was adamant that his (vs. *their*) new family was *not* a "stepfamily." His firm opinion was that "Labels aren't unimportant. *Love* is!" He came in to provide love, protection, and strong Christian male guidance to Sarah and Patty, while being a devoted absent father to his biokids, and a responsible health professional in their community. His *heart* was in the right place, but his wounds misguided it.

As I learned more about their stepfamily, it appeared that Jack had remarried (partly) to *save* Sarah and her daughter from chaos, stress, and worry. As with many of us from low-nurturance childhoods, he seemed to see his wife and step-daughter (and most things) in rigid, black-and-white terms. Jack's views implied that he saw Sarah as lovable and incompetent at just about everything, including raising Patty.

In Jack's eyes, their rewedding 18 months before instantly promoted him to the head of their new household. He had imposed a rigid code of discipline with Patty in their home, feeling that Sarah "was too soft" on her early-teen daughter. Jack felt genuine concern that Patty "was headed for (some unspecified) big trouble." He was critical and irate that Patty's dad Ted had "weaseled out" of his fathering responsibilities, leaving Jack to "clean up their mess." He had no wish to enlist Ted as a co-parenting teammate, despising him for having abandoned Patty—just as Jack's father had left him long ago. He rarely spoke to Ted or showed any real interest in his life. Both men ignored each other to avoid probable conflict and painful self-awarenesses.

Sarah and Jack demonstrated a mystery I've seen often: they each *unconsciously* chose a partner who gave them the chance to face and resolve major unhealed childhood wounds.

Sarah seemed to be overwhelmed with Jack's righteous, rigid forcefulness. Caught "in the middle," she had begun explaining lamely to Patty that Jack "really meant well," which he did! Sarah's timid attempts to get Jack to compromise and "be softer, and make friends" with her daughter earned condescending monologs on "correct parenting," "It's for her own good," and on Sarah's inadequacies as a mother and wife. Jack seemed unaware that he was continuing a devastating pattern of over-controlling and shaming that Sarah had experienced from both her father and Ted. This same attitude and denied denial had helped destroy Jack's first marriage.

I saw that neither Sarah nor Jack knew how to *listen* empathically or problem-solve effectively. Like many co-parent couples, they were locked in a corrosive, lose-lose *values*

conflict over "good parenting." Jack was unflinching, confident, and "assertive" (i.e. rigid and *aggressive*) in his judgments. Because Sarah felt unsure and poorly about herself as a
person and mother, she felt powerless, intimidated, shamed,
guilty, frustrated demeaned, and increasingly despairing.

She was losing respect for, and trust in, her husband, and
was becoming resentful and angry. Yet she didn't feel justified
or safe in expressing those feelings. One result was that Sarah
was withdrawing emotionally and physically, which made Jack
"irritable" (i.e. hurt, uneasy, and angry). As a deeply wounded,
shame-based man in major denial, he made no apparent conscious connection between Sarah's emotional and physical with-
drawals and his ex-wife Karen's decision to leave him.

Sarah brought Patty in that Saturday because the girl was
having trouble in her new school. She had begun hinting to her
Mom that she was thinking of running away. This is a common
clinical pattern: an anxious bioparent or concerned stepparent,
usually a woman, will initiate counseling to help a troubled
stepchild. This is safer than confronting a significant *re/marital*
problem.

I spent half an hour with Patty and her mom, building the
girl's initial trust in our process and me. When I asked to meet
with Patty alone, both agreed. As soon as Sarah left the room,
Patty's warm brown eyes filled with tears, and her mouth quiv-
ered. In escalating gusts and sobs she told me some of her
story. We met alone several other times, and a familiar heart-
wrenching saga emerged. She felt hopeless, unsafe, and overwhelmed by a set of tensions she could barely describe, let
alone cope with. She knew her mother loved her, and felt intensely angry and scornful that Sarah wouldn't "stand up" to
her domineering stepfather and protect her (Patty) from his
endless lectures, rules, criticisms, and groundings.

Part of Patty's stepfamily pain was periodic. When her
stepsibs Annie (13) and Roger (11) came to visit every other
weekend, she usually felt that Jack favored them over her, despite his indignant denial. Annie would leave her clothes strewn
around the house, and her father never yelled at her the way he

did at Patty. Jack was specially supportive of Roger's progress at school sports, while he alternated between indifference to, and criticism of, Patty's gymnastic efforts.

Eventually I asked Patty if either of her bioparents had explained to her why they got divorced. She dropped her eyes and said quietly "Well, sort of." Further gentle probing revealed that she really wasn't clear on that, and felt much inner confusion and conflict about the losses and stress her parent's divorce had caused. Patty said sadly that her "real" father (Ted) didn't seem to care much about her. I wondered: "is this false-self inability to bond, and/or blocked grief?"

She described several instances where her Dad promised to attend school parent-conferences and gymnastic meets, but never came. "He always has excuses," she said woodenly. When I asked about her father's drinking, the slender girl looked away. "It scares me, sometimes. Mom won't let him drive me anywhere now because she's scared we'll have an accident. That makes him real angry, because he doesn't think he has a problem." I asked, "Do you?" Patty nodded silently, looking away.

Much of Patty's story was about instances where she felt Jack was unfair and harshly critical "over *nothing*!" He often restricted her phone calls with friends as punishment for her "bad" school grades (Bs and Cs), cutting off her main source of human sympathy and support. "He never *listens* to me," she grimaced. "When Mom tries to argue, he just walks all over her. And she *lets* him! Our life wasn't all that great before he came around, but I *hate* it now!"

I asked if there was any adult in her life who understood how she felt these days. Patty's long brown hair swung as she shook her head. Her nearest relative was her mother's sister, who lived about 50 miles away. I asked if there were things that got in the way of her talking honestly with her mother. She nodded, and again looked away. In her soft voice, the girl eventually was able to tell me she thought her mom was miserable and scared. "So I can't tell her how much I hate Jack in our life. She has enough problems! You know, she's already taking some pills for depression." Then an angry part of Patty spoke: "Why did she ever marry that dumb jerk, anyway? This is really *her* fault!" She began to cry again.

The girl described sadness and frustration about her social life. "Jack won't let me have friends in my room. I don't like to have them over anyway, because he is such a dork! And Mom is such a wimp!" I asked how she got along with her stepsister and stepbrother. "Annie's all right, I guess. We can talk about some stuff, and we like the same music. She feels her father's too strict too, but she never talks back to him. Roger is *so* stuck up. He thinks he's so great! He sucks up to his Dad, and he (Jack) just eats that up. It makes me *sick!*"

At some length, Patty described her anguish over really liking a boy at school, and Jack and her mother saying he "wasn't her kind of boy." "What do they know about it?" she declared angrily. "It's *my* life, isn't it?" She hinted that she was sneaking out to be with him "no matter what they think!" I noted silently that Patty's big hoop earrings, tight clothes, and overdone makeup signaled both "growing up early in America," and her apparent desperation for some male approval, closeness, and social normalcy.

I worked with this stepfamily trio individually and together for perhaps 15 sessions before the adults quit. I suggested several times it would be helpful for Jack, Sarah, and me to meet with their other co-parents "to strengthen communications and teamwork," but both partners balked, for several (surface) reasons. By coincidence or Divine intervention, Jack's ex-wife Karen had enrolled herself and second husband Rick Cohen in a co-parenting class I gave during this time.

Over seven weeks, I sensed that the Cohens were a reasonably stable, moderately wounded couple. They had fully accepted their stepfamily identity, and were mutually eager to learn the ropes for themselves and their kids. An important factor in their home's stability was that Rick and his ex wife Sheila had a relatively co-operative relationship around raising their nine-year-old son Nicholas. They seemed to have genuinely resolved most major issues around their separation and divorce and his remarriage.

Karen and Rick Cohen were respectful to Jack and Sarah, and genuinely concerned about Patty. They rarely saw her, and were unsure on how to support the young teen. Karen had learned to set clear, firm co-parenting limits with Jack on visitation, support, and holiday issues around their kids Annie and Roger. She had talked empathically with Sarah about "how (rigid and critical) Jack can be." Karen was careful not to criticize Jack in front of their kids, camouflaging some strong disagreements with his personal and parenting values and methods.

I suspect that the Tilmons (i.e. Jack) stopped consulting me because we were getting too close to confronting the real causes of the tensions inside their skins and home. I think both Sarah and Jack sensed subliminally that they were heading towards psychological and legal redivorce, but their dominant false selves and unawarenesses blocked their genuine wish to reverse course. This struggling couple and their four co-parenting partners and five minor kids formed a classic example of the best and the worst in a normal, complex nuclear stepfamily.

The combined power of five re/divorce factors was clearly eroding the Tilmon's remarriage and home, but not the Cohen's. My guess was that Patty McLean's biofather Ted was a psychologically wounded man still struggling with his own conflicted subselves. I never spoke with him. His reportedly increasing alcohol addiction and protective denials demonstrated a classic (futile) attempt to self-medicate from his childhood legacy of shame, guilt, fear, confusion, and emptiness. This toxic stew caused him to avoid the pain he felt around his daughter Patty. His unexplained absence from her life was silently promoting her own set of similar psychological wounds, compounded by Sarah and Jack's major childhood injuries.

The Five Hazards at Work

How were the five common re/marital hazards combining to affect the McLean-Tilmon home? Here's an overview:

1) False-self Dominance and Wounds

As with over 80% of the hundreds of divorced and stepfamily co-parents I've worked with since 1981, Sarah, Jack, and (apparently) Patty's biofather Ted seemed to be significantly burdened by psychological wounds (p. 66), *and didn't know it*. As kids, they had each adapted to low psycho-spiritual nurturance deficits (neglect) by unconsciously forming a protective, reactive false self (p. 139). Their respective early caregivers were surely fragmented also. These ancestors gave their best, while burdened with significant psychological wounds and ignorance of what was needed for personal wholistic health, and a high-nurturance marriage and family.

Jack would have been surprised and "irritated" (insulted, defensive, and threatened) to hear that I saw him as "badly wounded." If I had been frank with him about this opinion, he'd probably have quit therapy earlier than he did. He would have gravely agreed that Sarah and her former husband "had major problems." Sarah acknowledged (some of) her emotional-spiritual wounds, but was bewildered about what to do about them. What wounds?

Sarah's deepest false-self wounds were **excessive shame and guilt**. Her sexual molestation at 13, lack of education and other childhood deprivations, and her early stressful marriage and later divorce, combined to give her a half-conscious core belief that she was a tainted, stupid, inept, *bad* female. This had many unconscious impacts on her remarriage to Jack and her bewildered daughter Patty. One impact was the distorted belief that Sarah felt the only way she could merit love and support from a man was through sexual co-operation.

That fit fine for Jack. He (his governing subselves) needed a dependant, compliant, desirable child-woman partner to "fix," so he could feel "good," and avoid looking honestly at himself. Sarah was torn between compulsively eating fats and sugars to temporarily numb her inner pain, and enduring Jack's (and her *Inner Critic*) ridiculing her extra 50 pounds and "looking like a pig." Her shame, fears, and other inner wounds locked her into a verbally abusive (shaming) marriage by crippling any belief that she could earn enough to support her and Patty without Jack's income. Sarah felt trapped, inadequate, confused, and depressed. This was increasingly burdening Patty, on top of the girl's complex teen-development and stepfamily-adjustment challenges (p. 454).

Like Sarah, Jack was clearly controlled by shame-based personality subselves. He was in classic protective denial of his deep inner wounds and their major effects on him, Sarah, and all three older stepfamily kids. He had camouflaged his inner chaos and pain by earning the public image of a successful, competent dentist, and a devoted non-custodial Christian-patriarch biofather. Where Sarah turned to compulsive over-eating, Jack used overworking and righteous religion (vs. spirituality) to distract from his relentless old inner pain and wounds. Sarah's ex husband had turned to ethyl alcohol to self medicate from *his* inner pain.

Another unseen false-self wound destroying Jack's second marriage was his **reality distortion**: i.e. perceiving things that weren't there (illusions), and not seeing things that *were* there (denials and repressions). For example, when Jack told Sarah "I love you," he really meant, "I desire and *pity* you. As a good Christian man, I will patiently *rescue* and *fix* you because you're incompetent and floundering." Just as her father had, Jack consistently sent Sarah mixed messages: "I'll gladly commit to you, and I want to support and love you;" and "You're stupid, inept, and hopeless. You'll never be able to stand on your own, so do what I say and be grateful." The latter (unseen) attitude doomed their communication effectiveness, because it implied "I'm 1-up (superior) to you." Sarah's shamed subselves agreed ("I'm 1-down").

Another of Jack's significant reality distortions (denials) was "I don't need or have time for self-exploration." A third was "We are not a *step*family, so we (I) don't need to examine our family roles, or special education and support. I'm acting like a responsible (bio)father to Patty. I am *not* a stepfather."

Implication: "She better treat me like a biodad and Sarah better go along, or I am a victim, and they are *wrong* and *bad*."

Yet another shame-based distortion Jack's Guardian subselves promoted was "I had little to do with my first divorce, and am a victim. Karen made a major mistake in leaving me, for which I'll generously forgive her." The biggest distortion of all (besides denying all of these) was "I am *not* majorly wounded by my father's early abandonment, and by my overwhelmed (wounded) mother's inability to consistently fill my nurturance-needs as a boy. I am OK enough!"

No he wasn't. It appeared that the five hazards were inexorably propelling him, Sarah, and Patty toward their second divorces, in mid-life.

Mixed messages are a common symptom of **significant false-self dominance**. There were many "Jacks" (subselves) living inside his body, well short of his being a full "multiple personality." One Jack was a truly thoughtful, patient, kind, decisive, adult man with a fun sense of humor. Sarah married this subself, who was very visible during their dating. A group of other Jacks emerged after the wedding toasts ended their courtship ritual. They had different needs and perceptions than *Courting Jack*. These newly-active subselves were arrogant, rigid, controlling, domineering, judgmental, and harsh with Sarah and her needy daughter.

A narrow-visioned *Righteous-Christian* subself supplied zealous black/white, moralistic justifications for *Controlling Jack's* behaviors at home. Because he was following Biblical scripture—an early childhood "must" based on instilled terror of eternal damnation (spiritual abuse)—*Controlling Jack* was allied with Jesus and God Almighty. As a result, he was implacable, unreachable, and inherently "1-up." I experienced Jack as defensively *religious*, not spiritual.

His dental patients and staff saw *Professional Jack*, who was competent, courteous, warm, and trustworthy. A fifth Jack (subself) was well hidden: a scared, lonely, abandoned six year old boy. *Orphan Jack* was certain that he was worthless and unlovable because his Dad had left him, and his mother had *let* him leave. The maternal *Good Mom* part of Sarah responded instinctively to this lonely young subself, and nurtured and comforted him when his other subselves let her.

The equally terrified, lonely little *Abandoned Girl* inside Sarah responded powerfully to the strong, decisive, protective side of his personality: *Nurturing Jack.* All these personality "sides," including *Magician Jack*, who justified his reality distortions, combined to form Jack's **false self**. The talented real leader of his inner family, his *true* Self (capital "S"), was seldom in charge of his life at home. Despite extensive professional education and licensing, Jack had no concept of any this, or of the impacts that his dominant subselves had caused in his adolescence and adult years.

Sarah also had major false-self wounds. Her psychological inner family included *Good Mom, Good Girl (People Pleaser)*, a *Rager*, and a guardian *Suppressor, an Overeater* (i.e. *Addict/ Comforter*), *Emotional Numb-er, Shamed Girl, Perfectionist, Catastrophizer, Inner Critic (Shamer), Sensual Woman, Beautician*, and several others.

As a veteran *inner*-family therapist, I felt that neither of these good people knew much about having their wise, grounded, empathic true Self run their lives and relationships. Like all unaware, psychologically-wounded people, Sarah and Jack unconsciously used "I" and "you" to refer to the *groups* of "Jacks" and "Sarahs" (false selves) which comprised their personalities. They were each normal (vs. "crazy"), badly wounded adults, who weren't aware of many aspects of their inner and outer worlds. What things?

2) Unawarenesses

On top of their hidden inner wounds, this typical struggling remarried couple was stressed by a lack of vital knowledge and awareness. As with most stepfamily couples, an overarching problem was that Sarah and Jack didn't know what they didn't know. So why should they have to learn anything?

Because they were "mature" adults and veteran spouses and *bio*parents, they understandably felt they knew enough to co-manage their complex new (step)family and their remarriage.

Jack's insistence that they were *not* a stepfamily (reality distortion), and Sarah's self-doubts, shame, and fears of conflict and abandonment, blocked them from *wanting* to learn about _ personal recovery, _ stepfamily norms, _ *effective* communications, and _ how to promote healthy grief in their home. They knew few of the quiz items in Chapter 5, or the stepfamily realities in Chapter 6. Neither was aware of the toxic implications of their unawareness.

Like most co-parents controlled by unseen false selves, Sarah, Jack, and Ted McLean could only superficially describe the requisites for a high-nurturance family (Chapter 3). They had only vague ideas about "parental neglect" (low emotional-spiritual nurturance).

These three adults knew *nothing* about the six inner wounds that were relentlessly shaping their lives and relationships. No one had ever modeled or encouraged them to develop a stepfamily mission statement, or "job descriptions" for their complex roles as effective bioparents, much less as novice stepfamily co-parents. They were sailing the stormy remarital ocean without land-school training, charts, weather reports, or compass, while young Patty played on deck. In stark contrast, Rick and Karen Cohen (Jack's ex wife) had accepted the key ideas in this book from our stepfamily class. They were actively tailoring the ideas to fit their situation, and experimenting with them creatively as true committed teammates.

Neither Jack nor Sarah could articulate more than five of the 70 differences between their multi-home stepfamily and typical intact biofamilies (p. 423). This left them unconsciously guessing at what was normal in their alien new roles, using unrealistic (biofamily) expectations of themselves and each other. For example, Jack's well-meant expectation that everyone would come around to behaving like a "good Christian (bio)family" under his wise, strong leadership wasn't happening. It *wouldn't*, without his genuinely accepting and working with Sarah and the other co-parents on the five re/divorce hazards and acceptance of the stepfamily realities in Chapter 6.

More than Sarah, Jack was unaware (vs. stupid) of the core mental shift that was needed for their stepfamily success: consciously changing from the identity of a two-parent, one-household "(bio)family" to a four home, six-co-parent *stepfamily* team working together to guide their kids toward adult independence and success. Rick and Karen Cohen and Rick's ex wife Sheila appeared to accept versions of the latter reality, but hadn't been able to "team up" with Sarah, Jack, and Ted as they wished.

I think part of the block was Jack's protective denial of his part in Karen's leaving (rejecting) him. As with many divorced non-custodial parents, Jack was denying the enormous shame, guilt, and pain he felt over "abandoning" his kids via divorce, specially his son Roger. He seemed numb to the pain I suspect he felt that another man was raising his only son, and the deeper old pain that his father had abandoned *him*.

Patty McLean's father, mother and stepfather could not name more than a few of the ~40 environmental differences between stepfamily co-parenting and traditional bioparenting (http://sfhelp.org/10/co-p-dfrnces.htm). Nor could they articulate the three levels and various stages of healthy grieving, or the common symptoms of blocked grief (p. 303). These three co-parents had only vague awareness of the major psychological losses that they and their kids had sustained in childhood, and from separation, divorce, remarriage, and cohabiting.

Sarah and Jack, and Patty's biofather Ted, had never seen a reason to learn the three sets of unique adjustment needs that typical post-divorce stepkids struggle to fill (p. 454). They didn't *really* know specifically what Patty, Roger, Annie, and Nick needed help with. These typical, burdened kids couldn't articulate their many family-adjustment tasks, nor could their hardworking school staffs.

Starting with their childhood caregivers and teachers, no one had helped these six co-parents learn the seven communication skills you'll read in Project 2. This doomed them to *fight, argue, defer, avoid, blame, defend,* and *ignore* conflicts, rather then *prob-*

lem-solve as "=/=" (mutually respectful) teammates. This blocked them from really resolving their many inevitable inner-family and mutual conflicts over core values, roles, rituals, membership, family titles and names, visitations, resources, priorities, and loyalties that complex stepfamily mergers generate.

These unresolved conflicts were accumulating like garbage in the Tilmon's home. Jack and Sarah's remarital bond, blooming from deep needs, love, lust, and dreams, was dying a death of a thousand cuts from this "garbage" and shrinking respect and trust. Like their uninformed, wounded parents, Sarah, Jack, and Ted weren't able to demonstrate or teach their kids the seven communication skills. This was a major unintended deprivation, with life-long personal and social implications for these vulnerable adults-in-training.

In addition to their combined psychological wounds and unawarenesses, a common third hazard was corroding the nurturance level of Sarah and Jack's stepfamily home and re/ marriage . . .

3) Blocked Grief at Work

From infancy, we all form mild to strong emotional bonds with people, rituals, freedoms, ideas, and things. Because of fate, aging, and forced choices, we all must eventually cope with these bonds breaking. Ideally, we learn how to accept these breaks (grieve well), and form new bonds. Kids raised in high-nurturance homes are taught and encouraged to do *good* (effective) grief. Were you?

All new stepfamilies follow two or three major sets of broken bonds (losses) for adults and kids. The first losses may occur from low childhood nurturance. The second set comes from the gradual or sudden reorganization (vs. *breakup*) of a biofamily from death, desertion, or marital separation and divorce. The third web of abstract and tangible losses comes from remarriage and/or people cohabiting and merging their prior families' roles, rules, rituals (customs), values, and assets.

Most significantly-wounded divorced or re/wedded co-parents like Jack, Sarah, and Ted have no consistent inner and outer permissions (shoulds, oughts, and musts) to grieve their respective losses effectively (p. 248). Sarah seemed to have never mourned the losses of childhood *safety* (via emotional neglect and molestation), and of her *self-esteem* as a worthy, lovable female. I believe Jack had never grieved the losses of childhood *safety*, and of his *identity* as a beloved son prized by his father and protected by his mother. In full denials, neither grieved the early loss of their psychological health, and all that it meant.

Over our meetings, I came to feel that Ted, Sarah, Jack, and Patty had been unable to mourn their three complex sets of invisible and physical losses. They had vague awareness at best that the happy event of Jack and Sarah's wedding, and their moving into a shared dwelling as a "family," caused each of them to voluntarily break a set of key bonds with valued rituals, privacies, relationships, prior identities, and some emotional securities. These typical mates were far more aware of their important *gains*, like securities, companionship, social *normalcy*, sanctioned sex, and hope . . .

As typical unaware adults dominated by false selves, Patty McLean's three main co-parents were repressing and denying intense anger and sadness from their respective sets of broken bonds and abandonments. The adults' unconscious terror of the intensity of these deep emotions (overwhelm) caused them to live a reality-distorted life, and to deny that. Ted, Sarah, and Jack each used self-medicating addictions (alcohol, eating, sugar and fat, prescription drugs, and work, to help numb their repressed grief feelings and thoughts.

I suspect that Sarah's "depression" was really her being stuck in the *despair* phase of enormous compound grief. Medication would mask, not heal this. Defending against feeling overwhelmed by their own grief, Sarah and Jack weren't able to make a pro-grief home for Patty and her visiting stepsibs. Jack's ruling subselves couldn't tolerate Patty or Sarah expressing the anger and sadness that was essential for their healthy mourning.

Sarah couldn't protect her daughter from Jack's tirades, so Patty's rage was going underground and fermenting. Underneath it was the deep, deep sadness that had brought tears to the girl's eyes when we first met. My sense was that part of Patty's pain and sadness was for her wounded, struggling mother, and perhaps for her troubled, alcoholic father.

Some clinicians feel that each generation bears the unhealed pain (specially shame, guilts, and fears) of all their ancestors. Unaware of this, they adapt as well as they can until their denials break, and true (vs. pseudo) inner-family healing begins (Project 1).

Blocked anger and despair (grief) over *many* key losses seemed to be silently playing a toxic relationship role in the McLean and Tilmon homes. It probably had in their respective parents' childhood families too. No one saw this. Until Jack and Sarah found the courage to admit their protective denials and repressions and the childhood nurturance deprivations that caused them, they would never be able to *really* bond as a stepfamily couple or group.

In contrast, Karen and Rick Cohen seemed to be helping each other and their three kids to do *good* (effective) *grief*. They steadily modeled and encouraged *feeling* and respectfully *expressing* their angers and sadnesses. They helped each other to vent repeatedly about their losses, and what they meant. This was freeing them and their kids to risk forming new psychological-spiritual bonds over time. The Cohen's little "ours" daughter Sharon was blessed by starting her life in a pro-grief home.

Given these combined psychological wounds, unawarenesses, and blocked grief, how did Sarah and Jack choose each other in the first place? The fourth re/divorce hazard had done its work:

4) Courtship Distortions

From 23 years' clinical study and experience, I believe that wounded co-parents choose other wounded partners *repeat-*

edly, until real personal healing occurs. Perhaps this is because shame-based false selves are instinctively uncomfortable with (feel inferior to and judged by) self-loving, wholistically-healthy partners. People guided by their Selves probably sense the danger in committing themselves and their kids to significantly wounded people, and avoid *rescuing* (taking responsibility for) them.

I believe protective false selves dominate most people who divorce. If so, the pool of potential re/marriage partners is heavily flavored with other wounded people. Few of them are aware of these five hazards, or are recovering from their mix of inner wounds. I suspect that Ted McLean's divorced "girlfriend" Tanya was a Grown Wounded Child (GWC) too, and that the cycle of (low childhood nurturance > false-self development > first divorce > re/divorce > low-nurturance family and relationships) was progressing inexorably in their lives also. In our co-parenting class, both Rick and Karen Cohen had courageously identified themselves as GWCs. Many others in my classes do too, once they understand the concepts and criteria, and accept that *there is no shame* to this common affliction.

The Cohens told the other students that they each had been in extensive therapy, "and were probably going back for more." This seemed to be helping them find the mental, emotional, and spiritual tools to avoid the relentless wounding > (re)divorce cycle; and to *intentionally* minimize passing on the six psychological wounds to their four fortunate kids.

Our culture's courtship ritual fills complex sets of surface and underlying true needs (p. 49). Couples unconsciously strive to fill primal needs for companionship, security, stimulation, sensuality, intimacies, hope, comfort, personal and social acceptance, and *belonging*. We label these combined needs *attraction* and *romantic love*. Some suitors also need to conceive and raise children. When widowed or divorced co-parents like Jack and Sarah court, they also need to protect and nurture each of their resident and/or visiting minor kids.

Again: in my experience, *most divorced and stepfamily co-parents seem to be dominated by a reactive, narrow-visioned false self.* Their mix of the other five inner wounds often causes partners to fill their courtship needs impulsively or ambivalently. Long-term needs (stability, harmony, security, mature love) take a back seat to intense short-term needs like legitimized sex, help with needy kids, social "normalcy," and an end to boredom, loneliness, doubts, and the stressful dating game.

I suspect that Sarah's nuptial commitment to Jack was primarily made by her needy inner children (plural). The most powerful of these were *Scared Sarah, Lonely Sarah, Unlovable (shamed) Sarah, Good Girl,* and *Fairy-tale Sarah.* They were each excited for various reasons by Jack's (perceived) inner family. *Sensuous Sarah* (probably an inner teen) delighted in Jack desiring her and his enthusiastic lovemaking. *Good-Mom Sarah,* the struggling, responsible single parent, admired Jack's inner *Good Dad* caring for his two biokids. Patterned after her Depression-era mother, Sarah's *People Pleaser* Guardian subself urged her constantly to "Be nice!" and not confront or disappoint Jack as they courted.

Uncertain (self-doubting) *Sarah* appealed to Jack's inner *White Knight.* That subself's core needs were to _ bolster Jack's weak senses of personal importance and male competence, and to _ supply missing life *meaning*, by finding someone agreeing to be "rescued." Sarah and Patty were perfect! Jack's *Abandoned Boy* was enthralled that Sarah's *Good Mom* seemed to be who he had longed for forever. His covert fear of growing old alone was powerful. Young *Shamed Jack* needed relief from the tormenting guilt and shame of being divorced and unmarried in his 40s.

Lusty Jack needed sexual conquest and periodic release. *Righteous (Christian) Jack* needed their sexual behavior to be religiously and socially acceptable. Jack's *Magician* subself needed a set of new responsibilities, complex relationships, and activities to help divert from the enormous pain that *Abandoned (Lost) Jack* and *Shamed Jack* endured. The dentist's inner *Anesthetist* had helped to numb his daily pain since early childhood. *Enraged Jack* seethed hidden in the internal shadows, kept at bay by *Controlling* and *Christian Jack,* and his relentless *Inner Critic.* He forced his way out soon after the honeymoon ended. The inner din from all these subselves ("self talk") drowned out the quiet voice of Jack's *Spiritual One,* and his wise true Self.

Like most stepfamily co-parents, Jack and Sarah's decision to remarry was probably a need-driven, impulsive decision between two clamoring inner *groups.* Intense inner children and their Guardian subselves dominated each partner. They remarried complementary illusions, not real people. Jack and Sarah each had an inner *Magician* who legitimized their protective distortions and made them seem reasonable and "OK." Sarah and Jack's courtship process was well behaved, exciting, and fun, delighting the *Playful Child* in each of their inner families.

Courting Jack and Sarah showed each other their best "face" (personality subselves), to maximize the odds of filling their false self's immediate needs. The calm, wise inner counsel of their *Adult* subselves and their wide-angle, long-visioned true Selves was repeatedly drowned out and discounted. Their courtship was like two vans of elementary and high school kids trying to decide where to go on a Saturday, while their supervising adults were tied and gagged in the back. Externally, the vans appeared "normal." Internally, there were frequent gusts of rioting, anxiety, laughter, and conflict going on. Patty and her biodad Ted also had "vans" of needy subselves who all contributed to Jack and Sarah's magical courtship fantasy dance. Their skilled "drivers" (true Selves) were overwhelmed and disabled.

In addition to these four courtship hazards, Jack, Sarah, and Patty were also hindered by a . . .

5) Lack of Community Co-parenting Support

This typical co-parenting couple drove almost 30 miles one way from their Chicago suburb (population ~85,000) to consult with me on a busy weekday evening. They could find no one closer.

Jack came to support Sarah, as he felt a good Christian

husband should (per *Righteous Jack,* and his *Perfectionist* and *Inner Critic*). Because his protective *Magician* subself blocked him from accepting his role as a *step*family co-parent, Jack didn't really see any value in using me as a stepfamily specialist "to help Sarah," compared with other therapists closer to home. Sarah felt that their problems had a "stepfamily flavor," and had looked diligently for "stepparenting" classes and clinicians near their home. She wanted to be a good non-custodial stepmom to Roger and Annie Tilmon, and timidly hoped that Jack would get interested in learning about stepfathering Patty.

Like most of my hundreds of clients and callers, she said she was "amazed" to find no credible *informed* stepfamily counsel or support near their home. The information she found in their library dealt (superficially, I suspect) with stepfamily weddings, stepmothering, and stepfamily anecdotes. Jack had read nothing, and only briefly scanned the educational booklets (many of these chapters and related class handouts) that I gave them in our first meeting.

From what this couple told me, the (unmarried) moderately-liberal Christian minister who sanctified their remarriage had no training in stepfamily differences, adjustment tasks, or co-parenting dynamics. He could offer no informed suggestions or realistic cautions to this appealing, idealistic, needy couple. Neither could either Jack's or Sarah's relatives or close friends. If others had offered cautions, this couple (i.e. their false selves) would probably have pooh-poohed them. Immediate needs, hidden wounds, and illusions covertly cast a magic spell over their courtship scene.

So this typical couple had little premonition of the stepfamily relationship challenges they all would experience together. Once their inevitable problems began to surface, Sarah could find no *informed* local help. "We can't be the only remarried parents (in greater Chicago) having problems," she said in an early session. They weren't.

Patty, Sarah, and Jack and the others in their four-home nuclear stepfamily are real people. This is part of a real story. It does not have a satisfying Brady-Bunch ending. The origins and complex dynamics of the McLean-Tilmon-Cohen relationship-web are similar to the high majority of hundreds of stepfamilies I've met. Their story is far different from those that successful co-parents tell.

Unlike Patty, minor kids in high-nurturance stepfamilies (Chapter 3) have three or more co-parents who are intentionally healing their own inner wounds, learning and applying stepfamily norms, problem-solving effectively, grieving well, and are there consistently with genuine encouragement, comfort, warmth, and mutual respect. Their co-parents and kin have learned to avoid the toxic mix of the five re/divorce hazards you've glimpsed working in the McLean-Tilmon homes:

+ Unseen false-self dominance and related psychological wounds; plus . . .
+ Unawarenesses; plus . . .
+ Blocked grief; plus . . .
+ Courtship neediness and romantic-love distortions; and . . .
+ Scant *informed* local and media co-parent support.

Successful courting co-parent couples like the Cohens intuitively do versions of the seven projects you'll learn in Part 2. After making three right re/marriage choices, the new mates help each other and their kids and kin to continue these efforts, and master five more stepfamily-building projects over time. They're described in *Build a High-nurturance Stepfamily* (xlibris.com). Chapter 8 summarizes all 12 projects.

When I last talked to Sarah alone several years ago, she was going to night school, and getting tutored in life skills like budgeting, vocabulary building, and checkbook managing. She sounded more self-confident, and said she was being more assertive with Jack. He (his false self) didn't like it. She said sadly that she didn't want to be married to him, and was working toward financial independence. Sarah said that Patty did try to run away twice, involving the police. She said that enraged Jack, rather than alerting him. This widened the emotional splits between Sarah and Patty, and Jack and Sarah. These lowered their home's nurturance level, which promoted Patty's false-self growth—i.e. passed on the psychological legacy from all three sets of her wounded, unaware ancestors.

Despite my best efforts, neither Jack nor Sarah was ready to grasp and accept their deep childhood wounds and what they meant. Their diligent, protective false selves were too scared, myopic, ignorant, and distrustful. These good people couldn't accept how the five combined hazards were inexorably corroding their remarriage and dreams and wounding Patty. These three people never really had a chance to bond well, because of false-self dominance, blocked grief, unawarenesses, and social ignorances and denials.

If this stepfamily couple breaks up legally as they were emotionally, I hope their new pain and the inexorable shifting of younger ideals to middle-aged realities will help Jack and Sarah break through their protective denials and illusions. Aging and second or third divorces cause *some* psychologically wounded co-parents to hit emotional bottom. From accumulating decades of pain and weariness, they finally accept their agonizing reality ("I was neglected psychologically and spiritually as a child, and I *am* affected by major psychological wounds!"), and begin true personal recovery.

Others whose Selves are disabled fall into "depression" (often blocked grief), and/or weary, resigned, *safe* social isolation. Some re/divorcers start or escalate self-medicating addictions. Still other fragmented, needy co-parents leap into another round of the inexorable (inner wounds > divorce > delusions and wrong re/marital choices > re/divorce) cycle. Their ruling false selves vow (again), "*This* time I'll get it right!" Until in true personal recovery and learning stepfamily realities, I fear that their and their kids' success odds are low. As their unaware, wounded ancestors' false-selves did, they'll unconsciously re-create low-nurturance environments, and pass the cycle on to their descendents.

The themes you've glimpsed in this McLean-Tilmon-Cohen vignette are common to the most of the hundreds of troubled divorced and stepfamily couples that I've consulted with since

1981. Though details always differ, some mix of the five re/ divorce hazards is usually causing early or mounting stress. Like Jack and Sarah Tilmon, typical courting and re/married co-parents are totally unaware of the hazards in Chapter 4, and the seven protective projects you'll read about in Part 2. Karen and Rick Cohen were *becoming* aware, and were helping each other patiently progress at their version of the 12 projects in Chapter 8. As a result, their re/marriage and stepfamily home seemed to be growing stronger.

Notice how you feel now. Be *aware* of what your inner voices are saying, without judgment. Reflect. If well over half of typical stepfamily couples re/divorce psychologically or legally, how many of them do you think knew of their version of the five toxic factors that were destroying Sarah and Jack's re-marriage? *If you're a courting co-parent, I believe you and your partner are as susceptible as they were.* Notice your thoughts and feelings as you read that blunt (compassionate) opinion.

The next chapter gives you an overview of the seven courtship projects, and five more to work on together if you re/ marry. You partners' patiently doing all 12 of these projects together over many years *can* beat the five hazards and re/ divorce odds, and help you harvest the wonderful satisfactions that high-nurturance stepfamilies can bring to all their kids and grownups.

These seven chapters have outlined the (your) problem: six psychological wounds, unawareness and ignorances, and epidemic stepfamily unhappiness and re/divorce. The rest of this book focuses on the first half of the solution: making three informed *right* re/marriage choices.

8) 12 Long-term Co-parent Projects
How to Build a High-Nurturance Stepfamily

Premise: partners who re/marry and form or join a typical multi-home stepfamily will need to do some version of each of these tasks over many years to succeed. Without _ clearly identifying as a multi-home *step*family, and _ seeking *informed* education and qualified help with these projects, well over half will eventually re/divorce or resign themselves to daily misery. The first seven projects are outlined in Part 2 of this book. The other five projects are described in "Build a High-nurturance Stepfamily" (xlibris.com). For an Internet version of this chapter and details on all the projects, refer others to http://sfhelp.org/12-overvw.htm.

These projects are concurrent with each other and with other life responsibilities and goals. Projects 1 through 6 usually continue after re/wedding and overlap with five new tasks.

Ideally, all three or more co-parents in your prospective stepfamily will work at these projects as teammates. Your shared *long-term* goal is to learn how to overcome the five hazards, and grow a high-nurturance stepfamily (p. 48). These 12 projects build on each other, so their order counts. Progress on all prior projects helps you master the later ones together.

What you're about to read is like viewing all the courses required for a multi-year higher-education degree. Feeling overwhelmed by what follows is normal. If you choose to re/wed, you partners will have many years to do these 12 multi-step projects. As mates, you can help each other along the way. Each project is composed of smaller steps, so you can progress in do-able stages. Before reading further, can you name the five pitfalls that put you at risk of making wrong re/marital choices?

To access the referenced Web pages below, add the pointers (..**/***.htm) to ..http://sfhelp.org/..

Seven Projects (Ideally) *Before* Re/wedding

The first six usually continue after re/wedding. They can be started at any time.

Project 1) Each co-parent (bioparent and prospective stepparent) _ learn the ~30 traits of high-nurturance family health (Chapter 3). Then _ overcome protective false-self denials and resistances, and _ **assess yourself for symptoms of up to six inner wounds.** If you find enough of them, _ evolve a self-motivated, high-priority personal healing plan, _ commit to it, and _ begin. Next, honestly evaluate the odds that _ your courtship partner and _ any ex mates are significantly wounded. If they are, and if at least your partner is not *clearly* in solid psycho-spiritual recovery, _ settle for friendship. *Survivors of low childhood nurturance unconsciously pick each other and often break up, repeatedly,* until in true (vs. pseudo) recovery from false-self control. (p. 137 and ..01/links01.htm)

Project 2) _ Accept that merging your three or more extended biofamilies will generate *many* major inner and interpersonal conflicts, for years. Couples _ honestly assess how well they accept and resolve _ values' and _ concrete-resource conflicts with _ each other and _ key others. _ Begin to **develop seven mental/verbal skills together**: awareness, clear thinking, digging down to true needs, "metatalk" (talking about how you communicate), empathic listening, effective assertion, and win-win problem-solving. *Typical false-selves don't resolve inner or interpersonal conflicts effectively.* Courtship romance often disguises major adult values-clashes on parenting, loyalties, finances and assets, family priorities, religion, and home management. These *will* surface after your re/wedding! As you hone these communication skills together, teach them to _ the kids and _ interested others in your life, like ex mates and grandparents. (p. 167 and ..02/links02.htm)

Project 3) Couples _ accept your (prospective) identity as a normal multi-home *step*family, vs. "We're just a (bio)family." Then _ all three or more of your co-parents help each other and all minor and grown kids to agree on who *belongs* in your _ nuclear and _ extended stepfamily. _ Use your Project-1 learnings to see "hostile" or "uninvolved' ex mates or kin compassionately as _ psychologically wounded, not *bad*. If any of you are not genuinely motivated to do this, then a false self probably controls you.

_ Admit and _ work to resolve major stepfamily _ *identity* and _ *membership* conflicts. _ Re-do these steps together each time any your family members move, die, divorce, marry, or conceive or adopt a child. Avoiding these steps blocks your members from doing Project 4, and promotes _ weak stepfamily bonding, __ ongoing relationship conflicts, and _ seeking stepfamily-unaware (or no) professional help. (p. 199 and ..03/links03.htm)

Project 4) Partners learn and accept _ stepfamily realities (Chapter 6), and _ how your multi-home stepfamily will differ in over *60* ways from typical one-home intact biofamilies (p. 425). Then _ discuss 60+ typical stepfamily *myths* and realities (..04/myths.htm), and _ **draft *realistic* expectations for each of your key stepfamily roles and relationships.** _ Find veteran co-parents, and _ reality-check your expectations with them. _ Help each other question and update your expectations as your complex stepfamily merger progresses (Project 9), and your experience, awareness, and wisdom grow. _ Learn how to respectfully confront members and others who hold unrealistic stepfamily expectations, and _ explain why your expectations differ, if that's useful. (p. 233 and ..04/links04.htm)

Project 5) While **all three or more of your co-parents _** work to resolve your co-parenting conflicts and wounds, **learn about _** bonds and losses, _ the three multi-phase levels of

healthy grieving, _ how the six inner wounds inhibit these, _ traits of effective grief supporters, and _ the *specific* symptoms of blocked grief (p. 303).

Then inventory _ yourselves, _ each of your co-parenting ex mates, and _ each of your minor and grown kids for their major prior divorce and/or death losses. As a team, _ **assess if anyone seriously blocked in mourning** their losses. If so, all your co-parents _ agree on a plan to correct that, and _ help each other act on your plan, over time. _ Identify specifically what each child and adult will *lose* by your re/marriage and cohabiting, as well as gain. **If you re/marry, _ evolve a clear family-wide** *Good-Grief* **policy, and** _ *use* it to guide and support you all through your inevitable stream of life losses. _ Help each other to use your evolving communication skills (Project 2) to master all these sub-steps. (p. 248 and ..05/links05.htm)

Project 6) Co-parents refresh yourselves on _ what comprises a high-nurturance nuclear-*step*family structure (p. 99 and ..09/map-str1.htm). Then _ compare your two or three linked co-parenting homes against that model to *learn*, not blame. Consult your other co-parents and key relatives, and _ work to agree on a shared vision of what you all want your stepfamily to be like in a decade. Then _ all your co-parents **rough draft a stepfamily** *mission statement* **together**. Use it as a foundation for the second half of this project:

Learn typical stepkids' _ normal development tasks, and _ family-adjustment needs (p. 454). _ Assess each minor child for their status with all these tasks (..10/kid-dx.htm and ..10/ co-pinv1.htm). Then _ all your co-parents negotiate specifically what each adult is responsible for with each minor child. Document your conclusions: _ **draft each of your co-parents' "job descriptions,"** and share them with _ key relatives, _ older kids, and _ other supporters (like counselors). _ If you re/wed, review and refine your _ mission statement and _ job descriptions over time, as all your co-parents manage your multi-year stepfamily merger (Project 9). Ignoring these steps *guarantees* escalating inner-personal, and intra- and inter-home conflicts and re/marital stress. (p. 325 and ..06/links06.htm)

Project 7) _ each courtship partner **explore six vital pre-re/marriage questions** by themselves:

+ "Is my Self leading my inner family?"
+ "Why should I (re)marry at all?"
+ "Why *now*?"
+ "Why commit to *this* person and their psychological baggage (and kids and ex mate, if any)?"
+ Bioparents: "In impasses, can I often put my partner's needs ahead of my own kid/s' needs *without major resentment or guilt*?" Stepparents: "Can I trust that my partner really *wants* to do that?"
+ "What are my other options now?"

Use _ all your knowledge and awareness from Projects 1–6 and prior life, and possibly _ the free re/marriage-evaluation course on the Web at http://sfhelp.org/07/bhsf/intro.htm to answer these complex questions honestly. Use the self-assessment worksheets at ..07/links07.htm to help you do this. This project gives you each the best chance to choose the right *people* to commit to, for the right *reasons*, at the right *time*.

If you decide to re/marry, then continue Projects 1-6 as needed, and add . . .

Five Concurrent *Post*-re/wedding Projects

Project 8) Partners protect your inner and outer child/ren from re/divorce by _ **intentionally nurturing your re/marriage often enough.** Make (vs. find) enough time for undistracted intimacy, play, sharing, planning, and problem solving. _ Keep your relationship consistently *second* only to your personal integrities, spirituality, and growth, including ongoing inner-wound recoveries (Project 1). Help each other _ improve your effectiveness at resolving the complex _ inner and _ interpersonal conflicts that will confront all of you all for years (Project 2); and _ intentionally model what a high-nurturance marriage looks and sounds like for your minor kids.

Your overall Project-8 goal is to _ shift from a (my needs vs. your needs) view to a shared, stable (*our* needs) focus, while keeping your _ personal boundaries and _ integrities clear and stable. People controlled by false selves often can't do this, until well along in meaningful Project-1 recovery. Option: _ based on your nuptial vows, evolve a mission statement together for your relationship, and _ help each other *use* it for guidance and inspiration in major confusions and conflicts. See *The Remarriage Book* (xlibris.com) or (..08/links08.htm).

Project 9) _ All three or more **co-parents** help each other _ **merge and** _ **stabilize your respective biofamilies'** _ assets, _ beliefs, _ habits, _ values, _ roles, _rules, _ rituals, _ priorities, **and** _ lifestyles ("cultures"). As you do, _ continue learning stepfamily realities and evolving realistic expectations of yourselves and each other. _ Use your Project-2 skills to help each other evolve an effective way to **resolve** the _ values and _ loyalty **conflicts, and** _ (persecutor–rescuer–victim) **relationship "triangles"** that *will* result from your complex merger. _ Accept that each of your bioparents *must* clearly decide which usually comes first with them in conflicts without workable compromises: their personal integrity, their re/marriage, or all else, including their kids.

If you excluded an ex mate and/or their new partner in Project 3, or if they or key relatives exclude themselves, this biofamily-merger project will be very conflictual or impossible. Each time one of your co-parent re/marries or re/divorces, and/ or any child marries, re-do parts of this project together, and re-stabilize over time. (..09/links09.htm)

Project 10) Continue Project 6 by building an *informed* co-parenting team over time. Ex mates _ continue working at admitting and resolving past hurts, guilts, disrespects, and distrusts. All co-parents _ refine your Project-6 job descriptions (goals and responsibilities), and _ agree on a collective definition of *effective* co-parenting. Over years, _ invent and stabilize up to 15 new multi-home stepfamily roles, and _ revise most of your old 15 biofamily roles. Concurrently _ evolve new intra- and inter-home *rules* for all 30 of these roles. Help each other _ identify and _ grieve key personal losses as you make these changes, using the pro-grief policy you drafted in

Project 5. _ Help each other **monitor each minor child's progress with their mix of developmental and adjustment needs**. As you do all these steps together, regularly affirm your multi-home stepfamily's specific _ strengths and _ benefits. Use a checklist like this to help: ..07/strnx-intro.htm. (p. 454 and ..10/links10.htm.)

Project 11) Because of the complexity of all these concurrent tasks and your other life activities, **build a support network** of _ successful stepfamily co-parents re/married five or more years, and stepfamily-informed _ relatives, _ friends, and _ professionals (clergy, counselors, school staff, and a family-law attorney.) _ Join or start a high-nurturance support group of like-minded co-parents. See http://sfhelp.org/11/sg-intro.htm for perspective and concrete suggestions. Option: _ explore the many Internet newsgroups, chat rooms, and message boards (forums) for nurturing stepfamily supporters (see ..11/resources.htm). A satisfying part of this ongoing project is _ passing on your growing stepfamily wisdom and guidance to courting, novice, and struggling co-parents and their supporters. (..11/links11.htm)

Finally: every day, help each other to do . . .

Project 12) Consciously *balance* **and co-manage all these ongoing projects**, plus myriad other responsibilities, well enough. As you do, _ keep your goals clear and ordered, _ build a solid, _ hi-priority re/marriage and _ high-nurturance stepfamily, _ enjoy your kids and each other, _ keep growing emotionally and spiritually as persons (based on recovery from false-self dominance, if needed); and _ laugh, play, relax, **and** _ *enjoy* **the whole adventure** together while you do all this! (..12/links12.htm)

This diagram below may help you visualize how these 12 projects fit together:

balance yourselves,
your relationships, and your homes,
as you do all these projects
and other life activities - and
enjoy the whole adventure!

| heal divorce wounds, & build a co-parent team | build a support network and use it together! |

if you re/wed, steadlily nurture your re/marriages,
as you merge 3 or more biofamilies over 4+ years
and resolve **many** conflicts and relationship "triangles"

develop 7 com-munication skills

learn stepfamily realities & tasks

learn grief basics; & assess all members for blocked grief

learn kids' needs & assess their status; then draft co-parent "job descriptions"

accept your stepfamily identity and your 5 hazards;
agree on who belongs to your stepfamily

assess co-parents for psychological wounds
and start needed recoveries

12 co-parent projects for building a high-nurturance
stepfamily, overmany years. Read from the bottom up.

 # Reality check: To clarify your initial reaction to all these many tasks and subtasks, check which of these feel true now. Consider journaling about these, and/or discussing them with key others. T = true, F = false, and ? = "I'm not sure now."

1) I feel some mix of *calm, centered, energized, light, focused, resilient, up, grounded, relaxed, alert, aware, serene, purposeful,* and *clear.* My true Self is leading my inner family of subselves now. (T F ?)

2) I can _ name and _ describe the five re/marriage hazards now, and _ I feel sure that they really *do* apply to me and those I care about. (T F ?)

3) I accept that without major sustained work on projects like these 12, the odds of my (and my kids') re/divorcing are probably well over 50%. (*Watch for protective denials or minimizings here.*) (T F ?)

4) I feel that the first seven of these projects are an effective way of evaluating _ how these hazards may affect us all, and _ whether we should re/marry. (T F ?)

5) I trust that with some tailoring, these 12 projects are a _ realistic and _ reliable guide to building a high-nurturance stepfamily over time. (T F ?)

6) I want to learn more about these projects now. (T F ?)

7) I feel comfortable inviting _ my partner and _ key others to review these projects now, and _ discussing how they apply to all our adults and minor and grown kids. (T F ?)

8) I feel confident enough that with more education and patient work, my partner and I can master these seven projects well enough, over time. (T F ?)

+ I feel skeptical about . . .

+ I feel upset or alarmed by . . .

+ I feel confused about . . .

+ Right now, I'm aware of . . .

Why Do These Projects?

Why should you elect to start or join a high-risk, stress-ful stepfamily and take on your version of all these 12 challenging, long-term projects with a partner? Long term, would you be better off not re/marrying at all, or re/wedding a childless partner? Recall my premise that families exist because they fill a set of core human needs (p. 49) better than other social groups. A stepfamily has the same potential for filling your and your kids' core needs as any other type of family.

A glass-half-full view says a stepfamily offers greater potential, because there are more people and resources available to help your kids and adults along the way. A glass-half-empty perspective (voiced by a *Pessimist* subself) says all the people and their "baggage" will *hinder* filling your needs, and stress your life with new needs and conflicts.

By definition, your situation is unique. Questions like these may help you decide **among the three options above: which is most likely to . . .**

+ Heal my personal wounds, and help me to discover and fulfill my real life purpose?
+ Fill my adult needs for _ belonging, _ support, _ companionship and _ fun, _ love, _ security, _ intimacy, _ appreciation, and _ nurturing others?
+ Give me the greatest life-satisfaction in old age, as I approach my death?
+ Provide each of my kids (if any) with the best long-term environment to fill their mix of the needs on p. 454?

+ (Add your own question/s)

Option: jot a reminder on p. 385 now to review these 12 projects and these questions. You'll know *much* more then!

Recap

This chapter overviews the whole grand stepfamily adventure you may commit to. It's a marvelously challenging, stretching, scary, satisfying *long-term* enterprise. Because most courting or re/wedded American co-parents like you can't name the five re/marital hazards and some version of these 12 projects, most re/divorce emotionally or legally within a decade of their earnest, idealistic vows. That leaves most of them in middle age with major confusion, regret, guilt, shame, sadness, and anxiety. I assume you want to avoid that!

These projects come from my study of divorced-family and stepfamily dynamics and realities since 1979. I've never seen a version of them or the underlying five hazards in any lay or clinical stepfamily literature to date. Some premises underlying these projects are not validated yet by methodical research, and they should be. Meanwhile, they offer you a coherent framework to evaluate stepfamily re/ marriage, and/or to strengthen your existing inner and outer stepfamily relationships.

Part 1 of this book aims to help you understand why typical stepfamily re/marriage is a very high-risk choice, and what's required for long-term re/marital and co-parenting success. I hope you're motivated now to study more, so you partners can make informed re/marital and co-parenting decisions for you and your kids.

The next chapters explore each of your seven re/marriage-evaluation projects in some detail. The last chapter in Part 2 sums up all seven and suggests some next-step options. Before reading more, I encourage you to mull the reality-check questions above. If your true Self is disabled, other subselves may urge you to do something else, like . . .

+ "Forget this psychobabble junk! Love really *is* enough!"
+ "This makes sense, but it sure doesn't apply to *me* or *us*."
+ "Stop reading, and go do (something else)."
+ "Wow, I'm so *tired*! Better take a nap . . ."
+ "This is *way* too complicated. Let's put the book down (for good)."
+ "Oh my God, I'm gonna die alone and unloved!"
+ "Hey, how about some (comforting sugar or fat) now?"
+ "All I/we need is God and our love;" and/or . . .
+ "I don't understand any of this." This is often a symptom of false-self anxiety. I encourage you to finish the book to see what you understand *then*.

What are your inner voices saying now? Do you know which subselves are "speaking"?

if you hilighted any Web links that looked interesting, explore them before continuing. Then get ready to learn about (what I believe to be) the biggest and least-recognized re/marital hazard you partners face: false-self dominance and five related psychological wounds. *Take your time here, pilgrim!*

Poll your inner team: do they need a break?

Part 2) Seven Courtship Projects

Note that each breaks down into sub-tasks:

Project 1) _ Learn about multi-part personalities, _ assess yourselves for significant pychological wounding, and _ act on your findings. _ Teach relevant others what you learn.

Project 2) _ Learn and _ use seven effective-communication skills to resolve your _ inner-family and _ mutual conflicts. _ Model and teach the skills to your kids.

Project 3) _ Accept your *stepfamily* identity, and _ seek peaceful agreement on who belongs.

Project 4) _ Change stepfamily myths into realistic expectations and _ apply them. _ Teach relevant others what you learn, over time.

Project 5) _ Learn about healthy grieving, and _ assess your adults and kids for blocked grief. _ Begin to free up any you find. _ Evolve a good-grief family policy and _ use it to build pro-grief relationships and homes together.

Project 6) _ Draft a stepfamily mission statement, _ learn what your minor kids need, and evolve _ co-parent job (role) descriptions together based on Projects 1 - 5.

Project 7) Use all you've learned to make three *right* re/marriage choices.

Chapter 17) Put it all together, and next steps

Project 1: Assess For Inner Wounds

> *"If you bring forth what is within you,*
> *What you bring forth will save you.*
> *If you do not bring forth what is within you,*
> *What you do not bring forth will destroy you."*
> —The Gnostic Gospels

> *"Go within, or go without."*
> —Neal Walsch

I estimate that 85% or more of ~1,000 typical divorced and/
or re/married women and men I've met clinically since 1981
have clear symptoms of the six psychological wounds on p.
66. Few knew it, and virtually *none* of them saw how the wounds
were promoting personal, relationship, and parenting problems.

If you are divorced, considering divorce, or seriously dating someone who has divorced, with or without kids, the odds
are very high that a "false self" (p. 139) significantly influences you and your current and/or past partners. If so, you
risk . . .

+ Unconsciously choosing similarly-wounded partners;
   having unsatisfying, stressful relationships; and divorcing emotionally or legally *again*.
+ Unintentionally promoting psychological wounds in your
   dependent kids, and continuing the ancestral legacy of
   toxic false-self dominance. And . . .

+ Dying prematurely, without realizing your true potential as a unique, worthy, gifted human being.

This keystone project helps combat two of the five reasons most Americans like you make wrong marital choices: partners' _ combined inner wounds, and _ their *unawareness* of them, what they mean, and how to build high-nurturance marital and family relationships.

This chapter offers a skeletal outline of a complex multi-step project. For far more detail on assessing for false-self wounds and an effective option for reducing them ("parts work"), read "Who's *Really* Running Your Life?" (Xlibris.com, 2000). You can get the gist of the book from the Web pages at http://sfhelp.org/01/links01.htm.

As we start, note your initial attitude: on a scale of 1 to 10, how likely is it that your life is significantly controlled by an uncoordinated, short-sighted, reactive group of "subselves"? Notice your thoughts . . .

Background

Advances in computer and medical technology since the 1980's (e.g. Positron Emission Tomography) make us the first generation in human history to *see* living brains in action. We see that "thinking" activates many different areas of our brains at once, without our awareness. One implication is that our ancestors' assumption that we have one brain, and therefore one personality, is as wrong as the old "truth" that the sun circled the Earth. Our brains have a trait now called *multiplicity*: the ability to automatically assign complex information-processing tasks to different neural regions that operate semi-independently, like a net of minicomputers.

In 1984 the prestigious American Psychiatric Association validated that "Multiple Personality Disorder" (MPD) is a real psycho-medical condition in about 5% of the American population. This condition has predictable origins (massive childhood trauma), discrete symptoms, and can be improved over time by skilled clinical treatment. The APA renamed MPD as

"Dissociative Identity Disorder" (DID) in 1994. *Dissociation* is the clinical word for personality "splitting."

What is dawning from these two recent developments is the awareness that *all* humans have the normal neural capacity to "split," or fragment their personalities a little or a lot, starting in early childhood. This isn't new: mindscape pioneers Sigmund Freud, Roberto Assagioli, and Carl Jung proposed personality splitting almost a century ago, and many others have agreed since then. Have you come across Dr. Thomas Harris's popular 1967 book "I'm OK, You're OK"? Dr. Erik Berne's "Games People (read *subselves*) Play" was a bestseller 35 years ago.

Premise: after 15 years' study and clinical practice, I believe the degree of splitting is proportional to the level of psychological-spiritual nurturance available to a young child (Chapter 3). Restated: the lower a child's environmental nurturance during his or her first three to five years, the higher their degree of adaptive splitting. I also believe that parents from low-nurturance childhoods (like Sarah McLean and Jack Tilmon) often pick each other, and reproduce low nurturance for their own kids *against their conscious will.* ("I swore I'd never discipline like my Dad, and I'm doing just what he did!"). Low nurturance and personality fragmenting pass unseen down the generations, and spread in our culture, until enlightened adults stop it via personal healing. That's the goal of this first co-parental project.

True and False Selves

After a decade of clinical research, *inner*-family pioneer Dr. Richard Schwartz proposed that adaptive personality splitting produces three functional groups of "subselves" or personality "parts." Based on his work, my books call these groups "Regulars," "Vulnerables," and "Guardians." I agree with Schwartz's opinion that there is a fourth group of "higher" selves. The members of these groups make up your **inner family**, troop, clan, or team of subselves. Like an orchestra's or sports team's performance, *your daily behavior is determined by which of your subselves leads your inner family at any time.*

Your Regular subselves control your thoughts, perceptions, and behavior when no crisis is apparent to any of your subselves. One Regular that all people have is called (here) your **true Self** (capital "S"). S/He is a naturally skilled leader, providing wide-angle, far seeing judgment and decisiveness to your other subselves in daily decisions. Because a young child's Self doesn't know much about the world, kids grow up following the subselves leading their caregivers' inner families. If parents' true Selves are often disabled, everyone's in long-term trouble. See this sobering summary of over 500 research studies that validate this: http://sfhelp.org/01/research.htm.

If parents are dominated by false selves, (the apparent American norm), the resulting low family nurturance promotes fears, shame, guilt, and confusion among a child's young subselves (**Vulnerables**). To survive, children's personalities fragment. They develop **Guardian** subselves, who are solely devoted to protecting the Vulnerables from present and future pain and harm.

Common Guardian subselves are the *Procrastinator, Perfectionist, Numb-er, Forgetter, Liar, Bully, Fantasizer, Sneak, Martyr, People Pleaser, Illusionist, Addict, Controller, Rescuer, Hero(ine), Star, Bigot, Critic,* and *Catastrophizer.* See anyone familiar? Like the young Vulnerables, each of these subselves has their own values, goals, and (narrow) view of the world. In adulthood, they often distrust the Self and other Regulars, since these parts were originally unable to keep the young person safe. These Guardian subselves feel they must take charge to avoid pain. Some appear to be stuck in the (traumatic) past, believing childhood dangers are real *now*, against all evidence to the contrary.

When Guardian subselves perceive that one or more Vulnerables are in pain or danger, they reflexively activate, and take over the inner family (personality). This is like students distrusting the teacher and taking over the class, or one or more disgruntled musicians forcing the conductor (your Self) off the podium. When this happens, you feel, think, and perceive what your dominant subselves do, not what your wise

Self does. In this series of books, your controlling non-Self personality parts are called your **false self**. Emotional Vulnerable subselves can take over, as well as their Guardians. Do you know any adult who seems *childish*, or a child who seems immature for their age?

Adults and kids can range from being controlled by a false self occasionally to some of the time, to *all the time*. Some people got so little childhood nurturance they have *never* experienced their true Self in charge. If you are such a wounded person, the idea that you have a competent true Self will seem like science fiction.

When their Self leads their team of subselves, people universally report feeling some mix of *light, "up," aware, alert, grounded, focused, purposeful, secure, confidant, clear, calm or serene, "happy," empowered, grateful, in the moment, sure,* and *"in the flow."* I've witnessed scores of clients describing this spontaneously, with no coaching from me. Other inner-family therapists (ref. the Internal Family Systems Association, IFSA) report the same thing.

Our language reflects how common these inner take-overs are. We describe each other as being or having . . .

+ Yellow or mean *streaks*
+ Rage, panic, or anxiety *attacks*
+ Blue *moods*, or mood *swings*
+ A *bent* or *talent* for something
+ Paranoid and neurotic
+ Obsessive and compulsive
+ Giving *double* or *mixed* messages
+ Putting on a different *face*, or being *two-faced*
+ Seeing *both sides* ("on the other hand . . .")
+ "Going ballistic, to pieces, or bonkers"
+ Addictive personalities
+ Illusions or delusions
+ Scatterbrained, unfocused, and "out to lunch"
+ Saying one thing and doing another
+ Personality disorders and "character flaws"
+ "Falling apart"

+ Finding our (true) Self (and inner harmony)
+ Being ambivalent, indecisive, torn, of two minds
+ "Getting my act (inner family) together"
+ "Losing *it*" (inner-family harmony)
+ Driven, or Type A
+ Controlling, manipulative, lazy, etc.
+ "Something came over me", and "I wasn't myself"
+ Hunches, "senses," intuitions, and fantasies

If we were unitary personalities, we English speakers would greet each other "Hi! How *is* you?"

Significant false-self wounding is all around us. It's so common that we don't see it. Our ruling subselves don't *want* us to see it, for they don't trust what might follow. We Americans spend billions of dollars treating the personal and social results of widespread false-self dominance, but ignore the cause: parental wounds and unawareness, and low childhood nurturance. One of the cultural results is our toxic epidemic of family "trouble," divorce, and re/divorce. As I write this, current headlines again feature a troubled teen "loner" who "lost it" and shot several high school classmates. Another tragic sign of our psychologically-split times.

Six Psychological Wounds

The symptoms of inadequate childhood nurturance seem to fall into six groups:

1) Local or chronic **false-self dominance** (loss of true-Self leadership), and inner-family conflict or chaos. This causes mixes of:

2) Excessive shame ("I'm inept, disgusting, worthless, and unlovable") **and guilt** ("I broke an important rule, made a mistake, or did something *wrong*."); and . . .

3) Excessive fears of _ rejection and abandonment, _ "failure," _ mental/emotional overwhelm (and therefore of conflict and intimacy), _ the unknown (and therefore of taking risks), and _ *success*; and . . .

4) Reality distortions, like denials, repressions, minimizing, exaggerating, idealizing, black-white thinking, projecting, "mis-remembering" and "forgetting," paranoias, phobias, and delusions; and . . .

5) Trust imbalances: trusting toxic others too much, or *dis*trusting reliable, safe others too often. Related wounds are *self*-distrust (ambivalence, doubts, "worry," and second-guessing), and distrust of a benign Higher Power.

Mixes of these five wounds combine to cause some people . . .

6) Difficulty attaching emotionally and spiritually (bonding) to some or all other people. That inhibits or blocks intimacy and giving or receiving *love*, despite most subselves' longing for it.

Does it make sense to you that needy, entranced courting partners who _ don't know what they don't know about re/marriage realities, low-nurturance and recovery from the six wounds, and effective communication (Project 2), and who _ each deny having significant mixes of these six wounds, are at high risk of making unwise re/marital choices? Does it also make sense that _ their ex mates and parents probably have these wounds to some degree, and that _ the courting partners' minor kids may have started to develop their own set of them?

Pause. Breathe well, and notice what you're feeling and thinking. I assume these ideas are new to you. If one or more Guardian or Vulnerable subselves control you, they may cause you to . . .

+ "Feel nothing," or . . .
+ "Forget what I just read," or . . .
+ Label it "stupid psychobabble" or "New Age nonsense," or . . .
+ Remember some pressing responsibility, and stop reading.

False selves are ceaselessly vigilant. They inherently distrust and avoid anything they perceive as threatening, including your Self becoming aware of them and their protective control of your inner family.

I believe that **unseen false-self dominance is probably the**

biggest of the five hazards you face in making a re/marriage decision. The rest of this chapter outlines steps you can take to initially assess of whether you, your partner, an ex mate, or a child, has significant psychological wounds. The last part of the chapter outlines *recovery* (healing) options, and points to relevant resources.

I fear that if your false self ignores this project, your other six courtship projects will be of little use. False-self dominance and unawarenesses relentlessly distort thinking, perceiving, feeling, and "good judgment." Protective Guardian subselves make impulsive, self-defeating, or harmful decisions seem rational and desirable. They're big on instant gratification: comforting upset Vulnerables *now.* The challenge is that their doing this feels *normal*!

Reality check: I'd be surprised if you weren't wondering if a well-meaning false self is holding your true Self hostage. For an initial estimate, use Resources A (p. 401) and B (p. 413). There are 10 more self-assessment checklists in "Who's *Really* Running Your Life?" and in the Web pages at http://sfhelp.org/ pop/assess.htm). I suggest you read through the rest of this chapter first, for more perspective.

Who Should Do Project 1?

+ Any mother or father, whether happily married, single, foster, adoptive, courting, cohabiting, re/married, and/ or re/divorced.

+ Any childless adult considering marriage, specially if you've had significant relationship, personal health, financial, and/or work "problems."

+ Any wife or husband who wants to guard against possible (re)divorce, and to protect dependent kids from psychological wounding and years of adult misery.

+ Any caregiver concerned about an "acting out" or troubled child.

+ Anyone _ recovering from an addiction or "depression,"

_ seeing a therapist, and/or _ taking prescription drugs for any reason.

+ Any grandparent or sibling who "senses" assessment "might be useful."

+ Any older teen or young adult who is troubled about their family and their life. And . . .

+ Any human-service professional in any discipline. My 20 years of clinical experience suggest that a high percentage of mental-health practitioners, clergy, educators, family-law professionals (including legislators, mediators, and police), medical professionals, and those who train, monitor, fund, certify, and evaluate them, are often dominated by false selves. Few know it. Significantly wounded people seem to gravitate to the "helping" professions . . . "Physician, heal thyself."

Project-1 Goals for Co-parents

1) Each courting co-parent assess _ themselves, _ their partner, _ each related minor or grown child, and _ the kids' other parent/s, *honestly* for significant inner-wound symptoms. This is not to see if anyone is *crazy*, *sick*, or *bad*!

2) If *you* have significant symptoms of false-self dominance . . .

_ Research, draft, and begin a high-priority personal recovery (healing) program, to restore the wise leadership of your true Self to your *inner* family of subselves.

_ Work to prevent, and/or assess and heal, false-self wounds in each dependent child in your life, whether custodial or not. And . . .

_ Alert your kids' other co-parent/s to this project, and appeal to them to assess themselves for psychological wounds, for everyone's' sakes.

3) If your courtship partner has significant false-self traits, invite her or him to join you in researching and doing this first project. If s/he's resistant, apathetic, or ambivalent, *settle for friendship!*

4) Long-term: if you believe you're often controlled by Guardian and Vulnerable subselves, **make personal recovery second only to current survival,** and any parental responsibilities. I propose that healing your psychological wounds, and breaking the unseen ancestral cycle of low nurturance and personality fragmenting, are the greatest long-term bequests you can make to your descendents. **The rewards are** *beyond price!*

Goals for Human Service Professionals

If you earn a living helping other people directly or indirectly . . .

1) Honestly assess yourself for traits of significant false-self dominance, *regardless* of prior education, certification, and personal healing work. Reluctance to do this, and/or denying such reluctance, suggests that your Self is disabled.

2) If you find "enough" symptoms of false-self dominance, **decide whether you want to work at freeing your true Self to harmonize and lead you inner team of subselves.**

3) Consider whether helping people in your family to _ learn about false selves, _ assess for inner wounds, and _ begin needed recoveries, is a priority. _ Act on your decision.

4) (Re)evaluate the nurturance-level of your work setting (ref. Chapter 3). If it's "low," ask yourself why you choose to work there. Such an environment will inhibit your recovery, and enable false-self control, denials, and low-nurturance environments in clients and co-workers. In my clinical experience, low-nurturance agencies and programs are headed by significantly-wounded people in denial, often with many credentials.

5) Re-evaluate your work goals and methods. Do they overtly or covertly enable or encourage false selves in those you serve? If so, do you want to keep doing that that? Which of your subselves is deciding?

Co-parents and professionals can achieve these goals over time via . . .

Five Main Steps

Because your personal situation, genes, upbringing, and ancestry are unique, you (your Self) may need to tailor these steps to fit you better: _ prepare your mind; _ assess yourself for the six inner wounds *honestly*; _ assess any courtship partner or key co-workers for the same traits, *honestly*; _ one at a time, assess each dependent child (custodial or not), and then each of their other co-parents, including stepparents. Then based on what you learn, _ start personal recovery, if needed; _ help your kids, if needed; and _ *re-evaluate any potential decision to (re)marry.*

Let's explore each of these steps briefly . . .

Prepare Your Mind

_ **Reread** Chapters 3, 4, and 7 in this book, using the ideas above to get new meaning from them.

_ For wider perspective, read and discuss several of the "splitting and recovery" books recommended in "Who's *Really* Running Your Life?" or http://sfhelp.org/11/resources.htm.

_ **Check your attitude.** Notice if you're approaching this project with short-range anxiety, cynicism, and pessimism, or the feeling that it's a worthy *long-range* effort that will enhance the quality of your life and the lives of others you care about. The latter suggests your Self is leading.

_ **Clarify your goals**, and keep aware of them. The purpose of this project is to see if one or more distrustful subselves control you too often, and block you from achieving the full potential of your life. A related goal may be to help make three right (re)marriage choices that will delight you for the rest of your days (Project 7).

Assess Yourself

In this keystone project, you seek answers to . . .
"Am I controlled by a well-meaning false self too often?"

"If so, which of the five other wounds do I have, and . . .

"How are all six wounds affecting _ my health, _ my key relationships (including my Self, my Higher Power, and my kids), and _ my life-quality to date?"

To answer these, use 11 checklists to identify symptoms of significant false-self control. *Significant* means "enough to cause me to act." The number of checklists is meant to overcome any protective reality distortions your Guardian subselves promote. An option is to use an objective professional counselor to help you see through self-protective denials. This book offers the three checklists asterisked below. All 11 are available in "Who's *Really* Running Your Life?" and on the Web at ..pop/ assess.htm. The checklists are:

1*) Assess for common false-self behavioral traits. (p. 401)

2*) Assess your birth-family's nurturance level (Chapter 3).

3) Assess for family-tree symptoms of low emotional/spiritual nurturance.

4) Assess how your target person behaves relative to their family.

5) through 10) Assess for common symptoms of each of the six inner wounds; and . . .

11*) Assess for symptoms of co-dependence: a potentially serious form of relationship addiction which indicates significant false-self control. (p. 413).

Once you fill out all 11 checklists and discuss or meditate on the results, you'll conclude . . .

+ *"I am clearly wounded, and my Self is disabled too often. I need to identify my wounds and recovery options;"* or . . .

+ *"I'm not sure if I'm significantly wounded;"* or . . .

+ *"I'm confident that I grew up in a high-enough nurturance family, and that my inner wounds are minimal."* Because of protective unconscious reality distortions, this may *or may not* be true!

Some significantly-wounded co-parents in denial will do the checklists, not evaluate (or ignore) what the results *mean,* and then deny doing this (reality distortion). Others will evaluate the results, decide that some follow-up is warranted, and their *Procrastinator* Guardian subself will defer *doing* anything indefinitely.

If you conclude that you *do* have significant inner wounds, your odds rise that any past or present intimate partners are also wounded. To find out . . .

Assess Your Partner for False-self Control

Prepare: read (at least) . . .
+ Dr. Harville Hendrix's useful book "Keeping the Love You Find,"
+ Hal and Sidra Stone's eye-opening book "Embracing Each Other," and . . .
+ One or more of the titles on *codependence* or *relationship addiction* recommended in *"Who's Really Running Your Life?"* or at *..11/resources.htm*. Then . . .

Use copies of the same 11 assessment tools (above) to honestly evaluate the odds that your present love-*partner* is often controlled by a false self. If you conclude s/he probably or surely is, then . . .

Discuss this together, show your partner the worksheets, and learn his/her reaction. If s/he seems genuinely interested in self-evaluating, encourage that, and share your own false-self assessment findings and plans.

If your partner concludes s/he *is* significantly wounded, _ discuss co-committing to long-term work at empowering your true Selves, and harmonizing your inner families. _ Continue building your relationship, and _ support (vs. take *responsibility* for) each other's recoveries. *Such relationships are often among the strongest!*

If your partner has any other reaction, _ meditate on the high risks of trying to build a lasting relationship with a psychologically wounded person in denial, and with any wounded kids and ex mates. Again: would you board a plane knowing the odds were better than half that it would crash? Your well-meaning false self will try to persuade you that it's safe enough. America has an invisible subculture of *millions* of anguished (wounded) adults and kids who risked "flying," and eventually crashed (re/divorced). Do you know any of them? Shamed subselves cause them to keep a low profile.

Beware of convincing false-self reality distortions. Excessive neediness and strong sexual excitement can mix to greatly skew your judgment here! Consider getting a qualified professional opinion on any relationship commitment decision you make. "Qualified" means someone with training and experience in stepfamily realities (p. 91) and recovery from low-childhood nurturance. See ..11/counsel.htm on the Web.

Next . . .

Assess Each Child and Each Other Co-parent

Despite painful results, needy adults controlled by false selves like Sara and Jack, and Rick and Karen, repeatedly choose each other for mates. My clinical experience since 1981 suggests that most troubled, divorced, and stepfamily co-parents seem to be significantly controlled by false selves. The high majority of them come from low-nurturance childhoods. Many of them (i.e. their false selves) minimize or deny this ("It wasn't all *that* bad . . .")

The more wounded and unaware the three or more co-parents in your potential stepfamily are, the higher your odds of making three *wrong* re/marital decisions. Your minor kids and their future kids depend on you and their other co-parents to take this vital courtship project seriously! If you're already re/married, assessing for inner wounds can significantly raise the quality of your future years, and help your kids begin to heal.

Evaluate the odds that _ each minor or grown child's other living or dead bioparent, and _ any new partner of theirs, is or was an unrecovering, significantly-split adult (Grown Wounded Child, or GWC). Use the same 11 checklists. If you conclude "probably" or "surely," expect frequent, ongoing co-parenting strife with them and related kids. Past, present, and threatened legal battles over parenting and/or financial issues are a sure sign of false-self control in all concerned, possibly including attorneys and judges.

If you're courting someone who's ex mate, parents, and/or kids seem significantly wounded, *RED LIGHT!* It's very likely that *you* are significantly wounded too. That means without your progressing well on true (vs. pseudo) recovery, committing to this alluring person will cause you all great heartache, and probably lead to emotional or legal re/divorce. Notice your reaction now.

If you have a dependent child, _ decide whether their wounded other parent would be open to learning about these Project-1 ideas and tools. If so, _ share them. If not, it can't be helped. They may become open to assessing and recovery as time goes on. Meanwhile, work at healing your own wounds and any your kids have.

<u>Evolve a Personal Healing Strategy</u>

If you feel *you* have a significant mix of the six inner wounds . . .

Learn about *inner* family therapy ("parts work") from "Who's *Really* Running Your Life?", and/or "Inner Family Systems Therapy," (Schwartz, 1995); and/or the 'inner family" Web articles at ..<u>01/links01.htm</u>. The former book and the Web pages go into detail about recovery options and resources.

Research other views and resources about personal healing (recovery). There are *many!* Use your findings to draft and practice a meaningful long-term plan to promote your true Self to inner-family leadership, and protect the kids in your life from psychological wounding from unintended nurturance restrictions.

Build recovery supports: Selectively tell safe (non-shaming) family members and friends of your learnings and recovery goals, and ask their help in your recovery. Expect major reactions, including congratulations, indifference, criticism, and defensiveness. Stay clear: this project is *not* about blaming par-

ents, other early caregivers, or their ancestors! They were probably unaware of their inner wounds, and gave the best they
could. Their social and religious communities knew much less
than ours do.

Rank recovery among your top personal priorities. If
you do commit to building a stepfamily (Project 7), _ accept
that your healing work will be concurrent with all 10 other
projects in Chapter 8. Your co-parents' degrees of wounding
and healing will greatly affect your ongoing and ultimate success with your other projects.

Use *recovery, adult child, and toxic parents* as **Internet
search** terms, and see what you get. There's *lots* of help available, though little will refer to "personality splitting," "inner-
family harmonizing," or "empowering your true Self."

Stay comfortably alert for chances to **identify veteran recoverers, and learn from them.** As with all social movements,
there is an evolving "recovery language" that helps recoverers
vent and problem-solve together. Be gentle and patient with
your inner selves. This is a *major* life-shift, and new experiential ground. Rest often along the way, and affirm your efforts
and outcomes. There are no recovery mistakes, only *learnings*.

Watch for the right time to **experiment with journaling
and meditation** as helpful sources of recovery awareness. Begin to identify and *trust* the "still small voice" within: true recovery is fundamentally a spiritual-evolution process. Learn to
listen to your "self talk" (thought streams), and start to recognize and get to know your different internal speakers.

Try out nonjudgmental inner dialogs with your inner-family members. Expect interesting surprises! Learn to discern when
your true Self is in charge, and when other subselves are. Develop a sense of which inner-family members are *really* running your life, and whether that's OK with your Self.

As you experiment, **notice and enjoy the changes that start
to happen** in your life.

Along the way, **update your personal identity** to include
something like ". . . and I am a wo/man who cares for myself
by exploring personal healing / growth / recovery / change /

development." Gently raise your awareness of how false-self wounds get transmitted, and spot this happening to any kids in your life.

Ask siblings, childhood friends, and knowledgeable others **for information about your early years,** specially from pre-birth through puberty. Learn what you can about your parents' and grandparents' childhoods through the eyes of compassion, empathy, and forgiveness, not *blame*.

Evolve your own clear **definitions of personal wholistic health, and "high-nurturance" relationships** and families. _ Develop your skill at spotting toxic relationships, situations, and groups that often generate anxiety, shame, guilt, confusion, and anger in you (and others), and question why you're in them. _ Expand your *emotion* vocabulary, and practice saying, "I feel . . ." and "I need . . ."

Become aware of how you react to inevitable life losses **(grieve)**. Restated: clarify your inherited grieving policy (shoulds, oughts, have to's, and musts), and update it to fit your unique personality and beliefs. See Project 5.

Over time, **identify and question all your core beliefs.** They may be someone else's! Also, _ affirm your unique gifts, limitations, and worth, and **clarify your life purpose.** Do you know clearly why you're on Earth? If not, what (or who) is in the way of discerning and acting on that?

I could go on, but I trust that you get the idea. The main purpose of this first re/marriage-evaluation project is to identify and *start* to heal any major psychological wounds you have.

What Is *Recovery*?

Healing significant false-self wounds is an organic, long-term, inner and social *process*, not an event. **True**, vs. pseudo, **recovery gradually . . .**

. . . **replaces** toxic false-self dominance with the expert wide-angle, far-seeing wisdom and leadership of your true Self, and your Higher Power; and . . .

. . . **changes** Vulnerable subselves' distorted opinion "I'm unlovable" (excessive shame) to "Despite my limitations, I'm worthy, valuable, special, and lovable; and *I always have been*." And true recovery . . .

. . . **helps** Vulnerable subselves burdened with excessive (unwarranted) guilt to release that burden, and avoid unwarranted new guilts; and it . . .

. . . **frees** Vulnerable and Guardian subselves from excessive fears. This happens as they gain trust in the ability of your Regular subselves and Higher Power to handle life crises effectively (unlike your childhood), and keep all subselves your inner-family members safe enough.

And over time, true recovery . . .

. . . **improves** your subselves' ability to consistently evaluate who is safe to trust, and who isn't. The practical outcome is less isolation, deeper nurturing friendships, increasing intimacy, and fewer betrayals and approach-avoid dances; and . . .

. . . **helps** you to see, accept, and enjoy life as it is, with decreasing needs to deny, repress, project, exaggerate, minimize, numb, or avoid. Reality distortions recede, replaced by calm awareness of what *is,* in the present moment.

Together, all these shifts **increase your ability to bond well** with selected other (nurturing) people, grieve your losses effectively, choose higher-nurturance environments, and pursue and enjoy your life mission with confidence, resilience, humility, gratitude, and enthusiasm.

Achieving these changes takes patience, dedication, courage, and considerable effort. What are the payoffs you can expect?

Typical Recovery Benefits

As your true Self becomes more trusted and free to lead, you'll experience increasing periods of feeling *grounded, centered, "good," "well," focused, alert, "up," clear, light, aware, confident, resilient, strong, energized, purposeful, calm,* and *serene.*

Your inner and outer lives usually become slower and less

frantic, and more thoughtful, spontaneous, and satisfying. Excessive perfectionism, worry, and needs to *control* drop noticeably.

Compulsively-social recoverers usually become more comfortable with solitude, and even relish it. Personal spirituality deepens, refreshing, calming, and nourishing your Soul.

If you're used to compulsively rescuing others, you'll start to relax and detach. You'll compassionately and respectfully give others responsibility for managing their own lives. Unconscious *enabling* (pretending troubled people are OK, and helping them avoid self-awareness and self-responsibility) evolves into compassionate confrontations and choices ("I'm sorry, Nina. I've decided I won't interrupt my life to drive you around any more because you choose to not learn to drive. I'd be glad to help you get to a driving school.")

Growing *inner*-family harmony allows you to become more real, genuine, confidant, and spontaneous: all the things that Jack and Sarah Tilmon's dominant subselves were too scared, distrustful, and numb to be. These changes in you invite increasing honesty and intimacy with those you care about.

Typical recoverers grow an interest in, and enthusiasm for, wholistic personal, relationship, and group health. They also can increasingly discern between feeling true unselfish *love*, and acting on unconscious *neediness, lust, excitement, pity*, and *duty*. This opens the way to truly nourishing, stable primary and social relationships, and higher parenting effectiveness.

Typical recoverers spontaneously start to treat their bodies, minds, and spirits more respectfully. They *want to* choose more balanced nutrition, exercise, health care, and anxiety-free rest periods. Journaling, meditation, self-reflection, and guilt-free playing usually increase, despite some others' protests, warnings, or jibes.

You'll *want to* start discriminating between shame and anxiety-promoting (toxic) jobs, churches and civic groups, and high-nurturance groups. This trends toward quitting the former, and satisfying participation in the latter, over time. This may include regretfully choosing to reduce co-dependent relations with wounded parents, siblings, and other kin, despite their (false selves') loud resentments, accusations, threats, pleas, manipulations, and demands. Old compulsions to "save" others, and "show them the light" are replaced by compassionate acceptance that others may or may not find the *light* (e.g. recovery awareness, true Self leadership, and High-Power communion) in this lifetime.

Finally, typical pilgrims in true (vs. pseudo) recovery gradually replace protective reality distortions with clearer awarenesses. We stop denying that we were seriously psychologically and spiritually neglected and perhaps abused as kids. We accept our and others' wounds, including our early caregivers, and the need and opportunity to heal our injuries. We acknowledge toxic (Self-defeating) inner self-talk and outer behaviors, and let go of our need to explain and excuse them. We confront fears, guilts, and angers more honestly, promptly, and directly. We begin to live from some version of this Bill of Personal Rights: ..02/rights.htm.

We honestly acknowledge our and others' addictions and compulsions, and begin to really manage (vs. "cure") ours. We discard the old delusions that we don't need others, or can't live without others. We learn to seek and offer help as equals, not sniveling incompetents. We recoverers learn to see the humor that surrounds us, and to belly-laugh spontaneously at our own foibles and silliness. Old habits of constantly or never apologizing, and our nervous, self-deprecating chuckling and smiling as we express our pain, fade away.

All these recovery changes happen gradually and organically, over some years. My experience is that when a recoverer breaks protective denial and commits to personal healing, s/he experiences some of the payoffs above within weeks or months. As our rewards grow and stabilize, the pace of healthful inner and outer changes usually escalates, then levels off. Genuine recovery from psychological wounds nurtures itself!

If you are a significantly-wounded person in normal de-

nial, you'll probably disbelieve, trivialize, or blank out what you've just read. If your protective *Inner Skeptic* disbelieves, try to be open to listening to others who may talk about their recovery experiences. They probably won't know the terms *personality splitting, true Self, inner family*, and *subselves*. They may or may not know about the concept of low and high-nurturance families (Chapter 3). True recoverers will identify immediately with *wounds, family dysfunction*, and *recovery*. They may know something about being an *Adult Child* of childhood trauma or "toxic parents."

Reality-check the ideas in this chapter with other people, at your own pace. If you experience some self-talk (thought streams) like "Well *other* people might be able to recover and get the alluring things above, but *I* can't," affectionately know that's one of your faithful, uninformed, Guardian subselves trying to spare you from disappointment, "failure," and pain.

You CAN start to free your Self to harmonize your inner family any day! For more information, see the Project-1 guidebook, or ..01/recovery1.htm

Two more key Project-1 concepts are *pseudo* recovery, and *addiction* recovery. Here's an overview:

Pseudo Recovery

If shortsighted, reactive Guardian and Vulnerable parts of your personality often control you, the former have worked ceaselessly for your security and comfort, for years. If some of your subselves commit to personal recovery, i.e. to *change*, that will probably evoke intense distrust, skepticism, anxiety ("worry"), and determination to *block* change in some Guardian subselves or frightened Vulnerables. Typical Guardians fear "losing my job," and vague or vivid catastrophes that they believe recovery will surely bring.

To protect themselves, such Guardians can tolerate you (your Regular subselves) learning intellectually about wounds and recovery, but they'll try to avoid *doing* it. To minimize the danger they perceive (reality distortion), they'll creatively deny that they're blocking your healing. When such subselves control your thoughts and behavior, it's called *pseudo* recovery.

I recall working with a highly intelligent, caring, divorced Mom I'll call Rosa. She declared proudly "I've read every dysfunctional-family and recovery book ever published!" (When denials first break, many early recoverers grow a temporary compulsion to know *everything* about these subjects.) She had attended a range of 12-step groups like Codependents Anonymous (CoDA) for over a decade. Yet at 40, she was over 100 pounds overweight, and gaining; diabetic and eating poorly; socially isolated; and had a history of menial, low-paying, short-lived human-service jobs, and related financial problems.

She had chosen a co-dependent, conflictual relationship with a majorly wounded, childless man for 12 years. Her false self periodically berated and disparaged him. Then when he (his Vulnerable subselves) cowered, her other subselves felt guilty, apologized, and became loving, passionate, and subservient. These alternating states and mixed messages drove both of them "crazy." Rosa had no relationship with one of her two biokids or their father. She was choosing to remain in a steadily shaming, highly conflictual relationship with her verbally abusive, demanding (highly wounded) mother.

Rosa is one of the invisible legions of strugglers who sense or acknowledge their wounds, but haven't yet *really* surrendered to what they mean, and what's *really* needed to heal them. Paradoxically, she was a genuine help to other recoverers. Her unacknowledged false self stopped her short of committing to true recovery for herself. She was addicted to fat, sugar, carbohydrates, a toxic relationship, and *talking* about recovery. She vehemently denied these (e.g. "My metabolism and thyroid cause my weight problem. I obviously can't control them.")

Rosa's pseudo recovery testifies to the relentless terror, guilt, and shame that some of her *inner*-family members have felt her whole life. She and her non-recovering partner regularly enabled each other (i.e. promoted avoiding recovery, and denying that). I believe Life will patiently keep offering each of them reasons to truly hit their bottom, and choose *true* recovery. That can happen literally any day.

Fear, distractions, and ignorance can cause our governing subselves to avoid the scary, alien inner work needed for true recovery. Seeking personal and social acceptance and *peace*, and wanting to avoid the pain of uncovering and recovering, some Guardian subselves learn how recoverers talk and act. They mimic these convincingly. Some Christians and recovering addicts describe this as "not walking the talk." Twelve-step people talk about "dry drunks" who have quit using toxic chemicals, but keep doing "stinkin' thinkin'" (false-self inner talk), and deny that and their denials.

So if you're often ruled by a false self, you risk moving into *pseudo* recovery instead of real healing, and denying that. A way of acknowledging this is to use Project 1 worksheets 1 and 5 through 11 periodically to see if your "scores" change. If you think you're in real recovery and your scores don't change, use "parts work" to discover which subselves are sabotaging your Self's competent leadership toward true inner-family harmony.

Changeless Changes

Paul Watzlawick taught me this helpful concept: A common symptom of false-self dominance and pseudo recovery is making "changeless changes." You probably know people who commit to trying a new diet to remove extra pounds. They work diligently, and eventually the pounds return. Then they try the next diet . . . Attempts to quit smoking and other addiction relapses are other common examples. **These are *first-order* changes**: false-self attempts to appease the subselves and/or outer people saying "change!" without *really* risking a shift in the underlying core beliefs and priorities.

A second-order (core attitude) change happens when a person voluntarily revises their basic priorities about work, play, rest, nutrition, and exercise. Then they don't need the artificial help of someone's "miracle pills or diet program" to re-tone and reshape their body and energy level permanently. Common second-order changes are shifting from atheism or agnosticism to solid faith in a Higher Power, and mid-life shifts from a high-pressure profits-and-power career to a human-service occupation.

True recovery from life-long false-self control (empowering your Self to harmonize and lead your inner family) is a second-order change. Previously-dominant Guardian subselves increasingly trust the Self to do what they used to do, and focus their energy elsewhere. Reading this book and doing nothing is a first order change.

Addiction Recovery vs. Full Recovery

A high percentage of my single and stepfamily clients have been recovering addicts, the child and/or mate of an addict, or seemed to have symptoms of addiction. The relationship between low childhood nurturance, unseen false-self domination, addictions, and recovery deserves a book of its own. Here are some key points:

An *addiction* **is a cycle** of compulsive, self-harmful behaviors that defies willful attempts to stop the cycle. All **four types** of addiction serve to self-medicate and distract from intolerable fear, shame, guilt, confusion, emptiness, aimlessness, and hopelessness:

+ *Ingesting mood-altering* **substances** (chemical addiction or dependence), including sugar, fat, complex carbohydrates ("comfort foods"), caffeine, nicotine, and illegal and some prescription drugs.

+ *Activities*, like excessive work, sex, gambling, spending, jogging, eating, worship, socializing, attending 12-step meetings, Internet surfing, etc. These are toxic because they unbalance the addict's (and others') lives and resources, and deflect from inner pain.

+ *Toxic (wounding) relationships*, like co-dependence and enmeshment. And . . .

+ *Emotional states* like (out)rage, power (domination), excitement ("thrill seeking"), and sensual stimulation and orgasm.

True addictions are _ progressive; _ life degrading and shortening; _ self-promoting, and _ instinctively aim to relieve the addict's relentless shame, guilt, anxiety, rage, and emptiness. Some chemical addictions like ethyl alcohol, nicotine, sugar, and cocaine are complicated by growing cellular dependencies. It's now known that at least alcoholics have a genetic predisposition to addiction, because their bodies metabolize ethyl alcohol differently than non-addicts.

Three more traits of a true active addiction are _ the addict guiltily or defiantly *denies* the reality, extent, or personal and social effects of their compulsion, despite undeniable evidence; _ s/he can't quit the toxic compulsion/s alone, despite repeated attempts; and _ s/he may "manage" (control) one addiction, and develop another to compensate for the loss of the comforting payoff (cross addiction).

I believe that *all* teen and adult addicts are suffering from significant psychological wounds, following inadequate childhood nurturance. Their addiction results from two Guardian subselves, the *Addict* and the *Magician,* or *Rationalizer,* focused intently on providing immediate relief to young Vulnerable subselves burdened with intolerable shame, guilt, fear, and loneliness. They value immediate relief more than long-term health, so "logical" attempts to stop their toxic behaviors can't work. This inexorably *amplifies* despair, anxiety, guilts, and shame.

Since the birth of Alcoholics Anonymous and the famous 12 steps in 1935, the public and our medical profession are recognizing that addiction is *not* caused by a "weak will" or "bad character." With increasingly informed professional help, and the true strength in 12-step support groups, millions of addicts have arrested (vs. cured) their compulsions, and led increasingly *sane* and *sober* lives. However, the 12-step program doesn't yet acknowledge the underlying psychological wounds that sobriety doesn't heal, so many struggle with re-

lapses and cross addictions. The "insanity" of addictive thinking and behaving is inner-family chaos and false-self control.

The revered Alcoholics Anonymous "Big Book" was last
revised in 1976. It mentions nothing about childhood
nurturance deprivations or wounds. The book promotes turning life over to a benign Higher Power, adherence to a set of life
principles, and compassionate service to others. For many, these
work (manage addictions), as far as they go. Many 12-step AA
meetings are blue with cigarette smoke. The caffeine pot is
always full. The inner pain and protective false-selves usually
remain, however camouflaged.

I propose that if an addict achieves lasting sobriety but
doesn't get into meaningful true recovery from false-self dominance, s/he's in *pseudo* recovery. Dominant false selves make
first-order changes: they creatively exchange obvious addictions for less obvious ones. A sober chemical addict begins
overworking, over-praying, and/or chooses comforting/aggra-
vating co-dependent relationships. Their lives do feel better,
and they've stopped short of full recovery because of unawareness that their Self is still held hostage by distrustful subselves.
Such people are called "Dry drunks."

Bottom line: I feel that any past or active addiction, and
enabling an addict (not confronting them respectfully), indicate major false-self control. A recovering addict may or may
not be controlled by a false self. Stable *addiction* management
is the gateway to *full* recovery from false-self dominance. Many
(wounded?) traditionalists will dispute this. Rigid, black-white
(bipolar) thinking is a common trait of false-self dominance . . .

Recap

Technological advances since 1980 show that our neural
systems have a normal trait now called *multiplicity*. This is many
brain regions operating together semi-independently to cause
a single response or perception. Multiplicity confirms what
psychiatric explorers have suspected for well over a century:
that the personality of normal people is composed of a group

of semi-independent *subselves* or *parts*. This poses the questions "Who leads my inner family of subselves in normal and crisis times, and how well do they lead?" Your recent wholistic health is a measure of the latter.

I estimate that over 85% of the ~1,000 troubled, divorced, and stepfamily co-parents I've worked with since 1981 were unaware of struggling with a mix of up to six psychological injuries from a low-nurturance childhood:

+ Frequent dominance of a well-meaning, reactive, short-sighted false self. This causes . . .
+ Excessive guilts and shame ("low self esteem");
+ Excessive anxieties and fears;
+ Reality distortions, including denial of these wounds; and . . .
+ Toxic dis/trust imbalances. These combine to cause . . .
+ Difficulty *bonding* with some or all other living things, which hinders exchanging intimacy and love.

The core wound is personality control by Guardian and Vulnerable subselves who distrust or don't know the person's true Self. Often, these subselves firmly believe they live in a traumatic time long past (reality distortion). Until recovery frees them, they guard every new day against menacing ghosts and illusions that will never return. "Logic" and persuasion are *always* useless against this survival reflex, and build mutual frustrations.

Most courting co-parents like you are in partial or full denial of their personality wounds, where they came from, and what effects they cause. Typically, wounded adults and teens pick each other repeatedly for short-term comfort, despite stressful long-term results. Most of them, specially in complex stepfamilies, ultimately (re)divorce. Until in true recovery from false-self dominance, typical wounded co-parents unconsciously replicate their low childhood nurturance, and pass versions of these wounds on to their kids, just as their unaware ancestors did.

Courting couples' mix of these wounds and their unawareness of them is probably the most powerful and least known of five factors that cause eventual legal and/or psychological (re)divorce.

Honestly assessing yourself and your partner for symptoms of the six inner wounds is the first of seven projects that I believe are essential for your making three *right* re/marriage decisions. Ideally, you two will do this well *before* a re/marriage commitment. It's also useful after re/wedding. As you read further, you'll increasingly appreciate how postponing or ignoring this pivotal wounded-assessment and recovery task will probably stress you and wound your kids.

This chapter outlines the goals of Project 1, and five steps to reach them. The goals for courting co-parents are:

1) _ Learn basic family nurturance and inner-family concepts. Then assess _ yourself, _ your partner, _ each related minor or grown child, and _ the kids' other parent/s, *honestly* for significant false-self wounds.

2) If *you* have significant symptoms of false-self dominance, begin an informed recovery (healing) program, and work with co-parenting partners to prevent, and/or assess and heal, false-self wounds in each dependent child in your life, whether custodial or not.

3) If your courtship partner has significant false-self traits, invite her or him to join you in researching and doing this first project. If s/he's resistant, apathetic, or ambivalent, *settle for friendship!*

4) Keep a vision of the long term benefits steadily in mind, and make your personal recovery second only to current survival, and any parental responsibilities.

This vital project also applies to human-service professionals personally, parentally, and in your workplace and practice.

The book "Who's *Really* Running Your Life?—Free Your *Self* from Custody, and Guard Your Kids" is entirely devoted to Project 1. It explains childhood wounding and a powerful recovery option called *inner*-family therapy ("parts work") in depth, and provides many resources and options. The bibliographies in that book and the Web site http://sfhelp.org/11/

booklist.htm offer other titles that can raise your awareness of your amazing, vexing inner family of subselves.

Pause and reflect now. Notice your feelings and thoughts. What are your inner voices saying? As you evaluate inner wounds and complex stepfamily co-commitment together, use this simple, powerful recovery resource that theologian Reinhold Niebuhr gave us in 1934. It has brought clarity, guidance, inspiration, and strength to millions of people in personal recovery around the world:

The Serenity Prayer

God grant me the serenity
to accept the things I cannot change,
Courage to change the things I can, and . . .
Wisdom to know the difference.

+ + +

Is your Self leading your inner family right now, or are some other subselves? How do you know?

Reality check: to sense your reaction to this chapter, see which of these feel *true* now. Take your time: haste and/or fudging puts you and any dependent kids at risk . . .

1) I _ understand and _ accept the concepts of _ family nurturance, _ "inner-family of subselves" (multi-part personalities), _ false self and true Self, and _ the six related psychological wounds now. I also understand the concepts of _ first-order and second-order change, and _ pseudo recovery. (T F ?) Can you clearly describe each of these to another person?

2) I understand that _ once these wounds are identified, there are effective recovery options and resources available. (T F ?)

3) I accept that _ I and my _ current and/or _ past partners,

may have some or all of these six wounds, and _ may not know it now. (T F ?)

4) I see personal (and perhaps parental) benefit to assessing myself for these wounds in the next month. (T F ?)

5) I know where to find resources that can help me self-assess for the six inner wounds. (T F ?)

6) I can name the common emotional symptoms of true-Self inner-family leadership now. (T F ?)

Now I'm aware of . . .

Option: reread the sketch of the McLean-Tilmon-Cohen clan in Chapter 7, and see if you react differently.

If your inner crew or body needs a break, take one! We're about to shift gears to overview Project 2. It reduces the second most potent block to your getting your needs met well enough, after freeing your Self: ineffective thinking and communicating.

On a scale of 1 to 10 (10 = "very"), how effective would you rate your recent communications with the most important people in your life, in __ calm times and __ conflicts? Would you agree that effective thinking, communicating, and problem solving are essential for making wise re/marriage and co-parenting decisions? Do your kids know how to think and communicate *effectively* yet?

Project 2: Learn Effective Problem-solving

"I know you believe you understand what you think I said,
but I'm not sure you realize that
what you heard was not what I meant."
—Poster, author unknown.

I've studied and taught communication skills for over 30 years, including clinical hypnosis. Since 1981, I've listened to over a thousand troubled divorced, single, and re/wedded co-parents describe their problems. I estimate that over 90% of these good people didn't know how to think and communicate *effectively* about relationship stressors. Typical co-parents like Sarah and Jack Tilmon don't know what they don't know about effective *inner*personal and interpersonal problem solving. That's one reason they and their peers (probably including you) seek no training in it before marrying.

Divorce starkly implies that the partners were _ probably neglected and wounded in childhood, _ didn't know key health and relationship concepts (Chapter 5), and _ couldn't communicate effectively enough to solve their problems. Unless co-parents have studied communication skills after divorce, they probably haven't improved. That means _ the communication among ex mates and their minor and grown kids is probably ineffective, specially in significant conflicts.

Paradox: we all depend on "communicating" more than

any other learned skill to meet our daily needs, yet few of us ever study how to *do* it well! The same was true for our ancestors, and now most of our kids. On a communication-effectiveness scale of one to 10, I'd guess most people average two to five with the adults and kids who matter the most to them. How can you tell if that's true of *you*? Having no yardstick to use and no reason to find one, few people are aware of their communication habits, abilities, and options. Communicating effectively is essential for long-term re/marital, co-parenting, stepfamily, and occupational success.

This vital second project applies to all people in all settings. Its importance merits its own book, which is the **recommended "text" for this co-parent project**: *"Satisfactions—7 Relationship Skills You Need to Know"* (Xlibris.com, 2001). Much of the content is available at http://sfhelp.org/02/links02.htm.

This chapter offers specific Project-2 goals and steps to reach them, and relevant resources to help you do that together. To begin our exploration, see how you feel about these . . .

Premises and Basics

See how aware you are by checking each of these ideas that you "already knew":

__ **All life forms communicate** to fill current needs—i.e. to lower discomforts. *Effective* communication fills all participants' current true needs well enough for now.

__ Ultimately **each of us is the only person who can fill our current true needs**. Adults' expecting or demanding other adults or kids to fill their true needs *always* breed inner and interpersonal conflict, unless the others *need* to do so.

__ Relationship **"problems" are up to three sets of simultaneous conflicting needs**: _ inside you, _ inside your partner, and _ between your two inner teams. The skills of *awareness, digging down, and metatalk* can clarify and separate these to help you resolve them in key situations.

__ **Communication between partners is a process**: a series of multi-level transactions with a beginning, middle, and an end. The process involves _ perceiving internal and environmental (social) information, _ making "sense" (meaning) of it, _ comparing the meaning against our current *conscious* needs, and _ reacting intentionally or impulsively. "No reaction" *is* a reaction. Our reaction triggers the same sequence in our partner, which triggers an ongoing spiral of interactions until someone stops reacting.

__ **Communicating** *effectively* **is essential** for co-parents to _ make wise (re)marriage decisions, _ resolve relationship conflicts, and to _ provide effective child nurturance.

__ (False-self dominance + unawareness) inexorably minimize the effectiveness of your inner and interpersonal communications. **You probably accept ineffective communication as** *normal.*

__ Your three or more related **co-parents _ will face a stream of** *many* concurrent innerpersonal and mutual **conflicts for many years.** _ Many of these conflicts are deferred, muted, or ignored during courtship, because most adults and kids are on "best behavior." They appear in full strength after re/wedding, startling and dismaying everyone.

__ **"Problem solving" means** _ mutual understanding of each partner's current needs, _ ranking them as equally important (=/=), and _ cooperatively brainstorming possible solutions toward win-win outcomes. Popular alternatives are arguing, fighting, avoiding, explaining, persuading, threatening, manipulating, and withdrawing, specially if false selves are in control.

__ When inevitable courtship ideals and illusions wear off after re/wedding, **most co-parents have trouble problem-solving effectively.** They don't know what they don't know about their communication habits, process, or ways they could improve their effectiveness. Evidence: over half of American re/marriers eventually divorce.

__ **Any motivated person can learn to use seven mental/ verbal skills** that will greatly improve the effectiveness of their *inner*, intimate, and social communicating. If you can't name and describe the seven now, you're probably not using them, or teaching them to your kids. Choosing which of the seven skills to use in any situation depends on partner's mix of **E(motion) levels**. .

Here are more communication premises and basics. Are these new to you?

__ Each communicator tries instinctively to fill **two to six current needs**. Partners' respective current need-mixes may mesh well or conflict. Most adults and kids _ can't name their communication needs (p. 182), and _ don't know what to do if their needs conflict. Do you?

__ Our ruling subselves semi-consciously **decode up to four messages at once** from our partner/s: what you seem to _ think, _ feel, _ need, and _ *how you seem to feel about yourself and me now.* The latter **"R(espect) messages"** largely control the outcome of our most important communications, yet most people aren't aware of them. Incoming R-messages are decoded as _ "I'm 1-up" (superior to you), _ "I'm 1-down" (inferior to you), or _ **"We're '=/='**: I see us now as equals in dignity and worth." *Your communications can be effective* only *when you and any partner consistently decode believable "=/=" R-messages from each other.* Does this make sense?

__ Until shame-based (wounded) co-parents are in effective recovery, their *Inner Critic* and *Perfectionist* subselves relentlessly judge them as "1-down." This distortion blocks their ceaseless need to feel respected enough in any situation, which wrecks communication effectiveness. Patient _ Project-1 recovery progress, and _ learning to use these seven skills, can significantly reduce this major problem over time.

__ Kids and adults exchange these **four messages over three "channels" simultaneously**: _ verbal (words), _ paraverbal (how we make sounds) and _ non-verbal (visual, tactile, smell, and *sensing.*). That means *we're each decoding up to 12 messages at once* as key communications unfold. Research implies that most face-to-face meaning is decoded *visually*, not from spoken words.

More communication premises. Did you know these?

__ When we decode **mixed (double) messages** on these channels ("I love you." / "You disgust me."), it's very likely one or both of us are controlled by a false self without knowing it.

__ **Any communication** exchange between two subselves or persons **can have 16 outcomes.** Only *one* is fully effective for both partners!

__ There are over **30 variables you can become aware of** to assess and improve your communication effectiveness, like: eye contact, "flooding," interrupting, defocusing, R(espect)-messages, voice tone, outcomes, *pace* conflicts, need conflicts, E(motion) levels, assumptions (mind reading), awareness bubbles, paradoxes, surface vs. true needs, and communication sequences and patterns. Can you define each of these? These concepts and labels are the tools for "metatalk" skill.

__ Assertion or aggression are ways we express our needs to other subselves or people. **Three keys to effective assertion** are _ your Self leads your inner family, _ you value your needs, dignity and worth as much as your partner's (=/= attitude), and _ you *expect* and listen empathically to your partner's resistances, and then calmly re-assert your needs.

__ **It's vital for** courting co-parents like **you to _ learn what** *effective communication* **means**, and then _ assess *before re/wedding* how effective you two are at _ thinking, _ communicating, and _ problem solving; _ generally and _ in conflict, as _ individuals and as _ co-parenting teammates.

__ Suitors considering re/wedding a divorced family also do well to **assess the ex mates' problem-solving effectiveness,** specially about co-parenting and money. The lower their effectiveness, the higher the odds of post-re/marriage relationship stress for you all, and eventual emotional or legal re/divorce. Legal battles between ex mates demonstrate that they can't communicate effectively. That usually means significant false-self wounding in *both* people, plus shared unawareness of _ the realities in Chapter 5 and _ what you're about to read. A final premise:

__ Ignoring or **postponing this second courtship project probably indicates significant false-self dominance:** a *major* re/marital red light.

Notice your self-talk (thought streams and feelings) now. What are your subselves saying? Who's "speaking"?

Reality check: Put aside current distractions for a moment, and get clear on what *effective communication* means to you now. Then answer these questions thoughtfully to help you assess whether this second project will be useful to you and those you care about. Use an effectiveness scale of 1 to 10 (10 = "consistently very high") to answer. Option: answer with a range, like "2 to 4."

Recently . . .

+ **My** general communication effectiveness with other people has averaged ___;
+ My communication in interpersonal *conflicts* at work or school has averaged ___;
+ My communication in interpersonal *conflicts* with family kids and adults has averaged ___;
+ My *internal* communications (among my subselves) has averaged ___;
+ My communication effectiveness in *conflicts* with my partner has averaged ___;
+ My communication effectiveness with my ex mate (if any) has been about ___;
+ I feel **my partner's** recent general communication effectiveness with other people has averaged ___;
+ Her/His communication effectiveness in interpersonal conflicts with me has averaged ___;
+ His/Her communication effectiveness in interpersonal *conflicts* at work (or school) seems to be about ___;
+ His/Her communication effectiveness in interpersonal conflicts with family kids and adults has averaged ___;
+ Her/His **communication effectiveness with her/his ex mate** (if any) has been about ___;

"?" below means "I'm not sure."
+ I have a very clear idea of what *effective* communication
is (True False ?).
+ My partner has a very clear definition of *effective* communication (T F ?).
+ My partner _ and I _ know what *values* conflicts are, and
_ agree how to handle them effectively: (T F ?)
+ My partner _ and I know _ the six needs we try to fill by
communicating, and _ we usually act effectively when
our *communication needs* conflict: (T F ?)
+ My partner and I can clearly define the difference between *problem solving* and *fighting* or *arguing*: (T F ?)
+ I feel very comfortable showing these rankings to my
partner, and discussing them Now: (T F ?).
+ Viewing my answers and considering what they mean, I
now feel _ content _ fairly calm, _ nothing special, _
somewhat uneasy, _ very uneasy.
Option: use this learning tool to help assess your Project 2
knowledge along the way: ..02/evc-quiz.htm.

+ + +

Seven Skills

In 23 years' research, I've never seen a book on parenting,
divorce, or stepfamily topics that outlines what you're about to
read. Most *communication* books and programs I've reviewed
don't either. This second re/marriage-evaluation project invites
all co-parents to learn and use seven mental/verbal skills co-
operatively. Add the pointers (..**/***.htm) below to http://
sfhelp.org/02/ to access Internet resources on these skills:

Awareness of what's happening _ inside you, _ inside your
communication partner, _ between you two, and _ around you
both. There are over 30 factors you can become aware of. Seven
are specially helpful. (..awareness.htm)

Clear thinking. Many people (you?) are used to fuzzy, unfocused thinking, and vague or ambivalent terms and phrases. It's their daily norm, often fostered by _ unawareness, _ a limited vocabulary, and _ a controlling false self. You can grow awareness and knowledge to illuminate fuzzy thinking in general and in conflicts. Inner-family chaos (false-self dominance) breeds fuzzy thinking. That hampers effective negotiating and problem solving. Progress on Project 1 can help improve them. (..fuzzy1-wks.htm)

"**Dig Down**" below surface problems to unearth _ the true needs beneath them, and _ who's responsible for filling them. Without this skill, personal and relationship "problems" keep recurring and may escalate. (..dig-down.htm)

Empathic listening: hearing with your *heart*. Thanks to Stephen Covey for this descriptive term. (..listen.htm)

"**Metatalk**": talking cooperatively about *how* you're communicating. This skill uses _ knowledge of communication basics, _ a special vocabulary, and _ your *awarenesses* to help identify inner-family and interpersonal communication problems. (..metatalk.htm)

Respectful assertion: _ saying what you need in a way your partner can hear you clearly, _ handling *expected* resistances with empathic listening, and _ calmly re-asserting (..assert.htm). The seventh skill is . . .

Problem solving or conflict reduction. This uses all six other skills to help each person _ identify and _ get their current true needs met well enough, _ in a way that pleases all partners well enough. *Arguing* or *fighting* are battles to fill *my* needs vs. *your* needs. Problem-solving focuses on filling *our* (co-equal) needs. (..prblmslv.htm and ..win-win.htm)

Appropriately used, these seven skills can help _ your Self harmonize your inner subselves, and _ nurture your "outer" relationships with adults and kids. If you couldn't name these skills before reading them, or if you can't describe them now, you probably _ are used to communicating at well below half of your potential effectiveness; _ don't know what's possible;

and _ haven't taught any dependent kids how to get their needs met effectively with other people. True?

This chapter outlines key goals and steps to help you partners learn and apply these powerful skills. It also explores a common stepfamily dynamic: *loyalty* or *inclusion* conflicts. Reminder: the guidebook and the Web pages at http://sfhelp.org/02/links02.htm provide much more perspective, and illustrations and resources on this vital courtship and re/marital project.

What Is *Effective* Communication?

This is really two questions: _ "What is *communication?*" and _ "What is *effective* communication?" See if you agree with this **premise**:

Anything you do or don't do that causes a physical, emotional, spiritual, and/or mental change in another person is "interpersonal communication."

A key implication is that **we can't *not* communicate.** "No response" *is* a response, containing an implied (1-up, 1-down, or =/=) R(espect)-message. Silence and the lack of a look, touch, phone call, or note, cause reactions just as much as speech, touch, e-mail, and greeting cards do. If someone says "S/He didn't say anything," there were probably some meanings *assumed*, like "You don't care much about me right now," or "You're too ashamed or scared to answer me." That may or may not be what the "unresponsive one" meant. Kids and adults controlled by shamed and/or fearful subselves are at special risk of mis-decoding what "no response" means.

All life forms are naturally *needy.* Human **needs** are dynamic combinations of mental, emotional, spiritual, and physical tensions or *discomforts*. **We communicate with others to meet our current** conscious and unconscious personal **needs** for comfort. This is true of infants, mutes, "mentally ill" (wounded) people, tycoons, hermits, deaf and homeless people, "criminals," world leaders, gurus, and everyone else. Do you agree?

Moment by moment, you and each communication partner have sets of major and minor needs that can conflict _ within and _ between you (*"I need to _ change my clothes, and to _ avoid conflict with you. You need us to leave now, and _ be on time. I feel torn."*). We constantly strive to reduce the discomfort of these combined tensions. So I propose that . . .

*Inner*personal and *inter*personal communications are *effective* when _ each "inner voice" (subself) and _ each person involved feels (1) they got enough of their present true (vs. surface) needs met, (2) in a way that feels good enough. How does this compare to your definition?

This two-part definition implies that to communicate effectively, _ all participants know their true present needs clearly (via *awareness*), and _ are aware of their feelings _ during and _ after the communication process. The word *true* is key. We're often not clear on or honest with ourselves or our partners about our *real* motivations, perceptions, and needs. Where true, this is usually because an unaware false self controls us. Practicing your awareness and "dig down" skills will empower you to identify your *true* (vs. surface) current needs. If kids don't experience their key adults doing this often, they usually won't either.

The psychological wounds of reality distortion and excessive shame, guilts, and fears cause conflicting perceptions, needs and feelings. Combined, these shroud both inner and mutual communications with vagueness and ambiguity. This causes mixed messages, self and mutual doubt, and significant anxieties and defensiveness. This is specially true in _ unfamiliar social situations and roles and _ inner and _ mutual conflicts. Typical stepfamilies are loaded with these for *years*. That's why your first and second co-parent projects are so vital!

When partners like Sarah and Jack Tilmon don't have a clear definition of *effective* communication (they didn't), they can't evaluate how well they're talking and listening or solve communication glitches. Incidentally, I use *effective* vs. *good* communication because the latter invites blaming someone for *bad* communication. We shame-based co-parents do *not* need more reasons to feel badly about ourselves or to criticize our wounded partners!

Why Do This Second Project?

You can't know what it's like to birth a baby, skydive, eat sushi, or raft through the Grand Canyon until you've done it. If you haven't been a stepfamily co-parent before, you won't really *know* how it will feel to have many simultaneous, alien, complex conflicts to negotiate if you choose to re/marry. These are common stressors you'll probably all encounter:

+ Post-separation _ resentments, _ hostilities, _ disrespects, _ anxieties, _ hurts, and _ distrusts between ex mates and minor and grown kids.

+ Resolving _ habitually ineffective communication habits between _ ex mates and _ some relatives.

+ Periodic or ongoing co-parent disputes over child _ custody, _ visitations, _ discipline, _ holidays, _ schooling, _ activities, _ vacations, _ health, _ religion, and _ financial support. In a large minority of stepfamilies, these conflicts often escalate into _ costly courtroom battles that polarize the entire extended stepfamily, and significantly stress re/marriages and finances. Legal fights are sure indicators co-parents aren't using the seven skills in this Project. Legal suits leave emotional scars that add to others and take *years* to heal. (http:// sfhelp.org/Rx/ex/legal.htm.)

+ Over time, your three or more co-parents will experience major clashes over _ parenting values, _ family rituals, _ customs, and _ priorities. These promote stepfamily _ inclusion (membership) conflicts, and divisive _ loyalty conflicts in and between your several related homes for years. And . . .

+ There are generally more minor children in nuclear step-homes than in biofamily homes. This means more _ sibling battles, more _ simultaneous need conflicts, and therefore _ higher ongoing needs for effective co-parent mediation, guidance, and problem solving. Typical stepkids need help with over 30 extra family-change adjustment needs to fill, compared to their intact-biofamily peers (p. 454).

Here's the point: **Typical** absent-parent biofamilies and extended **stepfamilies are extra-complex, high-conflict groups**. They're usually co-managed by well-meaning adults who aren't aware of key high-nurturance relationship basics (Chapter 3) and these communication basics and skills. Compared to Self-led, aware bioparents, single and re/married co-parents have more simultaneous current conflicts to resolve, and more hindrances to doing so.

I've heard lovestruck courting partners say proudly "Well, this may be true for most people, but not *us*. We agree on just about everything. We *never* fight!" (Implied reality distortion: ". . . and we never will.") Such declarations are a glaring red light for me. Average re/marriages and stepfamily relationships are significantly conflictual for years after re/wedding! Once romantic courtship's unrealistic politeness, idealisms, and tolerances fade, complex inner-family, interpersonal, and inter-home conflicts *will* surface. Romantic love and mutual commitment alone won't prevent or resolve them—specially if myopic false selves are covertly calling the shots.

The earlier you start practicing your version of these seven skills, the easier all six other courtship projects will be. *To progress on this skill-building project together, you partners must be well along on any needed personal recoveries from false-self wounds.* Single, separated, divorced, courting, or re/married, **it's never too late to start these two** inter-related keystone **projects**!

Where did you learn to communicate? Most of us did from watching our families, teachers, heroes, enemies, coaches, and friends. *None* of them knew what you're learning here. We usually think, talk, listen, and react unconsciously from old habits, even if the results don't please us. Taking a "speech" or Toastmaster class may grow your diction, public speaking confidence, or debating abilities. It will *not* impart the seven effective-communication skills above. In over 30 years' research,

I've never seen a school, business, or adult education program that teaches them. Have you?

The skills work between people and *within* you: between your subselves. Kids and adults experience *self-talk* all the time: a dynamic flow of thoughts, hunches, intuitions, images, feelings, and visions. These are **inner**personal **communications**. They can range from tumultuous and chaotic, to clear, quiet, and effective. Our inner conversations and uproars are so familiar that they often go unnoticed, until we (you) learn *awareness*. The next time you feel *uneasy* (anxious and confused) or *upset* (conflicted), observe the dialog or shouting match between two or more "voices" inside you objectively, as a reporter would. For example:

Voice 1: "I wonder how Bob is recovering. I'll call him today."

Voice 2: "But you know he'll talk your ear off, and he never asks about you. Talking to Bob gets boring, and it hurts every time. *Don't* call Bob!"

Voice 3: "Yeh, but friends should call! I'll feel guilty if I don't . . ."

Voice 4: "Listen, this is too hard and confusing. C'mon, let's get a donut."

Voice 5: "*No!* You're 20 pounds overweight as it is. Don't eat that junk, have some yogurt!"

Sound familiar? How often and when do your inner voices (subselves) argue and create (the feeling of) *confusion*? With practice, the seven communication skills above will work between your subselves as well as with other people. What would your life be like with more *internal* co-operation, compromising, and harmony?

Trying **these seven skills** is the only way you'll experience their power and usefulness. A thorough hands-on communication skill-building class takes at least 40 contact hours over many weeks, plus hours of homework and outside-class practice. By themselves, this chapter and the related resources will *not* make you a more effective communicator. They can _ alert you to what's possible, _ motivate you to learn, and _ provide a clear concept to work from.

Too little attention to harmonizing your inner crew (Project 1) and to learning how to problem-solve effectively will hinder your progress on Projects 3-12. *That* promotes wrong re/marital choices, years of distress, middle-aged re/divorce, agonizing personal losses, and unintentionally wounding another generation of vulnerable kids. Are your ruling subselves tired of reading that?

Project 2 Goals

Edit and use this checklist to guide you partners in doing Project 2.

__ **1) accept** (vs. deny, ignore, or minimize) that _ If you re/marry, you'll encounter many marriage-threatening *inner*personal and *inter*personal conflicts in your complex web of stepfamily relationships, for many years. Then _ accept that _ each of you is responsible for learning how to resolve these conflicts together, and _ teaching your dependent kids how to communicate *effectively.*

__ **2) Clarify** your definition of *effective* communication together, so you can tell clearly if you're *doing* it or not. Use my definition as a springboard (p. 176).

__ **3) Use the Project-2 book** *Satisfactions* or the Web worksheets at http://sfhelp.org/02/links02.htm to evaluate how effectively each of you communicate _ normally, and _ in conflict with key people. Pay special attention to conflicts between _ ex-mates, and _ parents and kids. *Do not expect that harmonious courtship communications accurately forecast post-re/ wedding effectiveness!* Option: validate this with veteran stepfamily co-parents.

__ **4) Factor your evaluation results** into your decision about whether to re/marry or not in Project 7.

If you do re/marry, then you partners continue this project by . . .

__ **5) Commit** to helping each other and other family members develop and use the seven mental/verbal communication skills to get more of your daily needs met.

___ **6) Help each other build a genuine "=/=" attitude of respecting** every adult and child, including ex mates, as a person of equal dignity and worth to yourself. Implication: "Right now and over time, your (non-emergency) needs, feelings, and values are co-equal with mine." *Without this genuine core attitude, communications don't work well! False selves rarely feel =/=, so personal recovery (Project 1) is probably essential for effective communication with those you love and need the most.*

___ **7)** Learn to **identify four types of conflict:** _ *internal* (inner family); _ concrete resource (like a checkbook, vehicle, device, or tool); _ values, priorities, and preferences; and _ current communication needs. Then you three or more co-parents _ build effective strategies to resolve each of these types over time.

___ **8)** Patiently **help all minor and grown kids** and interested others to learn and use the same seven skills.

Based on Project-1 progress, this vital second project combats at least two of the five re/divorce hazards: unawareness (of effective-communication skills), and excessive fears of assertion, conflict, and strong emotions.

How can you co-parents help each other accomplish all these goals, over time?

Main Steps

Edit these suggestions to fit your present levels of communication knowledge and skill:

1) _ Study all 12 of the stepfamily-building projects in Chapter 8 for context. Then _ study and **do enough of Project 1 to decide if personal recovery is warranted.** Unhealed false-self dominance in you and/or your partner will relentlessly sabotage effective inner family and interpersonal communication. Reading "Who's *Really* Running Your Life?" or the related articles at http://sfhelp.org/01/links01.htm) will help you perceive and resolve inner conflicts. That foundation skill will significantly help you partners resolve interpersonal conflicts.

Step 2) You and your partner **adopt the solid beliefs** that . . .

_ **"Communication" exists to fill two to six concurrent** *needs* in each partner:

+ To feel enough *respect* now, internally and from each current partner (a constant), and . . .

+ To give or get information; and/or . . .

+ To vent: express current feelings and thoughts, *and be respectfully understood and accepted* by an empathic partner; and/or. . . .

+ To cause action, change, or impact (feel potent, vs. powerless); and/or . . .

+ To cause excitement (prevent or end boredom and/or emptiness); and/or . . .

+ To avoid or reduce some other discomfort, like solitary or social silences.

Also adopt the beliefs that . . .

_ *Effective* communication requires that each partner truly believes "Your current needs and mine are equally important to me now" *That* requires that your true Self is leading your inner families. And believe that . . .

_ Communication skills are *learnable*: no Ph.D. required; and that . . .

_ Consciously investing time and effort in this project *will* harvest priceless personal and relationship benefits for yourselves and your kids, for many years to come. Adopt "the (open, curious) mind of a student," and . . .

_ Accept that *you partners will each have to change* some unconscious and/or beloved habits (e.g. interrupting others, or composing your response while they're talking), to reap this project's full long-term rewards. And help each other . . .

_ Accept that this skill-building project is an ongoing process that overarches your courtship and complex re/marriage evaluation. Based on Project 1, learning to use these seven skills will help you and your partner master the five other co-parent courtship projects in satisfying ways you can't predict.

Step 3) Begin to **notice the conversations or arguments that occur** *within* **you.** Experiment with identifying your different inner "voices," (thought streams), and try using these seven skills with their "owners" (subselves). When you do, watch what happens to your feelings and body over time. Notice that relationship "problems" (need conflicts) often have three concurrent parts: conflicts _ within me, _ within you, and _ between us (i.e. our dominant subselves).

Step 4) Help each other evolve and use Bills of Personal Rights. These are affirmations of your rights as a valuable human with unique talents, perceptions, and limits. Your core belief in such rights for you and every other person *may* sharply increase your success at *assertion* and problem solving. This won't work if shame-based subselves control your inner family. See the book "*Satisfactions*" or the Web article at ..02/rights.htm.

Step 5) Gain perspective: read and discuss each of the recommended Project-2 books on p. 539. Look for well regarded communication-skill classes in your community that might speed you along. They probably won't include all seven skills or mention recovery from false-self wounds as a prerequisite. They can still grow your awareness and knowledge!

Step 6) As individuals and partners, **clarify and refine your definition of** *effective* (vs. *open and honest* or *good*) *communication.* Evolve a meaningful way to measure whether inner and mutual exchanges *work well enough*. Use your learnings from the book *Satisfactions* and the definition above for reference and inspiration. A definition will work better for you if it's *yours*. While you're doing these . . .

Step 7) Learn from live communications around you, including interactive media like TV and Web chat rooms. Get *curious*, and . . .

+ Build the habit of noting non-judgmentally those relationships and situations where you communicate effectively, and *why*. Useful questions to ask are "Did each person _ get their main communication needs met well enough here _ in a way they each felt good about?" Do the same with people and situations where communication seemed *in*effective. Use your *awareness* skill to see *why,* and to start defining skill-changes you'd like to experiment with. This is about discovery, not blame.

+ Ask other people their ideas about effective communication, and watch others to see what "works" and what doesn't.

+ Identify **communication hero/ines** you'd like to emulate, and seek mentors to coach and encourage you. Do you know any *really* effective communicators?

+ Ask other people for feedback as to how they experience you communicating. Ask for and *listen* to constructive suggestions (e.g. "Your loudness and hand-waving tend to distract me at times.")

+ Consider keeping a Project-2 notebook or journal to capture things you want to remember and/or do about communicating, along the way. This becomes a great tool for affirming and celebrating your growing skills and results over time!

Step 8) Try out the powerful technique of *mapping* ineffective **communication sequences and patterns.** This assessment tool uses the first four skills to help you identify communication blocks together. All seven skills then empower you to resolve them. See the book *Satisfactions* or ..02/evc-maps.htm.

Step 9) Practice the seven skills often. You partners do this as fellow students and teammates in a way that fits your personalities and lifestyles. Practice the seven skills **in order:** they build on each other. *Awareness* skill gives you dozens of things to notice about typical communication exchanges. Metatalk skill gives you the vocabulary to discuss them and their outcomes with your communication partners. Consider practicing one new skill a month together for seven months and notice what changes in your lives. As teammates, become *aware* of how your stepfamily members and supporters react to these common communication blocks: ..02/evc-blox.htm.

Step 10) Help each other to **become aware of your "aware-ness bubbles"** _ in general and _ in conflicts. Including each other in these bubbles indicates both your Selves are in charge, and they value each others' feelings, needs, and opinions equally: i.e. you share genuine "=/=" attitudes. These are core requisites for effective communication. See ..02/a-bubble.htm.

Step 11) Use your learnings to answer the questions at the start of this chapter honestly. Use your answers to help answer the six re/marriage-evaluation questions in Project 7. How effective each of you partners are at _ building mutual-respect (=/=) attitudes, _ identifying your true needs, and re-solving _ inner and _ interpersonal conflicts, will powerfully shape your personal recoveries and re/marital and co-parenting relationships.

<u>If You Do Re/marry . . .</u>

. . . continue this and the 10 other ongoing projects in Chap-ter 8. Suggestions:

Step 12) Accept that this skill-building is continuous. Life will steadily present you all with new social situations, types of communication partners, and conflicts, to adapt your skills to.

Step 13) Watch for chances to practice and build fluency in the skills. As partners, use your definition of effective com-munication to grow the habit of noting the *outcomes* of impor-tant communication events. Enjoy your growing effectiveness! Affirm and celebrate what gets your and your partners' needs met, and patiently experiment at improving what doesn't. Do this together and with key others in your lives.

Step 14) Make this a co-parenting team project. If you haven't already, respectfully invite your kids' other co-parents and key relatives to learn and practice the skills with you. Doing this is a win-win-win decision: *Everyone* gets more of their true needs met more often! This becomes part of Project 10.

Step 15) Practice the fine art of **giving respectful, clear feedback** to others about *their* communication strengths and "opportunities to grow." Experiment with composing and delivering "dodge-proof" compliments (assertions), and enjoy what happens! See ..02/evc-feedback.htm.

Step 16) Model these seven skills for the kids in your lives, and coach them to learn and use the skills along the way. Whether you re/marry or not, the long-term value of you co-parents' doing this is beyond measure!

Step 17) Add and practice any other steps you feel would help you and your co-parenting partners and kids be more effective communicators over time.

If this feels like a lot to tackle, it *is*! So is graduating from high school, trade school, or college, yet you've probably done one or more. I suspect you've learned to break big projects like these into small steps, and work on them patiently one or a few at a time toward long-term payoffs. Your Self knows how to encourage patience . . .

Reality check: one at a time, think about the most important past and present family, social, and work relationships in your life. Use what you've learned here to compare the communication effectiveness in satisfying relationships, vs. any that haven't "worked well" for you, like divorces. What do you notice?

Among the web of common conflicts you'll encounter if you re/marry, one deserves special mention here:

About Stepfamily *Loyalty* Conflicts

How do you define *loyalty*? For me, it's "steady genuine guilt-free devotion to a person, relationship, group, or idea despite challenges." Do you agree that bonding, loyalty, and commitment promote each other?

Conflicts or problems are unclear and/or opposing needs. One of the many kinds of normal problems you will surely encounter if you re/marry is called a *loyalty conflict*. The basic clash is this: when a stepparent and stepchild or stepsiblings disagree, who does the bioparent (seem to) side with? Any choice upsets someone, including "not siding with anyone." These occur in divorced families, too.

In my experience, co-parents' (1) not knowing or discounting this stressor, and (2) lacking a unified strategy for resolving it together, are probably the most widespread *surface* reasons for stepfamily unhappiness and re/divorce. **Stepkids and some ex mates will test relentlessly** to learn who the bioparent will side with after choosing a new partner. The real causes of these conflicts are [false-self insecurity + communication-skill and stepfamily unawareness + post-divorce guilt + (often) blocked grief]. *All* of these can be mastered and resolved, with knowledge, commitment, and informed help!

Courtship idealism, neediness, tolerances, and politenesses usually camouflage *major* loyalty and other values conflicts that erupt during or soon after re/wedding. You lovebirds learning what these disputes are and how to resolve *before* any nuptials greatly increases your odds of making three right re/marriage decisions. _ Knowledge, _ recovery from any inner wounds, and _ these seven mental/verbal skills can empower you two to spot and resolve loyalty conflicts now and in the future. **Here's an overview:**

Most stepfamilies start with _ one or two (divorced) bioparents strongly bonded to one or more kids, and _ a new adult with or without kids and an ex mate. The initial loyalty (bonding) "map" is (me and my minor or grown child/ren) and (you and yours, if any). When conflicts occur between these two groups, many bioparents will instinctively rank the needs of their kids higher than the needs of their new partner or stepkids. They may be honest about that, rationalize and justify it, deny it, or do several of these if a false self governs them. Some can become paralyzed because *any* choice seems lose-lose.

This inherently sets up a c/overt stepparent conflict: **"Who comes first with you (the bioparent), me or your kids?"** This is specially likely with adults and kids ruled by fearful, shame-based false-selves. A major stepfamily development task is for co-parents to consciously change this "us vs. you" polarity to a genuine, shared "us partners and our prior kids" viewpoint. Many minor and grown kids will resists this shift c/overtly, un- til they have _ grieved well, _ stabilized their *inner* family, and _ feel they're really *safe* in this weird new multi-home stepfamily. Other kids' false selves will pretend to encourage the polarity shift from fear of rejection (abandonment) and conflict.

Many courting co-parents say "I understand that your kids often come first with you, and that's OK with me." If their dat- ing partner puts their kids' needs first "too often," more needy (wounded, shame-based) suitors feel resentful right away. A root of this is the stepparents' (subselves') instinctive needs to feel valued, respected, and *included as* (at least) *an equal*, by their new love partner. See Project 3.

Common Scenarios

Depending on many factors, one of several loyalty-con- flict situations starts to develop before or after re/wedding. See if you recognize any of these yet . . .

1) As insecure minor or adult **kids** become aware their bioparent's dating is turning serious, they **start to test their Mom or Dad's priorities** by *forcing* minor or major conflicts. Young kids do this blatantly; e.g. insisting they sit in the front passenger seat when their bioparent drives, or forcibly sitting between their parent and potential stepparent on a couch or in a movie.

Teens have more creative or subtle ways of forcing their parent/s to demonstrate "Who comes first with you now: me or this new person (and their child/ren)?" Kids do this **from an instinctive need for security** ("Are you going to abandon me?"), not malice. Some do this as loyal agents for their other bioparent, and/or to preserve their dream that their parents and biofamily will reunite somehow. False selves, inner wounds, and blocked grief can amplify this testing reflex, which hin-

ders accepting the nicest "new people." You'll learn more about
this in Projects 5 and 6.

2) One or both suitors _ deny there are loyalty conflicts
despite glaring evidence, **or** they _ **start blaming** each other
or themselves for them. I believe both of these are clear signs
of _ significant psychological wounds and _ stepfamily and
false-self unawareness *in both partners.* This protective denial
raises kids and ex mates' anxieties, and may increase their "acting out."

**3) One partner feels conflicted, and may or may not ex-
press their feelings**. The other partner _ rationalizes and defends, _ minimizes, or _ denies the conflict and/or who's causing it. _ Neither partner knows what loyalty conflicts or related
persecutor–victim–rescuer (PVR) relationship "triangles" are
or _ what to do about them. This was the situation for Sarah
and Jack Tilmon, amplified by Jack's need to deny they were a
stepfamily.

More common loyalty-conflict situations:

4) Both courting partners acknowledge minor to significant **loyalty conflicts, and argue** fruitlessly about _ who's at
fault and _ who must change. The conflicts get worse, and _
one or both may fantasize that "living together will work these
out, somehow." That false-self illusion rarely comes true, unless both partners commit to versions of these 12 projects (p.
122).

5) A courting or re/wedded bioparent is torn (inner conflict) between seeing their adult relationship or a needy child as
primary. Wounded, stepfamily-unaware ex mates and/or influential relatives, friends, or professionals say, "Your kids *must*
come first." **The stepparent feels confused**, guilty, anxious,
hurt, and resentful. No one knows what to do, and the conflicts
ferment. Kids may take advantage of this.

6) A courting bioparent accepts that putting their new adult
relationship first often enough protects them and their dependent kids and/or grandkids *long term* from (another) divorce
trauma. S/He starts to act on this, **and** _ kids' and/or _ other
family adults' **c/overt resentments rise**. The bioparent may

waver or remain firm and clear if their Self leads their inner family. Related conflicts may bloom, like ex mates suing for custody or fighting over child support or visitations, and kids "acting out" and/or threatening to live with their other bioparent.

I believe this was the case for biomom Karen Cohen and her second husband Rick (Chapter 7). She seemed genuinely clear that her re/marriage usually came first, for all four kids' long-term sakes.

7) Courting co-parents and supporters **may** _ acknowledge, **discuss, and research loyalty conflicts, or** _ **try to ignore them.** If they go to a professional counselor for help, s/he usually lacks stepfamily training and offers well-meant but ineffective or harmful (biofamily-based) advice. **Or . . .**

8) Some variation of these occurs, where the bioparent feels significantly torn between the needs of their new love and their kids. A jealous or insecure (wounded) ex mate can c/overtly pressure a courting or re/married parent to "side with" them in child-related matters, vs. the stepparent. The extreme version of this is becoming labeled "Parent Alienation Syndrome (PAS)." (..Rx/ex/split.htm.)

9) Significant loyalty conflicts normally cause stressful PVR *relationship triangles.* If unseen, ignored, or minimized these emotionally-complex relationship dynamics can stress stepfamily relationships before and after re/wedding. These role-triangles can form over many other topics like money, sex, power, status, roles, home chores, assets, pets, values, and health. Major PVR triangles are *always* symptoms of (false-self dominance + unawareness + ineffective communications) and other issues. Do you partners have a viable strategy for resolving them yet? See ..09/triangles.htm.

Do you see anyone you know in these loyalty-conflict scenarios? Do you think these pertain to you all? Guarantee: some of them *will*!

Loyalty-conflict Options

To master this common stepfamily stressor, I recommend that you partners commit to _ helping each other do Project 1 and _ learning these seven Project-2 basics and skills. Also . . .

_ **Accept your stepfamily identity** and _ agree on your membership (Project 3). Then accept that _ you adults and kids *will* experience loyalty conflicts and relationship triangles if you re/marry or before, and _ when they happen, no one is *wrong* or *bad*! Also accept that _ if you ignore or pooh-pooh loyalty conflicts and triangles, they can accumulate to wreck your integrities, your relationship, and your stepfamily dream. Biofamilies have versions of these conflicts, but they're usually simpler: they involve *our* kids, not *your* child or ex mate. Next . . .

Reality-check the premise above with veteran stepfamily co-parents. Ask them if they've had "Who comes first?" conflicts, how they feel to each person, how the co-parents handle them, and what results they get. If a false self controls them, they'll probably give you distorted answers ("Hey, don't worry about it!").

Work at these seven courtship projects honestly and patiently. If you're already remarried, work at projects 1-6, and 8-12. _ Read and discuss these articles at http://sfhelp.org/ for perspective and options: ..09/lc-intro.htm, ..09/triangles.htm, and ..Rx/mates/loyalty.htm.

You and your partner each **fill out the Priorities checklist** on p. 447 separately. Then compare your results honestly as co-learners. *If you're a bioparent and can't honestly say, "I want to put my kids first long term, by putting them second to our re/marriage and protecting us all from re/divorce," settle for friendship.*

If you're a (prospective) stepparent, be alert for _ feeling like you *should* sacrifice your relationship needs for your stepkids without complaint, or _ your partner expecting you to "because you're an adult," or _ feeling great guilt at resenting your feeling "second place." All three are signs of false-self control, ignoring step-realities, and unrealistic expectations. These can each be resolved, over time.

If you re/marry, spotting and resolving loyalty conflicts and persecutor-victim-rescuer triangles will be part of Project 9, merging your three or more extended biofamilies. I mention them here to alert you and to note an important focus for your seven mental/verbal skills. If your kids test you suitors early, you'll encounter loyalty conflicts and triangles well before you exchange vows (or don't). Even if they don't, an ex mate or relative may well do so.

Suggestions

Read the book *"Satisfactions"* together *slowly* for more detail, illustrations, exercises, worksheets, and perspective. Consider reading it out loud to each other, and discussing as you go. This summary chapter alone isn't enough to help you become effective problem-solvers. Gain more perspective by reading other Project-2 titles on p. 539.

Practice these seven skills with a partner. Having someone to try them with and exchange constructive feedback will speed your learning and make it more fun. If you don't have a learning partner now, you can still ask trusted others for constructive feedback on your communication behaviors. Once most people *experience* the options that these powerful skills provide, they become enthused and willing to safely risk trying them out. If your partner "isn't interested," I suspect their false self feels threatened in some way.

As these mental/verbal skills start to work for you, I encourage you to **avoid preaching** about or selling them to insecure or disinterested partners. Doing so implies "I'm 1-up. I know more than you, and you need to be 'fixed.'" This usually breeds resentment, defensiveness, and resistance, not co-operation. *Modeling* **these skills**, and describing their effects on your life informationally, may intrigue and motivate others, over time.

Common early reactions to these seven alien skills are that

_ they seem "phony" or "gimmicky," and that _ people trying them out are "pulling something" on their partners. **These skills can be used to manipulate,** rather than fill mutual needs. Manipulation sends a "1-up" R(espect)-message, and inexorably erodes trust and respect. If your steady goals are "*I want to* hear *you with my heart, and I want* both *of us to get more of what we need here,"* these seven skills <u>will</u> enhance your serenity and all inner and social relationships.

Tape or video recorders can help you learn these skills, and become aware of your present communication habits. They can also help you avoid the endless *"You said . . . No I didn't"* cycles that erupt when insecure and shame-based people get clear, specific feedback. Recorders can also scare and distract uneasy partners from communicating freely. If these tools are used to trap, beat, or shame, then your relationships and self-esteem will suffer.

You don't need all these seven skills all the time. Your goal is to grow automatic competence with them in important situations, specially in innerpersonal and social conflicts. You and your current communication partners decide at any moment what qualifies as "important."

Teaching these powerful mental/verbal skills to kids by modeling and instruction is one of the most priceless gifts you can bestow. If based on healthy self-esteem and genuine =/= (mutual respect) attitudes, these relationship skills will serve your kids a lifetime. Imagine them empowering generations to come . . .

Recall our larger purpose: learning to use these seven communications skills over time is the second of seven ways courting co-parents can help each other choose the right *people* to re/wed, for the right *reasons*, at the right *time* (Project 7). Progress on Projects 1 and 2 is essential to get value from the five courtship projects you're about to study.

Recap

Every waking hour, you and your loved ones communicate internally and socially to reduce current *needs*. Few kids or adults study the communication skills needed to do this well. Your communications are *effective* (vs. "good") when each person feels (1) they got their major true (vs. surface) needs met well enough, and (2) good enough about _ their communication process, and _ each participant.

Typical courting co-parents like you are controlled occasionally or chronically by myopic, reactive, protective false selves. They don't know what they don't know about their inner wounds or effective communications. This *unawareness* promotes suitors' making three wrong re/marital choices, years of domestic stress, and eventual re/divorce. This vital co-parent project aims to correct the second problem by guiding you suitors or mates to _ evaluate your problem-solving effectiveness, and _ learn seven communication skills to raise your effectiveness together. While the best time to begin this project is *before* deciding whether to re/marry, commitment to it brings benefits any time.

Compared to average intact biofamilies, typical stepfamilies have *many* more concurrent conflicts, among more people, over more topics. So co-parents' skill at effective problem-solving is specially crucial to building high-nurturance relationships in and between their linked homes. Does it make more sense now why well over half of typical U.S. re/marriages fail emotionally or legally?

The seven mental/verbal skills you can use to fill more of your mutual true needs well are . . .

Awareness: "What's going on now and over time _ inside me, _ inside you, _ between us, and _ around us?"

Clear thinking: using awareness to stay focused on identifying _ current needs and _ relationship dynamics, by _ intentionally using appropriate, unambiguous, emotionally-neutral terms. Use awareness and this skill in important situations to amplify the value of all five other communication skills.

Digging down below surface "problems" (need conflicts) to _ identify the true needs underneath them (p. 49), and _ get clear on who is responsible for filling these needs.

Metatalk: _ learn up to 30 key communication concepts

and related terms (..02/metatalk.htm), and _ talk clearly and co-operatively with your partner/s about how you're communicating now and over time. This skill enables you both to use the other six skills to resolve key communication problems.

Empathic **listening**: nonjudgmentally "listening with your heart" to learn "what's it like to be *you* right now?" Listening like this is not necessarily agreeing!

Respectful assertion, vs. aggression or submission: _ identifying and _ telling a partner specifically what you need, in a way s/he can hear you; _ expecting resistances without judgment; _ handling them calmly with =/= (mutually respectful) empathic listening; and _ consciously aiming for either clear agreement, refusal, or new information. And . . .

Win-win problem solving (conflict reduction): use all six other skills *respectfully* to _ get your and your partner/s' true current needs _ identified and _ met well enough; and to _ feel good enough about how you did it together. These two criteria determine the *effectiveness* of any communication exchange.

If you and your partner can't describe these seven skills in some detail, you're probably not using them. That means _ you're probably used to communicating at well below 50% of your potential effectiveness, _ you don't really know what's possible, and _ in conflicts, you're doing something other than win-win problem solving, like arguing, avoiding, explaining, defending, fighting, or fleeing. These seldom *really* satisfy true current needs!

These seven skills can help you partners master common stepfamily flashpoints over . . .

+ _ loyalty conflicts and _ persecutor-victim-rescuer (PVR) relationship triangles.

+ Stepfamily _ identity ("We are *not* a stepfamily!") and _ membership ("Your ex wife is *not* part of our family!") conflicts.

+ Child _ discipline, _ custody, _ visitations, _ financial support, _ conception, education, _ health, and _ adoption.

+ Individual and biofamily _ values and _ preferences: "We're proud Irish-Catholic Democrats. Your people are Germanic Lutheran Republicans. Your ex mate's people are a mix of liberal Californian, Unitarian and agnostic socialists and non-voters.

+ _ Roles and related _ rules: "You have no say in my son's dental care!"

+ Money and assets: "I'm not responsible for your daughter's health insurance or college; Get your ex off our dental insurance!"

+ Names and role-titles: "I don't think my son should call you (stepfather) 'Dad.'"

+ Family _ holidays, _ rituals, and _ traditions: "We always open presents on December 24th, so you and your kids should (want to) do that too."

+ Household _ choice, _ furnishing, _ decorating, _ maintenance, and _ chores: "I think you're *way* too easy on your kids about helping out here." And . . .

+ Communication styles: e.g. "I don't agree that we have to confront all major family problems before we go to sleep!"

There are other stepfamily conflict areas and many *concurrent* disputes within each of these topics. Many of these will probably feel alien to you all. With patience, humor, and flexibility, the seven skills will help resolve all of them *if* your Selves are leading!

Four gifts you can bequeath your minor kids are: _ a healthily respect for themselves and their current needs, feelings, and opinions; _ an equal (=/=)respect for every other person's worth, dignity, and needs; _ understanding these seven related skills and true needs; and _ knowing clearly how and when to use the skills to get *everyone's* current real needs met well enough.

Reading about these seven skills will do little for you. *Trying* them patiently, with cautious optimism, will lower stress; create new options; and raise personal and household satisfaction, trust, and bonding over time. These skills work equally well with adults, kids, and among the different voices (subselves) *within* you.

It's taken years to develop your present thinking, talking, listening, and negotiating reflexes. It will take time for these new skills to improve them. As you experiment patiently, let yourself feel alien, awkward, and even phony for a time, without guilt! You couldn't play a concert instrument skillfully the first time you try it. As with any acquired skill, these seven take practice, feedback, and patience before they become familiar and fully effective. As you work on this second project together, use guidelines like these along the way:

"Progress, not perfection!"
"The road to success is always under construction."
"There are no mistakes, only lessons."

This chapter overviews the problem (co-parent unawareness and undeveloped communication skills), **and the solution**: study and apply seven mental/verbal communication skills together, and use your learnings to help make three *right* re/ marriage decisions in Project 7. The chapter proposes clear Project-2 goals, explicit steps to reach them, and a buffet of experience-based suggestions and resources.

Caution: do *not* expect that learning and applying these skills will help you fill more needs if you minimize or ignore Project 1. Knowing these seven skills is of limited use if you and/or your partner are often controlled by a false self that _ focuses only on your immediate comfort and gratification and _ lacks a genuine =/= attitude!

 # Reality check: Flip back to the start of this chapter and review your initial estimates of your and your partner's communication effectiveness. Has anything changed? Option: review this set of common communication blocks, and see which you'd like to reduce in your key relationships: ..02/evc-blox.htm.

If you could get your daily needs met twice as often as you do now, how would that affect your self-esteem, relationships, productivity, health, and satisfaction? Patiently developing these seven skills makes this a real possibility for you and those you care about! It can also help you partners evaluate if and when you should re/marry or not. Notice your self-talk (inner voices) now . . .

Do you need to stretch and refresh? When you're ready for more, your third courtship project will help you avoid three common problems:

+ Misunderstanding what a stepfamily is and *feels* like;
+ You partners denying your stepfamily identity, and assuming you'll all operate like a biofamily ("Naw, we're just a *family!*"); and . . .
+ One or both of you denying that ex mates and their relatives are and will be full members of your prospective stepfamily for decades. Their opinions, needs, finances, genes, ancestry (ethnicity), and priorities will affect your re/marriage and household serenity well after the youngest child leaves home.

Do you still have "the mind of a student"? As you continue, recall your options to hilight and make notes on these pages as you read, and to keep a journal or log of your questions, awarenesses, and other reactions . . .

Project 3: Accept Your Stepfamily Identity

Resolve *Identity* and *Inclusion* Conflicts

In our consultations, Dr. Jack Tilmon (Chapter 7) fiercely declared "We are *not* a stepfamily. We're just a normal American (bio)family, *period*! I am Patty's second father, not her step-father!" He wouldn't discuss why he felt so strongly about this, or the possibility that this rigid (distorted) belief was contributing to the escalating tensions in his home and remarriage.

Like Jack, many courting and re/married men and women feel stepfamilies are *second best*, *abnormal*, and *unnatural*. Do *you* honestly feel people in stepfamilies can be as successful, healthy, and happy as members of a "regular" (intact biological) family? Are stepkids and stepparents just as *good* as "normal" (biofamily) kids and parents? Do stepmothers tend to be *wicked*? Do you see people who divorce as *losers*? Can you honestly say you'd be proud to be a member of a stepfamily or *blended* family?

Most people are unaware and biased about this ancient type of family. I suspect this is partly because of slanted parental and media portrayals (starting with fairy tales), and the Christian Bible's proclamation that God decrees that divorce is a sin. What's your opinion?

Co-parents' denying or minimizing their (your) stepfamily identity promotes ignoring _ the realities in Chapter 6, _ the five hazards in Chapter 4, and _ the high need for these seven projects. These promote _ unrealistic relationship expectations among everyone, stepfamily-wide _ role confusion, and _ major inner and interpersonal conflicts. Combined, these all promote eventual re/divorce. Do you believe this applies to *you* all?

Sarah Tilmon *did* accept that they were a stepfamily, and had given up trying to get Jack's agreement. His ex wife Karen Cohen had given up too. Jack's stepfamily-identity-denial amplified confusions in his 13-year-old stepdaughter Patty, and probably some in his two biokids also. I see Jack's rigid denials as classic symptoms of false-self dominance and reality distortion.

Your third co-parent project starts with two steps: _ accept your stepfamily identity, and learn what it means. Then _ you partners work to agree on who *belongs* to your (potential) stepfamily. If you hedge or ignore the first of these, you probably can't do the second. That guarantees major future conflicts and stress.

This chapter proposes . . .

+ Five goals for this project;
+ A definition of *stepfamily identity*, and why this should matter to you co-parents and kin;
+ What your stepfamily identity probably *means*;
+ Why some co-parents reject this identity;
+ Signs of step-identity acceptance; and . . .
+ How to resolve typical step-identity and membership (inclusion) conflicts.

Project 3 Goals

To make wise re/marital choices, courting co-parents like you need to help each other to:

1) **Fully accept** that . . .
   _ We are and will be a normal multi-home *step*family, not "just a (bio)family." So . . .

_ Without doing these seven courtship projects honestly, we're at high risk of making up to three wrong re/marital choices, because the five hazards in Chapter 4 apply to *us*. And we accept that . . .

_ Most of the realities in Chapter 6 and the series of Web articles at http://sfhelp.org/04/myths.htm apply to us all; and . . .

_ Each of our kids' other co-parents are full members of our (potential) stepfamily, and _ will remain so well after the youngest existing child leaves home.

Then you partners . . .

2) Learn if your _ kids' other co-parents and _ key relatives agree that you all are considering (or in) a *step*family. If they disagree or minimize this identity and what it means, *yellow light*!

Three more Project-3 goals are . . .

3) Firmly _ agree or _ agree to *disagree* on "Who is included in our stepfamily?" Whose needs, feelings, and opinions will we honor, and _ how will we mates rank these when we all conflict?

4) Use your step-identity and membership agreements to do Project 4: convert stepfamily myths into realistic role and relationship expectations. Finally . . .

5) Educate your key relatives and in-laws and minor and grown kids on your stepfamily identity and what it means to you all, and _ negotiate what titles and names you're going to call each other. _ Use your Project-2 mental/verbal skills together to resolve any major conflicts over these.

Though these Project-3 goals are best mastered *before* re/ wedding, your co-parents can do them any time. Avoiding these five targets raises the odds that despite your love and life experience, you lovebirds are considering stepfamily re/marriage without *really* knowing what you're committing to! Restated: if you don't see personal value in this two-part task, you'll have little reason to do any of the 11 other projects. That *steeply* raises your and your kids' risk that the five hazards in Chapter

4 will defeat any re/wedding vows you make. Note your self-talk now . . .

Why Is "Stepfamily *Identity*" Important?

Identity is a set of traits and a title or label which sets one thing apart from other things. For example, in the group called *animals*, a *poodle* is not a *giraffe*. Our ancestors invented these word-symbols to distinguish between (the identity of) these two four-legged mammals. The label *poodle* brings to mind a set of images, memories, expectations ("poodles don't sing or climb trees"), stereotypes ("poodles are hyper"), feelings and judgments ("I like beagles better"), and associations ("I associate poodles with rich snobs, diamond collars, and France.") If a poodle lives among giraffes and insists they *ought to act like poodles*, everyone's in trouble, including girafflings and poodlettes.

The word *family* stands for many things. Most people automatically connect this word with their birthfamily, or family of origin. In this series of books, these are called *bio(logical)families*. Typical stepfamilies and biofamilies *are* similar in a number of ways (p. 424) and ..03/similar.htm). At the same time, average multi-home stepfamilies *differ structurally and dynamically from typical intact biofamilies in over 70 ways* (p. 425 and ..03/compare.htm)!

If well-meaning re/married co-parents like Jack Tilmon label themselves as "a normal (bio)family," they're prone to trivialize or ignore many of these structural and dynamic differences. Then they risk having unrealistic relationship and family-role expectations, which cause mounting frustrations, conflicts, and disappointments. These accumulate and promote emotional and legal re/divorce—specially if co-parents can't problem-solve effectively. These also promote unintended low stepfamily nurturance and psychologically wounding dependent kids.

Like Jack Tilmon did, courting co-parents who deny or pooh-pooh their *step*family identity, and/or minimize what their identity *means*, won't admit this somber risk. They'll have little motivation to work at the 12 projects in Chapter 8. This is like blithely taking your whole nuclear family sailing down an unfamiliar river without checking maps to see if there are major rapids, whirlpools, and waterfalls ahead, because "a river is just a river." Well, yes *and no*.

Karen and Rick Cohen *had* accepted their identity as a multi-home stepfamily. What did that prepare them for?

What It Means To Be In a *Step*family

Review your mental definition of a *stepfamily*. If you're fuzzy, read the definition on p. 531. An overarching meaning of belonging to a stepfamily is: *many of the norms you've been trained to believe about (bio)families do not apply*. If you're considering forming a stepfamily or are already in one, it means that most or all of the *realities* in Chapter 6 will apply to you all. In particular, your **"step-hood" means that . . .**

1) Whether alive, dead, or uninvolved, *both* bioparents of each stepchild are full emotional, genetic, and legal members of your stepfamily. They will continue to be well beyond your youngest child's moving out. Unless your kids' other parents are dead, your nuclear stepfamily has three or more co-parents, living in two or more homes (p. 99). Your co-parents' homes will be linked tightly for *decades* by needs, genes and ancestral scripts, finances, emotional bonds, history and memories, holiday rituals, and legal contracts and laws.

2) Achieving solid adult agreements on co-parenting and co-grandparenting goals and strategies is often *much* harder in a stepfamily than in an intact biofamily.

3) Being in a stepfamily also means that reactive, narrow-focused false selves probably govern one or all of your co-parents and their parents. Most or all of you are probably in protective denial of _ this and the related psychological wounds, _ what caused them (low childhood nurturance), and _ how these wounds stress and limit you each every day. Until you break your denials of these and start to heal (Project 1), you co-parents are at high risk of _ unintentionally passing your false-self hindrances on to your minor kids like your unaware ancestors did.

4) For years or perhaps forever, the emotional bonds, caring and loyalties, and incest taboo between your stepparent/s and your stepchild/ren will be significantly weaker than those between typical bioparents and biokids. The bonding and loyalty among members of your extended (multi-generational) stepfamily will probably be significantly weaker, too. There are exceptions.

And your choosing to be in a normal *step*family means that . . .

5) Each of your minor kids probably has over 30 overlapping family adjustments to make that peers in typical intact biofamilies don't have. These concurrent needs (p. 454) are on top of your kids' normal developmental needs, and are probably hindering their progress with them. Even young-adult kids can't clearly describe their adjustment or developmental tasks, so they can't request help with them. Without education, most co-parenting partners, kin, and human-service professionals can't name most of these 30+ adjustment needs either. Can *you*?

6) You co-parenting partners each have many of the same adjustment tasks at the same time your kids do. Until you co-parents _ become aware of these tasks and _ accurately assess your kids' status with each of them (Project 6), your unawareness will promote unmet needs ("stress") in your kids; "acting-out" behaviors; family, school, and social difficulties; emotional wounding; and related co-parental and re/marital values conflicts, anxiety, frustration, and stress—for many years.

Being in a stepfamily also means . . .

7) Daily life will feel far more confusing and alien than living in the biofamilies you're used to. This is because of the combined effect of the 70+ structural and dynamic differences (p. 425), and the ~60 common misconceptions that go with them (..04/myths.htm). Your extended stepfamily can have up to 30 roles (e.g. step-uncle, half-brother, non-custodial biofather . . .), vs. 15 roles in traditional multi-generational biofamilies. Your stepfamily identity also means . . .

8) It will probably take your extended-stepfamily members four or more years after your re/marriage to merge, evolve, and stabilize these roles, related rules, customs, priorities, goals, and relationship expectations. Each re/marriage, re/divorce, birth, death, and major geographic move among your many three-generational members will cause ripples of change (losses) throughout your whole extended-stepfamily system, requiring another slow grieving and re-stabilizing process.

9) If you are or may be a stepparent like Jack and Sarah Tilmon, your child-raising goals are probably the same as a typical bioparent's. However, your personal, family, and social environments will differ from traditional bioparents' in up to 40 specific ways (..10/co-p-dfrnces.htm). Without stepfamily education, awareness, and *informed* support, these combined environmental differences will foster self-doubt, confusion, uncertainty, resentments, defensiveness, and frustration in and between your kids' homes.

Yet another *step*family reality is that . . .

10) If you're a bioparent and decide to re/marry, you'll often feel caught in the middle of a lose-lose *loyalty conflict* (p. 186). You'll be forced to choose repeatedly between pleasing _ your new mate, _ yourself, and _ one or more of your minor or grown biokids. Your kids will relentlessly test to see whom you choose. Choosing not to choose is not an option. You'll also be asked to choose whom you support among clashing bio-relatives, ex in-laws, and new step-kin.

If you _ don't want to choose your mate and relationship often enough to satisfy her or him, and _ can't see that choice as a major way of supporting your own kids by sparing them from (another?) traumatic family breakup, you'll probably re/divorce, psychologically or legally. This is specially true if you and/or your mate are governed by a false self, and haven't built effective communication skills. See the Priorities worksheet on p. 447.

11) Being in a stepfamily also means that if you and your caregiving partners look for *informed* co-parenting classes and groups, and re/marriage and stepfamily programs, media materials, and pre-and post-re/marriage counseling, you'll find little or none. It also means that . . .

12) You, your co-parenting partners, and your dependent kids will experience a social aura of *second best, odd,* and *weird,* compared to "normal" intact (bio)families. You'll probably never meet people in a stepfamily structured like yours, which promotes feeling *alone.* Unless you mates join (or form) a mutual-help group for stepfamily co-parents (Project 11), you'll learn to accept that few non-step people can really empathize with you about your co-parenting and re/marital challenges, confusions, satisfactions, and triumphs. One corollary is that if you vent to others about your ongoing stepfamily conflicts or uncertainties, your listeners (including relatives, friends, and many professionals) may offer sympathy, and well-meant but ineffective or toxic advice based on *biofamily* norms.

And having a *step*family identity also means that . . .

13) If you mates long for everyone in your home/s to share the closeness, loyalty, love, security, and pride that members of an ideal intact biofamily feel, you'll probably be disappointed and frustrated. Stepfamily relationships and homes rarely feel like biofamily relationships and households, even years after re/marriage. Adopting your stepkids and/or having an "ours" baby usually does *not* change this, though they *may* significantly increase inter-member bonding and solidarity. Co-parents from low-nurturance childhoods risk unrealistically expecting their new stepfamily to provide the nurturance they didn't get.

The overarching reality of your choosing to re/marry into a stepfamily is: you'll probably re/divorce within ~10 years, because of these combined factors and the five hazards in Chapter 4. **You partners can avoid this** by _ accepting your stepfamily identity and what that means, and _ doing all 6 other pre-re/marriage projects in this book. If you partners do re/ wed, and get reasonable cooperation from your other co-parents and relatives, your stepfamily can provide much of the care, securities, companionship, support, warmth, satisfaction, fun, and sometimes, the love that you all long for. Healthy, stabilized multi-home stepfamilies can offer unique strengths and advantages to adult and child members that typical biofamilies can't provide. Can you name them?

"Accepting your stepfamily identity" means solidly believing that these 13 factors really apply to you, your other co-parents, and your kids and kin. How many of the above *meanings* do you believe apply to you all now? If this seems like a lot of detail and work, it *is*.

So is re/divorce in middle age.

Recap: belonging to an average *step*family means that compared to an intact nuclear biofamily, you mates will have _ three or more complex extended families to merge (Project 9); _ more linked homes to harmonize; _ more people and roles to consider; _ more concurrent conflicts and stresses among them to resolve; _ more uncertainties to resolve, and _ more simultaneous adjustment projects for co-parents and stepkids to master, with _ less social guidance, precedents, and support. Together, these mean _ you're *at higher risk of re/divorce* than being in a typical intact biofamily. Are you getting tired of reading that?

Your stepfamily identity also means that if your co-parents accept all this and work together co-operatively (Projects 6 and 10), you all *can* build an exceptionally satisfying high-nurturance stepfamily together (p. 48), and fill your true needs well enough.

A poodle will never be a giraffe. It has its own life rewards, pleasures, and value to the world just the same.

How do your governing subselves feel now? For most needy suitors who have (finally) found Mr. or Ms. *Really* Right, this is pretty discouraging stuff. You can probably appreciate . . .

Why Some Co-parents Reject Their *Step*family Identity

Given the sobering realities above, why would anyone want to accept that they're in a complex, high-risk stepfamily? From the comments of hundreds of co-parents I've met since 1981, I propose that (wounded) people like Jack Tilmon resist fully accepting their stepfamily identity for some core reasons.

Two of the most powerful reasons are (denied) excessive *shame*, and personal **and** societal *unawareness*. In my experience, most separated, divorced, and/or re/married adults like the Tilmons and Cohens are governed by protective false selves. So our denied *excessive shame* wound already makes us feel badly about ourselves. We have longed our whole lives to feel and be clearly seen as *normal* and *OK*.

Though stepfamilies have been around since human prehistory, they're often dubbed *abnormal*. They have an aura of *failure* (prior divorces and "broken" homes). So admitting that "I'm re/married and in a stepfamily" can feel to shame-based adults like carrying a neon sign saying "I'm *not normal* and *not OK*."

Most stepfamily co-parents or kin don't identify themselves as such in public. Thus new co-parents' behaviors are covertly shaped by the *implied* social norm "If you're in a stepfamily, you don't say so." I've asked hundreds of typical stepfamily co-parents if they know other re/married co-parents. After reflecting, over 90% of them answer "No." This clashes with the reality that roughly one of every five U.S. families is a stepfamily. Many of us are unconsciously wearing social masks (false selves).

Unawareness of stepfamily norms and benefits blocks lay and professional people, including media pros, from accepting that _ stepfamilies are *normal*, and _ can nurture their members just as well as healthy intact biofamilies can. This ignorance flourishes partly because some people can't clearly define what a stepfamily *is*. For example, I've heard many well-educated co-parents say one or more of these:

+ "Well, we're not a stepfamily, because the kids are all grown and on their own."
+ "Her kids' father is dead, so we're not a stepfamily."
+ "We (re/married co-parents) have our own child now, so we're no longer a stepfamily."
+ "We don't see ourselves as a stepfamily, because it really upsets my Mother."
+ "His ex wife has nothing to do with their kids: no cards, no calls, and no contact. Therefore, we're not a real stepfamily."
+ "Her ex gave up his legal parenting rights, and I've legally adopted her kids. That means we're just a regular (bio)family!"

Each of these is wrong, and signals ignorance and/or diligent false selves at work.

Blocked grief in adults and kids **is a third common reason co-parents deny their stepfamily identity**. About 90% of U.S. stepfamilies form after the prior divorce of one or both new mates. Divorce causes *major* sets of tangible and invisible losses (broken bonds) for kids, co-parents, and kin. If a child or bioparent can't grieve and really release old biofamily and absent-parent family attachments, they often resist *really* accepting their new stepfamily identity, relationships, roles, and realities.

To accept these, they have to consciously confront *and* mourn their painful broken bonds. If even one member of a post-divorce biofamily is blocked in grieving, then personal, re/marital, and stepfamily stresses result. Adults from low-nurturance childhoods and their kids and kin often have trouble grieving well. These are among the reasons for Projects 1 and 5.

A special case of blocked grief and related step-identity rejection occurs with older wounded relatives. Older parents who can't fully accept and mourn that their child is divorced and remarried may openly or subtly resist accepting their step-grandparent, step-aunt, or step-uncle roles and identity. Their own shame, pain, guilts, and unawarenesses can fuel quiet or fierce insistence that "We're all just a *normal* (bio)family!" This is particularly likely when older parents' religious beliefs equate divorce to *shameful* "sin" and disobedience to God's commandments.

Usually some co-parents will accept their stepfamily identity superficially or fully, and other relatives or kids will be ambivalent or reject their "step-hood." Sarah Tilmon, Karen Cohen, and her second husband Rick accepted their stepfamily identity, and were working steadily to make the best of it together. Sarah's ex Ted McLean reportedly "didn't care" about being in a stepfamily. Jack Tilmon refused to accept that he and his wife Sarah were two of five co-parents trying to manage a three-home stepfamily (p. 99).

He rejected Sarah's ex husband Ted and Karen's husband Rick as co-parenting teammates in a common caregiving enterprise. Well-intentioned, Jack strove to treat his stepdaughter "no differently" than his biokids. He unrealistically expected her to respect and *obey* ("love") him like his biodaughter Annie. Jack's denials caused him to completely miss the fact that Patty had a cluster of special needs that typical biokids don't. His step-identity denial and the hidden wounds and ignorance underneath it promoted divisive loyalty conflicts among all five co-parents, and stressed all three older kids. Jack was _ wounded and controlled by a false self, _ unaware, and _ scared, *not* "a bad stepfather!"

Recap: many co-parents and kin resist *fully* accepting their identity as a stepfamily for several reasons. These include _ camouflaged shame and guilt, _ personal and social unawareness of what a stepfamily *is*, _ a longing to be socially and personally *normal*, and _ blocked grief.

Alternatively, stepfamily members may accept their role-titles ("Yeah, I'm a stepparent . . ."), but ignore or reject what their step-hood *means*. Both rejections steeply raise the odds that when conflicted or confused, re/married co-parents will unconsciously use inappropriate *bio*family norms and expectations. This often makes problems worse. Denials are reality distortions used by protective false selves to promote short-term safety. Are you denying any denials? How do you know?

Incidentally, **a clear sign of c/overt stepfamily identity-rejection and denial is** partners calling their enterprise a *blended* family, *co-family*, or *second family*. When I ask why co-parents prefer **non-step terms**, the common answer is something like "Oh, I just don't like the term *step*."

Some authors and publishers promote book sales by avoiding the unpleasant connotations of step-hood. Instead of *step-*, they write about *bi-nuclear, rem(arried), serial, bonus, co-, second,* and *combined* families. My bias is that using any title other than *step*, and/or avoidance of the role titles *stepmom, stepdad, stepson, stepdaughter, and stepsibling,* probably indicates moderate to major adult denial of stepfamily realities like those above and in Chapter 6. Condoning that enables false-self reality distortion, and promotes stepfamily ignorance and strife. Notice what your subselves think about this blunt opinion.

So the first step in this third co-parent project is you partners recognizing that *all* your members accepting your *step*family identity is vital. The next step is to assess other adults and kids in your extended stepfamily for _ identity confusion and/or _ identity barriers. The last step is to confront and dissolve these barriers respectfully.

Signs of Stepfamily-Identity Acceptance

How can you tell if people have really accepted that they belong to a multi-home stepfamily? Common symptoms include . . .

1) Co-parents' re/wedding ceremonies mention their status as a new stepfamily, and acknowledge the relationships of each adult to _ the other's minor and grown kids, and _ their kids' other co-parents.

2) In normal conversation, co-parents spontaneously use role-labels like . . .

+ "This is my stepson Allen."
+ "My daughter's stepsister Norma took a Latin-dance class."
+ "My children live with their biomom and their stepfather Rick;"
+ "We're a his, hers, and ours stepfamily;" and . . .
+ "My poor Mom is confused so far about how to be a step-grandma to Sharon and Keith."

Co-parents who accept their step-identity use these labels and phrases consistently and spontaneously, without apology, explanation, anxiety, or guilt. Similarly . . .

3) Co-parents socially acknowledge that they're in or considering a re/marriage, without undue anxiety, guilt, or shame. Partners talk about their prior-marriage families, relationships, and divorces or deaths realistically and pretty objectively, vs. defensively. Also . . .

4) Co-parents freely **acknowledge that their kids' other (bio and step) parents are** legitimate emotional, genetic, and legal **members** of their multi-home stepfamily, even if they're uninvolved, hostile, or dead.

5) On Mother's Day or Father's Day, primary-school stepkids can make gifts for their bioparent and their same-gender stepparent without significant anxiety, guilt, or confusion.

More symptoms of stepfamily-identity acceptance:

6) Family members may invent a "Stepmother's / Stepfather's / Stepfamily / Stepson's / Stepdaughter's Day, and/or exchange **"step" cards**.

7) If they seek **counseling**, co-parents make it a point to ask if the professional has training and experience in stepfamily dynamics, problems, and norms.

8) On school, medical, insurance, and tax **forms**, stepparents describe their relationship to dependent stepkids as *stepmother* or *stepfather*.

9) If they draw a family map (see below), co-parents and kids are genuinely comfortable including the two or three homes of all three or more co-parents, and everyone living in and related to them.

10) Courting or re/married adults who accept their prospective *step* identity **spontaneously seek books, TV programs, classes, and support groups** for stepfamily co-parents.

11) Such co-parents want to **meet and learn** from other (veteran) stepfamily co-parents and/or clinicians.

12) Co-parents and older relatives include key step-relatives in their **wills and estate plans.**

13) Identity-accepting co-parents can **describe, and genuinely accept, many of the realities** in Chapter 6, and the differences between stepfamilies and intact biofamilies summarized on p. 425.

14) These co-parents are genuinely motivated to **learn the many special adjustment tasks** they and most minor stepkids face (pp. 435 and 454), and are working together patiently to learn how to help each child with their unique set of these needs via versions of Projects 6 and 10.

15) Co-parents who accept their "step" identity grow an appreciation for, and **pride in, the unique benefits** found in high-nurturance stepfamilies. And . . .

16) After reading this book, co-parents are strongly motivated to adapt the seven courtship projects to fit their unique situation, and **commit to doing the projects** as partners, vs. adversaries.

Do these traits of identity-acceptance describe you and your co-parenting partners? If so, *congratulations*! If not (yet), here are some ideas about . . .

How to Resolve Stepfamily *Identity* Conflicts

There are two kinds of stepfamily-identity conflicts. The first is internal ("*I* don't believe or accept that we're a stepfamily," and/or "I'll agree to the label, but I sure don't accept what this book says that the label *means*!") The second identity conflict is interpersonal, like the Tilmons: "I (Sarah) believe we're a stepfamily, but you (Jack) don't." Admitting and resolving each kind of disagreement is vital to your making three wise re/marriage decisions.

Inner-family *Identity Conflicts*

My experience is that when one or more related co-parents deny, or are ambivalent or unclear about, their stepfamily identity and membership, the core reasons are _ unawareness (denials and ignorance), and _ false-self wounds: shame, fears, guilts, and reality distortions. These combine to promote a third possibility: _ blocked grief. Where true, the implacable reality is that the only way to really resolve this internal step-identity denial is through _ true (vs. pseudo) personal recovery via doing Project 1 over time, and _ Self-motivated education, like studying and applying this book.

If a co-parent, older stepchild, or important relative isn't ready to assess their inner wounds and start personal healing, I propose that trying to persuade them to accept their "step-hood" is futile and disrespectful. It's a personal choice whether planting the *seed* of why such acceptance is important is respectful and useful ("Jack, you may find benefits in the future to accepting that you all really are a three-home stepfamily"). What do you think?

If you're in a committed adult relationship and one or both of you have prior biokids, you are *in a stepfamily.* If your immediate reaction is "No I'm *not!*" or something like "I'm not sure about that", then meditate on or journal about, questions like these:

+ "If I did accept that we're all a *step*family, what, specifically, would that mean to me and/or people important to me?"
+ "If I publicly acknowledge that we are a stepfamily, who would get upset, and *why?*"
+ "To me, being in a 'stepfamily' means_____."
+ "The word 'stepfamily' makes me think of (or feel) _____."
+ "If I publicly said 'I'm in a stepfamily,' other people / my parent(s) / my child(ren) / my ex mate / my partner / my friend / would _____."

+ "If I don't like the terms *stepfamily*, *stepparent*, and/or *stepchild*, what is it that I find objectionable or uncomfortable about them—specifically? Where did I learn to feel this way? Are these my own reactions, or someone else's? Whose? Recall that titles like *stepmother*, *stepfather*, *stepbrother*, and *stepsister* describe family *roles*, not persons!

+ "If other people try to sell me on accepting that we're a stepfamily, I feel _____ because _____."

Discuss questions like these with your partner and a supportive, objective person. The ideal is a stepfamily-aware, veteran clinician without divorce, re/marriage, and stepfamily biases, whose main motive is to assist you in getting clearer on your own identity. See the Web article ..11/counsel.htm for suggestions on how to select such a consultant.

Another option is to invest time drawing a multi-generational, multi-family stepfamily map or *genogram* like the one on p. 96. Then consider "Does this diagram show what I call a biological family?" "If not, what *would* I call this group of people and relationships?" Settling for "I don't know" is probably protective false-self reality distortion (denial and avoidance).

If Partners Disagree on Their Stepfamily Identity . . .

If you accept your stepfamily identity but your primary partner doesn't, or is ambivalent or vague about it, what can you do? Here are several choices available to conflicted co-parents like Sarah Tilmon and Karen Cohen:

1) Get clear on what your partner's stance is about fully accepting stepfamily identity and what it means *before* re/wedding. If your partner needs to deny being "in step," your choice is whether to balance this pro-re/divorce factor against many others, and to re/marry anyway. Many co-parents controlled by a false self are too needy and intoxicated with romantic love to assess this rationally.

2) Check your attitude about your partner, whether you're courting or re/married. If you feel critical of them or their choice to deny your step-hood, your attitude ["I'm *right* (1-up), you're *wrong!*"] may be part of the problem. See if you can compassionately respect your partner's identity-denial as self-protective, rather then *bad, stupid, wrong, dumb, ignorant, stubborn,* or *silly.* Otherwise you'll leak these opinions, fostering resentment, hurt, anxiety, guilt, and resistance.

3) Beware sacrificing your integrity by not confronting or upsetting your partner, (i.e. don't *enable* them). Lacking personal recovery, Sarah Tilmon was a prisoner of her ruling subselves' shame, self-doubts, and fears of Jack's rejection and possible abandonment. By not confronting him firmly and respectfully about their stepfamily identity, she was enabling his reality distortion, promoting confusion in her daughter, and losing respect for herself. A high price to pay for the illusion of household and marital peace!

4) Calmly and consistently **use stepfamily terms in front of your mate, kids, and relatives**, *despite* their discomfort, irritation, or objections. Openly seek stepfamily education and support, assert your beliefs and concerns, and **hold firm** to treating your kids' other parents as legitimate members of your nuclear stepfamily. Let your partner witness that you'll act on your belief to protect your kids and your integrity, not to punish or torment them. If s/he's controlled by a false self, the related psychological wounds may block her or his understanding and/or accepting this.

Strengthen your listening and assertion skills (Project 2), and affirm your right to act on your beliefs, *even if your partner is uncomfortable.* **Evolve a Bill of personal Rights as part of Project 1** (..02/rights.htm). Remind yourself that your kids need you to do this for them. Which is more important to you: keeping your self-respect and integrity, or avoiding conflict with your partner (and potential abandonment and aloneness)? The latter *surely* signals a false self controls your true Self.

If you accept your step-identity and your partner (or another) doesn't, you have a *values* conflict. If you're both well along on building effective communication skills (Project 2), you'll know how resolve this (..09/lc-intro.htm). This is specially true if you can compassionately see the other's resistance as a symptom of fear, guilt, and/or shame, not *stupidity*, *stubbornness* (rigidity), and/or *badness*.

5) Another choice you have here is to **get clear on the** *advantages* **that being in a stepfamily offers you** and your kids, without diminishing the challenges and hardships. A well-led stepfamily can offer most or all of the priceless high-nurturance traits in Chapter 3. Look for ways to affirm these specific advantages with adults and kids in your extended stepfamily, not just your partner ("Honey, I'm so glad that you're able to confide in your step-uncle Frank. He really likes and cares about you, doesn't he?")

6) If your mate disavows or minimizes your stepfamily identity, or denies what step-hood *means*, another option is to **ask or demand** **that they join you** in working to exploring this important values conflict **with a** seasoned, **stepfamily-informed, recovery-aware clinician.** As you know, effective demands include clear, enforceable consequences.

Choices like these also apply if the person denying your stepfamily identity is a child, their other co-parent, or an important relative or friend. *Not* doing some or all of these options is a choice. "Choosing not to choose" is a self-defeating strategy to avoid scary responsibility, conflicts, and outcomes. It promotes eventual emotional and legal re/divorce.

Bottom line: for your best odds of making right re/marital choices and long-term stepfamily success, you and your mate must fully accept _ your *step*family identity, and _ what it means. If related co-parents, kids, and/or kin aren't able to accept these realities now, you can't *make* them. Keep inviting them, and avoid blame, if you can. If you re/wed, steadily make your re/marriage (Project 8) second only to your personal wholistic health and recovery (Project 1). If you can't, what's in the way?

Resolving *Membership* Conflicts

When you partners solidly agree, "OK, we are a *step*family," then you're able to tackle the second half of Project 3: resolving any major disputes over who *belongs* in your stepfamily. Why is this important? Can you imagine a sports team or orchestra functioning "well" if their members or leader disagreed on who belonged to the group? Everyone has the best chances for high-nurturance success if all your extended-stepfamily members agree clearly on _ who comprises your stepfamily, _ what you're all trying to *do* together (Project 6), and _ who can contribute what towards your common goals?" Building effective communication skills (Project 2) is a great help in negotiating these agreements *if* your Selves are leading.

There are **two kinds of stepfamily membership conflicts**: *exclusions* ("I / We don't want you in our home, our stepfamily, or in our lives!"), and membership *rejections* ("I don't *want* to be part of your household, your stepfamily, or your lives!") The obvious problem with excluding others who want co-equal membership is that they feel disrespected, discounted, and demeaned: "1-down." If they're shame-based survivors of low-nurturance childhoods, rejection pain and anger are amplified. These fuel serious arguments, hostility, and escalating conflict spirals. This is specially true if the people involved can't use the seven Project-2 communication skills effectively.

Co-parents like Ted McLean who exclude *themselves* cause at least two problems: _ the other co-parents resent their not assuming their "fair" child-raising responsibilities, including financial; and _ their biokids, like Patty McLean, feel abandoned, unimportant, confused, and shamed. That promotes false-self formation and five related inner wounds (p. 142).

Membership exclusions and rejections _ amplify psychological wounds, _ lower stepfamily nurturance (Chapter 3), and _ inhibit extended-stepfamily bonding, loyalty, and pride. These combine with other stepfamily tensions to lower personal serenities, stress re/marriages, and reduce minor kids' senses of household and family emotional security and well-being. In sum, **unresolved membership conflicts lower your stepfamily's nurturance level and raise your re/divorce odds.**

Membership exclusions and rejections occur in *bio*families too. They happen more often in typical multi-home stepfamilies, and are tougher to resolve because of the five hazards in Chapter 4.

Often, lovestruck courting co-parents like you don't "see" stepfamily membership conflicts or what they *mean*. They ignore, minimize, or intellectualize them, until adults and kids take a major vacation, plan a major holiday together with relatives, and/or start planning their commitment ceremony. The extent or intensity of stepfamily membership conflicts may not become apparent until planning your re/wedding, so *courtship is often not a reliable guide.* Re/wedding and reception invitation lists often reveal existing membership and loyalty conflicts, and cause new ones.

Even if re/married co-parents do acknowledge that some adults or kids are conflicted about inclusion in their stepfamily, idealistic new couples often believe "These tensions will surely relax as we all get to know each other and our love grows." That's usually a romantic illusion, unless no one has major false-self wounds. This is about as likely as your winning the lottery tomorrow.

Typical Membership Conflicts

Stepfamily exclusions and rejections come in many forms and combinations. For example . . .

+ A resentful, bitter, or insecure co-parent excludes their former mate ("Dorothy may be my son's mother, but she sure isn't part of my new family!")

+ A bioparent excludes a new stepparent ("Janine is your father's girlfriend, *not* your 'stepmother,' so you don't have to do what she says!")

+ An insecure new stepparent excludes their mate's former partner ("Jane, this is your family now, and I'm your husband. I don't want to hear about George, see pic-

tures of him, answer his calls, or have him in our house. Period.")
+ A bio-grandparent politely or bluntly excludes a new daughter or son-in-law, and/or their step-grandkids or relatives ("I'm sorry, Chris. I just don't care to have them here for Thanksgiving dinner.")
+ A stepchild rejects a stepsibling ("I don't want my idiot stepbrother in our house, and I won't let him in my room!")
+ A stepchild rejects the role, concern, and authority of a custodial or visited stepparent ("Read my lips: You are *not* my Mother, and I *don't* have to do what you say!")
+ Deeply offended, hurt, and angry over a parent's divorce-related behavior, a teen or grown daughter or son refuses any relationship with them and any new partner ("I will *never* forgive you for what you did to Mom / Dad / me / us!") Alternatively, the child may bitterly cut off relations with a brother or sister who sides with the offending parent. Such cut-offs are a sure sign of blocked grief, and probably indicate inner-family anarchy.

More examples of stepfamily membership conflicts . . .
+ A new stepparent's invitation to discuss a troubled stepchild is rejected by the stepchild's "other parent" ("I called Ingrid to talk about our concern over Ben's school grades, and she told me that was none of my business!")
+ A son or daughter tries to avoid visitations with their non-custodial biomom or biodad and stepparent ("But Mom, why do I have to go over there? Dad's gone a lot, and we never do anything that I want to do. Besides, I hate the food (stepmom) Margo makes.")
+ Relatives are rejected by their new step-kin ["I won't call (stepdaughter-in-law) Susan's mother again. Every time I do, she says she's 'in the middle of something,' and ends the conversation. I don't think she likes us."]

The opposite of these membership exclusions and rejections is mutually-respectful acceptances, and genuine (vs. dutiful) interest in some normal and holiday socializing. Over time, such open acquaintanceships *may* (vs. will) ripen into true =/= friendships and mutual caring.

Membership-conflict Options

First, get clearer on what *belonging* and *membership* mean to you all. To me, when an adult or child really belongs to a group, other members consistently . . .

+ *Want* to (vs. *have* to) acknowledge their existence ("Hello!"; "Goodbye," "How are you doing?", etc.)
+ Care genuinely about and respect their needs, opinions, beliefs, feelings, and values. One sign of such caring is respectful confrontations, vs. enabling.
+ Periodically appreciate and acknowledge what skills, energy, traits, and wisdom they bring to the group, and say so publicly.
+ Want to keep them promptly and honestly informed of group problems, changes, and key happenings, and to spontaneously (vs. dutifully) invite them to attend group gatherings.
+ Ask for and accept their help in times of threat, loss, and change.
+ Try to respect and accept their personal limitations and preferences *without excessive judgment.*
+ Expect them to either accept the group's main rules, values, and goals, or to work co-operatively to improve them.
+ Strive to balance respecting their individual needs and priorities against the group's goals and needs. And . . .
+ Encourage their individual health and growth, and those of every other member.

How does this compare with your ideas about belonging to a group? Because he disrespected Ted McLean as a man and a father, Jack Tilmon didn't want to do these things for Ted, who didn't assertively seek them for his own reasons. This caused _ ongoing mutual indifference, hostility, and distrust between their two homes; _ remarital tension between Sarah and Jack; and _ insecurity, confusion, hurt, sadness, and anger in 13-year-old Patty McLean.

Tensions were specially sharp around child discipline, visitations, and finances. Conversely, stepdad Rick Cohen included Jack and Patty, and tried hard to accord these belonging factors (above) to them, Sarah, and his ex wife Sheila, as legitimate members of his three-home nuclear stepfamily.

Group membership also brings responsibilities. Ideally, each stepfamily co-parent will *want* to share the responsibilities for guiding, protecting, teaching, encouraging, and financially supporting ("nurturing") each dependent stepchild and biochild. Re/married or not, divorced bioparents often disagree mildly or fiercely over who's responsible for what, and how co-parenting responsibilities are discharged. When one or two stepparents are added, specially if they have biokids, agreeing on co-parenting responsibilities is a major ongoing challenge. See Projects 6, 9, and 10 in Chapter 8.

Re/married bioparents usually feel they have more responsibility and authority for their dependent kids' welfare than stepparents do. Unresolved co-parental *values* conflicts over child-raising responsibilities, priorities, and methods often promote stressful old and new stepfamily-membership exclusions, loyalty conflicts, relationship triangles, and role confusions. Whew.

Note that membership exclusion/rejection struggles overlap other *inner*personal and interpersonal clashes. These include conflicts over stepfamily roles and rules, values, loyalties, priorities, assets (specially money and time); and "unfinished business" (e.g. "If you hadn't been unfaithful to me / a drunk / obsessed with your work / so irresponsible / gone so much / so over-focused on sex / verbally abusive / so wimpy with your father / such a lousy parent . . . we wouldn't have these problems!)"

This perspective suggests at least three stepfamily realities:

You three or more co-parenting partners need to accept that your extended-stepfamily relationships will probably be significantly conflictual for *years*. This will be specially true just before and after your re/wedding, holidays, vacations, and special occasions like birthdays, anniversaries, graduations, births, and deaths.

Second, for long-term successes, you co-parents will need to *want* to learn how to resolve conflicts effectively together, and *want* to help other stepfamily members do the same (Project 2). These are often second-order changes (p. 159).

Third, you'll need to help each other _ separate your simultaneous clashes, _ prioritize them, _ learn how to resolve each kind of conflict, and _ stay focused on one clash at a time until everyone's satisfied enough. This takes shared awareness, discipline, clarity, commitment, communication skills, and mutual and self respect. A tall order, eh?

Until they heal their inner wounds, co-parents from low-nurturance childhoods usually have trouble doing these three things, because of their false-self myopia, biases, and unawarenesses. Once clearly aware of their wounds and accepting responsibility for their own healing (Project 1), re/wedded co-parents can help each other overcome every one of them! Rick and Karen Cohen were inspiring examples.

In addition to these conflict-resolution basics, what can you partners do about *membership* conflicts? There are two sets of options: prepare, then act.

Prepare For Resolution

What does "get prepared" mean, here? You and your partner tailor these things to fit your situation *before* you decide to re/marry:

+ **Agree together** without ambivalence "We all will be (or are) a normal, multi-home stepfamily," and then learn and accept what that means; (above, and Project 4)
+ _ **Evolve** a clear, shared definition of "high nurturance families and relationships" (p. 48), and _ rough draft your stepfamily mission statement (Project 6).
+ **Agree on** your co-parenting and re/marital priorities. Suggestion: adopt a long-range view, and each of you

usually put personal wholistic health and recovery first, your re/marriage second, and all else third. See p. 447.
+ **Read** _ this book, _ "Who's *Really* Running Your Life?", and _ "*Satisfactions*;" and work together at making significant progress on Projects _ 1 and _ 2.
+ **Get clear together on** what _ "stepfamily membership" and _ "belonging" mean to you.
+ You and your partner **get clear and honest about your attitudes about** yourselves and each other on . . .

1) "Do we exchange true mutual respect ("we're =/="), competition and blame ("I am / we are 1-up"), fear ("you're 1-up"), or indifference ("you don't exist")? Restated: "Are we _ coparenting opponents, or _ teammates with a common, long-term mission?"

2) "Are our basic expectations about our stepfamily conflicts idealized, realistically optimistic, or cynical and pessimistic?" (see Project 4 and ..04/myths.htm.)

3) "Do each of us co-parents see relationship conflicts in _ black/white, win/lose terms, or do we believe _ there are usually many options open to us in any conflict?" The former usually indicates a disabled true Self.

4) "Do we tend to _ avoid and postpone confronting conflicts, or do we _ take prompt, proactive responsibility for resolving them together for our kids' sakes?" Ditto.

5) "Do we tend to focus on _ short-term resolution, or are we _ able to keep long-range goals and priorities clearly in mind as we problem-solve?"

A powerful way you co-parents can prepare to resolve identity and membership conflicts is to **draw and cooperatively discuss a multi-generational family map**, or *genogram*. Then use it to work toward agreement on your stepfamily identity and who's included in it. Study the example on p. 96.

This diagram shows the network of genetic, emotional, and legal relationships among many (not all) of the people that comprise this three-generational stepfamily. Horizontal lines are marriages, an "—x—" is a divorce, and "X" denotes a death.

Vertical or slanted lines show child conceptions. Circles represent females, and squares are males.

Take at least 30 minutes, and use a *large* piece of paper to draw your own map. See http://sfhelp.org/03/geno1.htm for more ideas on how to do this, and ways to use your genogram. Once you and your partner have each drawn your respective maps separately, compare them. Minimize distractions, and explore questions like these together:

Q1: "If our maps differ 'significantly,' what problems will that cause us if we re/marry?" Typical loyalty and membership conflicts erupt about holiday gifts and invitations, attending special events like graduations, homecomings, retirements, bar and bas mitzvahs, weddings, and birthdays.

Q2: "Are there any membership conflicts you and I need to resolve now?" A major challenge for many courting and re/wedded co-parents is really accepting that despite legal divorce, their kids' other bioparents remain long-term, co-equal emotional, genetic, legal, and financial stepfamily members.

Q3: "Who among all these people are of special emotional importance to each of us co-parents, and to each of our minor and grown kids?" Option: give each such person a unique symbol or color on your map.

Q4: "How does each adult and child on our map seem to feel about being in a multi-home, multi-generational stepfamily now?" Option: put a plus, question mark, minus, or zero (no apparent feeling) by each key person's symbol. If you and your mate are unsure if someone on your map is "in" or "out" of your stepfamily, *ask them* how they feel!

Q5: "Who among us has _ a stepfamily *identity* conflict (option: put a colored "I" next to their map-symbol), and who has _ a *membership* problem? (colored "M"). Among the latter, "Who are rejecters (self-excluders), and who are being excluded by someone else? By whom?"

Q6: "How are these identity and membership conflicts, individually and combined, affecting our relationship, specifically?" Settling for "I don't know" suggests that a false self is running someone's inner team . . .

Q7: "How are these identity and membership conflicts, individually and combined, affecting each of our minor and grown children?" Common effects are *guilt, resentment, insecurity* and *anxiety, confusion, defensiveness, anger, withdrawal, "acting out," avoidances, hostility, self-medication (addictions),* and so on.

Q8: "Which of the adults and kids we've identified as having stepfamily identity and/or membership conflicts may be blocked in grieving important prior losses (broken emotional bonds)? See Project 5 for more on this vital question.

You can't force someone to accept his or her membership in your nuclear or extended stepfamily. You can _ educate them about stepfamilies (e.g. show them your map), _ confront them ("we are related, now . . ."), _ invite them, and _ appeal to them with compassion, respect, and patience. Because of the sheer number of your members and the complex web of concurrent adjustment tasks that you all face, **it takes most steppeople four or more years after re/wedding** to grieve, adjust, learn, clarify, and solidly accept their new multi-home stepfamily's complex roles, rules, rituals, and goals (Project 9). An adult or child who resists stepfamily identity or membership today may be much more receptive two or three years from now, after their mourning has progressed (hopefully), and sub-groups of you all have shared some common experiences together.

These preparation steps are ideal. In the real world, most co-parents like the Tilmons and Cohens can't come close to doing these steps decisively, thoroughly, or co-operatively, They're blocked by their mix of the five hazards (p. 69). Can you name them now?

The hazards and emotional and logistic complexity of new stepfamily relationships and roles causes typical co-parents Like Sarah, Jack, and Ted to feel overwhelmed, confused, anxious, skeptical, or numb. These feelings promote protective avoidances, procrastinations, minimizations, and blamings, rather than motivation to work patiently on these preparation projects together as a co-parenting team. This in turn causes membership and other stepfamily conflicts to accumulate and amplify over time. As Barry Commoner has observed about Earthly ecology, the "TANSTAFL" principle applies: "There Ain't No Such Thing as Free Lunch." Do you relate?

For co-parents who do many of the preparation steps suggested above before or after re/wedding, the next options are action steps. Like what?

Action Options

These will work best if you partners or all your co-parents solidly accept their stepfamily identity and what it means.

Reflect on how relationships between strangers begin, how they grow (or don't), and what affects how fast and how deep they grow. Re/marriage creates reasons and chances to grow new high-nurturance relationships between the adults and kids in your several extended biofamilies. As a couple, you can range from passive to active in having members of your merging families meet each other and give "good chemistry" a chance to bloom.

Using your genogram, pick key stepfamily members that you mates want to reduce exclusions and rejections with. Prioritize them: "Which membership conflicts affect us and our (non/custodial) kids the most now? Why?" **For each key membership conflict, assess** (1) what factors are probably causing it, and (2) what would have to happen for it to shrink to "acceptable" (according to whom)?

At first, typical stepfamily membership conflicts seem to be caused by a variety of surface reasons, like unresolved prior marital or parental betrayals, disputes, blamings, and/or "inability to reason together." Other common surface reasons are about current arguments over assets; and/or child custody, visitations, finances, and co-parenting or other values differences.

In my experience, the *real* reasons underneath these **usually boil down to combinations of these**:

+ Unhealed childhood and first-marriage wounds including . . .

_ Being ruled be an overwhelmed (chaotic) false self, and unable to focus and problem solve effectively; i.e. scared or angry inner children control one or both sides of the exclusion or rejection conflict, rather than the person's calm, rational true Self.

_ Shame and guilts ("Talking with you forces me to look at my awful mistakes, failures, and personal defects");

_ Fears of confrontation and disrespectful conflict, loss, grief pain or rage, disapprovals, and/or of expensive, adversarial legal action; and . . .

_ Distrust of someone's motives ("You don't really care about my needs, or respect my values"), and/or of the effectiveness of communication attempts ("We always fight").

+ Other factors that promote stepfamily membership problems include . . .

_ Unawarenesses and denials ("We're not a stepfamily!");

_ Unconscious or semi-conscious biases ("We don't associate with people like that.");

_ Ineffective communications ("You never listen to me!," or "We always fight, never problem-solve," or an unconscious self-amplifying communication pattern: member "A" does something that upsets member "B," who reacts in a way that upsets person "A," who . . .);

_ Indifference and/or little true empathy ("I honestly don't care about _____");

_ Jealousy and resentment ("Why should you re/marry and get happiness when you couldn't be happy with me?");

_ Hostility ["I dislike and resent (some family member) and/or things about them"];

_ Unresolved or inappropriate sexual tensions ("I'm still attracted to you" or "My mate seems attracted to you," or "My child is sexually excited by you or your child.")

These examples illustrate some common real (vs. surface) causes of stepfamily membership conflicts. There are other possibilities and combinations. *Note that many of these root causes are not subject to "reason" or "logic,"* so explaining "rationally" what you need and why will be of little or no help. These core causes *can* be eased, over time, by genuine (vs. dutiful) empathic listening, understanding, acceptance, compassion, =/= respect, patience, and unambivalent forgiveness, and self-motivated true recovery from false-self control.

Review the Serenity Prayer (p. 165), and accept together that some membership conflicts are presently beyond your power to resolve. In such cases, your co-parental challenge becomes "What can I or we do to peacefully accept and *adapt* to these conflicts, until something beyond our control changes them?" You can't force someone to *want to* change. You *can* intentionally grow relationship environments that promote self-motivated second-order (core attitude) change!

For each membership conflict you co-parents *can* affect, **brainstorm options** that might help. If the conflict seems specially harmful to your home's nurturance level, and/or to a child's wholistic health, consider hiring a stepfamily aware clinical consultant to help you. See ..11/counsel.htm for suggestions on how to pick one.

Perhaps the toughest task here is admitting *your* part in stepfamily exclusion and rejection conflicts. Do you need to forgive yourself or another for some past hurt? Taking responsibility for past mistakes, and courageously making *genuine* (vs. dutiful) apologies can help free up the toughest relationship impasse. Are you blocked in grieving some prior losses? Work steadily on your own recovery and healing, and compassionately support other recovering members of your stepfamily.

Once you have a plan to resolve a specific membership conflict, **use your seven communication skills** (Project 2) to implement it together. Tackle one conflict at a time. Tell other stepfamily members, including your minor and grown kids, what you're doing, and why. If your efforts don't bring the results you wish, try to learn from the outcomes, and avoid blaming!

As with all your stepfamily-building projects, help each other to be patient ("Progress, not perfection!"), and keep your senses of humor and long-term perspective. Try using John and Emily Vishers' realistic motto as a touchstone along the way: **"In eight** (years after re/marriage) **it'll be great!"** Please don't see these suggestions for resolving your stepfamily identity and membership conflicts as a black/white cookbook! If you do, you'll probably miss some creative solutions that are unique to you all.

Recap

It's common for adults like you and kids to _ reject their identity as members of a stepfamily, and/or to _ minimize what such identity *means*. You partners are also apt to _ exclude other kids or adults as members of your extended stepfamily, or _ reject your own belonging. Each of these promotes unrealistic expectations, and escalating relationship and role problems.

Identity conflicts promote adults and kids unconsciously expecting their stepfamily relationships to feel and act like those in idealized or remembered intact biofamilies. Like expecting octopus to taste like meatloaf, this harvests escalating dismay, confusion, frustration, and conflict.

Membership conflicts cause ongoing and escalating personal and re/marital resentments; hinder extended-stepfamily bondings; and raise minor kids' anxieties and insecurities and their odds of emotional wounding over time. All these inhibit building stepfamily bondings and loyalties, and lower your household and stepfamily-wide nurturance levels.

Ideally your three or more co-parents will accept these two realities *before* any re/weddings. You all will agree to work some version of the above preparation and action steps together over time, to reduce the identity and membership conflicts that are healable. Some aren't. If you're courting, doing this third project thoroughly together will help you decide whether to re/marry or not. If you're already re/married, this project can help you raise the harmony inside your skins and homes, and between your homes, over time. Expect conflicts before that happens.

Most (all?) identity and membership conflicts bloom from unseen false-self wounds mixed with and unawarenesses (Chapters 5 and 6) and ineffective communications. Therefore, *many such disputes are* not *subject to logic, mediation, "reason," and negotiation.* In such cases, the challenge becomes for co-parents to accept the disputes with compassion (vs. blame and resentment), *adapt* to them, and work steadily to grow a pro-healing home and stepfamily environment.

Have you ever belonged to a well-led, harmonious team, committee, or group? Remember what that *felt* like? Recall what you all accomplished together, and how you did it. Would you like to have your kids and grandkids grow up in such a consistently harmonious, strongly bonded, purposeful, well-led, multi-talented group? Keep learning here, so you can trust your future decision about whether stepfamily re/marriage is the best way to achieve that vision for you and any kids, long term.

Reality check: Before moving on, reflect and perhaps journal about your reactions to what you just experienced. Check which of these feel true now . . .

1) I feel a mix of *calm, centered, energized, light, focused, resilient, up, grounded, relaxed, alert, aware, serene, purposeful*, and *clear*. (T F ?) If so, your Self is probably leading your team of subselves. If not, who *is*?

2) I feel clear on _ what a stepfamily *identity* is, _ why fully accepting it is important to me and those I care about, and on _ key signs that adults and kids have accepted this identity. (T F ?)

3) I'm also clear on _ what a stepfamily *membership* conflict are, _ the two kinds of membership conflicts, and key options toward _identifying and _ resolving them. (T F ?)

4) I feel that my partner is clear on the two items above, and that _ s/he and I can talk *effectively* about them in our situation. (T F ?)

5) I should slowly re-read this chapter to clarify and anchor _ what I've learned and _ what it *means* to me. I need to review _ the pre-re/marriage quiz in Chapter 5, and/or _ the stepfamily realities in Chapter 6 now. (T F ?)

6) I want to discuss the ideas here with (who?) (T F ?)

7) I'm genuinely motivated to _ identify any major identity and membership conflicts in our (prospective) stepfamily, and I _ feel confident enough that I'll see any clearly enough to help me make three right re/marriage choices in Project 7. (T F ?)

8) My partner (if any) _ seems genuinely interested in these first three courtship projects, _ is learning about them, like me; and _ I feel we're real partners in learning, so far. (T F ?)

9) Now I feel _ clear and confident, _ numb or blah, _ distracted and scattered, _ anxious or scared, _ locally overwhelmed, or _ something else.

Awarenesses . . .

We've covered a lot of abstract ideas here. When you chose this book, did you have any idea we'd cover what we have, so far? Are you glad you're reading this? Take a mind-body break, if you need one. When you're ready, your next project uses your stepfamily identity to justify transforming common myths you may hold into realistic expectations about your potential stepfamily roles, relationships, and adjustment tasks.

Patiently done, your fourth courtship project will help you partners expand the awareness you began here about what it *means* to re/wed and be "in a stepfamily." This will build your confidence making in the complex re/marital and co-parental decisions up ahead . . .

Project 4: Form Realistic Expectations
Avoid "I Never Thought It Would Be Like This!"

I recently co-led a re/marriage preparation seminar for 12 middle-class couples. Ten couples cautiously identified that they were about to form a stepfamily. The other four people had no prior kids. I asked the former to raise their hands if they expected that stepparents should "love" their minor and grown stepkids. Over half of the 20 adults raised their hands. Their faces registered a variety of reactions, when I said, "That's one of the most common of over 60 troublesome myths about typical stepfamily relationships. The more realistic expectation is: stepparents should work to build mutual *respect* with stepkids, not *love*. If one-way or mutual love does bloom, over time, that's a wonderful bonus."

One of five major reasons most stepfamily re/marriages fail or endure with daily stress is *unawareness*. Most re/marriers I've met don't know how different typical stepfamilies are from traditional biofamilies, and what those differences mean. Like the Tilmons, they rarely know what's "normal" in average multi-home stepfamilies. Such co-parents unconsciously rely on inappropriate *bio*family norms to resolve confusions and conflicts about their stepfamily goals, roles, rules, and relationships.

Over time, this usually causes escalating frustration, disappointment, hurt, self-doubts, and resentments among stepfamily members. Lacking factual information, typical psychologically-wounded co-parents try ever harder to force their square stepfamily peg to fit a round biofamily hole. They blame themselves or each other in frustration, rather than looking together for a square hole: realistic *stepfamily* expectations.

Reality check: if you haven't recently, scan the 72 common structural and task differences between stepfamilies and intact biofamilies on p. 425. With those differences in mind, explore the series of Web pages beginning with http://sfhelp.org/04/myths.htm. They'll show you over 60 common **misconceptions about stepfamily life**, and typical realities. After you've studied those, come back here, and muse on these . . .

1) I could have named over half of these differences and myths before I read these. (True / False / unsure)

2) Using Chapter 6 (step realities), Resource C (stepfamily-biofamily differences), and the Web pages above, I need to thoughtfully review and clarify my *stepfamily* expectations now, to help me make the best re/marriage choices I can. (T F ?)

3) Reading and thinking about all these items has changed my thinking about possible stepfamily re/marriage and co-parenting. (T F ?)

4) My interest in doing all seven of these re/marriage evaluation projects has changed. (T F ?)

5) I feel better, after reading all these and reflecting on what they mean to me. (T F ?)

6) I want to learn my partner's awareness and expectations about these stepfamily differences and realities now. (T F ?)

7) I'm confident my true Self is answering these questions now. (T F ?)

Awarenesses . . .

Your fourth courtship project has four steps: you and your partner _ learn what's normal in typical stepfamilies, *early*. _ Identify your co-parents' and key relatives' misconceptions (myths), and _ adjust your specific expectations to fit stepfamily realities. Then _ patiently encourage your other potential stepfamily members and supporters to learn and accept these realities too.

Courting or re/married co-parents who haven't made significant progress on the prior three projects will probably have trouble doing this one before experiencing painful real-life conflicts and disillusionments.

This chapter suggests why this fourth project is important, and options for doing it effectively.

Why Do This Project?

Like your expecting to sprout wings and fly with the eagles, an *unrealistic stepfamily expectation* is any un/conscious mental image or concept that's unattainable in real life. Some of the surprises that life constantly provides you are more impactful than others. Can you recall trusting that something was "true" or "sure," only to discover painfully that your belief was wrong? One of the painful truths that experience teaches typical co-parent couples is "Our stepfamily will probably never *feel* like the biofamily we would each like to have."

This courtship myth-busting project is vital because the sobering 60+% U.S. re/divorce rate *applies to you.* Your individual misconceptions about stepfamily roles and relationships may be trivial. The combined impact of inner wounds, ineffective communications, and several dozen unrealistic expectations can often promote entranced courting co-parents to make three wrong re/marital choices, and later deeply regret them. Self-awareness, self-motivated education, and clear, focused, *honest* co-parental discussion can prevent this.

Besides unawareness, a major cause for many co-parents' stepfamily illusions is the false-self trait of *reality distortion.* It manifests as minimizing and denying inner wounds (p. 142), prospective *step*family identity (p. 199), and stepfamily realities (p. 91) including your high risk of re/divorce. Typical wounded co-parents long for the happiness of a solid marriage and the (idealized, loving *biological*) family they've never experienced before.

Before reviewing the key steps toward mastering this fourth project, sharpen your perspective. Considering all the combinations of prior co-parent divorce or death, child custody, and conception, **there are almost 100 structural kinds of stepfamily.** This means that average co-parents and kids like you all will never meet another stepfamily structured like yours. So what? Courting couples in denial may say of other re/married co-parents "Well *they* have stepfamily troubles, but we're very different than them (. . . . so their norms and realities don't apply to us)." Paradoxically, that's both true and not true. The hazards and 12 projects in this series of books and Web pages apply to *all* stepfamilies, including yours, regardless of unique structure and circumstances.

Form *Realistic* Stepfamily Expectations

Ideally *before* deciding if you should re/wed . . .
+ **Fully accept** your stepfamily identity, and _ get very curious about what that *means* to you and the people you care about the most (Project 3).
+ **Prepare** your mind to learn; and . . .
+ **Get educated** on a range of stepfamily topics, _ clarify your expectations on how they'll apply to you (or won't), and _ validate your expectations with knowledgeable other people. Then . . .
+ **Apply your learnings** to your courtship or re/marriage as research partners.
Let's look at the last three of these . . .

Prepare to Learn

Athletes warm up before competing, and pilots do pre-flight checks before taking off. Choosing some key attitudes and beliefs can help prepare you partners to master this fourth project together. When you can check each of the following as being clearly true for you *and* your partner now, you're well prepared:

__ **1)** We can each _ name the six psychological wounds on p. 142, and _ we accept without ambivalence that each of us must _ assess for and _ heal some mix of these wounds, whether we re/wed or not.

__ **2)** We are now, or will be, *stepfamily* co-parents.

__ **3)** We each can name and describe the five hazards we face (Chapter 4), and _ we accept that they *do* apply to us, our minor or grown kids, and our ex mates.

__ **4)** We accept that each of our kids' other bioparents and stepparents are and will be full members of our stepfamily, whether they want or accept that or not. If we don't, we both *want* to learn what prevents our acceptance, and heal that.

__ **5)** We *want to* work at these seven courtship projects together now, to avoid making up to three wrong re/marriage decisions.

__ **6)** We *want to* learn which of the 60 common stepfamily myths we believe now, and what the probable realities are.

__ **7)** We believe our stepfamily roles and relationships will feel alien at first, and that we each must *want to* replace old biofamily "truths" and expectations with new ones.

__ **8)** We accept that if we re/marry, it will take us all four or more years to merge and stabilize our biofamilies *after* our commitment ceremony.

__ **9)** We see our 12 projects (Chapter 8) as a chance to learn, grow, and bring out the best in each of us, rather than a set of unpleasant, conflictual chores.

__ **10)** We each accept that to succeed long term, we'll have to *want* to talk regularly about our progress and problems with our version of the projects.

__ **11)** We solidly believe that stepfamilies are just "as good as" biofamilies. If we re/marry *and take these 12 projects seriously together*, our multi-home stepfamily can be just as enjoyable, high-nurturance, and productive as any traditional biofamily—though it probably will never *feel* like one!

__ **12)** We both *want to* learn the seven communication skills in Project 2 together, to resolve the values, loyalty, and many other conflicts we and the kids are *sure* to experience if we re/wed.

__ **13)** We accept that if our courtship experience is going "well," this is *not* a reliable guide to how we all will get along if we re/marry.

__ **14)** We accept that TV, magazines, novels, videos, and movies rarely represent average real stepfamilies.

__ **15)** We both agree now that in our family-relationship conflicts, our integrities and wholistic (spiritual + physical + emotional + mental) health come first, our adult relationship second, and everything else comes third, except in emergencies. Other priority schemes probably indicate false-self control, and/or major unfinished biofamily conflicts. See the priorities checklist on p. 447.

__ **16)** I look forward to discussing these items with my partner now.

If your Self is disabled now, other protective subselves may check these items as "true" to avoid facing that you're not prepared yet to do Project 4, or probably shouldn't re/marry. They may also numb or blank you out ("What did I just read?"), distract you, or say something like "Maybe for other people, but not *us!*"

Beliefs like these can prepare you to learn about what to *really* expect if you choose to be stepfamily mates. Notice what your subselves are saying (or aren't) now . . .

Keep Your Motivation to Learn

In warp-speed America 2000, it's very easy to put other goals and activities ahead of doing these challenging seven projects. How can you partners help each other stay focused and motivated? Options:

Several times a week, talk together about progress and obstacles on your first four projects when you're not distracted. If either of you is reluctant to do this, your Self is probably disabled.

Co-create a metaphor together that symbolizes preparing for stepfamily life, and refer to it as you partners think and talk. One metaphor you've read here likens stepfamily life to inland-lake sailors (or landlubbers) getting ready to put all their combined family members aboard an unfamiliar ocean-going sloop, and sailing around the world together over four or more years. You and your partner are co-captains and co-navigators.

Another realistic metaphor pictures you and your mate learning how to build a sturdy, comfortable multi-level home together for you and dependent others, on a rocky, sloping hillside *by hand*, with few tools and little professional help. If you think that these metaphors are far-fetched, reality-check them with several stepfamily co-parents who have been re/married at least five years.

Picture your (step)children as adults, say in their mid thirties. Vision clearly _ how you'd like them to feel about themselves, and _ what you'd wish for them then. Imagine clearly _ what you want to give your children to empower them to be effective, serene, productive people and parents of your grandkids. Acknowledge that the stepfamily decisions you and your co-parenting partners are preparing to make now will promote or hinder that vision from manifesting. If it feels helpful, write down these visions, and reread them to each other and your co-parenting partners and kids (!) from time to time.

Finally, find and **ask veteran re/married *and re/divorced* stepfamily co-parents** something like: "What did you expect your stepfamily life to be like, specifically, and what did you get?" This assumes that they accept their *stepfamily* identity. You may harvest clearer answers if you break your question into chunks, like "What did you expect about . . .

+ Re/marriage in a stepfamily?"
+ Co-parenting relationships and responsibilities?
+ Relations with and between your stepkids?
+ Money and assets?
+ Loyalties and priorities?
+ Harmony and contentment?
+ Love? And . . .

+ Other people's empathy and support?"

If false selves control your consultants, they're likely to describe their experiences as being better or worse than they really were (reality distortion). Unless they've read this book, they won't know about the five hazards and seven projects.

Adapt the proposed set of steps below to fit your circumstances and styles, or devise your own plan. Part of your plan should include an answer to "How will we know clearly that our stepfamily 'shoulds' and expectations are realistic enough?" Like seeing how a child "turns out," you can only do your best, trust the process and your own judgments, and wait for the outcome to emerge over some years . . .

Choices like these can help you partners stay motivated to build realistic stepfamily expectations, and progress patiently on your other courtship projects. Accept that periodically you partners will need to rest, regroup, and refresh your commitment as your courtship research adventure unfolds.

After preparing and recharging your motivations to learn, you two are ready to gradually . . .

Convert Myths to Realistic Expectations

Most courting co-parents can't name their stepfamily expectations, other than generalities like "It'll be a challenge," and "Sure, we'll have some problems." Other unaware, numb, or serene people literally have no expectations. From 23 years' study and experience, I offer the following aids and options to help you become aware of what you (your subselves) think would happen if you re/marry and become co-parents. Pick the options that fit your unique situation best.

Find the stepfamily maps (p. 96) you each made in Project 3. If you didn't make them, do so now using the guidelines at http://sfhelp.org/03/geno1.htm. Discuss any questions or disputes that come up, and refresh your definitions of "Who belongs to our (potential) extended stepfamily?" Imagine gathering all the people represented by your diagrams into one comfortable place, like a retreat center. With *all* of them and per-

haps any unborn "ours" kids in mind, read and discuss the
items below one at a time.

I recommend that you thoughtfully **read these out loud to
each other,** and discuss them as you go. As you do, hilight or
asterisk any items that specially concern either of you partners
for future exploration. Also, be alert for *values* and *loyalty* conflicts (p. 186) that may emerge. If they do, see if you use your
seven Project-2 skills to resolve them or not. Doing this is a
preview of *many* such conflicts you all will discover if you
choose to merge your three or more extended biofamilies.

Options:

1) An item at a time, reread and discuss _ the 14 danger
signs on p. 9, _ the stepfamily realities in Chapter 6, and _ the
"meanings" outlined on p. 203. Your reaction to each item
springs from your current beliefs, priorities, needs, and expectations.

2) Reread and discuss Chapter 3, and test your expectations about your prospective stepfamily against each high-
nurturance factor. Without blame, note which factors seem unlikely or uncertain in your situation, and why.

3) Review the summary of typical new-stepfamily adjustment tasks on p. 435 (also at ..09/sf-task1.htm). Which of these
tasks do you expect to confront, specifically, and how well do
you expect to do at them?

4) If you two haven't recently, read and discuss the summary of stepchild developmental and adjustment needs on p.
454. Your reactions as persons and partners to individual items
and all of them together indicate your current stepfamily expectations. If these child-tasks seem realistic and relevant, you'll
be motivated to do Project 6 together (if your Selves are in
charge).

5) Slowly and thoughtfully, go over each of the ~60 common myths and realities you'll find linked from http://sfhelp.org/
04/myths.htm. Identify and discuss each time your expectation
or intuition differs from the proposed reality. Take plenty of
time to do this, and don't try to finish in one session. Notice
your emotions as you do this. They're your subselves signal-

ing which of these realities they feel are specially important in your unique situation, as they see it.

    6) Read and discuss each of these Web articles at http:// sfhelp.org/. Note which items seem probable or credible in your situation, and which don't. Your judgments form part of your stepfamily expectations.

+ The ~ 40 environmental differences between stepparenting and traditional (intact) bioparenting: ..10/co-p-dfrnces.htm. Do you expect these to cause you stress?

+ These typical stepfamily developmental paths: ..09/develop1.htm. Which do you expect to follow, and *why*?

+ This introduction to the multi-family merger all your co-parents will work at for years if you decide to re/wed: ..09/merge.htm.

+ This introduction to *values* and *loyalty* conflicts and related persecutor-victim-rescuer relationship "triangles": ..09/lc-intro.htm, and ..09/triangles.htm. Do you expect these to be significant problems for you?

+ This "structural mapping" tool, which can reveal how the relationships in your present or future stepfamily homes "work" together: ..09/map-str1.htm (a series of pages). Who's needs do you each expect will most affect each of your co-parenting homes?

+ This detailed inventory of stepfamily *strengths*: ..07/strnx-intro.htm. Which do you expect to develop together?

+ Do you expect *money* to cause any of you significant problems? See ..Rx/mates/money.htm, ..Rx/ex/money.htm, and ..Rx/kin/money.htm.

+ Do either of you expect a co-parent in your prospective stepfamily will want to *adopt* a stepchild? See and discuss ..Rx/spsc/adopt.htm.

+ Do you expect to have any serious arguments over (step)child *discipline*? Many typical co-parents do. Explore by reading and discussing ..10/discipline1.htm.

+ Do you expect to have several or many of these typical *communication blocks*? ..02/evc-blox.htm.

+ Do either of you expect significant "conflicts" with a stepchild's "other parent/s"? See the menu of "ex mate" problems and solutions at http://sfhelp.org/Rx/dx.htm.
+ Do you expect any sexual feelings to develop between a stepparent and a stepchild, or between stepsibs, in or between your homes? See ..Rx/spsc/lust.htm and ..Rx/sibs/lust.htm.
+ Do you expect to forge a *pro-grief* home and stepfamily together? All your members need them! Read and discuss _ ..05/grief-6steps.htm, _ ..05/grief-permits.htm, and _ ..05/griefpol.htm. You'll focus on these in Project 5.
+ Do you partners expect each of these relationship premises to apply to yours? ..10/premises-rln.htm.
+ Do you expect any minor (step)child to change custodial residence, if you re/marry? It happens in about 30% of U.S. stepfamilies. See ..Rx/spl/kid-moves1.htm.
+ Do you expect any conflict over conceiving or raising an "ours" child? See ..Rx/spl/ourschild.htm.
+ Is it possible that an ex mate will file a child-related court suit against either of you? See ..Rx/ex/legal.htm.
+ Could you co-parents have major stepfamily disputes over religion? See ..Rx/spl/religion1.htm.

Do you find this list sobering? It comes from 20 years' experience listening to hundreds of typical re/married parents describe their problems. Often, one or both partners said, "We never expected this!" Be reassured: typical stepfamily couples have several, not *all* of these potential stressors. I encourage you partners to review each one of these items honestly to see what each of you expects if you re/marry. You can view differing expectations as *enriching* and *challenging* (glass half full) or *problems.*

Validate What You Learn

If your and/or your partner's Self is disabled, other subselves may urge you to skip reading the Web articles above or to dismiss what they say. You can guard against that by reality-checking your new expectations with relevant other people. It's unlikely any of them will know of the five hazards and these seven projects. Nonetheless, expand your awareness by checking your research findings by . . .

+ Seeking and listening to other veteran co-parents, individually or via a co-parent support group and/or Internet message boards (http://sfhelp.org/11/resources.htm).

+ Watching for media programs, articles, or local classes on stepfamilies. While *most* are uninformed and unrealistic, they can still raise your shared awareness.

+ Reading and discussing several of the stepfamily titles on p. 540. You may also . . .

+ Hire an *informed* stepfamily clinician, and ask for selective verification of your expectations. See http://sfhelp.org/11/counsel.htm for suggestions on selecting such an effective professional.

The overall goal here is to develop your own store of *realistic* information and beliefs about "What's normal in a typical multi-home, multi-generation U.S. stepfamily?"

Really converting unrealistic (biofamily-based) expectations to stepfamily realities is a second-order change (p. 159). Your false selves will probably resist making them. Do you each now know how to discern these from first-order (changeless) changes?

More Options

Review your personal history and **describe *how* you each change your expectations.** I believe most of us may prepare to change if we hear or read relevant new information (like this book and related Web pages), but we don't *really* "change our minds" until we experience something new. For example, you won't *really* expect significant confusion and stress over stepfamily loyalty conflicts until you're aware that you're *in* one. If that's true for you good people, then reading these printed words and pixels will *prepare* you to make true second-order changes in your expectations.

Re-read this chapter and any related materials you locate **periodically**, e.g. every three months until you both feel solidly "done." Progress on your projects will change how you react to these Project 4 ideas. Notice what stays the same, and what changes in and between you. As you do, notice your emotions: they're subselves trying to tell you something!

When you partners each feel that your expectations are real enough, **ask your _ co-parenting partners and _ key relatives and _ friends about *their* expectations**. Give them copies of any of the materials above that you think would raise their awareness and/or promote constructive discussion. If any of these people hasn't *really* accepted that _ you all are or will be a normal *step*family, or that _ s/he is (or will be) a full member or supporter, s/he may resist or discount your invitation.

Potential and new stepfamilies usually pose *many* questions for minor and grown stepkids. Use what you've learned (above) to **probe what each minor and grown child is wondering, and what *they* expect** will happen if you re/marry. This lays important groundwork for Project 6.

As you encounter major stepfamily conflicts or decisions individually or together, **build the reflex of asking questions** like these:

+ "What do I expect of myself and of other members, here, specifically?"
+ "What shoulds, oughts, and musts ("rules") are we each using to guide our decisions, specifically?"
+ "Are my expectations and these rules *bio*family-based, or stepfamily based? How do I know?" And . . .
+ "Is a false self creating my or my partner's expectations? How do I know?"

Finally, **see this fourth project as ongoing**, rather than something you'll eventually say "There, we're *done*." The seminar co-parents who heard me suggest "Aim to exchange respect with your stepkids, not *love*" wouldn't convert their beliefs or desires because I suggested they should. They each had to experiment with their relations with their stepkids, to begin to reality-check my opinion and decide whether to alter their expectations. I assume you'll have the same reactions to each of the articles and books above. Yes, this is a *lot* of work. *So is re/divorce.* Nag, nag, nag.

Converting your family members' semi-conscious stepfamily myths into shared realistic expectations is a long-term process. As you become more experienced, realistic, and aware, you co-parents will become valuable teachers to unaware co-parents and professionals.

Recap

This chapter offers you a framework of ideas, options, and resources to help you convert common misperceptions about stepfamily life into realistic expectations. This fourth courtship project will have limited value unless you have each fully accepted that you, your ex mates, and all your genetic and legal kin are now a complex stepfamily *that has high odds of re/divorcing* if your governing subselves ignore these 12 projects and the hazards that justify them.

You just read options to . . .

+ **Prepare** to form valid expectations by adopting some key beliefs and identifying any barriers to them. Then . . .

+ **Learn** a range of stepfamily topics, clarify your expectations on how they'll apply to you (or won't), **and validate** your expectations with knowledgeable other people. Then . . .

+ Creatively **apply your learnings** to your courtship or re/marriage together, and teach relevant others along the way.

Recall your main goal is to prepare to make three *right* long-term re/marital decisions in Project 7. The factual stepfamily knowledge you partners acquire now and how it shapes your conscious *and unconscious* expectations will largely determine whether you're a happily-re/married couple years from now or not. A more potent factor is who leads your respective inner families as you court.

How effective are you and your partner at grieving? How do you form an answer? We're about to focus on Project 5: avoiding the widespread re/marital hazard of blocked grief. Single parents and courting co-parents like you and your ex mates profit greatly by becoming *good grief* experts. Doing so benefits your and your descendents' wholistic healths and happiness. The next chapter will tell you how well your caregivers, teachers, and society taught you about good-grief basics. The following chapter offers a framework you can use to _ identify and _ thaw any frozen mourning in your stepfamily's adults and kids. Could any of you be "frozen" now? Many (most?) divorced and re/married people seem to be.

Do you need to reduce any discomfort before continuing? Do you know who's leading your inner family right now? Who is answering?

Project 5A) Learn Good-Grief Basics

This chapter exists because of our toxic national denial that we adults need to understand attachments, losses, and healthy grieving concepts. This denial and related ignorances powerfully contribute to our national pandemic of divorce and other ills. Have you ever attended a lecture or course on *effective mourning, grief and your wholistic health*, or *how to make a pro-grief home*? Has your partner? Did your parents?

To rouse your interest here, I propose that (1) the length and quality of your and your kids' lives are directly proportional to how well you each know how to grieve, and (2) If you're blocked in grieving, you probably won't know it or what to do about it. Notice your reaction . . .

True story: Philip and Sharon had lived well together for 17 years. They had four children, and were a close, loving family. At 47, Sharon developed a malignant tumor. She died a year later at home, surrounded by her sorrowing family. Phil fell into a deep depression, and gratefully accepted the compassionate support of friends and relatives. The youngest children mourned in their own ways. The oldest son Jason appeared remarkably steady, and often helped the others while excelling in high school.

Three years later Phil remarried a lovely divorced woman. Janice and her two daughters moved into his home, making a high-energy household of eight. Janice had known Sharon and their family from their church. She empathized that her stepkids found it hard to have her "replace" their mother, especially in their own home, so she worked to include Sharon's spirit and memory in their stepfamily life.

On the anniversary of Sharon's death, Janice made a special family dinner. Phil and her stepkids reminisced about things they had all loved about her. Janice suggested they all go to the cemetery to honor and share remembrance of Sharon. All agreed but Jason. He had eaten very little, and had been unusually quiet. He snapped at his younger stepsister rudely in a way that no one had seen before.

Despite repeated invitations of friendship and attempts at support, Jason maintained a cool distance from his stepmother over the next several years. He began to drink and smoke heavily at college, and his grades declined. He sharply maintained "*Nothing* is wrong!" Jason always found reasons to be absent from the annual meal celebrating his mother. He never visited his mother's grave, and would change the subject or leave if conversation focused on her. He grew sullen and isolated, and scornfully refused suggestions of professional help.

The young man became rude and sarcastic with his stepmother and stepsisters. He pointedly ignored them when he came home, despite his father's requests, then demands, for courtesy and respect. Janice gradually lost patience with Jason's behavior, and admitted her hurt and growing resentment. She became protective of her two daughters around this stepson, which began to split their young stepfamily.

Philip felt torn and confused. Caught in a classic stepfamily loyalty conflict (p. 186), he began to blame Janice for being "immature" and "insensitive." His drinking began to increase. Even when Jason was away at college, mention of him often provoked blame, defensiveness, resentment, anger, and fighting in their home. No one had a clear idea what to do about this.

Things came to a head on their fourth stepfamily Thanksgiving. Jason had had too much to drink by dinner, and blew up at Janice in front of the family. He screamed, "*You don't belong here! You never did! This is* <u>my mother's</u> *house, not yours!"* He raged at his father, face distorted, *"You betrayed us, Dad! Betrayed* <u>me</u>*! You're a coward and a traitor! How could you get married so soon? How dare you bring them to live here? How could you* do *that to Mom?"*

Everyone was stunned: Jason had never said a word to anyone about his cauldron of feelings about his mother's death and father's remarriage. His avoiding the agony of truly saying *goodbye* to his mother and birthfamily, and denying his avoidance, had brewed a major re/marital and stepfamily crisis. His blocked grief prevented him from accepting relationships with Janice and her daughters for four years, through no fault of theirs. Jason's rejections had repeatedly forced his father to choose between him and his new wife and stepdaughters. Phil's indecisions and mixed messages had hurt and outraged Jason beyond words. His grief had "frozen," and the adults had not understood his many signals. The awful holiday explosion began Jason's real mourning, and improved the odds of their stepfamily's full bonding.

This intense loyalty conflict with Philip "in the middle" had manifested in a pair of contentious relationship triangles: Jason as *persecutor* (blamer), and his father and Janice alternated between being the *victim* and the *rescuer*. There was a dynamic web of other loyalty conflicts and triangles too, as each of the other five kids took sides. All eight adults and kids experienced surges of major *inner* conflicts and confusions among their groups of polarized subselves.

If Philip and his first wife had divorced, this story would have been similar and more complex. Jason would have resisted accepting the reality and finality of his parents' divorce, and the shattering of his fantasy of birthfamily reunion. This resistance would have hindered his growing a cordial, respectful relationship with his stepmother Janice and his two stepsisters. That would promote her increasing resentment and frustration and her pulling away from Jason, just as it did here. Her withdrawal would foster major inner and outer loyalty conflicts with her husband, increasingly stressing their re/marriage.

This common post-divorce dynamic is even more complex and tense when one or both ex mates and/or several sibs and relatives can't mourn their losses well. When several members of a stepfamily are blocked in grieving major broken bonds, significant personal and relationship tensions (surface "problems") result.

Why This Fifth Project?

Human life is rich with emotional attachments (bonds), and chosen or forced broken bonds (losses). Nature endows us each with a built-in psycho-spiritual healing reflex: *grief.* **Every** re/marriage and multi-home **stepfamily is based on two or three sets of major losses** from...
+ (Probably) low childhood nurturance: e.g. losses of emotional security, normal psychological development, self esteem, and wholistic health; and...
+ Biofamily separation and divorce, or the death of a spouse; and complex family reorganization (changes); and...
+ Parental re/marriage, cohabiting, and complex extended-biofamily mergers.

Typical co-parents (like you?) have neither the training nor the wish to fully identify their losses from these, and/or evaluate their grieving progress. This is specially true amidst courtship excitement and dreams of a new love. **Four factors can combine to block** divorcing and re/marrying people from **healthy mourning**:
+ Distrustful, short-sighted false selves trying to protect us from pain;
+ Inhibitions learned in childhood against feeling and expressing anger, confusion, and despair; and...
+ Our media-induced American idealizing and obsessively seeking "the *good* life;" which all combine to...
+ Promote *unawareness* among your family members and supporters of what you're about to read.

Frozen grief can slow or stop personal growth, and the healthy bonding of a new couple and stepfamily. It fosters chronic sickness or depression, addictions, obesity, "endless" rage or sadness, ongoing hostility between ex-spouses, promiscuity, repeated law-breaking or school troubles, and divorce. My research and experience suggests that blocked grief plays a major role in America's ~50% first-divorce rate, and has a lot to do with our billion-dollar "depression" industry.

To prepare you partners to assess whether you or any important others are blocked in grieving, **this chapter provides** . . .

+ What average co-parents need to know about bonding, losses, and healthy three-level grieving. The checklist below will help you assess your own knowledge now;

+ Summaries of the emotional, mental, and spiritual phases of healthy mourning;

+ An outline of six ingredients needed for healthy grieving; and . . .

+ Perspective on why typical people from low nurturance childhoods have trouble grieving. In my experience, this seems to apply to many divorced and/or re/married adults, their minor and grown kids, and sometimes close kin like grandparents.

The next chapter uses these good-grief basics to describe six steps you partners can take to spot and free up blocked grief in your stepfamily adults and kids. These two chapters and their supporting materials aim to help you _ develop good-grief *awareness*, and _ pro-grief homes and family environments. Co-parents working at this vital two-part project together will learn how blocked mourning can seriously hinder their wholistic healths and forming new step-relationship bonds.

I propose that **the three taproots of typical blocked grief are** _ significant false-self dominance and related emotional numbing and denials, plus _ lay and clinical ignorance of good-grief basics and blockage symptoms, plus _ ineffective thinking and communication among family members and supporters. What do you think? Projects 1, 2, and this one (5) aim to empower you to reduce all three of these.

Reality check: see if these two chapters are relevant to you by interviewing the subselves who rule you. See how aware

they are about "good grief." T = true, F = false, and ? means "I'm not sure, or "it depends on . . .":

1) I can now clearly describe _ the three levels of healthy grief, and _ the specific phases that comprise each phase. (T F ?)

2) I _ know how to grieve my losses thoroughly and well on all three levels, and _ I always do so. (T F ?)

3) I can clearly describe the factors that determine whether _ a home or _ extended family is "pro-grief" or not. (T F ?)

4) I can _ name at least five of the common symptoms of blocked grief now, and I _ know clearly what to do about them. (T F ?)

5) I know _ what a "grieving *policy*" is, and I _ can describe mine clearly now. (T F ?)

6) I'm pretty clear on how _ my partner, _ ex mate/s, and _ each of our living parents would answer each of these five questions now. (T F ?)

7) My partner and I have already evaluated whether blocked grief is a significant hazard in our (potential) stepfamily. (T F ?)

8) I'm content that the young people in my life _ accurately know good-grief basics, and _ are healthy-enough grievers now. (T F ?)

9) I feel comfortable _ reading about grieving, and __ discussing how it applies to our adults and kids with all of them. (T F ?)

10) I understand the probable connection between false-self dominance and blocked grief, and __ I can describe this clearly to other people now. (T F ?)

11) My true Self is answering these questions now. (T F ?)

How many typical divorcing and re/wedding co-parents do you think could answer "true" to most of these? How many family-professionals could? For a Web version of these questions, see http://sfhelp.org/05/grief-quiz.htm.

Awarenesses . . .

Good-grief Basics

Let's start by building a grief vocabulary. As you review definitions for *attachment (bond), loss, mourning, and grief policy,* think of the kids and other key people in your personal life. Could they accurately define each of these?

Our Emotional-Spiritual Bonds (*Attachments*)

A *bond* **is** an adult or child's person's emotional/spiritual caring for, and sustained interest in, something precious. The something may be a prized relationship with a living thing or group, an object, a role ("I *love* being the first-chair violin!"), a freedom, an idea or dream, a beloved ritual, a physical place, or an emotional state. A bond is not a dependency, but may cause one. For example, a physiological craving for sugar, fat, nicotine, or alcohol is not a bond. Compulsive eaters or drinkers can become bonded to the ritual of obtaining and ingesting those chemicals, and to the short-term emotional-physical high from doing so. "I need you" may or may not include ". . . and I care deeply for and about you." Feeling *used* is a sign of being needed but not cared for.

Your bonds grow naturally over time or they don't, depending on many factors. One key factor is whether or not the bonder gets consistent comfort, pleasure, and satisfaction from the bonding "thing." As you know, our emotional-spiritual attachments range from weak and transitory to intense and life-long. Healthy parental and marital bonds are among the strongest in the relationship world. Fear-based dependencies can *feel* like bonds. Wounded people in *enmeshed* (boundary-less) relationships can feel bonded. ("Norman is like a part of me.")

Some divorcers feel a genuine caring and concern (vs. love) for their ex mate for many years after an unhappy marriage and a bitter divorce struggle. Others feel nothing (indifference). Most minor kids of divorce (i.e. some subselves) fight to preserve the bond with their *dream* of parental and family reunion, against all real-life evidence. Our primary bonds are emotional and spiritual, not logical. Is that your experience?

The time needed to attach may be hours or many years. Special events like births, anniversaries, graduations, refusals, deaths, certain phone calls or letters, traumas, and awards can imbue seemingly mundane objects with high emotional significance: think of your own most cherished mementos. Our most prized friendship-bonds often take many years of shared experiences to develop. Some people may live or work together for years, and form no significant emotional bond at all. Or one partner may bond while the other doesn't. Apartment or office wall-mates may never know or care who's on the other side.

Typical courting co-parents (like you?) fantasize together about building a closely-bonded stepfamily home, and maybe a web of growing attachments among all potential steprelatives. Re/marriers are often disappointed, because some or many of their stepfamily members don't develop mutual appreciation, enjoyment, caring, empathy, trust, and respect ("good chemistry"). Members who don't like or accept this stepfamily reality may try to pretend or force bonding for various reasons. That usually signals a false self is ruling and *hinders* step-member bonding. On the brighter side, some stepfamily relationships evolve into prized lifelong friendships. Like amateur photographs, it's hard to predict whether any pair of steppeople will "turn out well" (bond mutually) over time. Courtship politeness is *not* a good predictor.

Most humans and many other animals seem to come ready-made with this marvelous, vexing ability to selectively grow emotional-spiritual bonds. Research suggests that our life-long personal and social welfare is primally shaped by the constancy and quality of our infantile attachment to our main caregiver, usually Mom. Infants deprived of this essential attachment may survive, but often don't *thrive* and develop their full wholistic potentials.

I've evolved a strong bias from my clinical experience and 15 years of personal recovery from major ancestral neglect. It is that very young children deprived of this primal nurturing attachment often develop significant psychological wounds (Project 1). We suffer repeated personal and relationship failures and inhibitions that affect our core values, expectations, choices, and goals. One of these wounds is a crippled or undeveloped ability to bond. Do you know any people who are *emotionally unavailable, self-centered, cold, insensitive,* and *heartless*?

Barbra Streisand poignantly sings, "People who *need* people are the luckiest people in the world." From early-childhood neglect and terror, some psychologically-wounded people literally don't know *how* to bond with (genuinely care about) other people. They live frantic, false, or apathetic, empty lives, *and have little to grieve.*

Do you know anyone who expresses love by giving material things? Do *sociopath, self-centered, loner, egotistical,* and *Narcissism* take on new meanings here? Some psychiatrists diagnose such people as having *Reactive Attachment Disorder* (RAD). There are several Web sites and a national association (ATTACh) currently devoted to it. Use your favorite search engine to find them if they affect your inner family and life.

The blessing of being able to bond carries a price tag. It is that across our years, our bonds *break*, and we need to heal.

Losses: Broken Bonds

A *loss* **is** any sudden or foreseen, voluntary or involuntary change in or ending of, a significant emotional/spiritual bond. Dr. Jack Tilmon (Chapter 7) suffered a set of sudden massive emotional losses when his biofather left him and his mother at age six. Jack's second wife Sarah had survived agonizing psychological losses from her early sexual abuse, and related family-nurturance deprivations before and after that.

I suspect that neither of these good people had ever either acknowledged or grieved their respective losses. They had been living in personal, re/marital, and stepfamily distress partially because of that. Their loss-denials and blocked mourning *unconsciously* created an "anti-grief" household policy that will probably numb young Patty McLean until she gets help in adulthood. I also suspect her father Ted's reported alcoholism was a false-self strategy to self-medicate *his* major ungrieved losses, shame, and guilt.

We experience *positive* **losses too**: tangible and invisible endings that bring us relief, comfort, security, and joy. *Celebration* is the flip side of grieving: a chance to proclaim, affirm, and enjoy a positive ending. We celebrate _ completing a circle around the sun with a birthday or New Year's party; _ ending a long school effort with a graduation ceremony; _ ending a hospital stay with thank you's, goodbyes, hellos, hugs and grins. I can't think of anyone who suffers from "frozen celebration" syndrome, though some wounded people do have trouble *feeling* genuine pleasure or joy. The clinical name for that is *anhedonia*.

Note the difference between *loss* **and** *change*. Any shift in our mental, emotional, spiritual, and physical balances is a *change*. We spend much of our lives trying to keep our inner and outer balances because of the ceaseless changes in our inner and outer worlds. A change may or may not cause a significant *loss*. For example, as the seasons change slowly, or the price of eggs goes up unexpectedly, you probably *adjust* your clothing and eating patterns without significant emotional agony unless you're an omelette-aholic.

If your child, minister, counselor, or a good friend moves away, you *adjust* your worship, personal growth, and social behaviors, and you *grieve* the rupture of your prized relationship bonds with her or him. Kids and adults have *many* things to adjust to and many things to mourn, when their biofamily separates and divorces. Childless adults have *many* changes to adjust to and a complex set of losses to grieve, when they commit to live with a bioparent and their clan of kids and relatives. Moving out of your home and into someone else's always causes mixes of changes, losses, and gains for everyone.

Grieving (Mourning)

Grieving and *mourning* both refer to the natural multi-phase, (mental + spiritual + emotional) process that allows accepting and adapting to a major broken attachment, over time. **Healing** from a loss means "to move through the phases of all three grief levels (below) to reach stable genuine (vs. pseudo) acceptance." Healthy grieving allows us losers to _ eventually regain our stable inner balance, and _ frees up our psychic energy to form new bonds. Without enough of six factors (below), this healing process can be slowed or blocked in adults and kids. **Blocked grief** is serious psychological constipation. It promotes a wide range of mental, emotional, physical, and relationship problems, until freed up and allowed to complete.

Many unaware people associate grieving only with the death of a loved one. They don't consciously appreciate the many other types of broken bonds around them that need the same kind of grief healing, empathy, and support.

Grieving Policies

From our earliest years, we each grow complex semi-conscious *policies* about bonding and grieving values, norms, and behaviors. A policy is a set of conscious and unconscious rules and values (shoulds, oughts, and musts) that people, families, organizations, and societies use to shape their choices, tolerances, and actions. Most adults' personal policies about bonding and grieving are strongly influenced by perceptions of their early caregivers' attaching and mourning behaviors vs. their words.

These may have been nurturing (pro-grief) or toxic (grief-inhibiting). Have you ever identified your own semi-conscious values and policies about bonding, and mourning your broken bonds? See p. 297 for a sample family good-grief policy.

What You Need to Know About *Losses*

Grieving effectively yourself, and giving meaningful comfort to a grieving adult or child, depends partly on your understanding the nature of our inevitable broken bonds. Here's some perspective on that.

A lost "thing" can be physical (tangible) or invisible. Usually, biofamily separations and parental re/marriage and cohabiting each create complex sets of tangible and invisible losses for kids and adults. It's often much easier for us to identify physical things we miss, like prized mementos, homes, people, and pets, than invisible things like lost dreams, hopes, freedoms, abilities, youth, health, personal identity, roles, and relationships. Invisible losses range from minor to massive, and need the same three-level mourning that our tangible losses do. Did you know that?

The breaking of a bond **can be gradual or sudden, and foreseen or unexpected**. The loss of childhood innocence, security, and self-esteem may come from one massive trauma, or over a period of months or years. The agonizing loss of a beloved adult's personality and self-sufficiency from progressive Alzheimer's disease occurs over years. Sudden losses, even positive ones like winning the lottery, usually cause emotional and mental disorientation ("shock").

Expected losses are less shocking *if* awareness of them is gradual. Imagining a future loss and actually experiencing it may feel very different. Does an example come to mind? The loss of youthful agility and abilities is gradual and foreseen. The losses that erupt when a mate comes home to find an unexpected "goodbye" note, and perhaps key belongings and/or kids gone, is traumatizing. Most divorces and stepfamily household mergers each create complex sets of expected and unexpected losses for everyone, including bonded siblings, relatives, and friends.

Foreseeing losses lets us do *anticipatory* **mourning**, if we're not emotionally numbed out or over-distracted. We "process" (experience waves of) the anger and sadness, and regain mental clarity, before the loss actually happens. When it does, we may actually feel relief and release from the dread we've carried ("closure"). People unaware of anticipatory grief may mistakenly assume that such a veteran mourner is *uncaring, cold,* or *insensitive.* Except for their son Jason, Philip and Sharon and their kids and supporters began their grieving when they first learned the diagnosis of her imminent death.

Losses often come in clusters, so mourning one of a related group of physical and invisible losses may still leave other broken bonds to process and accept.

The importance of a given bond to a griever, and the impact of breaking it, **can range from minor to massive.** Massive loss-clusters may take many years to heal before *enough* stable (mental + emotional + spiritual + physical) balance returns.

The emotional impact of concurrent losses can add up. An adult or child may not have had one massive loss, but still feel overwhelmed by many small current losses and changes. A job promotion (usually a positive loss), a painful tooth infection, a crucial bounced check, and running out of gas are all individually-manageable losses of personal equilibrium. Their cumulative emotional effect in a single day can be greater than any one of them. Remember the last "bad hair" day you had?

Broken bonds can have immediate and long-term effects. So grieving is typically not a smooth process, and may not feel truly complete for months or years. For instance, Jack Tilmon re-experienced (muffled) surges of old anger and deep sadnesses over the long-past desertion of his father when he married, divorced, conceived each child (specially his son Roger), and on most Father's Days. The common phenomenon of "anniversary depression" (i.e. cyclic, recurring grief) testifies to the real length of our primal three-level mourning process.

People may process a group loss differently because personalities and the intensities of their emotional attachments differ. Thus the death of a family pet may devastate a child for weeks, and cause only passing sorrow in a sibling or their caregivers. Unaware adults promote shame, guilt, and anxiety in a griever by assuming that the other person should mourn like they do ("You should be over that, by now!"). And . . .

Well-mourned losses enable forming new bonds. Normal grief diverts personal motivation and physical-emotional energy from other life activities, over time. As we really *accept* our losses on all three grief-levels, that energy is freed to invest in new emotional-spiritual attachments. This is why some new stepfamily members seem "cool" or "detached" from each other, specially stepparents and stepkids. A stepchild that seems to ignore a kind new stepparent may not have grieved what s/he needs to, and *can't* emotionally bond with the newcomer. This is a central reason for co-parent Project 5, and what you'll read in the next chapter.

Staying consciously aware of these loss "basics" can help you feel appropriate compassion and empathy for yourself and other mourners. Your knowledge also provides a foundation for forming a pro-grief policy in your home. Do your kids know these realities about bonds and losses? Does your current or past mate? Do your parents? All of them can profit from getting clearer on bonding, losses, and our three-level mourning process.

See how many of these "Good Grief" basics you already know:

What *Is* "Good (Healthy Three-level) Grief"?

Breaking significant emotional-spiritual bonds interrupts the rhythm, focus, and harmony of kids' and adults' inner and outer lives. I believe that every newborn has the innate abilities to bond, accept losses, and re-bond. Typical grievers experience emotional, mental, and (perhaps) spiritual changes as they mourn. Let's look more closely at your three grief levels and the phases that comprise them:

Level 1: Phases of *Emotional* Mourning

The media and tradition cause most people to assume this is the *only* level of grieving. British researcher John Bowlby documented that young children's grief over a multi-day separation from their biological mother has three emotional stages: protest, despair, and detachment (numbness and uncaring). Dr. Elizabeth Kubler-Ross has studied and written widely on reactions to the death of a loved one. The five (emotional) phases of mourning that she proposes are widely accepted, and apply to *any* broken bond to a physical or invisible thing. She suggests that people who are able to bond all experience . . .

- Shock (emotional/mental disorientation) >
- Distorted or "magic" thinking >
- Anger or rage >
- Deep sadness or despair >
- Acceptance

Phase 1) The **shock** of an unexpected loss can include _ hysteria (loss of Self-leadership, and inner-family chaos) or _ mental disorientation or _ unusually clear mental focusing, and _ temporary protective emotional numbness. This instinctive mourning reflex is particularly intense and long-lasting if the loss is unexpected (e.g. a flood, fire, murder, car wreck, stroke, or tornado), and the broken bonds are deep and/or many at once. When *foreseen* losses actually occur, they may not evoke this grief phase at all, or only a mild version.

Phase 2) "Magic thinking" may include some or all of these: _ *denial* ("This isn't really happening!"); _ *irrational bargaining* or *pleading* with a person or Higher Power ("I really will stop my addiction now, so *please* bring back my mate / job / legal freedom / reputation / health . . ."); _ *fantasizing:* "I know that someone or something will restore what I've lost!" and/or _ *withdrawing* from reality: being emotionally "not there" (false-self dominance).

This second emotional grief phase may last a few minutes, a day, or recur periodically over days or weeks. It may manifest as temporary "strange behavior" like mumbling, praying, "sleeping a lot," spacing out ("daydreaming"), disorientation, experiencing the lost thing vividly, and so on.

Phase 3) Anger and *rage* about a loss may feel "free floating" (have no focus), or may be "irrationally" aimed at one's self, another person, Fate, God, prior situations, "laws," the "government," and/or other specific or vague targets. If a mourner learned to repress anger as a child, or to feel scared or guilty about feeling or expressing anger in public (or at all), s/ he'll have a hard time allowing this vital grief phase to happen and complete. Do you know anyone like this?

Many wounded kids and adults have trouble feeling and/or expressing intense anger. They have to learn how to be constructively angry *without guilt, shame, or anxiety* as a part of their recovery from a low-nurturance childhood. Other people need to learn how to restore Self-control over impulsive rage outbursts (dominant subselves) which hurt other people, relationships, and things.

Such people can seem stuck in this *anger* phase of grieving. They're labeled as "sitting on a lot of anger," having "explosive tempers" and "rage attacks," or being "difficult," "an angry person," or "rageaholic." Does "road rage" take on a new perspective now? If overdone, the Christian value of meekness and admonition to "turn the other cheek" risks (false-selves) repressing *healthy* anger and assertion. Were you praised as a child for feeling and expressing anger *constructively*? Have you congratulated your kids for doing this? ("Marcy, I am *so* proud of how you choose to express your anger!")

Phase 4) The best-known emotional mourning phase is *sadness* and apathy, perhaps flavored with despair (loss of hope). This phase and shock are why losses *hurt*. Each child and adult has their own way of feeling and expressing their *sorrow*, and their own pace for that. Some may "get over it" quickly, and others slowly. I believe the symptoms of this grief phase are often mislabeled as "depression." My bias is that many people taking medicine or "treatment" for depression are survivors of low childhood nurturance who really need informed help accepting early and recent losses, and restoring

their Self to inner leadership. I know of no research that validates this, so far.

By the way, medical research reveals that tears of happiness differ chemically from tears of pain, because the latter
contain compounds that cause depression and stress. By shed-
ding these chemicals, crying is one of our body's natural ways
of re-balancing from great (neuro-chemical) upset. Blocking
the natural urge to weep *stresses* us! Were you encouraged or
praised for crying, as a young child? Have you encouraged
your kids to weep? Remember your last *good* (vs. a *bad*) cry?
Have they experienced you crying without guilt or anxiety?
Can you describe your childhood and current families' policies on crying?

Phase 5) Acceptance. Three-level mourning usually has
no clear black/white ending point. As we move through the
four phases above, we eventually reach a state of stable *emotional* acceptance of our loss and its impacts on our life. Our
anger, despair, sadness, and apathy gradually lift, energy returns, and we resume our life goals and activities *if* we've
mourned on the other two levels. Our *sadness* may recur, specially when life reminds us (e.g. on anniversaries) of a cherished bond that we'll never experience again.

You and your loved ones can move through these four or
five emotional stages in order, skip one or several phases for a
while, or may move back and forth between them over time.
There is no right way to progress, other than "natural." Your
unique ancestral rules, social experiences, and inner teams of
subselves create your own mourning style. Expecting or demanding that another person grieve "right" (*my* way) is inherently futile, toxic, and disrespectful. It usually signals personal
(false-self) discomfort with the griever's behaviors, and/or lack
of true empathy.

While emotional grief is progressing in your "heart," (brain
and glands) what needs to happen "in your head"? It's easy to
overlook or minimize this vital process:

Level 2: Phases of *Mental* Mourning

People free to mourn gradually shift from mental chaos
(inner-family uproar) to stable clarity on key questions like
these:
+ "What have I lost, specifically?"
+ "Is it really gone for good?"
+ "How and why did my loss/es happen?"
+ "Could I or others have prevented it?"
+ "Why did this (loss) happen to me?
+ "Why did this (loss) happen now?"
+ "What does this loss *mean*: how will it affect me?"
+ "How will this loss impact others I care about? Will they
     be OK enough?"
+ "Can I replace my loss/es? How?"
+ "At what cost or risk?"
+ "Do I (all my subselves) want to do this?"
+ "When?"
+ "What support do I need to accept my loss/es?"
Recall the last major loss you experienced. Do you recall
inner questions like these? Have you experienced kids asking
them?
Mental grief progresses through four phases: _ cognitive chaos, when the loss is first experienced or perceived; _
questions like those above emerge and become distinct; and _
trial answers are formed and reality-tested, partly depending
on the perceived feelings and behaviors of others affected by
the loss; and the answers are accepted or recycled. Eventually
_ the inner and outer worlds stabilize enough (or don't), no
new questions emerge, and the answers to most loss-related
questions feel stable and credible enough. This promotes emotional and spiritual *acceptance*. Distraction-free times and empathic listening by others (vs. advice) can promote "getting
clear" on these questions and their answers.
Moving through these four mental phases, and observing
the post-loss world to understand "how things are now," takes
time. You and your kids may "complete" this grieving level as

fast as the slowest of the other grievers you care about. If others don't display how they're progressing with the impact of shared losses, it can delay *your* processing. If a child is anxious how a parent or sibling is doing after a cluster of divorce or re/marriage losses, and the other person is stuck in some part of their grief, the child must adapt to living with ongoing anxiety about the other person. Young kids don't have the concepts or vocabulary to express what they feel and need. Often their sibling, relative, or parent doesn't either.

Aware, grief-savvy co-parents can patiently help young mourners and each other answer these questions over time. Suggestions usually help mourners more than "right answers," even with young kids. Having no clear, credible answers to questions like those above can block the final emotional grief step of acceptance. Consciously acknowledging and accepting realities about big loss clusters can take a long time, because they can be so painful ("I'll *never* have my birthday again the way we used to do it!").

Some wounded people, specially males, have Guardian subselves who ceaselessly protect against feared emotional overwhelm. Such people may over-focus on this mental side of grieving their losses without *feeling* anything. They over-analyze ("analysis paralysis") or intellectualize, in order to not feel the shock, rage, sadness, guilt, and despair. Doing this unconsciously blocks full grief, for we losers need to think *and* feel!

As you or a loved one move through these emotional and mental grief phases, you or they may or may not need to progress through . . .

Level 3: Phases of *Spiritual* Mourning

In a seminar I led for divorced and separated Catholics, a father in his 40s spoke for many in the group. He said "There is *absolutely* a spiritual side to grieving. When I divorced, I totally lost my faith in a loving God. I felt alone on a *soul* level: totally abandoned, angry, and scared. Now, some years later, my faith has returned, and is even stronger. In an odd way, my divorce was a long-term blessing."

This third level of grieving is vital when a loser needs to **grow or re-stabilize their spiritual attitudes and beliefs** to fully *accept* a cluster of broken bonds. This is necessary when there are no credible answers to the mental loss-questions above, ("I can't explain why I married an addict.") We're left to rely on faith for solace, acceptance, hope, and the courage to go on. Like the emotional and mental levels, spiritual grief can't be forced or willed. Spiritual mourning can be specially helpful in accepting losses that "make no sense," and could not have been prevented.

You've probably met people who couldn't reconcile the reality of a cruel, "senseless" loss (like marital and biofamily breakup, premature death, murder, or child abuse) with the idea of a truly loving, compassionate God. Their spiritual faith and resilience had fractured, depriving them of a core inner and social resource for healing from major losses, including those from childhood.

Other grievers discover a new awareness of, and reassurance from, a "higher Self," Higher Power, or Guardian Angel, as they move through their rebalancing process a day at a time. Such spiritual sources help provide significant meaning, comfort, and *hope* in the hard journey toward full emotional and mental acceptance, regaining hope and purpose, and moving on.

So I suggest that *good* (healthy, complete) *grief* occurs when a child or grownup moves through these phases to reach _ stable emotional *acceptance* of, _ mental clarity about, and _ spiritual serenity with, their physical and invisible losses. Each of your loved one's unique needs, traits, experiences, perceptions, and environments determine if and how this completion occurs and how long it takes. Because mourning involves mind, body, and spirit our conscious mind (our *will*) can't hurry the process. However . . .

Healthy grieving in a child or adult *can* be unconsciously slowed or blocked, when one or more of these factors are absent *too much* . . .

Six Requisites for Healthy Mourning

To promote full loss-acceptance, rebalancing, and new bonding (*good* grief) in our lives and homes, I believe we kids and adults need all of these factors in our lives, consistently. See what you think . . .

1) Conscious awareness of _ our specific invisible and tangible losses; their main personal impacts on _ us and _ key loved ones; and of _ our natural three-level grieving process. These awarenesses allow us to *vent*: i.e. to clearly tell our grief story over and over again to any empathic listeners we're blessed with. If you can't _ name your tangible and invisible losses and _ what they *mean* to you, you don't have this ingredient yet.

2) Enough confidence about growing through and beyond our losses, based on knowledge, experience, and faith. "Enough" is a subjective judgment. Do you trust this natural three-level process to heal your own losses well enough? Do each of the people you care about? How do you know?

3) Commitment to healthy grieving as a personal priority, without excess anxiety or guilt.

4) Enough inner and outer supports: i.e. genuine _ inner-family and _ social permissions and encouragements to grieve thoroughly at our own pace. I believe that ignorance of healthy grief factors and too few accessible or accepted supports are probably the biggest causes of blocked grief. The latter seems to be based on widespread psychological wounds.

5) Enough undistracted solitudes to _ feel and _ vent anger and sadness, again and again, while we meditate, sort out, and _ evolve our mental clarities and rebuild spiritual trust; and . . .

6) Enough time, patience, and courage to *feel* the recurring waves of rage, confusion, regret, guilt, and sorrow; *express* them; and progress through them toward stable three-level acceptance.

Pause and reflect. Would you change this menu of good-grief ingredients? I suggest that the more these six factors are present consistently, the more likely it is that a child or adult will spontaneously move through fully mourning their shattered bonds. What do you think? Could you have named all six of these before reading them? They can be part of your good-grief policy (p. 297).

I believe that Jack and Sarah Tilmon and young Patty McLean (Chapter 7), didn't know what you just read, and had lacked these six factors. Each adult had clear symptoms of blocked grief, and the false-self dominance that usually underlies it. I believe this contributed to Sarah's needs for mood-control medication, sugar, and fat; being addicted to eating and her (co-dependent) relationship, and being overweight and guilty. All these promoted her low self esteem, aggravated by her husband's patronizing criticisms.

Before exploring why typical co-parents and their kids often lack too many of these six factors, let's learn more about each of them . . .

Naming Our Losses and Their Impacts

It helps you and your loved ones grieve if you can identify and describe (express) _ your tangible and invisible losses, and _ your related *feelings*, clearly and specifically. It also helps if you can _ say clearly how each significant broken bond affects your inner and outer lives. These conscious awarenesses help you to sort out, discuss, and vent about your losses, answer your mental questions, and eventually accept them and move on.

In this chapter's opening story, I suspect young Jason couldn't name the set of major losses he experienced from his mother's death, or the new ones from his father's remarriage. Even if he had internally identified the *impacts* of these sets of losses on his life, his false self had prohibited venting his thoughts, feelings and needs about his losses to family members, for years. The terror some of his subselves felt about allowing him to experience his grief rage and despair was overwhelming. Some family-systems theorists would say he (his false self) unconsciously took on his whole family's grief over his mother's death and father's remarriage, and his subselves felt duty-bound not to dishonor it or let it (her) go.

To be able and willing to name our losses, we must accept that *loss* and *grieving* have to do with a far wider range of broken bonds than someone's death. Our appliance-free pioneering ancestors depended on daily *action* (work) to survive. Many hadn't the luxury or encouragement to meditate or take "quiet times," and had practical reasons for minimizing losses other than deaths. Even when we understand the full range of our losses, we usually find it easier to name those that are tangible. Broken *invisible* bonds, like lost trust, security, respect, freedom, love, and hope, are much easier to minimize or ignore. Did your early caregivers ever talk about, or grieve, losing these?

With this wide-angle perspective and the desire to grieve well, kids and adults like you can become adept at naming their tangible and abstract losses before or after they occur. It may be a tougher challenge to identify the inner and social *impacts* of key losses. Here, an *impact* means a shift in the griever's inner and/or outer worlds that s/he judges to be "significant." Some loss impacts are more obvious than others. A grieving husband can easily see "Since Marla told me she doesn't love me and moved out with our son, I've lost my appetite, I sleep poorly, and I'm having a hard time staying focused at work."

It takes much more self-awareness for the same man to think or say "I'm suddenly less secure about where my life is going, my self-esteem has taken a major hit, and I'm battered by guilt-attacks and anger about the pain and anxiety our son is feeling. I suddenly distrust God . . . No, I'm *enraged* at Him, and I feel really guilty, anxious, and confused about that. I'm emotionally chaotic all the time and feeling crazy, I'm drinking too much, and I'm isolating socially, so I'm missing support I need because I'm so ashamed. I feel like a total failure as a man, a father, a husband, and a son."

Most minor kids and psychologically wounded adults usually need patient encouragement and empathic guidance on clearly identifying their key losses, and what they *mean*. How many pre-teens do you know who could say something like:

"Since my Mom remarried and we moved into my stepdad's house, I've lost clarity on who I am, who's in my family, and what the new house rules and their consequences are. I'm really confused about these, and feel anxious all the time. I don't know what I'm supposed to feel about my stepsister, so I avoid her. I'm afraid that I'm bad or wrong for doing that. Then I feel angry: I didn't *ask* for this! I'm often scared Mom's going to abandon me like my Dad has, and I feel guilty and ashamed for feeling that. I've also lost a lot of trust that I'll be safe and OK in the future as an adult, and that really scares me too. And nobody understands that I feel these things, and I can't talk to anyone about them because I'm scared they won't understand, or they'll say I'm weak, stupid, and weird." Do you know any *adults* who model this kind of self-awareness and articulation? (Easy does it!)

Losers whose Self leads their inner family need no formal grief training, any more than wholistically-healthy people need to understand their breathing, sleeping, or digestion. However, when grief gets blocked, the conscious knowledge of _ normal mourning dynamics and _ the common symptoms of blocked grief help us decide what's wrong, and how to fix it. Prospective and re/married stepfamily co-parents and their supporters all need at least clear knowledge of the symptoms of frozen grief to assess for it in this fifth pre-re/marital project. You'll learn about this in the next chapter.

For typical co-parents, getting clear on the differences and similarities of clinical depression and the sadness phase of normal mourning is useful. This clarity helps allay anxiety that "This (apathy, sorrow, and despair) will never end," and promotes getting appropriate supports.

Any caregiver or friend can help kids mourn major endings by helping them name their specific losses and the losses' impacts, and perhaps explaining the grief process in age-appropriate, factual terms. Did your caregivers do this for you? Neither Jack nor Sarah Tilmon's ancestors did, and they hadn't been able to do these for Patty, Roger, and Annie. This two-page worksheet can help you identify (name) someone's losses: http://sfhelp.org/05/physical-loss-inv.htm.

The second ingredient for *good grief* is . . .

Confidence in Surviving Losses and Intense Emotions

This grief resource is like the confidence we grow from experience that a stomach, head, or toothache *will* "go away;" and that skin cuts and broken bones will heal *automatically*, if we let them. Without similar faith that broken emotional bonds will eventually heal, the related rage and despair can feel literally paralyzing or fatal ("If I let myself get angry, I'll *kill* someone!" or "If I cry, I'll never stop!") Such fears (i.e. dominant fearful subselves) block our mourning process, even though our common sense and trusted others say "That's not true!" This is specially common for typical wounded people in denial like young Jason, and Jack and Sarah Tilmon.

Conscious confidence that our pain and sadness *will* subside, and new bonds *will* grow, nurtures patience and hope. It helps us endure grief's confusion, doubt, rage, sorrow, and despair. Key people around a griever who lack solid confidence in the healing process can be a powerful *external* block to good grief. Mates, relatives, or friends whose false-self wounds (e.g. numbing) have blocked mourning their searing childhood losses may have little reason to trust the grief process.

Once aware of the value of grief confidence, they (you) may need to rely on faith in human nature's restorative power, and in a potent, caring Higher Power. People in true recovery from inner wounds can add these faiths to borrowed confidence from respected grief "mentors."

Think of those you call "my family" one at a time. Do you think each is able to form bonds? Does each feel personal confidence in their ability to eventually adapt and rebalance from major or cluster losses? Did you include yourself?

The third requisite is . . .

Commitment to Doing *Good* Grief

What does *commitment* **mean** to you? I associate it with
consciously choosing to speak for and *act* on a core principle
or value, despite anxieties, discouragements, distractions, and
scorn. In contrast, an *obsession* or *compulsion* is not a conscious choice. Clear awareness of life losses and their impacts,
and firm faith in the three-level grief process, probably won't
help survivors of low childhood nurturance who aren't committed to their own wholistic health (self neglect). Do you know
any shame-based people who often put their needs and
wholistic health *last*? ("Mike nags me to see the dentist, but he
never goes.")

Many (most?) divorced and/or re/married co-parents like
Ted McLean and Sarah and Jack Tilmon are unrecovering,
shame-based people. Some widow/ers are too, specially those
whose mates sickened and died "early." They were taught as
kids to help others and devalue themselves, or be called *selfish*. By definition, people from high-nurturance childhoods have
internal and social permissions to develop and use these six
good-grief factors, *without anxiety, guilt, or shame.* Such *Grown
Nurtured Children* don't need to intentionally assess whether
or not they're committed to healthy mourning, or to discipline
themselves to "do it" as an important part of their wholistic
health. They grieve their broken bonds well instinctively, and
empathically encourage others to do the same.

Three-level grief seems to be partly instinctive and partly
conscious choice. Conscious mourning is *work*: e.g. going to
retreats, cemeteries, grief workshops, and/or therapy; reading
relevant books; meditating and/or journaling; discarding painful mementos; saying real or symbolic good-byes; and choosing to fully experience ("be in") uncomfortable feelings at the
moment. Doing these things takes awareness, commitment,
time, patience, support, and courage (below).

We mourners may or may not decide consciously how to
use our free times. You can invest time to reflect, feel, and realize, or you can semi-consciously *medicate* (distract) yourself

from the pain and confusion of loss with activities, substances or stimulation. In the long run, broken bonds heal better and faster if we give our grief-work, and that of close others, high priority and commitment. Do you agree? How you use your free times is one indicator of your grief priorities. Like other addicts, people who are "hustle-aholics" ("Type A's") are often governed by subselves frantically trying to avoid feeling and expressing their rage and deep sorrow from *many* major losses. So are people struggling with *mind churning*, whose thoughts and inner families are rarely quiet.

Our profit-minded American media ceaselessly glorifies *speed, youth, sex, stimulation (excitement), possessions,* and *fun.* We're persuaded incessantly to pursue these rather than to prize the six good-grief factors above. Recall the last commercial or billboard urging *"Enjoy life. Live longer. Take time to mourn!"?* Were your ancestors and early caregivers committed to practicing healthy mourning? Are *you* now?

Kids and adults who can name their losses and what they *mean,* and who trust and commit to healthy mourning, can still be blocked in accepting their broken bonds. What else do they need? The fourth vital *good-grief* ingredient is . . .

<u>Inner and Outer Encouragements to Mourn</u>

Because attachment and loss is so primal, every person and human group like you and your family evolve a set of *shoulds* and *musts* about how to "handle" them (think, feel, and act). The personal and social attitudes and values ("rules") that form our grief policies are conscious and unconscious. Some rules nourish healthy personal mourning, and others hinder or block it. We kids learn our grieving rules from personal hero/ines among our family, friends, church, schools, community, nation, and race. TV, sports, music, and fantasy heroes can powerfully model or inhibit *good* grief for kids and teens.

Do the Chicago Bears, Ninja Turtles, Barbie and Ken, GI Joe, Batman, Joan of Arc, Harry Potter, Madonna, Colin Powell,

Santa Claus, Abraham Lincoln, Captain Kirk, Led Zeppelin, Jesus, or the Masters of the Universe *have* losses? Obsess, vent, cry and rage? Meditate and journal? Get deeply sad and apathetic? Seek counseling? Who were your childhood hero/ines, and what did they teach you about bonding and mourning?

Let's look briefly at what "*inner* grief support" means:

Inner Permission to Grieve

Our dynamic thoughts, feelings, attitudes, values, and bodily functions form an invisible *inner* world. Most modern Westerners focus on our *outer* world, and ignore this bustling internal realm until some notable discomfort occurs. Part of our inner world's government is a "legislature" of subselves, which creates or imports and organizes our inner laws. All but sociopaths have an inner *Judge, Moralizer,* and/or *Perfectionist* who strive to apply and enforce our laws.

Some laws (shoulds, oughts, musts, and have to's) regulate if, how, and when we *feel* and *express* the marvelous range of our human emotions. Many people in or from low-nurturance childhoods have inner laws and stern *Judge* or *Critic* subselves that forbid _ feeling and _ expressing shock, anger or rage, sadness, and despair: the essentials of emotional grief. Other inner laws (beliefs) govern what we think and perceive.

Your core attitudes about strong emotions in yourself and other people may have crystallized by your fifth birthday. They silently shape your grieving behaviors via emotions and "inner voices" (thought streams). Your *inner* "laws" are probably somewhere between these basic beliefs:

Inner permissions: "It is always absolutely OK, safe, and good for me to fully _ *feel* and to _ *express* all intense emotions as they happen; to _ evolve clear, believable answers to all my questions about my invisible and physical losses and their impacts; and to _ take as long as I need to do these things every time I have a loss that's significant to me, *even if this causes other people discomfort*, without guilt, shame, or anxiety."

The other pole of our possible grief-belief spectrum is **inner inhibitions**: "It is *never* safe or acceptable for me to do these things privately or in public."

Between these two extremes is a wide range of possible un/conscious sub-rules like:

+ "It's OK for me to get angry, but *not* OK to cry;" or vice-versa.
+ "It's OK to cry, but only (alone / at night / in the car / silently . . .)." or
+ "Grieving is women's work." or
+ "I have to be strong (block my emotions) or (some person) will collapse."
+ "It's proper to *feel* anger and sorrow, but I selfishly burden others if I *show* them;"
+ "Grieving should take no longer than three or four weeks at the most."
+ "I'll never be able to cry."

Inner permissions and inhibitions that include *never* and *always* are specially powerful. They're examples of black/white (bipolar) thinking that suggests that a protective false self is in charge.

The good news is that you and your loved ones can chose to identify and replace inherited grieving inhibitions with healthy permissions, any time your ruling subselves choose to. You can also proactively model and teach kids in your life to forge their own clear (vs. vague or ambivalent) *inner* permissions for healthy mourning. Like teaching effective communication skills, this is a major, life-long gift!

Inner Encouragement

Think of the last time someone encouraged you, because they cared about you and wanted to help. What did they say or do? How did you feel? Can you imagine feeling the same compassion and motivation to help *yourself* move patiently through the difficult phases of healthy grief?

For each of the emotional, mental, and spiritual levels of grieving, what kind of thoughts would you choose that would significantly comfort you, and strengthen your commitment, patience, and courage? An inner-*permission* thought might be "I allow myself to evolve and practice my own unique way of grieving my life-losses effectively." Inner-*encouragement* thoughts might sound like "Sarah, why don't you block off an hour this afternoon to meditate and journal about the things you lost when you were molested? It would feel good to call Nina today, too, and just 'check in' with her. You know these are really more important than doing the laundry and cleaning the kitchen floor! Your long-term recovery really *counts*! You'll feel better if you these, and you'll have more patience for Patty (Chapter 7). Go ahead, Hon, and don't let Mom's misplaced guilt hook you, this time!"

Most of us, specially shame-based survivors of low childhood nurturance, routinely give ourselves *discouraging* self-talk. Another popular option is to get snarled in endless debates between two or more inner-family members:

"Go ahead and (take care of yourself)!"

"*NO*! It's too scary / selfish / expensive / shameful . . ."

"I know, but . . ."

Sound familiar?

With skilled help, the recovery process of "parts work," (*inner* family therapy), can identify subselves who hinder or block inner permission to grieve well, and can safely retrain them to become genuine supporters. See "Who's *Really* Running Your Life?" or ..01/ifs1-intro.htm.

Outer (Social) Permissions to Mourn

How do you feel around someone who's raging, weeping, or despairing? How is your tolerance, honestly, for someone who needs to rehash a loss-related saga in great detail, for the umpteenth time? If you can _ keep centered and calm, _ keep your boundaries ("Your rage is not my rage, and I don't have to 'fix' you"), and _ *listen*, or *be there* with real patience and empathy, you're providing priceless *outer* permission to mourn. Has anyone provided these comforts for you consistently, unselfishly, and without a hidden price tag? ("I was really there for *you* when you were so down, so you . . .").

People who can provide steady empathic permission and encouragement to active mourners are in short supply. One reason the U.S. therapy/psychiatry industry thrives is because (effective) clinicians provide the grief support and other things that are lacking in many wounded clients' homes and lives. This is one cost of our national decision to ignore (enable) ineffective parenting.

People can withhold permission for others to grieve well in many overt and subtle ways. Some are **verbal** and unmistakable, like . . .

+ "Oh Jeez, stop being such a wimp!"
+ "What is the big deal, anyway?"
+ "Aren't you over moping yet?"
+ "Come *on*; get on with your life!"
+ "Isn't Jean great? Nothing gets her down!"
+ "Depressed people are such a drag . . .!"
+ "I hate it when you get so upset."
+ "How's big Chief Black-Cloud today?"
+ "I'll come back when you feel better."
+ "Max just can't get a grip, can he?"
+ "Well, cheer up! It could be a *lot* worse. Just look at George's situation . . ."
+ "You stay in your room until you get a better attitude, young lady!"

People also send powerful **non-verbal** grief-disapprovals via a withering glance, a silence, a turn of the head, an interruption, an eye roll or sigh, an overdue or curt phone call, or a demeaning voice tone. Still other people's false self sends non-comforting mixed messages like "Oh you poor *Baby* . . . (pause) . . . I think whimpering and whining shows character weakness, don't you?"

There are layers of cultural, national, family, and personal reasons why people discourage others' mourning behaviors. Most motives are unconscious and reflexive, their origins lost in history. Some inhibitions have cultural roots: For example, some Asian, Native American, African, European, and Oriental cultures prize stoicism, among males or all people.

Other Mediterranean, Latin, Slavic, Arabic, and Asian groups expect males and females to feel and vent passions intensely and spontaneously. Some "permit" showing anger but not weeping, and some the reverse. Can you think of cultures that discourage females from healthy mourning, or encourage them to amplify and hang on to it? What culture/s do you identify with? Do you know what ethnic traditions are shaping your and your kids' reactions to bonding and mourning? Can you discuss this together?

A widespread cultural work ethic, with exceptions, is that personal problems and emotions should be left at home with the breakfast dishes. The implied rule is "We're here to get a day's work done." This means that most school kids and employed adults are discouraged from grieving openly from "9 to 5" or equivalent. The overarching social ethic many of us learned before we were six or so is "(We think) you're *bad* if you're loud and/or express strong emotions in public. Do not upset other people!" Until we validate or update this rule as an adult, we "can't" show grief-related rage, despair, or other intense emotions in the supermarket, drug store, church coffee hour, library, or the mall without a toxic stew of guilt, anxiety, and shame (embarrassment). We'll also probably lack compassion for (or envy) others who break this shame-based taboo.

Some dependent people (like a child of divorce) block another's grief (like an emotionally-fragile custodial parent) because they covertly fear the griever will "collapse" and won't be there to lean on. Other wounded (co-dependent, and/or enmeshed) people with only misty personal boundaries deeply feel *others'* intense emotions. They (their ruling subselves) dread feeling overwhelmed if they permit others to express intense rage, sorrow, and/or despair around them. Stressed and guilty single parents may covertly discourage their child's grieving, fearing it to be a "last (emotional) straw." An elderly or infirm parent can fear loss of vital support because of "probable" emotional collapse of their newly-divorced or widowed adult child. They can unconsciously hinder their child's inner focus and grief by increasing their calls for attention.

Whether blatant or subtle, grief blockers usually lack solid confidence in their and/or the griever's ability to *survive* intense rage and/or sorrow. Many haven't learned that full grieving is needed for losses other than someone's death. Grief critics and blockers are unaware and/or *wounded*, not "bad" people! Most are survivors of a childhood of great emotional deprivation, fear, confusion, loneliness, and pain. As such, if they're confronted about discouraging another's healthy grief, they (their Guardian subselves) will automatically react defensively to hide their ancient guilt, anxiety, and shame reflexes.

As some subselves do, "outer" people may *tolerate* grief behaviors (a weak form of permission), but stop short of genuinely *encouraging* them. I believe all of us kids and grownups need verbal and tactile encouragements like hugs, strokes, and affirmations from others, to go through the levels and phases of healthy grief. What do you think?

Getting consistent *outer* permissions can be specially complex for stepfamily grievers. There are more people, more daily inner and outer distractions, and three or more sets of biofamily and cultural customs about feeling and expressing confusion, anger, and sorrow. These sets can clash, sometimes starkly. One family's tradition may be "Boys grieve alone, and real men don't grieve," while the new partner's ancestors taught, "Males who cry, rage, and vent about losses openly are strong and healthy." Simply living with new people can impede natural grieving, because full trust in their acceptance and support hasn't formed yet.

Paradoxically, **close friends may *not* be the most helpful comforters** along our mourning path, specially if they're wounded. If friends _ have a high stake in the griever's quick recovery; _ don't understand the grief process; and/or _ carry strong biases about divorce, "sin," death, and re/marriage losses, they can unintentionally hinder the three-level healing process. Some well-meaning clergy can accidentally discount loss impacts and grief feelings by urging exclusive focus on God's blessings and grace. Parents of divorced kids can feel flayed by their own guilt, doubts, anxieties, and sadness, and seem impatient or unsupportive. Grief-support groups like "Compassionate Friends," "Rainbows," and "Kaleidoscope," (some) divorce-recovery groups, and qualified therapists can usually provide more balanced and effective support.

If you or a loved one have "It's OK to grieve well" *inner* permission, and get "It's *not* OK to grieve well" *outer* messages from key other people (or vice-versa), confusion and stress can be high. This is specially true without clear, shared awareness of this dynamic and conflict. If chronic, this inner/outer schism promotes false-self dominance. Do you know anyone with this kind of stress?

The bottom line: along with (1) clearly naming our tangible and invisible losses and their impacts on us; and (2) confidence in and (3) commitment to, our grief process; we grievers need (4) consistent inner and outer acceptance and encouragements as we move toward stable acceptance and re-balanced lives. Even with all those, I feel there are two more resources we need along the good-grief path. The first is choosing to get enough . . .

Distraction-free Solitudes

Good grief happens when we experience our feelings and confusions fully and repeatedly, and express them honestly, over and over until they subside. Being mentally and physically busy all the time interferes with this. The alternative is to intentionally give yourself or another mourner quiet, undistracted times to meditate, sort, pray, and be open to feeling and expressing the emotions that need to surface, especially confusion, disbelief, anger, and sorrow. Doing this with a centered, attentive, empathic supporter is also healing, and different.

At such healing times, we mourners benefit from being free of mind and emotion-distorting chemicals like alcohol, nicotine, sugar, fat, caffeine, tranquilizers, and sleep medications. Minimizing distractions like TV, phones, physical dis-comforts, appointments, and other people moving or talking, helps. So does writing in a journal or diary. For many people, being in Nature or in a personally sacred, peaceful place dur-ing such solitudes helps to get clear, quiet, and focused on the present moment.

Members of typical single-parent homes and multi-child stepfamily homes can have major trouble finding enough dis-traction-free solitudes to process their losses. *Where healthy grieving is a priority, co-parents will* make *(vs. find) such heal-ing times for themselves and their minor kids.* They'll also *want* to empathize and offer genuine mourning permissions and en-couragements to their kids' other co-parents, when they have broken bonds.

The last key ingredients for healthy mourning are . . .

Time, Patience, and Courage

Our marvelous natural ability to recover from broken emotional-spiritual bonds takes its own time, like the chang-ing of the seasons. Just as "nine women can't have a baby in a month," our three-level grief will not be hurried. In their book "Second Chances," Judith Wallerstein and Sandra Blakeslee observe that it takes some minor kids and young adults 10 to 15 years to fully adjust to the complex set of losses and changes from parental separation and divorce. Mourners who accept this reality will not burden themselves or other grievers with impatience to "get this (process) over with." Once again, the Serenity Prayer (p. 165) provides us grievers with wise guidance.

As you know, accepting the painful reality that cherished things are gone forever is *hard*. It takes resilience, emotional strength, and courage to endure the intense emotional periods that our losses bring. Where do people get *courage*? Where do *you* get it? Can you help younger mourners in your life find their own? Do you or they have a *Courageous* or *Brave One* among your inner crew?

We just reviewed six proposed ingredients for wholistically-healthy grieving. Do they make sense to you? Would you add any other factors? Did you get these as a child? Have your kids had these ingredients consistently? What does that mean?

Why Do Wounded People Have Trouble Grieving?

Recovery expert Claudia Black suggests the answer in her book "It Will Never happen to Me." She proposes that typical kids from alcoholic (i.e. low nurturance) families learn three survival rules from caregivers and key relatives very early: don't *talk*, don't *trust,* and don't *feel*. Wounded adults who teach these (unconsciously) can't model, teach, or encourage healthy mourning. Few are aware of the good-grief basics you're study-ing here, and most lacked their own inner permissions to grieve in *their* childhoods. School experiences often compound this: Unaware, wounded, uncomfortable peers may jeer at any ex-pression of grief sadness, or misunderstand, criticize, and/or withdraw from expression of mourning *anger* or the need for solitude. Other balanced students can lend genuine empathic support.

Restated: typical *Grown Wounded Children* (GWCs) are raised in homes and communities governed by ignorance and anti-grief policies. So what? **Until you and your partners work honestly at Project 1**, you risk your false self protectively de-nying that you survived a low-nurturance childhood. That means you may have major unconscious inhibitions against healthy grief, and may be *unintentionally* hindering your beloved kids and others from moving through their three-level mourning phases. If so, you're already taking a powerful first step by reading about healthy mourning, and what happens when it's blocked!

Recap

Every stepfamily is founded on two or three sets of losses for all kids and adults: _ childhood deprivations (probably); _

divorce or death losses; and _ re/wedding, cohabiting, and biofamily-merger changes. Personal and relationship health depends on adults' and kids' ability to mourn their tangible and invisible losses thoroughly on three levels: emotionally, spiritually, and mentally. People in and from high-nurturance (pro-grief) families tend to do this naturally.

My experience since 1981 is that most divorced and/or re/married co-parents like Jack and Sarah Tilmon come from low-nurturance childhoods. For them (i.e. you?), blocked grief is one of five major hindrances to their divorce recovery and successful stepfamily re/marriage. Most co-parents are unaware of _ their and _ their kids' losses, _ the grief basics in this chapter, and _ the toxic personal and relationship effects of blocked grief.

This chapter describes the first part of co-parent Project 5: healthy-grieving basics. Learning and discussing them *before* deciding on re/marriage empowers you partners to assess your co-parents (including ex mates) and kids for frozen mourning. If you find that any of you are significantly frozen, I propose that's good reason to be cautious about making nuptial plans. If you partners have ignored or minimized assessing for false-self dominance (Project 1), or haven't *really* accepted your stepfamily identity and what it means (Projects 3 and 4) you'll probably not be motivated or able to do Project 5 effectively even with the knowledge from this chapter.

For those of us who have to relearn our natural ability to grieve well, I believe that recovery from inner wounds and conscious attention to these good-grief basics can help. We can learn to understand and accept our broken emotional/spiritual bonds over time, and move ahead with our life purpose. Once in any needed personal recovery from inner wounds, six ways you others can re-learn how to grieve well are . . .

- Intentionally become aware of _ what you've lost, _ what your losses *mean* to you and key others, and _ how three-level, multi-phase grief flows *if it's allowed to*.

- Grow your confidence in the natural multi-level grieving process.

- _ Value and _ commit to the three-level mourning process, despite many daily distractions. You can also . . .

- Choose nurturing pro-grief environments and supports; i.e. find inner and outer permissions and encouragements to move through your grief phases.

- Choose undistracted solitudes to reflect, pray, sort out, and feel, without anxieties or guilt. And . . .

- _ Take your time, with _ patience and _ courage, to do what we must do to honor and accept our broken bonds, and move on.

Your unique combination of these factors can forge *effective* good-grief policies for you personally, and your households. When too many of these ingredients are missing too often, healthy three-level mourning gets blocked, and personal and family distress blooms.

Reality check: using the ideas above, learn something about yourself and your partner now: Get a pencil, slow down, breathe well, and thoughtfully answer these: (circle T = *true*, F = *false*, and ? = I'm not sure)

+ I grew up in a family where all six of these good-grief factors were consistently present. (T F ?)
+ All these factors have been consistently available to all residents and visitors in my home now. (T F ?)
+ My kids' other parent/s (if any) grew up in a family with all six of these factors. (T F ?)
+ My current partner grew up in a family with all these factors. (T F ?)
+ I can clearly describe _ what a "grief policy" is (p. 297), and _ what my current *personal* grief policy is now. (T F ?)

+ I can clearly describe my present *family's* grief policy
   now. (T F ?)
+ I can clearly describe my partner's current grief policy
   now. (T F ?)
+ My partner is clear on his or her personal grief policy. (T
   F ?)
+ I believe that blocked grief can be a valid reason to defer
   or decline re/marriage. (T F ?)
+ I want to learn about _ the symptoms of blocked grief
   now, and _ how to assess all of us for them. (T F ?)
+ I'm confident that my partner will *want* to _ join me in
   this assessment, and _ act on what we find. (T F ?)
+ I'm clear my true Self is answering these questions now.
   (T F ?)

Awarenesses . . .

Use these basics to help you make three *right* re/marriage
decisions by assessing for blocked grief and what caused it. If
you're already re/married, this is just as vital. If you're a single
parent or concerned grandparent, your inner and outer kids
depend on you to help them find and free up any frozen mourning.

Before you study how to do that, do you need to stretch,
relax, shift mental gears, and refresh?

Project 5B) Free Blocked Grief

Work through the denial that hides the anger
Work through the anger that hides the pain
Work through the pain that hides the loss and loneliness
Work through the loss and loneliness that hides the shame
Work through the shame that hides the fear
Work through the fear that hides our unwillingness
to give up our own control, and
surrender our lives to the Creator.
—Anonymous

Do you know anyone who has intentionally checked themselves and their family members for blocked grief? I'd be amazed if you did. I suspect that most homes would benefit greatly by family leaders' courageously doing this assessment and acting on it. Most don't, because of unawareness, misguided false-self interference, and our media relentlessly urging us to seek a superficial "good life."

This chapter uses the concepts in the prior chapter to help you avoid one of the five re/divorce hazards: unseen blocked grief. You're about to read . . .

- Why blocked grief can be a major re/marital and stepfamily problem.

- Why most divorced and/or re/married co-parents and their kids are specially susceptible to blocked grief.

- Five steps toward spotting frozen mourning in your adults or kids.

- Suggestions on what to do with any blocked grief you find.

- How blocked grief can promote tension in and between ex mates and/or their relatives, and eight things you can do about that; and . . .

- Practical ideas on how to evolve a pro-grief home and stepfamily.

The best time for you to assess for blocked grief is well *before* making re/marriage decisions. Generally, any person or caregiver can profit from working on this project at any time.

Why Is Blocked Grief a Major Re/marital Hazard?

Some reasons are general and others are unique to stepfamilies.

<u>Generally</u> . . .

Based on my (non-medical) clinical education and experience since 1979, I strongly suspect that interference with our natural three-level mourning process contributes to many physical and emotional problems in kids and adults. Repressing our normal urges to express grief confusion, anger, and sorrow takes energy from other life processes. That may affect our immune system, and diminish or defocus productive mental and physical activity. I suspect that in our hectic new-millennium life, blocked grief combines with other life traumas and stresses to promote . . .

+ Eating disorders (anorexia, bulimia, addiction)
+ Digestive problems
+ Social isolation
+ Rage-remorse cycles
+ (Some) sleep and breathing disorders
+ Approach-avoid relationships
+ Suicidal thoughts and actions
+ All addictions, including codependence
+ "Hyperactivity"
+ (Some) allergies
+ Anxiety "attacks"
+ Separation anxiety
+ Overcontrolling
+ Non-organic obesity
+ (Some) chronic pain
+ Abandonment fears
+ Psychosomatic "illness"
+ Chronic "depression"
+ Excessive religiosity, and . . .
+ Intimacy difficulties

I believe symptoms like these are specially likely in kids and adults in or from low-nurturance families. The symptoms become major secondary problems themselves. They're far easier to see and focus on than the underlying repressed emotions and false-self dominance.

In typical multi-home stepfamilies, such blocked-grief symptoms often compound with other stressors, and cause extra problems . . .

Effects of Blocked Grief in Typical Stepfamilies

Let's look briefly at each key stepfamily role to see typical ways that blocked grief can cause significant direct and indirect conflict. These examples are for illustration, not comprehensive.

If a minor or grown child is blocked in mourning their losses from parental separation or death and re/marriage, they may reject even the nicest stepparent/s and stepsiblings. That causes hurt, resentment, persecutor-victim-rescuer (PVR) relationship triangles and loyalty conflicts (p. 186). Some kids can angrily reject their own bioparents, siblings, or key relatives who "take sides"; specially if the child's other (blocked) parent encourages this. Extreme cases promote relationship cut-offs, which usually signal major inner wounds.

Kids, specially if they're shame-based or fear-based, can also develop "depression," psychosomatic maladies, interhome visitation anxieties and resistances, and/or school-avoidance behavior and achievement problems. Amplified by normal needs for independence, grief-blocked teens may act out with chemicals, violence, running away, unsafe sex, social isolation, excessive rebellion, or law breaking. These dramatic surface problems often mask the real issues: psychological wounds, ignorance, and an anti-grief environment. Patty McLean's pain and behaviors (Chapter 7) are classic examples.

If a bioparent's grief is blocked, they (their false self) can feel excessive shame and guilt for their child's divorce or parent-death pain. That can promote either their unconsciously favoring their own biokids over their new mate and/or their stepkids, or becoming paralyzed in trying *not* to favor their kids. Grief-blocked bioparents can also feel endlessly critical and distrustful of, and angry at their former mate. That may generalize to their ex mate's new partner, if any.

Rejected ex-mates who are stuck in their post-divorce grief can generate endless subtle or blatant conflicts with "the other household" over child-related financial support, custody, visitations, and parenting agreements. This is specially likely in co-parents from low-nurturance childhoods. False-self dominance causes their behaviors to send confusing mixed messages like: "I don't like or love you, and I don't want to live with you;" and "I can't bear to let you or our relationship go, so I'll stay connected through stressful conflict with you."

This is like a lonely neglected child acting defiant to get craved attention, despite painful punishments and rejections. Such hostile ex-mate dynamics usually trap minor and grown kids in the emotional crossfire, and foster stressful loyalty conflicts and PVR triangles. Empowering your true Selves (Project 1) and using the seven skills from Project 2 can reduce such conflicts and double messages.

For many stepfamilies, this **post-divorce war between ex mates** includes a series of expensive, adversarial, child-related court battles. These inevitably cause great long-lasting hurts, resentments, angers, and distrusts to flare in and between the co-parents' homes. Bitter counterattacks and responses escalate. Kids, kin, and some friends take sides or emotionally distance, and acrid divorced-family or stepfamily uproar increases. This *increases* the distrust, disrespect, hurt, and anger left from unfinished pre-divorce conflicts and denied childhood wounds.

Post-divorce legal warfare snares stepparents and often minor and grown kids in toxic emotional turmoil that they have little control over. As professional aggressors, lawyers *escalate* family strife. Emotionally numb or volatile (wounded) co-parents can be unconsciously attracted to this strife and excitement, because it _ feels painfully familiar, _ distracts from their pain, and _ they feel temporarily *alive*.

Marrying a divorced or widowed bioparent and their child/ren and ex mate/s causes **previously-single new stepparents** to lose much of their privacy; home quiet and tidiness (or mess); and control of their meals, slumber, assets, socializing, and leisure routines. Childless adults also lose loneliness, social "oddness," financial insecurity (maybe), and anxieties about living alone. They *also* may lose some physical possessions with special emotional value ("OK, we'll use your couch / plates / mattress / . . .").

Typical never-married stepparents give up many things for these positive losses, a prized committed adult relationship, and the (idealized) dream of a warm, loving family. If such stepparents don't grieve their invisible and tangible losses from re/wedding and cohabiting well, they risk growing hidden resentments, "depression," and significant psychosomatic and social problems.

More stepfamily impacts of blocked grief . . .

Like many children of divorce, **grandparents may uncon-sciously resist grieving** the lost dream of their adult child's marital and family reconciliation. If a guilty or shamed grand-parent is frozen in mourning their child's divorce and/or re-marriage, they may icily or sweetly reject the most appealing new step-kin. If they lose confidence about access to their grandkids, grandparents can become intrusive, critical, or hos-tile. A bio-grandparent may not want to end a prized emotional bond and frequent intimate talks with a wonderful former son or daughter-in-law ("After all, s/he *is* the parent of our grand-children!")

Reactions like these block stepfamily-wide bonding, and can turn family gatherings and holidays into tense, conflictual experiences for kids and adults. They are rich fertilizer for rag-ing extended-stepfamily loyalty conflicts and divisive relation-ship triangles. With naturally increasing health problems, older people are specially at risk of psychosomatic conditions par-tially fueled by long-hidden blocked grief. Seniors who are unrecovering survivors of low-nurturance childhoods are at higher risk of this.

Blocked mourning in co-parents and kin promotes ***unin-tentional* household and stepfamily anti-grief policies.** The semi-conscious terror of admitting their own losses and *feeling* the related rage and emotional agony, can prevent them giving others permission to mourn. Long term, this can be specially harmful to young people by crippling their *inner* permission to feel and express intense grief (and other) emotions. I believe this was happening silently to 13 year-old Patty McLean (Chap-ter 7), because of unseen blocked grief in her bioparents Sarah and Ted, and her stepfather Jack.

This is a small sample of the many interactive impacts of frozen mourning in stepfamily adults, kids, and relationships. Once you know the telltale symptoms of blocked grief below, such impacts are easy to spot. Uninformed co-parents, doc-tors, lawyers, pastoral and school counselors, and clinicians often focus only on the symptoms like those above. This often causes mounting confusion and frustration when their well-meant help doesn't reduce surface discomforts, over time. Such professionals were never trained to see the underlying *true* problems, and may suffer them personally.

False Selves and Blocked Mourning

Study and clinical experience since 1979 has forged my belief that unhealed personality wounds + unawareness + unintended family anti-grief policies combine to cause blocked grief in co-parents and their kids. In any stepfamily role, many (most?) psychologically-wounded people can't mourn old and new losses until well into true recovery (Project 1). There seems to be several reasons:

Failure to bond as an infant with an unavailable or wounded caregiver (Reactive Attachment Disorder) may stunt a co-parent's ability to form real emotional/spiritual bonds, even with their own biokids. Desperately seeking social approval, normalcy, and emotional connection, such impaired people must guess what real bonding looks, feels, and sounds like. They artfully pretend friendship, commitment, and intimacy, but don't really *feel* them. Their partners inevitably feel ignored, used, and unimportant, and fill their relationship needs with other people, isolate, or become "depressed."

An attachment-impaired person's history usually shows _ excessive isolation and/or _ superficial friendships, _ one or more addictions (including workaholism and/or co-dependence), and _ failed primary relationships. They often _ choose partners who are "emotionally unavailable," (controlled by false selves and can't bond) like their early caregiver/s. Survivors of childhood emotional neglect who can't bond don't *need* to mourn much, because they (their false self) can only form weak emotional attachments. Do you know anyone like this?

Secondly, **typical unaware, wounded people** like Jack and Sarah Tilmon, and re/married widower Philip and his son Jason, **have long lacked solid *inner* permission and self-encouragement to mourn.** This stems from an unspoken stern birthfamily anti-grief policy and our societal (media) denials.

Until they amend their own *shoulds, oughts, and musts* about expressing normal rage, confusions, and sadness, such people aren't aware of risking significant relationship and health problems.

A third reason that Grown Wounded Children have trouble mourning has three roots: their mixes of _ **reality distortion**, _ **excessive fear** of overwhelm and abandonment, **and _ protective emotional numbing**. Unconscious fear of intense anger or despair promotes repression, avoidances, and manipulations. Reality distortion causes half-perceived anxieties about some emotional catastrophe that will happen if the wounded co-parent allows their rage or sorrow to surface and vent, like "If I let myself cry, I'll never stop!" Distortion also manifests as denials ("What losses?"), projections ("You're the one with the anger problem, not *me!*"), and numbing ("I'm not sad, just tired.")

False-self dominance may cause embarrassing, scary "crying jags;" or rageful "explosions." Shame-based adults and kids with wobbly "impulse control" (reactive false selves) cause personal and social anxiety because they seem *extra sensitive, explosive, hostile, thin skinned,* or *very touchy.* Ignorance of what losses and healthy grief are ("It's what you're *supposed to* do when someone dies"), and excessive shame and guilt over raging or crying, add to co-parent grief paralysis. Symptoms like these suggest that one or more subselves are stuck in a past traumatic time, and need to be compassionately "rescued" via skilled inner-family therapy (..01/ifs7-rescuing.htm).

Because typical wounded co-parents unconsciously choose each other ("Birds of a feather flock together"), they often don't get genuine permissions and encouragements to mourn from each other, family, friends, and co-workers. Added to co-parents' unconscious lack of *inner* permissions, lack of outer support impairs or blocks healthy mourning. That promotes complex, stressful stepfamily-relationship problems like those sketched above.

Minor and grown kids of emotionally-blocked co-parents are often emotionally inhibited or volatile too. Once such blockage is seen and accepted and any needed inner-wound recov-

ery is underway, people can gradually free up their repressed
feelings and frozen grieving reflexes.

How's your inner family doing, right now? This is a *lot* of
abstract ideas to absorb and integrate! Stretch, breathe well,
and take care of any distractions (needs), before you continue.

We've just covered *why* blocked grief can be a serious problem in typical divorced families and stepfamilies. The heart of
Project 5 is assessing for it honestly, and working patiently to
free it up. How can you partners "assess for it honestly"?

Five Steps to Identify Blocked Mourning

These steps can be tailored to fit your unique situation, and
woven into your (step)family's Good-Grief policy:

+ Co-parents make significant **progress** on courtship
   projects one through four. Then . . .
+ **Learn and discuss** the "good grief" basics in the prior
   chapter. Option: do further research via other readings
   (p. 542). Then . . .
+ **Identify your** current _ personal, _ household, and _
   family beliefs and values ("**policies**") about losses and
   mourning (pp. 258 and 299). _ Intentionally revise them
   to fit your new loss/grief awareness, and your stepfamily
   goals (Project 6). Co-parents _ discuss your policies
   together to see what you agree on, and where you conflict. _ Work towards respectful compromise. Then . . .
+ **Inventory** each of **your** co-parents' and kids' prior major **losses** from _ childhood, _ biofamily separation or
   death, and if you're already remarried, _ from stepfamily
   cohabiting and mergers. Then . . .
+ **Check** each adult and minor or grown child **for symptoms of blocked grief** (below), relative to their losses.
   Option: consult with a professional grief counselor to
   resolve any uncertainties, and guard against unconscious distortions.

From steps like these, you co-parents will conclude that
either _ someone needs help thawing frozen grief, or _ your

adults and kids seem to be mourning their sets of losses well enough.

After exploring each of these steps, we'll look at options for freeing up any blocked grief that you find.

Progress on Your First Four Projects

Project 1 helps co-parents from low-nurturance childhoods acknowledge their psychological wounds and start to heal them. This is essential to help identify adults' and kids' grow genuine inner and outer encouragements to grieve. An early step in this project is agreeing on a definition of what a *high nurturance* family is (p. 48). Building your communication skills (Project 2) empowers you all to discuss and co-manage this good-grief project effectively. Project 3 validates your stepfamily identity and the need for this project, and clarifies *who* you should check for blocked grief (e.g. other co-parents). Project 4 helps your co-parents' to see this good-grief project in realistic stepfamily (vs. biofamily) perspective.

Courting co-parents who try assessing for blocked grief without progress on all four prior projects risk making wrong re/marital choices. Re/married co-parents who ignore this project risk escalating stress in and between their homes. Sarah and Jack Tilmon represent *millions* of burdened stepfamily co-parents and children struggling with this. Without a second-order (core attitude) change in average co-parents' knowledge, motivation, and values, the five re/divorce hazards sweep them and their dependent kids relentlessly toward *another* set of agonizing, demoralizing broken bonds.

You partners can avoid this! The next thing you can do is . . .

Learn Good-Grief Basics Together

As your inner-family harmonies and stepfamily awarenesses increase, work to dissolve your misconceptions about losses and healthy mourning. Validating the ideas in the prior chapter can empower all your co-parents to evolve a clear, shared definition of "healthy three-level grief." Are you willing to discuss the prior chapter with your other co-parents, and forge a common definition? Option: learn what you each know about good grief by discussing the "quiz" on p. 253 and http://sfhelp.org/05/grief-quiz.htm.

This learning step _ provides clear reasons to assess your kids and adults for blocked grief, and _ strengthens your motivation to free it up. Ignoring this promotes you co-parents using vague, unrealistic, and/or conflicting definitions of effective mourning, and *not knowing that*. Because our patriarchal Puritan ancestors passed on their values of *work*, *piety,* and *obedience*, an inherited *unhealthy* definition sounds like: "Well, *good* grief is not whining, moping, or blubbering over stuff that can't be changed. We should all get on with our lives, and not wallow in the past!" That's psychological arsenic. Our immigrant ancestors were too busy trying to survive to grieve well.

Whatever you believe, you and others in your family *do* have personal definitions of *good grief.* They're probably unconscious. Until you're aware of your definitions, they silently shape your reactions to your and others' significant losses. Learn more about your personal and family mourning values at ..05/griefval.htm.

Once you co-parents learn the basics and your current values about grieving, you can . . .

Update Your Grieving Policies

Recall that a *grief policy* is a set of personal, household, or family beliefs and rules about "acceptable" and "good" reactions to our inevitable life losses. Every child, adult, and family has a grief policy: s*houlds*, *musts*, and *oughts*. From tradition and social unawareness, most adults can't name them, and don't teach their kids to do so. Use your knowledge of the three grief levels and the six requisites for healthy mourning (p. 268) to see if any co-parent in your multi-home (step)family needs to

revise their policies and grieving behaviors. Like Jack and Sarah Tilmon, co-parents dominated by a false self will often unconsciously avoid, defer, or pooh-pooh this step, because it
threatens old protective repressions and denials.

An *effective* personal and household grieving policy will give
clear guidelines on some key questions for your kids and adults:

+ "Specifically how do we now define 'personal loss,'
   'healthy grief,' and 'effective mourning support'?"

+ "In our home, what are our specific beliefs (*shoulds,
   musts,* and *oughts*) about:

_ Naming and discussing broken emotional bonds (losses)
   together;

_ *Feeling* strong anger, deep sadness, confusion, and despair;

_ *Expressing* each of these, privately and socially,

_ Expressing and answering our loss-related mental questions, and . . .

_ Supporting each others' expressing normal grief emotions, confusions, and questions?"

+ "In our home and our stepfamily, how long can grief
   take without members getting impatient or judgmental? Can our members mourn differently and still be
   accepted by us all?"

+ "Who's responsible for ensuring that each of our members is encouraged to _ name their losses, and to _ grieve
   thoroughly in _ this home, and _ our multi-home
   (step)family?"

+ "_ Who among us is responsible for teaching and coaching our family members on how to support a mourner
   well? Is everyone on their own? _ Should (or do) we
   have a stepfamily 'grieving specialist' or coordinator?
   _ If so, who? _ What's their job? _ How did they get it?
   _ Are they doing it 'well enough'? _ Do they feel appreciated enough? _ Does s/he need help? "

+ "In our home and family, what priority do we normally give
   healthy mourning: i.e. what goals and activities are gen-

erally more important to our household and stepfamily members than grieving broken emotional bonds?"
+ "Is it OK to ask for grieving help _ in our home? In _ our stepfamily? _ Generally, how should we support each other in recovering from personal losses?
+ _ How do we pick 'safe' grief supporters, and _ what should we ask for and expect from them? _ Do we 'owe' them anything? _ If so, what?"
+ "_ When should we get aid in grieving, _ for whom, and _ from whom? _ Who should make this happen in our home? _ In our stepfamily? _ Who should monitor such help to see if it's effective? _ Who should pay for the help? _ How and _ when? _ Within what limits?"
+ _ "Who's responsible for making this grieving policy? _ Giving feedback on it? _ Resolving conflicts about it? _ Amending it? _ Implementing it? _ Appreciating good grievers among us? _ Finding blocked grievers?"

All members of your extended stepfamily have *unconscious* opinions on these questions now, or they haven't thought much about them. These opinions and "I-don't-knows" form your current personal, home, and family grief policies. If you haven't discussed questions like these together, it's likely that your mourning policies are semi-unconscious, conflictual, and un-coordinated. That's probably promoting blocked grief, and disabling your true Selves. If so, that's fertile ground for high personal and nuclear-stepfamily stress, and making wrong re/marital decisions. "You can run, but you can't hide . . ."

A family good-grief policy might look like this:

Our Family Policy on Healthy Grieving

"All our adults and kids will experience major losses (broken emotional attachments) throughout our lives. We will consistently, courageously, gently, and lovingly help each other to . . .
+ Learn clearly what healthy three-level grieving is; and . . .

+ Grow genuine inner(personal) and outer (family) permissions to mourn; and . . .

+ Evolve a family good-grief language, and use it to think and talk about our losses and their impacts on us, as they happen.

And when any of us lose something or someone dear, we'll work together to . . .

+ Fully *feel* and repeatedly *express* our normal shock, confusion, anger, and sadness, until these natural feelings subside; without anxiety, guilt, or shame; and we'll help each other to . . .

+ Gradually evolve clear answers to the questions that our losses cause, and to . . .

+ Help each other rebuild our spiritual faith that may be shaken by major "senseless" losses.

+ Respect and dignify every child and adult's unique way of saying their final goodbyes to precious tangible and invisible bonds that break.

+ And because people outside our family need effective grief support at times, we'll do our best to provide that compassionately, without sacrificing our own personal and family needs, or losing our identities and boundaries.

+ We'll help each other remember that each of us grieves differently, and that grief cannot be rushed. We adults accept the responsibility of grieving their own losses well, and compassionately modeling and teaching healthy three-level mourning to our children.

If you displayed such a policy in plain sight in your home, and/or read it out loud at key events and anniversaries, what do you think might happen? Note that co-parents' having no clear household and family-wide policy on good grief *is* a policy. "No policy" is our toxic national norm, so far. Note also that your personal good-grief policies may be different than your partner's, your parents', your siblings', and your extended (step)family's.

Recall: we're reviewing five steps to identify blocked grief. Once you partners _ progress on Projects 1 to 4, _ learn good-grief basics, and _ draft a clear, conscious pro-grief policy, you're ready to . . .

Inventory Your Co-parents' and Kids' Prior Losses

Scan http://sfhelp.org/05/physical-loss-inv.htm. It's a worksheet to help you identify specific intangible and tangible losses that each member of your several stepfamily homes has had from biofamily separation or parent death and stepfamily formation. This inventory can also alert you to possible future losses. Because most ancestors weren't taught grief basics and didn't teach us to name our non-death losses, it can feel alien to "inventory" them. That's specially true for invisible losses like these:

+ Lost _ relationships or _ relationship quality
+ Lost family _ roles, _ status, and _ identity
+ Lost respect for _ yourself and/or _ others
+ Lost _ faith and _ trusts, including intimacy
+ Lost _ dreams, _ hopes, and _ ideals
+ Lost _ accesses and _ freedoms
+ Lost personal _ privacy and _ solitudes
+ Lost family _ rituals and _ traditions
+ Lost emotional securities
+ Lost "states of mind" like serenity

Note that mixes of these 20 invisible losses often occur with each other and with significant *tangible* losses ("I sure miss having a back porch."). The compound impact of all of these broken bonds can feel overwhelming to kids and adults for days or many months. How many divorced, widowed, and re/married people do you know who could clearly *name* specific invisible losses like these?

Identify specifically *what* tangible and intangible things you've lost. Then one at a time, do the same with or for _ your present partner, _ each important child or young adult in your life, and _ each other co-parent in your stepfamily. Trusted companions or professionals may help you identify your losses, to guard against protective denials. Because you prize different things, your losses will differ also.

Consider losses from biofamily reorganization (vs. "divorce") or death, *and* (potential) re/marriage and/or cohabiting. If your list is long, **try grouping losses** as high, medium, and low-impact (on whom?). You partners' building this loss-inventory together can foster real household and extended-stepfamily empathy and closeness. It can also promote your exchanging empathic *outer* permissions to feel and express good grief *if protective false-self denials have been dissolved* (Project 1).

Once your losses are named, discuss their *meanings* to (impacts on) you with empathic supporters (p. 310). Talk over questions like those in the previous step. This talk can sound like . . .

"Because of my divorce, I feel like I've lost some of my main 'roots': I feel less secure emotionally, financially, and socially. I feel confused, too, about who I am; my identity is less clear to me now."

Encourage your kids to talk about the personal impacts of their losses *often*, and affirm them, without moralizing, correcting, evaluating, or trying to "fix" them. Demonstrate how to talk about significant broken bonds, and help resident and visiting youngsters understand the grief process and what life-losses *mean*.

The language of healthy mourning is rich with phrases like these:

+ "I really miss . . ."
+ "I keep thinking about . . ."
+ "I'm so *sad* that . . ."
+ "I remember . . .
+ "If only . . ."
+ "Every time I hear . . ."

+ "I cry when . . ."
+ "I'm so *angry* that . . ."
+ "I'm not ready to . . .
+ "I need to be alone."
+ "I can't understand . . ."
+ "I'm not up for . . .
+ "I've lost my . . ."
+ "I really need to . . ."
+ "Would you just hold me now?"
+ "If you can't listen to me (vent), will you tell me?"
+ "How could God let this happen?"
+ "I *hurt* (vs. 'it hurts') when . . ."
+ "No, I'm not over with . . ."
+ "I'm not sure you can understand how I feel."

People whose false self blocks inner permissions to *feel* and *express* often use *you* and *we* instead of "*I*." Do you know anyone who does this? What has the grieving language in your home sounded like recently? In many post-separation and stepfamily homes, it's the sound of *silence*.

These four Project-5 steps are a lot of work! You'll learn or clarify grieving basics; evolve clearer understanding and definitions of healthy grief, and draft meaningful personal and stepfamily mourning policies. You partners will thoughtfully name your and your kids' main tangible and invisible losses, and will reflect and talk openly about these losses' real impacts on your inner and outer lives. Doing all these together, over time, empowers you suitors or spouses to . . .

Check for Symptoms of Blocked Grief

Wounded people may not start their natural emotional-mental-spiritual grief process, or they can get stuck in any phase of the three levels. When either of these happens, there are clear behavioral symptoms. Use the list below to check for frozen grief in yourself or someone you care about. Look for repeated patterns over time. Also note that the person you're assessing may be so wounded they're not able to bond, so they have little to grieve. See ..01/bonding.htm for perspective.

__ 1) Seeming 'forever" sad, angry, or depressed, or often feeling numb or "nothing," in general, or about their loss/ es. People who always seem very intellectual, analytical, "dry," or unemotional are probably frozen grievers controlled by false selves.

__ 2) Repressed anger. Signs include repeated _ procrastination; _ lateness; _ sadistic or sarcastic humor; _ cynicism; _ sighing; _ inappropriate cheerfulness; _ an over-controlled, monotone ("flat") voice; _ insomnia or _ excessive sleep; _ waking up tired; _ tiring easily, _ inappropriate drowsiness; _ chronic "irritability"; _ clenched jaws ("TMJ") or _ teeth grinding, specially at night; _ (some) back pain; _ (some) muscle spasms, _ tics or twitches; _ road "rage," _ fist clenching, or other unconscious behaviors. Some of these may have primary or shared medical causes. Our mind-body-spirit interaction is a relevant mystery here.

__ 3) Minimizations or denials. Consistently downplaying either the broken bond itself ("___ wasn't *that* important to me"), or feelings *about* the loss ("No, I'm not angry, just tired and crabby.") The master denial is of one's own denial.

__ 4) Chronic weariness, "depression," or apathy. It takes a *lot* of personal energy to steadily repress scary or forbidden emotions and awarenesses. Recovery mentor John Bradshaw likens this repression to trying to swim while holding a big beach ball under water. Therapist Virginia Satir suggested it's like constantly holding a swinging kitchen door closed against pack of starving dogs . . .

__ 5) Addictions to one or more of these:
_ *Activities* like compulsive work; hobbies or sports; worship, committees, socializing, TV and/or personal computers; fitness and health; sexual excitement; cleaning, shopping, or gambling; reading or "endless" education; *and recovery*; and/ or . . .
_ *Substances* like nicotine; caffeine; fatty, salty, and sug-

ary foods; alcohol, marijuana, or other hard drugs; and/or mood-altering prescription medications. And/or . . .

_ "Toxic" *relationships* that consistently produce significant shame, fear, rage, pain, guilt, anxiety, or unhealthy dependencies; and/or. . . .

_ *States of mind* like rage, anxiety ("worry"), and/or sexual or other emotional excitement.

Often, people using addictions or obsessions to put off grief pain have several of these at once ("cross addiction"). An "addict" is someone in significant pain who is ruled by two or more protective subselves. His or her false self will deny, minimize, or rationalize their compulsive dependencies, until real (vs. pseudo) personal recovery begins. Partners or relatives who may be addicted to their addict's feelings and welfare (co-dependence) will join them in such denial (enabling). Others may acknowledge their partner's addiction and fiercely deny their own. In my clinical experience, *all* active addicts and their chief enablers are ruled by false selves (p. 139) and don't know it.

More symptoms of blocked grief . . .

__ **6) Repeated avoidances**. These can be verbal, mental, and/or sensory (physical). If the loss or something associated or similar comes under discussion, a blocked mourner will often become silent or irritable, tune out, try to change the subject, or leave. They may reflexively shun certain . . .

_ *Places*, like former dwellings, neighborhoods, worship centers, cemeteries . . .

_ *People* or mention of them;

_ *Activities or rituals,* like holidays, vacations, births, death, graduations; and/or . . .

_ *Painful mementos* like pictures, videos, movies, music, old letters, names, phrases, foods, holiday ornaments, special clothing, etc. that remind them of that which is gone.

Blocked mourners will often protectively deny, minimize, or intellectually explain such avoidances. Absent-parent families and stepfamilies abound with such painful reminders. Are there any in your life? In your kids' lives? Your partner's? Your ex mate's? Your parents' lives?

___ 7) (Some) **chronic pain or illness,** specially without clear biological cause. A growing number of professional healers feel that recurrent asthma, migraine or other headaches, digestive or colon problems, back pain, shoulder pain and neck stiffness or soreness, breathing or swallowing troubles, panic attacks, nightmares, allergies, and the like are body signals that emotions are being repressed. Typical wounded-mourners' false selves will scoff at this.

___ 8) **Obesity and eating disorders.** It's been said of significantly overweight adults and kids that "Every fat cell is an unshed tear." Some adults or kids numb their pain from unacknowledged losses by compulsive overeating or other eating disorders. Others are metabolically unbalanced. I believe that long-term, grief-work can be far more helpful and healthy than endless diet/regain cycles. The latter typically build guilt, shame, self-doubt, and eventual depression, despair, and resignation. Other eating problems, anorexia (self-starvation) or bulimia (compulsive binge-purge cycles), may signal blocked mourning and other psychological wounds like excessive shame and fears.

Obesity **can be a symptom of childhood sexual abuse**. This massive psycho-spiritual trauma ensures false-self control and the losses of innocence, trust, security, and self-respect in a child too young to understand and protect themselves. Often, molestation victims are too shamed and scared to say what happened, or if they do, wounded caregivers may disbelieve or even punish them. Informed clinical and family support can help to gradually heal the deep inner wounds that underlie eating disorders and non-organic obesity.

Another symptom of blocked grief is . . .

___ 9) **Anniversary "depressions."** Major apathy, sadness, sluggishness, sickness, sleep disorders, irritability, or feeling gloomy "for no reason" may recur annually at the time or season a major bond was broken. This can appear to be (or be increased by) "Seasonal Affective Disorder" (S.A.D.), where people explain recurring despondence by having too little sunlight in the winter months.

__ **10) Enshrining or purging mementos.** People who obsessively display, revere, discuss, or protect special reminders of a prized attachment long after it was broken are probably blocked mourners. Mementos can include foods, music, clothes, pictures, furniture, letters, jewelry, perfume, gardens, furniture, clothing, rituals, and many more. Revering or reacting to such reminders to perpetual *excess* is the key clue.

The opposite behavior may also signal blocked grief. People who compulsively throw away every tiny reminder of the lost person or thing can be avoiding the intolerable rage and anguish needed to accept and release it and move on.

__ **11) Often having strong reactions** to the losses or traumas of strangers, acquaintances, animals, or fictional characters. Reactions can include uncontrollable sobbing, depressions, rage outbursts, insomnia, obsessive thinking (perseveration), and over-identifying ("becoming" the hurting person). Such symptoms can have several roots, not just blocked grief.

Wounded young and adult mourners may have one or more of these symptoms, and their false selves will hide, mute, or disguise them from their excessive shame, guilts, and anxiety. This is specially true when key people around them discourage grieving behaviors. Having one or several of the signs above doesn't *prove* a person is blocking their grief. It justifies exploring the possibility.

Pause and reflect: have you ever read anything like this before? Did you ever hear your childhood adults or teachers discuss three-level grief, and these blocked grief symptoms? Did your partner? Does it seem more credible that [unawareness + inner wounds + blocked grief + romance illusions] promote unwise re/marital choices?

What If You Find Blocked Mourning?

If you co-parents decide that one or more of your adults or kids are blocked in their grief process, what are your options? If you're courting, _ factor the extent of the frozen mourning into your re/marital decisions in Project 7. _ Decide if you need to take any personal action to help unblock the grief, specially if *you're* blocked. If you're already re/married, then do the latter as partners. Caution: dominant false selves doing this can cause loyalty conflicts (p. 186) and relationship triangles! (..09/triangles.htm)

Here's a buffet of options to select from in evolving an effective "unblocking plan:"

Foundations

1) Learn your "roots." Compassionately explore your respective ancestors' habits about emotional attachments and losses, specially invisible ones. Research whether their personal and family grieving policies promoted or discouraged healthy mourning. Compare your present grieving beliefs and behaviors to your perception of theirs, nonjudgmentally. If you're unsure of your ancestors' mourning policies, and senior relatives are accessible, ask them! This is about finding information, not *fault*!

2) Co-parents check your attitudes: _ do you each clearly see *losses* and *grieving* as normal and positive, or as "negative" things to be avoided? If the latter, help each other to build "pro-grief" attitudes. _ Is your attitude about each blocked griever respectful and compassionate, or resentful, anxious, impatient, and/or judgmental? If the latter, examine what's causing that, for it will surely hinder helping the others to unblock.

3) Keep your perspectives clear:

+ Each of us is responsible for our own grief, so avoid feeling responsible for the blocked person ("I must help you grieve!"). Focus on what *you* need.

+ Mourning can be encouraged but not forced. Help each other use the Serenity Prayer (p. 165).
+ Blocked grief is usually a symptom of significant un-awareness and false-self control. Therefore, _ education (Projects 1, 2, 4, and 5) and _ recovery from inner wounds (p. 142) are the real targets.
+ Chronic "depression," addictions, and (some) physical symptoms can indicate frozen grief.
+ Each of us has our own grief pace and style, so avoid expecting others to mourn *your* way.
+ For major and multiple losses, grief takes time! It won't unblock over a weekend . . .

4) Learning and doing Project 5 together can help all your adults and kids bond and heal, over time! Use this vision as motivation to keep at this challenging task.

5) Identify and **draw inspiration from good-grief hero/ines and mentors**: adults and kids you feel are clearly healthy mourners. Identify specifically why you think they are. Note that *you* and each of your stepfamily members can become such a hero/ine!

6) Develop a pro-grief attitude and a good-grief vocabulary. Encourage each other to _ talk honestly and often about your attachments and losses, and your grief emotions, confusions, and progress or troubles. _ Affirm and encourage kids and adults who are grieving successfully. _ Use family gatherings as opportunities to raise everyone's awareness about this fifth project; grief basics; and individual losses, impacts, blocks, and progress. Like discussing shared recovery from a natural disaster, this doesn't have to be gloomy!

Once your Project-5 foundations are solid, then for each blocked mourner you've identified . . .

<u>Use the Six Good-Grief Factors to Assess</u>

These factors (p. 268) provide you with an effective framework to diagnose what's missing for each blocked mourner, and then to work together to provide it. Options:

7) If s/he doesn't **understand** the **good-grief basics** in the prior chapter and doesn't know that, respectfully invite her or him to learn ("I need you to learn, because . . .")

8) If s/he **can't name her or his** specific _ invisible and _ tangible **losses**, encourage her or him to do that. See ..05/physical-loss-inv.htm for help.

9) If your blocked mourner **can't clearly describe the _impacts_** of each major tangible and invisible loss on their life, encourage them to see value in _ reflecting on the effects, and _ talking about them with *feeling*. If they do, listen empathically without judgment or proposed "fixes." See ..02/listen.htm.

10) If the blocked person **has no confidence** in their own three-level grieving process, _ affirm that *without judgment.* Then _ proactively do what you partners can to encourage his or her trust in the healing process over time. Talk openly about what resources and experiences would build this trust. Settling for "I don't know" enables toxic blocked grief!

11) If the blocked griever **doesn't seem committed** to allowing their mourning to progress, ask if they're willing to explore that with you and/or a qualified professional. Except for people ruled by a false self, good grief can be a conscious choice.

A stuck person may have mourning awarenesses and confidence, but put most other life priorities ahead of self-healing. This often stems from repressed shame and related self-neglect ("I don't deserve to feel happy.") This neglect is often minimized, explained, joked about, or denied. Acknowledging and working to heal these inner wounds is an essential personal and co-parental project (#1). Avoiding it risks unintentionally passing the six wounds on to your descendants.

More options to unblock frozen mourning:

12) Respectfully **evaluate the blocked person's *inner* grief supports.** Ask them to describe their attitudes (inner permissions) about _ *feeling* loss-related confusion, anger, and sadness, and _ *expressing* each of those, privately and publicly, until they gradually diminish. One way of doing this is to ask the blocked person some specific questions, and then listen to them, *without judgment or moralizing*:

+ "How should (men / boys / women / girls) *feel* and *express* _ anger or rage, _ confusion, and _ sadness or despair?"
+ "_ When and _ where?"
+ "If you feel and show these emotions, will you or someone else get hurt?"
+ "How, specifically?"
+ "Why, specifically?"
+ "How do you know?" or "What makes you think so?"

Reflective questions like these are good focal points for journaling, praying, and meditating. Note: kids and grownups ruled by a false self often have *several* answers to each of these questions which may conflict. Project 1 and Project-2 *awareness* can help reduce this, over time.

If your blocked person lacks inner permissions and encouragements to grieve (p. 274), respectfully do what you can to build those *without feeling responsible*.

13) Evaluate the blocked person's *outer* (home, family, and social) **grief supports.** This is probably the most impactful and toughest aspect of thawing a family-member's frozen grief. It requires each of you co-parents to look honestly at your own attitudes and behaviors about acknowledging personal broken bonds and their impacts, and feeling and expressing your own grief emotions.

__ **Are *you* anxious** (fearful or worried) about allowing or encouraging the blocked child or adult to mourn? If a false self controls any of you three or more co-parents, odds of *unconsciously* withholding permission to grieve rise. Common ways of doing that are _ criticizing, _ ignoring, _ nagging, _ rushing, or _ lecturing losers about feeling and/or expressing confusion, anger, sorrow, and retelling their loss-story "too often." Avoid *enabling* your blocked person by telling them honestly and respectfully how their grief behaviors affect you ("Bill, I feel like you're not facing your feelings over being fired. I can empathize with you, and (not *but*) I'm losing patience and respect for you for not being honest with yourself. Will you talk with me about this?")

15) If a stepfamily adult or child is unconsciously impeding other members' grief, expect them to deny this, and/or to rationalize that "it's really best, because . . ." **Respect their resistance,** *and don't* **enable** *or accept it.* They mean no harm— and hindering a loved one's grieving *is* harmful, just as chronic constipation is. Prolonged blocked grief can make them emotionally, relationally, spiritually, and/or physically sick.

16) What **if an anti-grief family member can't accept** what they're doing and stop it? The stuck mourner can courageously **choose to reduce or end contact** with her or him, and choose supporters who spontaneously give true grief permissions and encouragements. Chronically unhappy and codependent people can help themselves by limiting or ending relationships that impede healthy grief. Doing so requires mastering guilt, self-neglect (shame), and fear of abandonment (progressing on Project 1). If the grief-blocker is a parent, spouse, old friend, religion-spokesman, or employer, such decisions are scary, and ultimately healing. They offer the other person a chance to accept responsibility for their own healing and growth.

17) Being with others who have experienced similar losses and are grieving well can really help your kids and adults mourn. Research your community for well-regarded **grief-support groups** like Rainbows and Compassionate Friends. National and/or professionally-led programs and groups are often the most grounded, focused, resourceful, and effective. Check local hospital outpatient programs and mental-health agencies. If you can't find any, check the Web for similar groups.

Still more options to help you free up blocked grief . . .

18) High-nurturance **personal and family** *spirituality* (vs. religion) is a major support for good grief. It accesses private and shared spiritual strength, courage, and inspiration. If the blocked person has few or no spiritual resources, encourage her or him to consider developing some now. Then accept their decision without judgment. Model your own spirituality for them openly, without hidden agendas (like persuasion). I believe spiritual indifference, cynicism, numbness, and fanaticism are signs of low childhood nurturance and psychological wounding.

19) Each griever needs to personally define what "outer support" is right for them now. We mourners often fear that "endless" sadness or rage will burden or annoy our supporters. This is specially true for shame-based and fear-based people with an overactive *People Pleaser* subself. To minimize this, invite your (step)family members and other supporters to tell each other honestly *without guilt* if they can't listen to, or be with, a griever at certain times. **Help each other to take responsibility for your own limits**, so that your grievers don't have to be.

Letting concerned others share your anguish is a gift, for it gives them a real way to help. Do you agree? How do you feel and act when a dear one shares their confusion, rage, or sadness with you? Can you tell them without guilt and worry when you've had enough for the time being? Typical survivors of low-nurturance childhoods have trouble with this, until they're in true recovery.

20) Help your mourner be clear on when they currently want _ empathic companionship and acceptance, or _ solitude. Help them get clear whether they need _ to vent, _ to clarify, or _ to problem-solve. When well-meaning supporters offer the latter at the wrong time, mourners need *inner* permission and maybe outer encouragement, to say, "Thanks, but that's not helpful now. Just hear me and be with me, please." or "I need time alone now to sort things out." We grief supporters need guidance at times on what our mourner needs at the moment. Your good-grief policy may include: "It's OK _ for our supporters to **ask what a griever needs**, and for _ us grievers to tell our supporters what we need if they don't ask!"

21) If the blocked person agrees, **co-design a one-time or annual ceremony or ritual** to honor that which was lost, and help the loser say good-bye. Ideas:

+ Have a special farewell meal with selected people.
+ Make imaginary or real calls or letters to key people.
+ Create or review a memorial poem, story, song, prayer, sculpture, collage, or painting.

+ Select people review a memorial book of pictures, me-
mentos, and remembrances.
+ Hold a memorial church service or group meeting.
+ Plant, bury, or burn something symbolic.
+ Reverently give away a symbolic object or memento.
+ Make a last or special visit to a place tied to the loss.
+ Write in detail about those things that will never be again,
and share that with a trusted friend.

Designing a grief ceremony and doing it together can grow
empathy and bonding for all (step)family members. Have you
ever participated in a ritual like this? What was it like?

22) Does your blocked person **avoid undistracted solitudes**
that would help them clarify and process their grief confusions
and emotions? If so, see if you co-parents are unconsciously
promoting that somehow (e.g. by not doing it yourselves), and
consider changing. Also consider confronting them compassionately on their avoidance and discussing it. Compulsive
"business" and "mind-racing" are often clues that the child or
adult's true Self is disabled. Her or his governing subselves are
terrified of what they imagine would happen if they got really
quiet ("I'd never stop crying!") Encourage journaling, meditating, and praying, without feeling responsible for the griever's
decisions.

You've just reviewed over 20 options you co-parents have
to help unblock a (step)family member who's stuck in one or
more of the three levels of mourning. You'll probably see more
options. Typical courting and re/married mates like Sarah and
Jack Tilmon aren't aware of their grief-unblocking options, or
the reasons they're important. Wounded co-parents like them,
specially wounded men, resist these *good*-grief steps despite
truly caring for their partners and kids. The steps feel too scary,
until true recovery from false-self dominance progresses and
subselves trust their true Self to lead.

Before summing up your fifth co-parent project, let's hilight two special cases of blocked grief . . .

Hostile and Uninvolved Ex Mates

Many of the hundreds of courting and re/wedded couples I've listened to since 1981 have denounced _ ceaselessly-bitter ex mates or _ non-custodial bioparents who "don't care about" their minor kids after divorce. I believe both suggest inner wounds, ignorance, and blocked grief. If you have either of these in your situation, here are some options:

"Hostile" Ex Mates and Frozen Grief

Unaware people can believe that legal divorce proceedings and documents "end" a marriage. Some think that the death of a spouse "ends" a committed relationship. Socially, legally, and physically, both are (usually) true. However, if surviving adults don't grieve their lost relationship, status, identity, rituals, and dreams well, they risk staying emotionally bonded, unless they didn't bond in the first place. Divorced parents must keep a relationship for years because of child support, visitation, education, health, church, holiday, and custody negotiations, and later weddings and grandkids.

Compulsively hanging on to a former mate or relationship, even if bitter and hostile, often masks a deeper terror of truly saying good-bye to a cherished marital *fantasy* or an idealized childhood caregiver symbolized by the ex spouse. This may follow having felt agonizingly abandoned by early caregivers. It can also mean subselves are avoiding goodbyes with an idealized childhood caregiver, whose qualities and/or identity ("Imago") is projected onto the ex mate.

It's sadly common to find an ex-spouse or ex in-law who seems dedicated to persecuting a former mate and perhaps their new partner, regardless of the pain it causes their kids. This lose-lose-lose behavior is often rooted in blocked-grief rage, combined with shame and repressed anger at their early

caregivers. I suspect the high majority (or *all*?) of such "vindictive" people are tormented, wounded survivors of low-
nurturance childhoods. They typically don't know that (denial),
minimize it ("Naw, my childhood wasn't *that* bad . . ."), or *intellectualize* it to numb out related hurt, anger, guilt, shame,
and anxiety.

If you have such an endlessly vindictive other parent, child,
or relative in your potential or present stepfamily, here are some
representative options:

**1) Partners steadily help each other view such a tormented
person as *wounded*, not *bad*.** Work hard to not discredit them,
specially in front of minor and grown kids. When the adult's
behavior is frustrating and offensive, use assertive, factual "I
messages" (Project 2) to describe their specific behaviors and
how they interfere with your needs. Stay alert to your R(espect)
messages too (p. 170)! See ..02/a-bubble.htm.

**2) Don't expecting logic, reasoning, or retaliation to
change them.** These make things worse because the core problem is probably unseen false-self control and related personality wounds. No matter how "sensible," *logic* is usually decoded
as an attack: "So you're right (1-up) and I'm wrong (*bad*), huh?"

**3) Do everything possible to avoid legal and court con-
frontations** with hostile ex mates. These are *always* adversarial
and generate clusters of stepfamily-wide emotional, financial,
and loyalty conflicts and losses *that usually take years to heal.*
A stepfamily reality is that sometimes an ex mate's wounds are
so deep there is no avoiding their using legal force to fill their
complex needs. Everyone loses, without exception. See this
article for more perspective: ..Rx/ex/legal.htm.

__ **4) Consistently practice the seven communication skills**
(Project 2) with your wounded co-parent, specially awareness,
digging down, empathic listening, and respectful assertion (limit
setting). Offer chances to problem solve, rather than avoiding,
arguing, explaining, defending, complaining, whining, or blaming. If your wounded co-parent refuses, **stay clear and firm
on your personal, re/marriage, and household boundaries**
without anxiety, guilt, or shame. Consider diagramming your

typical communication sequences with the ex to find improvement options (see ..02/evc-maps.htm). Stay clear on your *and their* rights as co-equal (=/=) worthy persons: see ..02/rights.htm. If a false self rules you, you won't be able to do this consistently or at all until you choose true Project-1 recovery.

5) Avoid using kids as spies, messengers, weapons, or "bargaining chips" to get your way with your hostile (wounded) co-parent. Doing so puts your kids in stressful relationship triangles, and avoids confronting your real issues. These are usually mixes of psychological wounds, ineffective thinking and communication skills, and blocked grief.

6) Invite (vs. demand) the wounded adult to join in professional post-divorce counseling. See this as a win-win-win (you / me / our kids) goal. If you do this covertly thinking, "You need to get fixed" (R-message: "I'm 1-up"), it will probably cause *more* hostility, resentment, and distrust. If the "hostile" co-parent is unwilling, accept this without judgment as being out of your control. Use the Serenity Prayer, and look to your own needs and balance.

7) Respectfully offer your wounded co-parent information about high-nurturance families (e.g. Chapter 3), inner-wound recovery (Project 1), stepfamily realities (e.g. Chapter 6 and Resource C), and the 12 projects (Chapter 8)—specially about this good-grief project. Appeal to their genuine love for their biokids to join you in converting distrust, antagonism, and resentment to co-parenting teamwork for the kids' sakes (Project 10).

The resentful, rageful, and distrustful members of their inner family may be too conflicted and distrustful to co-operate with you. If so, *you can't control this.* Blaming, pitying, and/or scorning this "hostile" person for their hidden psychological wounds *always* makes relations worse. A natural law: attack *always* causes defense and counterattack, withdrawal, or resentful submission. Your minor and future (grand)kids depend on you to *want to* break this cycle.

8) If you partners obsess about your "hostile" person, see if that's a covert way of avoiding something that scares you, like a personal, relationship, or co-parenting stressor. Meditate honestly on "What would I (we) be spending time on if I (we) weren't focusing so much on (the wounded person)?" An objective person may help you evaluate this. If one or both of you partners *are* avoiding something, that's a false self at work!

9) Overall, **you partners keep your personal and re/marital priorities clear** (p. 447), **and live by them as best you can.** Keep your perspective and balance on all seven of these challenging courtship projects (or 11 if you're re/married), rather than over-focusing on the wounded person's actions (a sign of false self control). If necessary, seek stepfamily-informed professional help in trying to balance your inter-home stepfamily relationships in the face of the wounded ex mate's behavior. For other ideas, see the series of "ex mate" articles at http://sfhelp.org/Rx/dx.htm.

The other end of the wounded ex-mate spectrum is . . .

"Uninvolved" Bioparents

Do you know a divorced family in which the absent bioparent "has little contact with" or "is way behind in paying support for" their minor kids? The latter is common enough in Millennium America to warrant laws, investigators, and collection agencies. Can you think of a stepfamily in which the custodial bioparent (usually the father) leaves most of the childcare to the new stepparent? If you have either situation, consider the options above and these:

The "uninvolvement" may be a *symptom* of the true problem underneath: unbearable [guilt + shame + remorse + self-disgust + sadness] that the bioparent is currently unable to face and adjust to. I've witnessed many tearful non-custodial fathers and mothers saying, "It hurts too much to walk into our house and see or talk to my child/ren!" Moralists who have never been in this position and know nothing about shame-based false selves will righteously sermonize, "Get over it!" or

"You wimpy scumbag, you're shirking your responsibility as a parent!" This is like reviling a person for having leukemia.

"Uninvolvement" may be **also a way of avoiding the agony and relentless guilt and remorse** of being _ "an unfit parent;" _ conceiving an unwanted child; _ "failing" as a mate, an adult child, and/or a parent; _ watching someone else raise my child; _ missing most of my child's growing up; and/or _ being unable to bond and feeling *empty* and *abnormal*. Examining the roots of each of these usually discloses blocked grief, underlying inner wounds, and unawarenesses, *not* a "bad parent." Compassionate assertion and respectful consequences work far better than blame and scorn here, long term.

Unwillingness or inability to pay legal child support can mean many things. I suspect that if you dig down far enough, you'll usually find low-childhood nurturance and some mix of the six psychological wounds on p. 142. Amplified by personal and societal ignorance, these often manifest as blocked grief, escalating attack-counterattack (or avoidant) communication spirals, toxic court fights, and fruitlessly focusing on surface problems rather than root causes.

In my experience with hundreds of stepfamilies, **bioparents who leave nurturance of custodial kids to a new stepparent** or a nanny, relative, sitter, au pair, or day care staff . . .

_ probably remarried for the wrong reasons (e.g. to gain a caregiver and reduce parental guilt, anxiety, and frustration).

_ may have an impaired ability to bond, and must deny that.

_ aren't very empathic with the needs of their new mate and/or their kids, and _ may have been abandoned as kids themselves.

_ probably deny or minimize being in a stepfamily, and/or what that means; and . . .

_ are at high risk of eventual emotional or legal re/divorce.

Such impaired parents wouldn't read this book, unless they're in true recovery.

So if you have "hostile" or "uninvolved" ex mates in your

stepfamily situation, you can _ revile, curse, and obsess about this "bad" person, or you can _ compassionately see them as severely wounded and ignorant, and assert respectful boundaries with them to protect your kids as best you can. If they're your former mate, you can ponder why you chose them as a mate. It probably means you're a low-nurturance survivor whose Self was or is held hostage by other protective subselves.

Recap

After 23 years' research, I believe that frozen grief in one or more family members is one of five related causes of U.S. divorce and re/divorce. Typical mates and kids have *many* losses to grieve, from _ low-nurturance childhoods, _ biofamily separation and divorce or _ the death of a spouse or parent, _ parental re/ marriage and cohabiting and related _ biofamily mergers. These broken bonds are to precious physical and invisible things.

Grieving is an instinctual emotional-mental-spiritual survival and healing reflex. The normal *emotional* process moves through shock > confusion and denial > anger > deep sorrow > eventual acceptance (tolerable emotional discomfort). The concurrent *mental* level of grief moves through confusion > emerging questions > trial answers > stable, credible answers > clarity and *understanding*. For many people, major losses often need spiritual mourning. This involves moving from stable faith to disbelief to anger and rejection of a benign Higher Power, (and perhaps a personal religion) to gradually rebuilding trust and faith in the presence and power of a caring Creator. Success at this depends partly on the griever not being dominated by a short-sighted, distrustful Guardian subself that fanatically tries to *control* life.

This three-level mourning process can be blocked in a child or adult by the consistent absence of some inner and outer factors:

+ Mental clarity on _ what was lost, and _ clearly understanding what the losses *mean* to the griever and others they care about.

+ Personal awareness of the normal mourning process, _ faith in it, and _ steady commitment to it in _ one's own life and _ in others.
+ _ Enough inner and _ outer permissions and encouragements to move through the three-level mourning process, in one's own way.
+ Enough undistracted solitudes to allow the healing process to happen at it's own pace. And . . .
+ Time, courage, and _ patience in the both the mourner and their supporters.

I believe an unseen false self controls many post-divorce, widowed, and stepfamily co-parents and their kin. Until well into true personal recovery from this (Project 1), they often lack the inner permission to *feel* and *express* normal grief emotions. Such wounded people also have trouble tolerating and encouraging others to do the same. As their own caregivers did, many injured co-parents like Jack and Sarah Tilmon have *unintentionally* deprived their kids of understanding and experiencing the healthy grief process, and guidance on how to "do it" well.

This fifth co-parent project aims to find and free blocked grief in kids and adults. It has five steps:

1) Co-parents and key supporters make significant progress together on the prior four projects, over many months.

2) Learn healthy-grief basics together and teach them to your kids and key supporters.

3) Evaluate your current personal, household, and stepfamily "policies" (*shoulds, have to's,* and *musts*) about grieving behaviors, and grief support. Amend your policies as needed to promote *healthy* three-level mourning in all your stepfamily members.

4) Inventory each of your co-parents' and kids' tangible and invisible losses from biofamily separation or death, and stepfamily re/marriage and cohabiting. Then . . .

5) Assess each family co-parent, and minor and grown child, for symptoms of blocked grief.

If you're courting, factor in who's blocked and what that's likely to mean in drafting your co-parenting role descriptions

(Project 6), and in answering the six re/marriage questions in Project 7. Then consider doing what re/married co-parents need to do:

Try to get all your co-parents to agree on _ who the blocked grief person/s are, and _ a plan to help them unblock. Then _ help each other work your plan together over time *as teammates*, using steps like those outlined above. _ Include your respective responsibilities in your evolving co-parental job descriptions (Projects 6 and 10).

You co-parents can only do this effectively if you're free to grieve yourself. That implies that if you and/or your partner are ruled by false selves, you must be well along in true personal recovery (Project 1).

There are lots of resources available to help you all with this vital good-grief project. One is the set of self-discovery **worksheets** at http://sfhelp.org/05/links05.htm. Another is the suggested reading list on p. 542. There are probably professionals who specialize in grief counseling near you, though it's likely they're not informed about inner-wound recovery (inner-family therapy) or stepfamilies. There may also be lay-led or professionally led grief-support groups for kids and adults nearby, like *Rainbows*. If not, consider starting one! Ask your local mental health agencies, churches, and hospitals for suggestions on grief-support resources.

Evolving informed pro-grief policies (p. 297 and ..05/griefpol.htm) and _ living from them are *essential* preparations for your re/marital and stepfamily success. Doing both parts of project 5 thoroughly, while you progress on the prior and following projects, will greatly improve your odds of making re/marriage decisions you'll treasure in old age.

 # Reality check: can you recall what your knowledge and attitudes about attachments, losses, and healthy grief were before you read the last two chapters? We've covered a *lot* of ideas and premises on them! To get a sense of where you stand on this fifth project now, (re)take the ..05/grief-quiz.htm and/or mull, discuss, and/or journal about questions like these:

1) I believe now that it's highly valuable for me and my

minor and grown kids (if any) to understand the phases and three levels of healthy grief. (T F ?)

2) I solidly believe that my partner feels the same way. (T F ?)

3) I believe that human grief *can* be blocked by lack of inner and outer permissions, and _ I feel my partner fully agrees with this. (T F ?)

4) I can _ name and _ describe the six factors that promote effective three-level grieving. (T F ?)

5) I'm strongly motivated to _ do this grief-assessment project _ with my partner and _ key others now. (T F ?)

6) I can _ clearly describe my personal good-grief policy now, and I can confidently _ guestimate my partner's policy. (T F ?)

7) I can clearly _ name and _ describe the five steps that my partner and I can follow to assess for blocked grief in our (step)family. (T F ?)

8) I know where to find the set of 20+ healing options we have, if we find blocked grief in one or more of us. (T F ?)

9) I have enough _ inner and _ outer permissions to grieve my losses well now. If not, _ I know what to do about this, and _ I'm motivated to act. (T F ?)

10) I strongly believe my partner has enough _ inner and _ outer permissions to grieve. If s/he doesn't, I believe _ s/he knows what to do about this, and _ is motivated to act. (T F ?)

11) I feel no hesitation in discussing this good-grief project with _ my partner and _ with our other related co-parents now. (T F ?)

12) My true Self is clearly in charge of my inner family as I answer these questions. (T F ?)

Awarenesses . . .

Your next-to-last courtship project builds on the prior five. It provides the keel, ribs, and rudder for your (potential) stepfamily love boat. In my research and clinical practice since 1979, I've never read of or met any stepfamily co-parents who have done it! Often that's because they didn't realize or accept how complex and conflictual stepfamily-building is (reality distortion plus unawareness).

Before turning the page, identify who, specifically, comprises your present family? What is the *purpose* of your family: why does it exist? Does whoever leads your family have a conscious set of long-term family goals? Does s/he or do they have a long-term *personal* mission statement (a life purpose) that guides their daily decisions? Do you? Do you know any families who have and use a *vision statement*?

Do you think your potential stepfamily has a better chance of success with a consensual mission statement, or just reacting to daily events as they happen? Which is more likely to reward you with contentment and satisfaction in old age? What are your subselves saying now?

Give them a mind/body break if they need one before continuing . . .

Project 6: Draft a Mission Statement and Co-parent "Job-descriptions"

If You Don't Know Where You Want To Go,
You'll Probably End Up Somewhere Else
— David Campbell

Imagine that you and your beloved partner, all your minor or grown kids, and all their other co-parents and key relatives are boarding an ocean-going yacht. Picture your friends waving from the dock as your sails catch the wind and you head for the horizon. The shoreline disappears, and everyone's excitement wears off after some hours. Imagine your having no navigation charts, compass, or weather information; no agreement on who's in charge of what on the boat; and no idea where you're all heading.

Would you do that? In my experience, most romance-dazed, needy, re/marrying co-parents do. A tragic result is that over half of our U.S. stepfamily love-boats sink in mid-ocean with all hands on board. You can avoid this happening to *your* crew!

As you saw in Chapter 3, co-creating a high-nurturance *bio*family is challenging enough. Typical multi-home nuclear stepfamilies like the McLean-Tilmon-Cohen clan (Chapter 7) are far more complex in structure, roles, adjustment and merger tasks, and interpersonal dynamics. Their multi-generational (extended) stepfamily is even *more* complicated: close to 100 kids and adults trying to fill up to 15 alien new roles "well," with little experience or informed help.

Unless the leaders in each of your kids' co-parenting homes share a clear vision of what you adults are trying to do together short and long term, you're likely to spend your days and nights struggling with endless sets of conflicts, and feel like "We're riding off in all directions."

You co-parents and kids *can* **end up where you want to go** over the coming years by (1) clarifying *early* what you want your stepfamily to achieve, over time. Then (2) evolve clear ideas together about who among your three or more co-parents is responsible for what, along the way. This assumes you all have accepted your stepfamily identity, settled major membership disputes, and are well along converting key stepfamily myths to realistic expectations (Projects 3 and 4).

This sixth courtship project focuses on the two tasks above. First, you partners thoughtfully draft a brief description of your main stepfamily objectives together: a shared *mission* or *vision* statement. Based on that, _ assess what each of your minor kids and any grandkids need, and _ evolve a specific set of goals and responsibilities for each of your stepfamily's co-parents on how to meet these needs: i.e. draft caregiving "job descriptions."

Well used, these two resources will help you co-captains sail your stepfamily vessel safely through many storms calms to satisfying, interesting ports along the way. Have you ever heard of re/married mates doing this together? Recall: most U.S. stepfamily re/marriages flounder and sink.

This chapter provides perspective, examples, and suggestions on creating an effective mission statement and co-parent role descriptions.

What is a Stepfamily *Mission Statement*?

It's a brief, well-deliberated document or charter describing the basic principals and goals of a person or group. It declares clearly "This is what we stand for, and what we're dedicated to doing." It may or may not include key guidelines (vs.

specific steps) on how to achieve the goals. As the U.S. Constitution underlies our government and system of laws, a mission statement is the foundation for all basic policies, roles, and decisions. It's a blueprint for guiding a person's or team's activities steadily towards consistency, order, and desired long-term outcomes. Four kinds of mission statements are personal, relationship, organizational, and national. The U.N. and related groups have international charters.

A personal mission statement is a concise written declaration of what a person (like you) is trying to do with her or his life over time, and how they want to do it. It implies that the author wants to take responsibility for the long-term direction and outcome of his or her choices and actions. Most of us don't think seriously of drafting such a statement. We never saw our parents or key teachers do it, nor any hero/ines. Paradoxically, we feel best when acting on our "integrity": living consistently from our core values and principles (e.g. "I will never take what doesn't belong to me.") These base values are elements in our (implied) personal mission statement. Do you know anyone who has a written personal mission statement? If so, do they *use* it?

One answer to the universal question "Why am I alive?" is to believe "I have unique gifts and talents. My life's mission is to find, develop, and use them creatively to benefit the world, within my limits." A personal mission statement might succinctly expand on that theme by naming your key talents, and describing generally what you wish to do with them across your years. I propose that such a personal statement is a powerful aid to, and comes true from, recovery from inner-family anarchy.

People who aren't self-motivated to define their life purposes clearly and to work patiently toward them, live aimless, reactive lives. They "ride off in all directions," and live each day as it comes, without a goal other than to survive and avoid or resolve local problems. They risk agonizing guilts and regret as they're dying, reflecting on lost opportunities and undreamed dreams. Do you know anyone like that?

Have you ever thought about what vision or standard you'll measure the success of your life against as you approach death? Without a clear long-term life goal, our lives evolve as a mosaic of small plans and achievements, often well below what we're really capable of. Effective re/marital and *stepfamily* mission statements are much more viable if the co-authors are each living from self-aware (vs. idealized) personal vision statements. Do you agree? Does this describe you and your partner?

In Western cultures, **wedding vows** are the traditional example of a *marital* (relationship) mission statement. Ministers provide a generic statement ("I John take thee, Teresa . . .") for couples that haven't devised their own. Re/marriers seem more likely to create their own vows. These may include pledges of loyalty to and support for their partner's child/ren, but rarely to the kids' other parent/s. Whether wedding vows are generic or personal, most couples seem lose track of them over time, as courtship thrills fade into humdrum daily living and dousing brushfires.

Do you know a couple that framed and displayed their nuptial pledges in a prominent place in their home as a reminder? Most mates and true friends each have a general idea of what they're trying to "do" with their relationship, but rarely refer to their goals except perhaps on anniversaries, retreats, crises, others' weddings, or in a counselor's office.

What might happen to the epidemic U.S. divorce rate if most couples made and *used* a meaningful relationship mission statement—specially if it were based on two thoughtful personal life-charters? What would be different in your life if your parents had devised and used a *parenting* vision statement? If you're a parent, do you know *specifically* what you're tying to do with and for your child/ren, long range? Does your daughter or son know?

In our culture, **organizational mission statements** are far more common than personal and relationship statements. Many religious orders, businesses, colleges, charities, and financial institutions, publish brief declarations of their main values and objectives. For example, here's the current mission statement of a Midwestern health center:

"West Suburban Hospital Medical Center is a community-based, not-for-profit, non-sectarian provider of high quality health care which is sensitive to the needs of people in our immediate and surrounding communities.

West Suburban Hospital Medical Center prepares and educates health professions to take their place in the health care system.

The Medical Center has an ongoing commitment to the well-being of the community we serve, our charitable trust, and individuals we employ."

Ideally the organization's personnel, financial, and operating policies and decisions are consistently based on a guiding declaration like this, specially in times of conflict and change.

We normally associate organizational charters with businesses, not families. Yet the leader/s of every home and multi-home stepfamily, including yours, have basic principles and at least short-term objectives that shape their daily decisions. These unwritten principles and goals still govern how the family operates. In all families, the members' personal, relationship, home, and family charters interact. When they harmonize "enough" with each other, local social values, and Natural laws, the family *works*, over time: it fills the core needs of each member well (Chapter 3), and adds value to its local and larger communities.

The odds of your family being *effective* (vs. low nurturance, or dysfunctional) go way up, when your leaders are consistently clear and united on, and steadily dedicated to, what they're trying to do together. Do you agree? Have you ever been in a family, team, or group like this? How did it feel to you? Did it *work* well? Note that the absence of conflict doesn't necessarily mean that a group or family is *working* . . .

Stepmom Jeanette Lofas, the founder of the Stepfamily Institute in New York, has proposed that forming a typical stepfamily is like merging several small companies. Usually it's three or more, including all related co-parents' biofamilies. Sane executives of merging businesses wouldn't try to blend their people, roles, assets, cultures, objectives, and customers without a clear, consensual set of merger goals, and agreeing on a phased plan to reach them. Yet that's exactly what most step-couples I've met do. They idealistically assume "Our love will see us though." Usually it doesn't.

Before looking at factors that shape how well a (step)family mission statement works, read the sample below out loud slowly. It's from the "Personal Leadership Application Resource" for Stephen Covey's excellent book "The Seven Habits of Highly Effective People":

"The mission of our family is . . .
to create a nurturing place of order, truth, love, happiness, and relaxation; and . . .
to provide opportunities for each person
to become responsibly independent, and effectively interde-pendent, . . .
in order to achieve worthwhile purposes.
Our Family Mission
To *love* each other . . .
To *help* each other . . .
To *believe in* each other . . .
To wisely use our time, talents, and resources to bless oth-ers . . .
To worship together . . .
Forever."

This brief charter says a lot. It clearly states what the leaders of this family want to do. In crises and major decisions, do you think rereading and reaffirming this would help partners decide what to do? What would it feel like to take part in a family whose leaders really *followed* these ideas? Would a charter like this work as well for a stepfamily as a biofamily?

Perhaps the co-authors of this declaration started with a shared high-priority need or dream to fashion a "good life" for themselves and their children. It looks like they felt responsible for making this dream happen, rather than assuming that it would "somehow." Finally, the co-authors evidently spent a lot of time thinking and talking about specifically what comprises the "good life" they wanted to co-create over time. Do you agree?

Notice your feelings and thoughts now. Are you curious, interested, and energized, or skeptical, bored, or indifferent? Think about the most challenging, risky event you've ever tried. Did you have clear goals and a well-research plan, or did you just jump in, trusting that "somehow" you'd be safe enough? What was the outcome?

What is your partner's style about complex life decisions: impulsive, prudent, or over-cautious? If either of you are divorced, did you approach your first marriages with a plan and key principles or did you "wing it"? Can you image going through another divorce with your dependent kids? How would you feel about yourself? What would your kids think about you? About marriage? About themselves?

Draft an *Effective* Mission Statement

Some mission statements *work* and others are just ink patterns on paper. I suggest three keys to making an effective stepfamily vision statement are:

+ Co-parents' clarity on their basic priorities, values, and stepfamily knowledge;
+ The document itself; and . . .
+ If, how, and when stepfamily members *use* the statement for guidance and inspiration.

Let's briefly explore each of these. Focus on the rest of your life in your mental viewfinder, or the lifetimes of each child you care about. Assess yourself thoughtfully on these factors as we go, and build an honest report card with your partner. This is pretty dry, so permit yourself to digest it in chunks. This is about *learning* and *visioning*, not blaming . . .

Your Priorities, Values, and Knowledge

Listening carefully to hundreds of contented and troubled co-parents since 1981 has revealed some common themes. Option: use what follows as a checklist to learn about you and your partner.

Relationships: Successful partners each genuinely _ prize and _ demonstrate interpersonal equality, dignity, and *respect*. Each mate consistently ranks their own personal needs, health, and worth as being just as important as those of other prized people in their lives, including their kids. Their concepts and practices of *self* love and loving others are founded on a true "equal-equal" attitude (p. 170).

From long habit, we men and women from low nurturance childhoods often rank our own needs and worth *last*. Over time, we usually grow dissatisfied and resentful, or resigned, depressed, and apathetic. Many step-adults (including grandparents) are such people. People who feel genuine self-love with little guilt or anxiety have no trouble in composing a Bill of Personal Rights, (..02/rights.htm) and in honoring the equal rights of others, including their kids' other co-parents!

Priorities: Successful co-parenting partners generally value their personal wholistic health (including spirituality) first, their committed relationship second, and everything else third. Successful re/wedded bioparents usually do *not* put their kids' needs before their mate's, other than in crises. These priorities are reflected in a genuine, long-term commitment to themselves, each other, and their kids. See p. 447.

Identity: Successful re/married partners like Rick and Karen Cohen clearly acknowledge that they, their kids, and their ex mates are in a multi-home stepfamily. They work diligently to learn stepfamily norms, tasks, and realities. Jack and Sarah

Tilmon we're struggling partly because they didn't know or care about Project 3 (p. 199).

Leadership: Successful co-parents clearly accept that they and their kids' other parents are each a co-leaders in their multi-home nuclear stepfamily, and a mentor for their minor kids. They fully (vs. "sort of") commit to the many responsibilities that come with those roles, because they *want* to, rather than *have* to. This usually implies that each child was a mutually desired conception or adoption.

Vision and planning. All successful co-parenting partners I've met agree that they're working on a complex *long-distance* project. They each feel that making and using clear, long-range personal and family goals is vital to their eventual stepfamily and re/marital success. Effective co-parents maintain a shared clear vision of specifically what kind of a multi-home stepfamily they want to build. From that, they form and use a co-operative plan to bring their vision to life a day at a time.

Acceptance of interpersonal conflict. Typical stepfamilies have *major* conflicts over needs and values in and between their related homes, for years. Successful co-parents each _ accept and _ expect that reality without undue blame, guilt, or anxiety. They patiently develop and use some version of the seven mental/verbal communication skills (Project 2), and teach them to their kids. A mission statement that works will probably clearly state co-parents' attitudes and aims on resolving stepfamily-members' conflicting needs. What are your *values* and *goals* on this?

Knowledge. Successful co-parents can clearly describe what wholistically-healthy, high-nurturance (vs. dysfunctional or toxic) persons, relationships, and families are. They're also reasonably informed on healthy grieving (Project 5), effective parenting, and the special needs of their minor and grown stepkids (p. 454).

Commitment. All three or more related co-parents are firmly dedicated to making their own lives, their relationships, and their whole multi-home stepfamily wholistically healthy. They take these seriously, without being obsessive. Adults who value themselves too little or too much, can't really bond, and/or have no clear life purpose, usually have trouble making meaningful family-purpose statements. Finally, successful co-parents keep their . . .

Balance: Daily and over time, mates help each other to blend family life, couple-time, careers, socializing, personal growth, and other obligations with personal and family playtimes (Project 12 in Chapter 8). They do this naturally with good humor and little anxiety, guilt, or shame. Usually their Selves provide *inner* balance among their dynamic teams of subselves. One result is consistent serenity and contentment.

In my experience, these nine values and traits seem to be common to contented co-parenting couples. They provide a solid base for designing a stepfamily mission statement that guides and inspires in times of need. If you co-parenting partners don't have some version of each of these factors now, do you *really* want to make the effort to acquire and live from them? Typical needy, idealistic false selves will vow "Yes!", yet their actions show otherwise.

Whatever your core values and knowledges, I urge you to draft your own stepfamily vision statement together, vs. adopting someone else's. You're far more apt to respect your own heart-values and shared goals than those of other authors, no matter how venerated or articulate. Even changing, adding, or deleting several words can make someone else's inspiring thoughts more *yours*.

The second key to your stepfamily mission-statement's effectiveness is . . .

The Document

I suggest up to nine traits will shape the effectiveness of your family mission statement:

Brevity. Each of the two examples above is under one page long. Charters that are too wordy and detailed risk being confining, rigid, cumbersome, and uninspiring.

Clarity and simplicity. To keep your statement short and simple, every word counts. The family charter above probably went through many drafts and adjustments before getting it *just right*. It may need periodic changes to reflect personal and environmental changes.

Flexibility and Balance. Effective vision statements *guide* rather than confine. They're general enough to avoid black/white rigidity, and specific enough to provide clear direction.

Relevance. Creating a meaningful family mission statement requires each co-author to first get clear on four fundamental questions: _ "What is a family?" _ "Who is, or may be, included in our (potential) stepfamily?" _ "What traits distinguish a high-nurturance (functional) stepfamily?" (Chapter 3), and _ "What are the main long-range purposes of our multi-home nuclear (or extended) stepfamily?"

For perspective on these questions, mull these: "What's the difference between our stepfamily and a sports team? A travel agency? A school? What basic things can only be done in and by our stepfamily?" The co-parents' I've polled on these questions mention "patiently preparing all dependent children to be safe, loving, independent, and productive," and "empowering each family member's love, self-respect, wholistic health, personal growth, security, support, and spirituality." Other family topics like home decorating, car maintenance, savings accounts, and pet care are minor compared to these, and are irrelevant to your mission statement.

Four more shaping factors to consider:

Reality. I hope Project 4 convinces you that typical courting co-parents like you have many potentially-harmful misconceptions about stepfamily roles, relationships, and lifestyles. A realistic stepfamily charter, then, will probably be a little longer than a typical biofamily mission statement. It will describe key goals that biofamily charters wouldn't include. For instance:

+ Adult and kids *grieving* major divorce or death, and re/marriage losses.

+ Rebuilding damaged interpersonal securities, trusts, and self-esteems.
+ Child visitation, support, and custody values and goals.
+ Relations among stepsiblings and with other step-relatives, especially with absent bioparents.
+ Handling household and stepfamily conflicts over stepfamily identity, membership, loyalties, and values. This includes conflicts over drafting a mission statement!
+ Doing these 12 co-parent projects together.

Focus. An effective stepfamily or personal mission statement will highlight values and key long-term targets, rather than related plans and strategies. Family *role* descriptions (below) may include the latter.

Integrity. There are no self-contradicting goals in an effective vision statement. The stated stepfamily goals are in clear harmony with all co-parents' personal life-values and goals, and with Natural, civil, and social laws.

Scope. I believe the potential for good from a mission statement rises if it's designed with the welfare of *all* members of your entire extended (multi-generational) stepfamily in mind. If you include all your kids' living legal and genetic grandparents, aunts, uncles, and cousins the scope of your mission statement can include 60 or more people living in over a dozen scattered homes.

Format. A ninth key aspect of your mission statement document is its physical appearance. A penciled declaration on a grocery bag has a much different emotional impact than silver-framed, manuscript-quality calligraphy on fine parchment. Some appropriate graphics or artwork (like a stepfamily crest you all create) can add dignity and importance to your vision statement.

Besides your co-parents' _ priorities, values, and stepfamily knowledge, and the _ nature and appearance of your document, the final effectiveness factor is . . .

Using Your Mission Statement

Personal, marriage, co-parenting, and stepfamily charters are either aging pages in a dark place, or truly helpful reference documents, like Holy books, address books, calendars, checkbooks, and dictionaries. What makes the difference is the motivation, thought, and cooperation that went into the charters, and how often family leaders and members *use* them in making daily and special decisions. By definition, your vision statement is unique. The "right" way to make and use it depends on what works for you partners and your stepfamily members.

Some **basic decisions you partners face together** here are: _ Shall we co-create a vision statement? _ When? _ Where do we put our mission statement in our home/s? _ How often do we refer to it, and why? _ Who do we give copies to, and why? And _ do we demand compliance with our declaration from all our stepfamily members, or request and encourage cooperation? Suggestions:

Your first chance to *use* the draft of your stepfamily mission statement is drafting **co-parent job descriptions** (below). Doing this sixth two-part courtship project together will reveal a lot about you partners' respective personal goals and priorities, and your ability to work as far-sighted teammates.

If you choose to re/marry, the second chance to use your vision statement is in **your commitment ceremony.** Your wedding may be one of a few times most members of your extended stepfamily will be together. Reading your mission statement out loud together in your ceremony, and/or including a copy in your invitations or programs, can boost its emotional power when you refer to it later across your years. These options also may help your family members "connect" emotionally to your statement, and may inspire them to make their own!

Display your statement prominently in your home, where residents and visitors will see it when they enter or socialize together. The alternative is probably "out of sight, out of mind."

Review your declaration as a couple and family regularly,

e.g. at anniversaries and rites of passage like childbirths, christenings and bar or bas mitzvahs, graduations, housewarmings,
Thanksgiving, and major lifestyle changes. Authorize yourselves to revise earlier drafts, as your re/marital and stepfamily
experience and wisdom grow.

More options on *using* your mission statement . . .

Consider giving a copy of your vision statement to your
kids' other co-parent/s, if they weren't involved in drafting it.
That's probable because of unhealed prior bitterness, hostility,
and/or indifference between your ex mates. If the language of
your statement specifically includes honoring the needs, feelings, and rights of your other co-parents, they may be more
receptive to adopting or contributing to it. They may need to
draft their own vision statement. Option: give a copy to your
kids' grandparents and/or other key relatives too, if only to
promote awareness, empathy, and family dialog.

Read your mission statement together, perhaps out loud,
**when you encounter serious stepfamily or re/marital con-
flicts**. This can provide a steadying beacon in emotionally confusing times, when one or more of you have temporarily lost
your bearings. It can also lead to important updates. Speaking
and hearing your statement can be more impactful than reading it silently.

Avoid *demanding* that all stepfamily members follow your
stated goals, or adopt the values in your declaration. Evolve a
statement that acts like a guiding keel for your stepfamily ship,
rather than a confining, narrow channel. A glass-half-full statement, vs. half-empty, will probably be more inspiring and "user
friendly."

Finally, use your mission statement as the foundation for
designing your alien new co-parenting roles. More on this below . . .

Add your ideas . . .

So the first half of your sixth courtship project is to thoughtfully compose a brief written statement with your partners describing what you want to accomplish with your nuclear or extended stepfamily over time. If false selves control your inner crews, this may have no practical value for you all. If your true Selves are usually leading, this can be a high-reward process of agreeing on the long-term ways you partners want to benefit the people you care most about, including yourselves.

As you mull and choose among these options, I suggest you review the traits of a high nurturance family in Chapter 3 together. Your grandkids and their kids will be significantly affected by whatever you partners chose to do here. Not choosing *is* a choice.

This first half of Project 6 can help you neutralize two of the five re/divorce hazards: unawareness, and romance-altered (idealistic) mind states. If you suitors don't share fundamentally similar values, priorities, and goals for your lives and future stepfamily relationships, you want to know *before* pledging your commitments. I've shared thousands of painful consultation hours with horrified stepfamily couples confronting major core relationship values-differences, months or years after their enthusiastic wedding vows and champagne toasts. Coparents with significant psycho-spiritual wounds are at special risk of this tragic unconscious self-deception.

 # Reality check: invest a few minutes in raising your awareness. Get quiet, reduce inner and outer distractions, breathe well, and . . .

Imagine yourself as an old person who is about to die naturally. You're preparing to end your long life journey. You're reflecting on your main choices along the way, and their effects on you and others. If you have kids, they're middle-aged and probably have kids of their own. Perhaps they're with you now, as you all get ready to say goodbye.

Do you have a life-partner with you in your image? Who is it? If you all reflected on the experiences and challenges you've shared together across the years and how they turned out, how would you want that conversation to go? If someone mentioned

David Campbell's book ("If You Don't Know Where You Want to Go, You'll Probably End Up Somewhere Else"), would you all smile and glow, or feel guilty, sad, and remorseful?

If it suits you, journal about your reactions to this image, and/ or share them with someone before continuing. Invite your partner to do this exercise, and learn what her or his experience is . . .

If you partners draft clear long-term goals for your (potential) stepfamily, what's next? The second half of this courtship project is to use your mission statement to . . .

Draft Your Co-parents' Role Descriptions

Co-parenting in an intact biofamily is an ongoing challenge. Three or more stepfamily co-parents trying to agree on what their young people need, who should provide it, when, and how, is *far more* challenging. There are more people, more special needs, and far more chances for distractions and major conflicts. This often doesn't really become clear to everyone until after couples return from any honeymoon. So courting partners like you do well to _ learn each minor child's status with their set of needs, and _ define which of your several caregivers should do what to help the kids with them, *before* deciding whether to re/marry.

Typical minor stepkids face a daunting array of over 20 normal developmental needs, plus up to four *concurrent* sets of family-change adjustment needs. Before reading further, write down as many of these as you can. Then bookmark this page, check your knowledge against Resource E (p. 454), and return here. The same list is on the Web at http://sfhelp.org/10/kid-needs.htm.

A *role* **is the set of responsibilities** that each family member tries to carry out, to promote personal and group harmony and success. To do this second half of Project 6 . . .

+ All your related co-parents must agree _ that you're in the same *step*family, and on _ who belongs to it (Project 3); and . . .
+ All your co-parents must also agree on _ which child(ren) each adult will take primary responsibility for, and _ what each of those kids need in the near future. This opens the door to your . . .
+ Negotiating what each co-parent _ will and won't provide for each child, _ when, and _ how, while _ maintaining the rest of her or his life priorities and goals.
+ Doing this effectively requires _ your Selves to be in charge (Project 1), _ sharing effective communication skills (Project 2), _ accurate stepfamily knowledge (Project 4 and Chapter 6), and _ consensual long-term stepfamily goals (above). Whew!

One of the most widely quoted reasons for stepfamily stress and eventual re/divorce is co-parents' inability to achieve these things co-operatively, over time. Disagreements manifest as major loyalty conflicts (p. 186) and bitter relationship triangles.

This second half of Project 6 aims to help you and your partner _ understand the four points above, and then _ work on them together. Doing this will help you preview how much co-parenting harmony or conflict to expect if you re/marry, mixed with other potential stressors. Evaluating this is vital for Project 7.

The rest of this chapter outlines key ideas on how you can rough-draft meaningful co-parental "job descriptions."

Guidelines

Tailor these ideas to fit your unique group of adults, kids, knowledge, and circumstances. If your Selves are in charge, you won't use this rigidly like a cookbook. This is a complex, high-emotion project with lots of chances for inner and mutual conflicts. So take your time and small steps. The *process* of drafting your job descriptions together is as useful as the result!

1) Accept that your kids' other bioparent/s and their current or future new mates *will* **be actively involved** in guiding and financing your minor and young-adult stepkids, for years. You partners must respectfully include these other adults' values, needs, and goals in your local and overall stepfamily plans, *even if they reject nuclear-stepfamily membership.* The inescapable alternative is increasing antagonism and conflict in and between your co-parenting homes. If that happens by intention or default, your present and unborn kids are guaranteed losers. If you can't agree on this now, the following steps probably won't work for you and the kids who depend on you all.

2) Review the realistic expectations you forged from Project 4. Use them and your mission statement as foundations for your job descriptions. Keep wondering "Why do well over half of typical re/married couples *like us* divorce?"

3) Gain perspective from several sources together. Each of you partners . . .

+ **Read and discuss** at least three of the stepfamily titles on p. 540. I specially endorse the books by Margaret Newman, Dr. James Bray, Patricia Papernow, and John and Emily Visher. If either of you partners identify as coming from low-nurturance childhoods, I also recommend the titles by Diaz and O'Gorman, and Mastrich and Birnes. Then use these Web resources at http:// sfhelp.org/ . . .

+ **Preview** what's ahead if you re/marry: three or more biofamily cultures over four or more years (..09/ project09.htm and ..09/merge.htm), while you build a co-parenting team (..10/project10.htm). Finally . . .

+ **Read** and discuss the ~40 environmental differences between stepparenting and traditional bioparenting at ..10/ co-p-dfrnces.htm.

+ **Discuss** how this overview of stepparent-stepchild relationships applies in your situation: ..Rx/spsc/basics.htm. And . . .

+ **Clarify** your strategy on spotting and resolving *loyalty*

conflicts and related *relationship triangles* (p. 186, ..09/
lc-intro.htm and ..09/triangles.htm). The following steps
will almost certainly generate these stepfamily stressors. Your co-parents' inner families will need reasonable fluency in the seven skills from Project 2 to master
both of them.

4) Each of you partners draft your own definition of an
effective **co-parent.** How can you distinguish between an effective co-parent and an ineffective or *toxic* co-parent? For
awareness and inspiration, think of one or more parenting hero/
ines: people you see as specially talented and effective childcare
providers. Identify the traits that promote your picking that
person. In contrast, think of others who aren't gifted caregivers.
Why do you think so? For ideas, see p. 478 and ..10/co-p-
goals.htm.

5) Use Resource E together (p. 454) to _ build a list of the
normal developmental needs that each of your minor (live-in
and visiting) kids needs to fill as they grow. Then scan the
several sets of typical stepkids' special adjustment needs. One
at a time, _ assess each of your kids to see how they're doing
with each relevant need. Try to _ agree on what kind of support
they need, but not who will help them yet. Consider giving
copies of these lists to your other co-parents and key supporters. Discuss them together as *teammates*, to raise your
awarenesses. Watch for and confront _ loyalty conflicts and _
relationship triangles that occur. Option: _ discuss your findings with each child, if they're old enough.

6) Stepparents-to-be: _ **get familiar in detail with any**
current legal parenting agreements that regulate your partner's
rights and responsibilities to each of your stepkids. If you're
unclear or conflicted about any aspect of such an agreement,
or a related legal document like an Order of Protection, _ discuss this honestly and clearly with your partner. Such documents are often powerful sources of past and ongoing resentment, frustration, and combat. They can cause periodic emotional firestorms in and between co-parents' homes, and in your
whole extended stepfamily. _ Get clear together on who's re-

sponsible for _ resolving present and future conflicts on such documents, and for _ paying any associated legal costs.

7) Honestly and *without blame*, **identify any specific current barriers** that block _ true cooperation and _ effective communication among your co-parents (..10/co-p-barriers.htm). Typical barriers are jealousy, resentment, distrust, disrespect, indifference, fear, guilt, anger, misperceptions, and "family politics." These usually come from seething brews of unacknowledged inner wounds, prior marital and divorce hurts and resentments, ineffective communication skills (..02/evcblox.htm), blocked grief, and various old and new reality distortions like denials and mis-assumptions.

Post-re/wedding **Project 10** (..10/project10.htm) **offers ideas on reducing** such barriers, over time. For now, simply acknowledge *without judgment* any specific barriers that you feel get in the way of co-parenting teamwork, child by child. *Your current goal is to draft initial realistic co-parental role-responsibilities that accept these barriers, vs. deny or minimize them.* If either or both of you feel the barriers are "significant" or want to ignore them, or if you have a strong disagreement about this, yellow re/marital light!

More co-parent job-description guidelines and options:

8) Most new stepfamily co-parents are confused about disciplining minor residential and visiting kids. Typical re/wedded couples like Jack and Sarah Tilmon have very different values, standards, and habits about setting behavioral rules, and enforcing related consequences. The best time to discover where you co-parenting teammates stand on **child-discipline similarities and differences** is *before* re/wedding. Courtship usually does *not* reveal what may be deep adult conflicts on this key aspect of co-parenting. For ideas and options, see the Web articles and worksheets starting at ..10/discipline1.htm.

9) **Get specific and honest about child-related expenses together.** Who does each of you co-parents feel should finance which _ daily costs (e.g. food, clothing, and school) and _ special costs for which child—now, and long-term? Learn each other's values about, and status with, _ estate planning and

wills. _ Whose insurance should cover each child's dental, medical, hospital, and optical care? Discuss _ providing weekly allowances for each child, and whether they should earn those or not. _ Get very clear on expected and actual child-support payments, allocations, and frequencies, including any back-due amounts. Who owes who how much, and when? If any of you three or more co-parents disagree on any of these financial points, who's responsible for resolving the conflicts? When? See ..Rx/mates/money.htm, ..Rx/ex/money.htm, and ..Rx/kin/money.htm.

10) Discuss the pros and cons of your stepparents' legally adopting their stepchildren. This is a complex emotional, legal, and financial matter that may merit *stepfamily-informed* professional counsel. In most states, without legally adopting their stepkids, typical custodial and non-custodial stepparents have few or no legal parental rights, and fewer legal responsibilities than bioparents. Usually the other bioparent must agree. See ..Rx/spsc/adopt.htm for perspective.

11) Courting couples talk honestly about child conception together. A sure recipe for eventual household polarization and corrosive stepfamily stress is one co-parent wanting to conceive, and their partner "going along" or feeling ambivalent. *Unlike healthy intact biofamilies, stepfamily* mates' *conceiving an "ours" child may wreck their re/marriage* unless they've progressed well on all 12 projects in Chapter 8.

My 20-year clinical experience is that having an "ours" child will probably *not* heal false-self dominance, resolve current loyalty conflicts, cement a wobbly re/marriage, or cause your stepfamily to bond and feel like an idealized biofamily. An "ours" conception probably *will* bring out new major anxieties and dormant stresses in and between your co-parenting homes. If you doubt this opinion, reality-check it with re/married veterans. Read and discuss ..Rx/spl/ourschild.htm.

12) All your prospective co-parents **discuss the possibility that child custody, and/or child primary residences, may change in the future.** Build an initial "what-if" strategy. Residence changes happen in roughly 30% of typical U.S. nuclear stepfamilies within 10 years of re/wedding, sometimes suddenly. This can happen because a child is "acting out" as a teen, and/ or their custodial parent is disabled or dies. Another trigger is increasing disrespect and conflict in and between a child and their custodial stepparent, and/or residential stepsibs. How likely is this in your case? Why, or why not? When might such changes happen? Specifically, how would such changes affect your web of co-parents' legal, financial, and emotional responsibilities, motivations, and satisfactions? See ..Rx/spl/kid-moves1.htm.

13) Admit and heal prior-relationship guilts. One or more of you co-parents are probably divorced (vs. widowed) bioparents. Are any of you burdened by significant guilt and shame about the hurts that kids endured from biofamily reorganization? If such guilt is excessive and chronic, it can semiconsciously cause a bioparent' to favor their biological kid/s, and discount their new mate and any stepkids. If not admitted and healed, this inevitably breeds accumulating hurt, resentment, new guilts, loyalty conflicts, and emotional distancing between mates and other stepfamily members.

A similar dynamic occurs when a bioparent had a marital affair, and/or is harshly self-critical for "selfishly" abandoning a wounded spouse despite their wedding vows. If any of you adults feel that some co-parent has significant guilt and/or shame issues like these, who is responsible for healing them? A powerful antidote to toxic guilt is true self and mutual forgiveness, which may grow after genuine (vs. dutiful or pretend) apologies are made. See ..Rx/ex/guilt.htm and ..Rx/ex/ forgive.htm.

14) As you partners research and reach decisions on each of these important co-parenting factors together, **keep** the draft of **your** relationship and stepfamily **mission statements updated and in mind.** If you haven't drafted these yet, I urge you to do so now.

15) Ask veteran stepfamily co-parents how they have divided caregiving responsibilities. Their decision *process* is as important as the division. Don't expect to find a stepfamily that is structured like yours.

Now . . .

16) Using your vision statement and all that you've learned, **draft the key caregiving responsibilities for each co-parent** in your (potential) multi-home stepfamily. Learn from your process: is it conflictual or co-operative? Do anxieties, loyalty or values conflicts, and/or ambivalences appear? If either of you has bioparent and (potential) stepparent roles, describe your key responsibilities for _ each role, and _ each dependent biochild and stepchild. See this sample inventory (http:// sfhelp.org/10/co-pinv1.htm) and the sample job description at ..10/job1.htm for perspective and ideas. Discuss your drafts with each other co-parent in your stepfamily, and perhaps with co-grandparents Are you courting partners open to input from these key people?

17) Family roles occur in pairs, like uncle-nephew, brother-sister, stepdaughter-stepfather. As you evolve drafts of the co-parents' roles in your multi-home nuclear stepfamily, a companion step is to **draft the key role-responsibilities of each of your minor and grown stepkids.** What are *their* main responsibilities in your stepfamily homes, and to whom? A rewarding option here is to make drafting *everyone's* stepfamily "jobs" (roles) a shared nuclear-stepfamily project. Keep the kids' complex sets of tasks in mind (Resource E).

18) Ideally, **include the thoughtful comments and requests of each dependent child—even young ones.** If you were a stepchild like Patty, Roger, or Annie, would it feel good to be consulted by your key adults on what you need from them, and what they're providing? This can get dicey. What if a stepchild says ". . . and I need my Mom and Dad to stop fighting and being so *mean* to each other;" or "I only want my *real* Mom and Dad to tell me what to do"? The alternative to this step is avoidance, which usually breeds anxiety, doubt, and guilt.

+ + +

Do you think typical romance-entranced co-parents would

discuss these co-parenting points in detail before deciding to say "I do"? Is it likely they'd intentionally invite their kids and other involved caregivers to discuss the points, and consider their opinions and needs? Do you think typical clergy or pre-re/marital counselors would know enough to encourage couples' discussing and negotiating these specific, complex issues before the ceremony?

My experience with hundreds of troubled couples is "Usually no." Result: average newly-re/weds and their partners start taking these co-parenting topics seriously *after* re/wedding. Co-parents are often antagonistic and confused then, and win-win problem solving is harder to do than before exchanging vows. The stakes are higher.

You just read 18 steps you partners can take together to _ learn what each of your custodial and non-custodial kids need, and _ co-operatively rough-draft each of your co-parenting role descriptions (responsibilities). Reflect. What are you feeling and thinking now?

If you partners agree that Project 6 is a useful, practical way to expand your personal, relationship and stepfamily awareness, then green light. If one or both of you resists drafting your mission statement and role descriptions, I suspect false selves are in charge. If you discover that any divorced bioparent (including ex mates) says to a potential stepparent "Hands off my kids. You (will) have no authority or right to co-parent them," *red light!* Ditto if a potential stepparent seems uninterested in helping to nurture their partner's kids, specially teens.

Most stepfamily researchers recommend that it's usually best for bioparents to do most of the child limit-setting and enforcing for many months after re/wedding, while stepparents, stepkids, and any stepsiblings are learning to trust, respect, and befriend each other. Stepparents like Jack Tilmon who demand immediate family changes and/or impose disciplinary rules and consequences too soon usually harvest resentment, hurt, and c/overt defiance.

These breed stressful loyalty conflicts and relationship triangles, and tend to polarize young stepfamilies into opposing adult-child camps. Take it easy, and consider the advice of stepfamily veterans Emily and John Visher: "In eight (years after re/wedding) it'll be great!"

Recap

The vital job of effective co-parenting is *far* more complex and challenging in average multi-home stepfamilies than in intact biofamilies. There are more adults and kids, more conflicting values, and new sets of concurrent, complex, alien adjustment tasks that typical first-marriage adults and kids don't face. Unless re/marrying co-parents foresee this complexity and prepare for it, accumulating conflicts between adults, kids, and kin will relentlessly fertilize hurts, antagonisms, distrusts, and potential re/divorce.

Your sixth co-parent project counteracts this gloomy probability in two ways. Your success with it depends on you partners progressing well on all five prior projects. The first way is (ideally) all three or more of your co-parents working together to _ agree on the key goals of your complex stepfamily enterprise, and then _ document these goals in a well-deliberated mission statement for all members to see and use.

Based on this initial vision statement, the second half of Project 6 is _ all you co-parents learn and agree on the normal and special needs of your dependent kids, _ resolve significant values and loyalty conflicts about these, and _ discuss and initially agree on "who among us is responsible for what, for each of our kids?" Ideally, this effort produces verbal or (better) written guidelines and targets for each co-parent's role in your (potential) stepfamily.

Investing time and energy in these two tasks together after working for some months on the prior five courtship projects can yield major long-term benefits. These six efforts are like you co-captains acquiring charts, weather lore, and a compass; and agreeing clearly on who will do what, as you all prepare to sail the unknown stepfamily ocean with your kids and kin. Your personal, re/marital, and stepfamily mission statements are like the North Star and a sturdy keel and rudder. They'll guide you safely and truly, when your officers and crew each know what their main jobs are.

Jack and Sarah Tilmon and Rick and Karen Cohen had never attempted these steps together or with their two other co-parents (Ted McLean and Sheila Cohen). Three results were that _ the Tilmons wound up in my office in major personal and remarital discord, _ Sarah began planning for life after her second divorce, and _ Patty McLean ran away from home twice. The Cohens seemed to be doing well enough, and Ted McLean was reported to be progressing in his toxic addiction.

If you're already re/married, this and the prior five projects are still highly worth your time and commitment.

 # Reality check: See where you stand with this sixth court-ship project now:

1) I can _ describe a stepfamily mission statement to some-one who doesn't know what that is, and I can _ say clearly why courtship partners drafting such a resource *before* deciding on re/marriage helps protect them against the five re/divorce haz-ards. (T F ?)

2) My courtship partner can do both of these now, too. (T F ?)

3) My partner and I _ each have a clear idea of our respec-tive life purposes now, and _ could draft a *personal* mission statement if we wanted to. (T F ?)

4) Based on our life purposes, we both are motivated to draft our _ re/marital and _ stepfamily mission statements, or _ we've already begun doing that. (T F ?)

5) My _ partner and _ I can each name at least five reasons that co-parenting in a typical multi-home stepfamily is signifi-cantly more complex and stressful than in a traditional intact biofamily. We also can each describe what _ loyalty conflicts and _ (persecutor-victim-rescuer) relationship triangles are, and _ why they stress typical re/marriages. (T F ?)

6) We have _ read and _ discussed the developmental and adjustment tasks that typical stepkids face in Resource E, and

_ are firmly motivated to assess the status of each of our minor kids with those tasks soon. (T F ?)

7) We partners _ solidly agree that our kids' other parent/s are equal members of our (potential) stepfamily, and _ we agree well enough on who comprises our multi-generational stepfamily. (T F ?)

8) We have _ begun researching what's *normal* in typical stepfamilies (http://sfhelp.org/04/myths.htm), and _ converting our myths to realistic expectations. (T F ?)

9) My partner and I can each _ describe what a "co-parent job description" is, and _ why thoughtfully drafting our set of them *before* getting engaged will help us decide wisely if we should re/marry. (T F ?)

10) We each _ *expect* to discover significant values and loyalty conflicts as we do this, and _ have begun to clarify how we want to resolve them using the communication skills from Project 2. (T F ?)

11) My partner and I are each _ interested in learning how veteran stepfamily co-parents have divided their caregiving responsibilities, and _ have begun learning in person and/or via the Internet. (T F ?)

12) My partner and I _ clearly agree that to build a successful stepfamily over many years, we each have to *want to* put our personal integrities first, our relationship (often) second, and all else third. We _ agree that these priorities protect our minor kids and us from the trauma of re/divorce, and what causes it (a low nurturance stepfamily). (T F ?)

13) I believe my true Self is answering these questions right now.

Awarenesses . . .

You've come a *long* way since you opened this book! Your investments in doing the first six projects can pay off richly if and when you partners are ready to make a very complex, far-reaching life decision: "Should we re/marry and form or join a stepfamily now?" Your final courtship project suggests how to make three *right* re/marriage choices, by using all that you've learned to answer six personal questions.

Ready?

Project 7: Decide If You Should Re/marry

"Remarriage is the triumph of hope over experience"
—Samuel Johnson

Imagine this: full of love, hope, determination, and commit ment, you and your wonderful partner re/marry. Some years pass, and you're approaching or past the middle of your life. You've accumulated some wonderful couple and family times together, and an increasingly painful collection of disappointments, disillusionments, frustrations, hurts, and resentments. You're courtship expectations and dreams have gradually become middle-aged anxieties, confusions, bitterness, soul-weariness, and despair (lack of hope). You and/or your partner have lost substantial trust, respect, empathy, and care ("love") for each other. You no longer feel that you're your attempts to problem-solve these together will work.

At a moment in time, you or your spouse decides, "I can't do this (stepfamily re/marriage) one more day. You or s/he decides that someone must move out, and calls a divorce attorney (again?). Your heart is breaking for your young people, and you're flooded with sadness, guilt, shame, anxiety, anger, and confusion. You may or may not appeal to your Higher Power and/or close friends for support, as you consider what re/divorce will mean to those you care about the most. You break your denials, and starkly admit it has become a better option than continuing to try fruitlessly to resolve insurmountable sets of personal, re/marital and family problems.

Alternatively, you and/or your mate decide: "I can't tolerate (another) legal divorce at this time in my life, but I no longer feel any love, hope, or marital commitment. I'm resigned to living with my stepfamily, but I've detached emotionally and must fill my core personal needs (p. 49) elsewhere." Millions of disillusioned, tormented middle-aged re/married mates choose this *psychological* divorce option. Do you know any?

Most courting American stepfamily couples eventually re/ divorce, emotionally or legally. I believe this is because of the five interactive pitfalls outlined in Chapter 4. Can you name them now? Despite couples' prior biofamily experiences, common sense, maturity, and their rosiest dreams, well over half of the partners like the Tilmons in Chapter 7, and potentially *you*, each make one to three wrong decisions. Their false selves unconsciously pick the wrong *people* (vs. person) to re/wed, for the wrong *reasons*, at the wrong *time*.

This chapter aims to help you make three *right* decisions for you and your kids, based on all that you've learned in your prior six projects. Here you'll read . . .

+ What's different about re/marriage involving prior kids and ex mates?
+ Options to help answer six vital re/marriage questions effectively.
+ Extra considerations for homosexual and bi-racial couples and widowers, and . . .
+ Key suggestions for your commitment ceremony.

If you're already re/married, projects 1-6 and 8-12 may help strengthen or save your relationship. See the comments at the end of this chapter.

What's Different About *Re/marriage*?

Paradoxically, re/marriage is exactly the same as, and *very* different from, first marriage, specially if prior kids are involved. Again, the "/" notes it may be a stepparent's first union. Before continuing, bookmark this page review the *10* meanings of *marriage* on p. 518. In addition to those, *re/marriage* often means **some or all of the factors below**. Option: read these out loud to your partner, and note your reactions:

+ Less adult and child idealism and naiveté about marriage, and more acceptance that re/divorce may happen to you all.
+ You partners have more marital and life experience, which shapes your priorities, communications, expectations, and tolerances.
+ More familiarity with, and less (or more) anxiety about, emotional, legal, financial, and social divorce.
+ Higher adult motivation to try to heal re/marital problems, vs. bailing out when relationship times get tough.
+ A natural reflex to compare your new relationship and mate with the prior one/s. This can evoke anxiety and/or resentment in your new mate, and dissatisfaction, regret (or relief), and guilt in you.

And getting re/married means . . .

+ Stepparents having to accept (grieve) that you're not, and never will be, your partner's "only" love or sexual partner.
+ Stepparents living with daily reminders of being mate number two (or three): children, mementos, legal agreements, and ex-mate communications.
+ Stepparents' relating to your stepkids' "other relatives," and working to merge their needs, opinions, and customs with your own extended (bio)family's. These relatives will be an asset or a stressor to your re/marriage, or both.

And re/wedded mates . . .

+ Have different life priorities than you had in your 20's, and (probably) more financial assets and/or debts.
+ Must resolve complex, concurrent inner and mutual conflicts over sex; money; religion; stepfamily identity and membership:, roles, rules, rituals, names, and customs; asset ownership and allocation; legal contracts (e.g.

parenting and prenuptial agreements, wills, and insurance policies); home management; co-parenting; loyalties; and complex relationship triangles. Typical first-marriers don't experience these individually or collectively. And re/wedded mates . . .

+ Repeatedly face emotionally and financially complex decisions over (step)child visitations, custody, financial support, adoption, conception, and parenting, complicated by the needs and emotional baggage of kids (Resource E), one or more ex mates, and influential relatives. Typical first marriers have none of these.

You'll also experience . . .

+ Possible ambivalence or resistance to your union from kids, ex mates, biased friends, kin or ex in-laws, and perhaps your church community;

+ Various social reactions from "Getting married again? Wonderful!" to "Oh . . . this is your *second* marriage?"

+ Low biofamily, social, and professional understanding of all these differences, and therefore less support in uncertain and conflictual times.

+ Less undistracted couple-time to nurture and stabilize your new marriage, because of many responsibilities to, and relationships with, custodial and visiting kids, and their other co-parents' needs, priorities, and activities.

And ultimately, committing to stepfamily re/marriage means . . .

+ Truly accepting that your odds of long-term relationship success are less than 50%, unless you partners work *hard* on preventive measures like the seven projects in this book, and five more after re/wedding.

So the *re/marriage* you're considering is the same as first marriage, with more wisdom, more concurrent distractions and conflicts, (often) higher motivations, different (e.g. mid-life) priorities, and a *much* more complex family system, and less supportive social environment. Each stepfamily situation has other unique re/marital differences.

If you've never married or parented before, and you're in love with the biomom or biodad of living kids, you're taking on two of our most complex modern social roles concurrently: spouse and co-parent. That's like learning competencies as a surgeon and a jumbo-jet pilot at the same time. Your odds for "role-strain" (emotional overwhelm and anxiety) are *significantly* higher than if you were marrying a single partner.

Notice your thoughts and feelings now. What are your subselves saying?

Six Pre-re/marriage Questions

If you and your prospective re/marital partner have prepared well enough, you'll be able to discuss and answer these sets of core questions now *honestly*:

1) _ Who is making my three re/marriage decisions: my true Self, or some other needy subselves? _ Is my partner's Self making her or his re/marital decisions? _ How do I know? *These are the most difficult and important questions you each face.* Your living and future kids' future welfare depends on thoughtful, informed answers.

2) Why should I re/marry at all? _ What specific needs am I really trying to fill? _ Do we each have the right *reasons* to re/marry?

3) Why re/marry now, vs. months or years from now?" Are we each healed and knowledgeable enough? Is this the right *time*?

4a) Bioparents with one or more minor or grown kids: _ When no viable compromise appears, am I consistently willing to put my new re/marriage relationship ahead of my kids' needs much of the time, without "too much" guilt, resentment, worry, and shame?

4b) Prospective stepparents without living kids: _ Do I really trust that my bioparent partner will *want* to put our adult relationship ahead of their children's needs often enough for me, when we can't find a workable compromise? If so, will s/he do that _ out of duty, or because _ s/he solidly believes this is a healthy long-term way to protect the kids from re/divorce trauma? _ Will s/he feel too anxious, guilty, and resentful about often putting us ahead of the kids or others?"

Some courting co-parents are bioparents and potential step-parents. If you're a dual-role suitor, you need to research and answer both these questions. Honest answers are *essential* to you all, because the most common surface reason for stepfamily re/divorce is either . . .

_ a stepparent feeling "second" (or fifth) to a stepchild or ex mate too often, and/or . . .

_ a re/wedded bioparent feeling too tired of having to choose between their mate and their kids.

This is specially true for needy co-parents controlled by a shame-based false self.

5) Why marry this person? If your partner is a bioparent, the question becomes _ Why should I marry this *family*: _ my entrancing partner, _ her or his minor and grown child/ren, _ their living or dead ex-mate/s, _ their biological and legal kin-folk, and _ all their combined emotional, physical, financial, and legal histories, contracts, debts, and conflicts? Am I re/marrying the right *people*?

The final question for each of you to mull is . . .

6) What options besides stepfamily re/marriage do I have to fill my and my dependents' main current needs?

None of these questions is trivial or simple. If you're a cus-todial or non-custodial biomom or biodad, each minor child depends on you to think clearly and honestly on these ques-tions. If you and your beloved hope to conceive "ours" kids together, the quality of their lives-to-be hinges largely on the wisdom, honesty, and courage you and your partner each bring to deliberating these six questions now.

Judging by our U.S. re/divorce estimates, why do most mature co-parents like you either avoid these questions or an-swer them wrong? My experience since 1981 suggests that most encore suitors are controlled by false selves, who aren't aware (or don't believe) that the five hazards on p. 69 apply to them, so they need to prepare by doing a meaningful version of the first six projects you've read about here.

Partners' shared ignorances of family-nurturance traits, false-self dominance, stepfamily realities and risks, blocked grief, and effective communication skills, shrouds the questions in fog. Even if courting partners have clear, accurate *knowledge*, their combined psychological wounds, specially [excessive shame + fear of aloneness and abandonment + reality distortions], make realistic answers to these six questions impossible. Could this include *you two*?

Romantic love, uninformed (stepfamily) advice, and media fairytales add major distortions to your decisions. They turn complex, sobering stepfamily-relationship challenges and risks into fun adventures where the good guys and their kids always win. Can you think of a media portrayal of stepfamily conflicts that didn't have a happy 60 or 90-minute ending? Most courting co-parents like you must deliberate these six complex, far-reaching questions alone, because there are no stepfamily-trained pre-re/marriage counselors or classes like this one: http://sfhelp.org/07/bhsf/intro.htm.

Self-motivated education replaces unawarenesses with conscious knowledge. False-self dominance can be greatly reduced over time, once co-parents become aware of it and assume personal responsibility for their own recovery. Many custodial single parents find this education and healing tough to do, on top of co-parenting and full-time jobs. With clear goals, patience, help, and true commitment, it *can* be done!

Let's put these ideas to work for you.

How to Answer These Questions *Effectively*

Like your prior co-parent projects, this seventh one breaks down into manageable steps:

1) You partners work steadily together at Projects 1 through 6 for many months. If you don't, you're at high risk of needy, protective false selves distorting your goals and perceptions and sabotaging this vital project.

2) Re-motivate yourselves: scan Part 1 before you take the following steps, noting which topics or parts raise your anxieties the most.

3) Thoughtfully fill out each of the three Project-7 worksheets at ..07/links07.htm, and discuss the results together *honestly.*

4) Consider using a computerized pre-marriage evaluation service like "Prepare/Enrich MC," and "FOCCUS (for Catholics and others)."

5) If you haven't yet, read several or all of (at least) the seven books on healthy relationships recommended below, and discuss them together as co-students. If you're "not a reader" (often a sign of false-self control), ask someone to read them to you.

6) Consider using an informed, experienced stepfamily counselor to reality-check your responses to these six pre-re/ marriage questions.

7) Be cautious and discerning about acting on re/marital advice from friends, relatives, and helping professionals, unless you judge them to be Self-led, and well grounded in high-nurturance traits, healthy grieving, and stepfamily basics.

8) Question veteran stepfamily co-parents (re/married at least five years) about their re/marriage stressors and satisfactions. Stay compassionately aware that if false selves control them, what they tell you is apt to be unconsciously distorted. Finally . . .

9) If you live together before re/wedding, do *not* take your experience to be a realistic guide to how your post-re/marriage stepfamily relationships will be, no matter how illogical that seems. Your 30-minute re/wedding ceremony will change some core things in your adults, kids, and kin!

10) If you and/or your partner are significantly "torn" (uncertain) about choosing stepfamily re/marriage now, take your time!

Let's look more closely at these steps . . .

Take Months to Do Projects 1-6 Together

This is essential if you want to make informed, wise re/ marriage decisions that you and your kids will cherish the rest of your days. You and your partner must want to devote considerable time and energy to each of the six prior tasks, to offset the five hazards you and your kids face together. Your and others' false selves will try earnestly to convince you otherwise.

As basic carpentry, electrical, cement, glazing, and plumbing courses would prepare you to build a home by hand, these six projects alert you to inevitable stepfamily "construction problems." They prepare you to avoid or master them, and to lay a solid foundation for patiently building and enjoying a high-nurturance re/marriage and multi-home stepfamily.

Reality check: Again, T = true, F = false, and ? means "I'm not sure."

+ My partner and I _ understand these seven re/marriage-evaluation projects clearly, and _ are strongly committed to working on them together now. (T F ?)

+ I'm very sure my true Self just answered the prior question. (T F ?) Can you name the emotional traits that suggest your true Self is leading your inner family? If you haven't yet, see how many of the traits of significantly-wounded people (pp. 401 and 413) apply to you. If you're ruled by a false self, your protective subselves will try to dissuade or defocus you or distort your answers.

Reread Part 1 in This Book

Remember what it was like as a high-school graduate to talk to new freshmen? Recall how much you knew about school that they didn't yet. You've spent hours reading several hundred pages here on scores of ideas, checklists, opinions, recommendations, and questions. You're about to "graduate"— i.e. to decide if and how to put all these to work in your life. If you've read for meaning, you now have a much wider perspective on the contents of the chapters in Part 1. Reread them now to get new meanings that you didn't see the first time through, and to refresh yourself on *why* these seven projects are vital to you, any dependent kids, and your future generations.

With these early chapters fresh in mind . . .

Do the Three "Right Choice" Worksheets *Alone*

You and your beloved each take periods of undistracted time to thoughtfully and honestly fill out the Right *Persons*, Right *Reasons*, and Right *Time* questionnaires at http://sfhelp.org/07/links07.htm. You can preview them via Chapter 3 and the summaries on p. 481. To avoid hedging your answers, I urge you to do this alone, not side by side. Only you can decide the answers that best fit you and any biokids, and what your answers mean. Pick thoughtfully among the options in these worksheets, and add up your results. Then discuss the outcomes at length together and with any trusted, *stepfamily-aware* advisors.

These three long, detailed worksheets aim to guide you partners towards answering the six stepfamily-re/marriage questions above factually and accurately. I can think of no way to avoid some bias and subjectivity.

Consider Pre-re/marriage Evaluation Services

There are at least two useful services to evaluate. "**Prepare/Enrich MC**" is a research-based, computer-scored questionnaire about an engaged-couple's strengths and "growth opportunities." To use it, find a local clergyperson or counselor who is certified to guide you in using this service. S/He will give each of you a questionnaire, send the results to a computer center for a modest fee, and help you evaluate and use the returned results. Call 1-800-331-1661, write Life Innovations, Inc. at P.O. Box 190, Minneapolis, MN, 55440, or see the Web site at http://www.lifeinnovation.com for any trained counselors in your area. I am trained to do this.

The "MC" (previously married with child/ren) version of the Prepare/Enrich questionnaire includes some items on childhood, prior marriage, existing children, and co-parenting values. These questions are very basic, and miss much of the relevant detail in _ Projects 1 through 6, and _ the three right-choice questionnaires for Project 7. Though informative, I believe this resource alone *cannot* give you adequate guidance on whether to choose stepfamily re/marriage.

The second re/marital evaluation service is abbreviated as **FOCCUS**: Facilitating Open Couple Communication, Understanding, and Study. This is a self-diagnostic questionnaire designed to help Catholic and other couples learn more about themselves and their unique relationship. Like Prepare/Enrich MC, it is not a test or a predictor of marital success or failure. It aims to help partners identify and work through potential problem areas *before* co-committing. After reviewing it, I believe there is real but limited value in this program.

A FOCCUS-trained couple or parish priest administers the questionnaire and discusses the results with you. Some Catholic dioceses also offer a related pre-marital program called "Pre-Cana II" for re/marrying couples. FOCCUS is similar to Prepare/Enrich MC, and (I believe) lacks vital, relevant questions about stepfamily knowledge and the five re/divorce hazards. I doubt that most priests or couples are either life-experienced or trained in these or what you're reading here.

So I suspect that unaware, love-dazed couples can get encouraging results from FOCCUS, and still be at high risk of stepfamily distress and ultimate re/divorce. From my Chicago-area experience since 1979, my impression is that few clergy of any religion are currently taught key stepfamily realities, or are personally experienced in co-parenting challenges and norms. For information on this resource, visit http://www.foccusinc.com on the Internet, call 1-888-874-2684, or e-mail FOCCUS@foccusinc.com.

If either of you suitors travels to foreign lands, do you re-

search what they'll be like before you go? If so, you'll probably be motivated to . . .

Read At Least Seven Books, and Discuss Them

The first two titles I recommend to you partners are mine:
"Who's *Really* Running Your Life?—Free Your Self From Custody and Guard Your Kids"; (Xlibris.com) and *"Satisfactions—
7 Relationship Skills You Need to Know"* (Xlibris.com, 2001).
These offer clarification, perspective, detailed examples and
suggestions, and resources that will help you master Projects 1
and 2 here. You can get many of the ideas and worksheets in
these books from http://sfhelp.org/01/links01.htm and ..02/
links02.htm on the Web.

Third, read *"Keeping the Love You Find,"* by Dr. Harville
Hendrix (Simon & Schuster, 1992). This veteran (remarried) pastoral counselor proposes that we each unconsciously construct a
mental template ("Imago") for our *ideal* adult partner from the
best and worst qualities of our main childhood caregivers. Hendrix
feels that we're unconsciously attracted to adults who match our
Imago template over and over again, until we're aware of doing
so. Hendrix and his many supporters believe that we suitors are
usually not able to see our partners for who they *really* are (hazard
4), and can't make healthy partner choices until we become
consciously aware of our Imago template. Common evidence of
his theory is a mate saying something like "I can't believe it—I
married my father (or mother)!"

This idea matches my experience. I see this reflexive, unconscious attraction to the same type of person as a form of
false-self reality distortion. While very useful, Hendrix's book
doesn't address the added factors in stepfamily-mate selection.
His book and the related audiotapes and classes offer a clear,
structured way to help partners learn and discuss the features
of their respective Imago-ideals. Well used, these ideas and
tools minimize your chances of making largely unconscious
mate choices, and regretting them later. Hendrix has another
book for married couples.

A fourth book I encourage you to study together before your "I do's" is *"Embracing Each Other,"* by veteran clinical psychologists and mates Hal Stone and Sidra Winkleman-Stone (New World Library, 1989). They propose that every person routinely has a group of "inner voices," or "selves" that provide us kids and adults with inner dialogs (or shouting matches) all the time. Having such "voices" (thought streams and emotions) in no way suggests we are "multiple personalities," though an estimated 5% of our population bears that very real, extreme disability. Learn about them on the Web at http://www.delos-inc.com.

Part of the Stones' theory is that unconsciously we are strongly attracted to or repelled by people who manifest unpleasant personality traits that we have repressed ("disowned"). The authors believe that the semi-autonomous selves within in us react to the selves in our partner in complex ways, strongly influencing our perceptions and decisions. Their ideas mesh with those of both Dr. Hendrix, and psychologist Dr. Richard Schwartz, an articulate spokesman for our *inner* families. See *"The Mosaic Mind"* by Schwartz and Regina Goulding (W.W. Norton, Co., New York, NY; 1995).

After 17,000 hours of clinical experience and 64 years on Earth, I agree with these authors. Though their terms and focuses are somewhat different than mine, these seasoned professionals' key proposals seem to validate the commonality of psychological wounding from a low-nurturance childhood.

The fifth book I suggest you both read and discuss is the paperback *"Is It Love, or Is It Addiction?"* by psychologist Brenda Schaeffer (Hazelden, 1987). This is one of many books since 1980 on the apparently widespread emotional condition of *relationship* or *love* addiction. Similar books focus on *codependence*, which has become a widely used and misused buzzword in the last 20 years. The theme of this harmful condition is that the needy person becomes compulsively overfocused on the welfare and behaviors of their partner. In doing this, they lose healthy awareness of, and attention to, their own needs, emotions, priorities, identities, and personal

goals. As with all true addictions, an unrecovering co-dependent will deny, rationalize, or minimize this self-harmful compulsion, if confronted on it.

My experience is that men and women suffering from co-
dependence are *always* dominated by a false self, and don't
know it. I write from personal experience. This destructive compulsion seems to be caused by the combined inner wounds of
false-self control, terror of rejection and abandonment, excessive shame and guilt, and reality distortion (denial).

Adult relationship addiction is common enough to warrant
a national recovery organization and local groups in many
towns called "CoDA," Codependents Anonymous. The philosophy and lay-led group meetings are modeled after the 12-step
Alcoholics Anonymous program. Relationship addiction can
be managed (vs. cured), via the 12-step philosophy, lifestyle,
and group support. Then it can be significantly reduced, over
time, via true recovery from psychological wounds via Project
1 here, or equivalent.

See Resource B (p. 413) for a two-part checklist of co-
dependence symptoms from CoDA.

My next recommendation to you lovebirds is *"The Good
Marriage—How and Why Love Lasts,"* by psychologist
Judith Wallerstein and Sandra Blakeslee (Warner Books,
1996). These authors propose the keys to sustaining a happy
and long-lasting relationship. From intimate interviews with
50 couples who describe themselves as happily married, this
book describes four basic types of union, and explores nine
basic couple-tasks needed to achieve a good relationship.
The authors look at marriage in general, not *stepfamily re/*
marriage. Be aware that your false selves are likely to ignore what you read here. Dr. Wallerstein writes this after
having studied a group of typical U.S. divorced families for
over 15 years. The authors don't comment on the couples'
childhood nurturance-levels.

Finally, I recommend *"Becoming a Stepfamily,"* by Patricia
Papernow. This is the most helpful stepfamily book I've read.
Other stepfamily titles have valuable perspective to offer, and

say little or nothing about the five hazards and the 12 projects proposed here. *Unawareness* at work!

There are many books on successful relationships and marriage. A small subset focuses on re/marriage. These seven books and this one provide a conceptual foundation for your understanding what you're trying to do together as a couple, and what factors are causing your attraction to each other.

Reading and using the ideas in books like these offers some protection against picking the wrong stepfamily mate, while blinded by romantic love, unawareness, and unseen false-self distortions. If either of you partners is ambivalent or reluctant to do this research before re/vowing your lifetime commitments, *you probably have protective false selves shaping your relationship and your life.*

Reading and discussing the other titles on p. 538 will raise your odds of making three right re/marriage choices even higher. Your decision is complex, far-reaching, and highly emotional. To optimize your chances for making wise decisions . . .

Use an *Informed* Counselor to Help You Decide

Your responses to the three "Right Choice" questionnaires and the six questions above have high odds of being distorted by over-needy personality subselves + romantic love + lust + emotional weariness + loneliness + (perhaps) rescue fantasies + personal and parental insecurities + and maybe social pressures. Using an objective, *stepfamily-informed* professional to help you evaluate _ how you arrived at your questionnaire answers, and _ what the answers *mean* to you and any dependent biokids, can offer some protection against these distortions.

The professional most likely to provide effective support here . . .

_ Is a state-licensed, stepfamily-aware clinician (pastoral counselor, clinical psychologist (MS, MSEd, or MC), or social worker (LCSW), marriage-and-family therapist (LMFT), licensed professional counselor (LPC) or psychiatrist (M.D.) who . . .

_ Clearly displays the traits of a Self-led adult: centered, grounded, calm, focused, aware, alert, genuine, "up," resilient, realistically optimistic, physically healthy, good humored, balanced, and purposeful; or is clearly in true recovery from false-self dominance; and . . .

_ Meets most of the stepfamily-knowledge criteria in this Web article: http://sfhelp.org/11/counsel.htm. To my knowledge, the Stepfamily Association of America is the only organization that now provides a two-day intensive training class in stepfamily therapy for clinical professionals. See their Website at http://saafamilies.org for a geographic list of graduates. Their training program includes little on the five hazards and 12 projects, so far.

If you work with a pre-re/marriage counselor, tell them of this series of Xlibris books and related the Web-site resources at http://sfhelp.org. Ask if they'll scan or read them, if they haven't yet. They'll probably have their own recommended resources, too.

Another way to help you answer your project-7 questions well is to . . .

Be Wary of Re/marriage Advice from Others

Appreciate and *beware* well-meant re/marriage suggestions from other people, including your dependent and grown kids. Emotionally biased, unaware relatives, friends, clergy, and counselors, rarely offer objective, knowledge-based advice on stepfamily re/marriage decisions. If they *do* provide realistic warnings and meaningful suggestions (like these seven projects), needy, impatient, blissed-out wounded couples (you?) often ignore them, and sail off together with their kids anyway.

This implacably sets up a new round of the (low-nurturance

wounds > re/marriage > stepfamily stress > re/divorce) cycle, replicating and spreading psychological wounds and shattered dreams. If others who care about you are willing to educate themselves on the books recommended above, their counsel really can provide valuable challenges, affirmations, and suggestions. Each such person has their own agenda as they offer you counsel and feedback (or don't).

A lot of what you're reading here is abstract theory and my (experience-based, biased) opinions. In deciding whether to re/marry or not, you partners can increase your awareness and confidence if you . . .

Question Veteran Stepfamily Co-parents

In listening to several thousand co-parents since 1981, I've been startled at how often I hear "No, I (we) don't know any other stepfamily adults." This clashes with the recent U.S. census estimate that about 1 of every 5 or 6 U.S. families is "in step." I'm confident there are *many* re/married co-parents in your area, unless you live in Death Valley or on a mountaintop. Such people are often semi-consciously uneasy about admitting they're in this "odd" form of family, so they don't socially identify as stepfamily co-parents.

If you can find stepfamily veterans (re/married over five years), ask about their experiences and any re/marriage recommendations. I've found that most co-parents are glad to vent and advise, once they feel invited and respected. Because there are almost 100 structural types of multi-home stepfamily, don't expect to find other adults in a situation like yours. Listen anyway, for the themes, like confusion, frustration, disillusionment, and loyalty and role conflicts, are universal.

Build on questions like these:
+ "Do all your adults and kids think of themselves as being in a *stepfamily*"?
+ "Did you all identify as being in a stepfamily before you re/married?"
+ "What do you *like* about being in your stepfamily?"

+ "Did you know what you were getting into when you re/married?"
+ "How does being in a stepfamily affect the quality of your re/marriage?"
+ "What aspects of your stepfamily generate the most conflict between you mates?"
+ "What (specific) factors do you think are most important in building and keeping a healthy stepfamily re/marriage?"
+ "How did your adult-adult and adult-child relationships change after your re/wedding?"
+ "What would you recommend we do to prepare for our stepfamily re/marriage?"
+ "What do you wish you'd known before you re/married?"
+ "What resources have you found helpful in keeping your re/marriage strong?"
+ "If you've ever used professional help with your stepfamily problems, did it help? Why (not)?"

Caution: unless you're close friends, most veteran co-parents will minimize or be vague about their major problems. If a false self dominates them, they'll probably distort their realities unconsciously. Some will make things sound worse than an unbiased observer would conclude. Other wounded veterans will guild their stepfamily situation with gold, specially if they're denying their personal, and re/marital problems. Most (unaware, wounded) troubled co-parents focus on their kids, not their adult relationship. Bottom line: take veterans' tales and advice with a large dose of salt, and expect to learn useful things anyway!

If local seasoned co-parents are hard to find, try contacting other veteran co-parents via any of the many Internet forums (message boards) or chat rooms for stepfamily adults. Expect to find most of them focused on stepparents, specially stepmoms. See p. 548 and http://sfhelp.org/11/resources.htm for some stepfamily Web site addresses. These change often, so use your favorite "search engine" to locate the current array.

Research studies and hundreds of re/married-couple testimonies have convinced me that . . .

Cohabiting Experience is Not a Reliable Guide

Since 1981, I've heard hundreds of troubled co-parents like Sarah and Jack Tilmon spontaneously describe painful disillusionments about their stepfamily relationships after their re/wedding. Many chose to live with each other well before their nuptial vows. They were lulled into false optimism and security by unrealistic romantic tolerances, excessive politenesses, and cautions in asserting personal needs. The powerful legal, social, and emotional re/wedding ritual seems to instantly transform co-parents', kids', and relatives' expectations of themselves and each other. "Half an hour ago I was your kids' pal. Now I am their stepparent, with new responsibilities and expectations of myself, you, their other parent/s, and each of them."

Each minor and grown stepchild, co-parent, and emotionally-bonded relative goes through an invisible change like this after vows are exchanged and the toasts are enjoyed. This unexpected shift is one reason that rough-drafting co-parents' and stepkids' roles *before* re/wedding (doing Project 6) can reduce stressful disillusionments afterwards. This is specially true on the complex challenge of stepfamily child guidance and discipline.

Finally . . .

If You're Unsure, *Take Your Time*!

Deciding to re/marry and form (or join) a multi-home, multi-task, multi-role stepfamily is one of the most complex, far-reaching decisions you'll ever make. Like researching a multi-year hike through the Amazon Jungle, or sailboating your family around the world, thorough preparation is *essential* here for your and your kids' long-term welfare. Romantic love and lust are intensely impatient, specially if you're lonely, empty, weary, and longing for companionship, love, and a warm home refuge of comfort and fun.

To raise the odds that you'll all get what you want long term, I encourage you to stay focused on the vision of the *future* you want, and beware making impulsive, uninformed short-term re/marital decisions. All seven of these multi-step projects take *lots* of time, commitment, focus, realistic optimism, courage, and energy. Consider these as investments in your contented retirement as a loving couple, and in your kids' and grandkids' lifetime happiness. Remember the image of your older (dying) self reviewing your life choices and outcomes (p. 38)? Your re/marital decisions will greatly affect your satisfactions or regrets, as you prepare to end your Earthly journey.

As with all complex life decisions, your re/marriage outcome depends on how thoroughly you partners prepare.

Widowers, Same-gender, and Bi-racial Couples

If these describe you, this book fully pertains to you and your loved ones. Your co-commitment decision is apt to be significantly *more* complex than other couples for a number of reasons. Each of these three merits its own book, so these are summary comments:

If Either of You Is a Widowed Parent . . .

You're among the ~10% of re/courting U.S. co-parents adapting to the death of their former mate. Most U.S. re/marriage candidates are divorced or never married. Stepfamily adjustment tasks following the death of a child's bioparent are the same as, and different from, those in post-divorce stepfamilies. Compared to post-*divorce* couples, key pros and cons of potential stepfamily re/marriage include . . .

Re/marriage Pros

Courtship and post-re/wedding logistics and finances are usually simpler and less conflictual. There are no child visitations to manage, or disputes over child support, child custody, first or last names, holidays, stepchild adoptions, new wills, insurance, schooling and conferences, or geographic moves, unless genetic relatives have been active caregivers.

There is no chance the other parent will move closer or farther away, go bankrupt, reject a custodial child, sue for custody or money, or re/marry a troublesome new stepparent and clan.

If kids and surviving relatives _ grieve well, and _ aren't significantly wounded, **real closure (acceptance) is more likely** than in parental divorce. That *may* mean faster bonding between the new adult and any kids.

Stepkids are less apt to reject or act ambivalently toward a new stepparent because of bioparent-reunion fantasies. They may reject the new stepparent (and any stepsibs) if they haven't grieved their dead parent well enough yet.

Child-related **expenses** like medical and school costs *may* **be less stressful**, if the dead parent bequeathed significant (uncontested) assets to their survivors.

In high-nurturance stepfamilies, **having three active co-parents is a major benefit** in helping each other and minor kids with their many tasks.

The odds of re/maritally-divisive loyalty conflicts involving ex mates **are lower** than in post-divorce re/marriages. Other factors being equal, the long-term odds for high stepfamily nurturance levels are greater.

_ (Add your own Pros)

Re/marriage Cons for Widow/ers

The new stepparent may feel s/he is **competing with a ghost**, if a stepchild glorifies a dead bioparent ("My *real* Mom knew how to make *perfect* chocolate frosting!")

Widow/ers ruled by an unseen false-self may say they've grieved, but some personality parts really haven't. That can generate confusing mixed messages to the new partner, and/or cause resentment and frustration ("I'm getting real tired of you calling me by your first husband's name, Jan.")

Ex in-laws and/or minor or grown **stepkids may be blocked in grieving** _ their dead relative, and _ related losses like holiday and reunion rituals; so _ they don't accept the new stepparent or step-grandkids. This is different than post-divorce situations, because relatives and kids may periodically talk to or spend time with the "other parent."

Loyalty conflicts can erupt over mementos of the dead person. Photographs or other reminders may become intra-home or inter-home flashpoints: "I think you're harsh and selfish, demanding that I take the oil portrait of my kids' Father (vs. *my ex husband*) off the wall." "Yeah? If you had any sensitivity, you'd understand what it feels like to me to walk into the house and see your former mate's face staring at me from over our fireplace. I'm not thrilled about being reminded every day for years that I'm number two." The picture is not the true problem here; unawareness, inner wounding, and a lack of communication skills are!

Because the surviving parent has full custody, the new couple will have a **harder time getting time alone.** This can be a big re/marital stressor.

If the dead parent had few assets to bequeath, the **new stepparent will probably be asked to pay for more** of their stepkids' daily and special expenses. That may or may not be a financial and/or emotional problem.

Stepkids will never have a chance to ask their "other parent" questions about their childhood, or feel their parent's pride and encouragement, as they move into adulthood. They'll also miss the potential richness (or stress) of having stepsibs or half-sibs and step-kin they might have had if the dead parent had re/married.

Psychologically-recovering (older) **stepkids can't discuss or confront a dead toxic parent** about childhood traumas or neglect, and vent their anger and sadness. The parent will never have a chance to apologize. These can slow (vs. block) recovery and healthy mourning.

(Add your own Cons)

Each courtship situation after an ex-mate's death brings unique pros and cons to partners' complex re/marriage decisions. Similar pros and cons emerge if a stepchild's sibling died before their parent re/marries.

Same-gender Co-parent Couples' Pros and Cons

To respect the fierce (false-self) debate over legal lesbian and gay marriages, I'll use *re/commitment* instead of re/marriage here. I also avoid the term *straight* for heterosexuals. It promotes covert shame by implying that homosexuals are *bent* or *crooked*. Also note the different associations between "same sex" and "same *gender*." See the proposed definition of *marriage* on p. 518.

The five re/commitment hazards in Chapter 4 apply fully to you and any minor kids. The seven projects can help you decide whether to exchange vows or not. In Millennium America ("land of the free . . ."), **you'll have extra stressors to contend with** compared to heterosexual mates and kids. These Pros and Cons are shaped by my clinical learnings from a number of childless and stepfamily homosexual partners.

Re/commitment Pros

With some extra resources and awarenesses, I believe **homosexual co-parents and their kids can gain the many benefits** of a high-nurturance union and stepfamily. Research repeatedly shows that adults living stably with a love-partner are healthier and live longer than single peers, regardless of sexual preference.

If _ both partners are led by their true Selves, and _ have unambivalent acceptance and encouragement from their key relatives and friends, then _ **custodial or visiting minor kids probably get more needs met more often** in a two-partner home than in an absent-parent family. Those are big *ifs*.

As with heterosexual couples, **the chance for true recovery from false-self control is probably higher** with a loving

376 Project 7: Decide If You Should Re/marry

committed partner than without one, specially if both partners are recovering psychologically. I suspect that the odds that typical homosexual co-parents came from low-nurturance childhoods are higher than for heterosexual peers. If true, _ their need for recovery from false-self wounds, specially toxic shame, is higher, and _ the odds of their kids have significant inner wounds is probably higher. This is speculation.

After 20 years as a therapist, I'm not aware of any credible evidence that suggests kids raised by one or two same-gender parents are more likely to be homosexual themselves. So I see **the chance for effective co-parenting** here as a potential plus. There may be a relevant genetic connection: see the well-researched, provocative book "Brain Sex," by biogeneticist Anne Moir and journalist David Jessel.

Re/commitment Cons

The odds of higher stepfamily conflict and eventual breakup and wounding kids are probably higher for homosexual co-parenting couples, because of a mix of ongoing stressors like these:

The likelihood of **excessive personal shame, confusion, and guilt in same-gender parents**, their ex mates ("My wife left me for a *woman!*"), and their parents ("What did we do wrong?") **is probably higher** than for re/wedded heterosexual peers and their kin. These combine to promote _ significant inner wounds in adults and kids, _ ineffective communications, and _ blocked grief. *These* combine to raise daily stress, lower home and stepfamily nurturance levels, and promote emotional or legal breakups. Projects 1, 2, and 5 offer hope, and ways reduce these crippling psychological wounds, to gain the benefits (pros) above.

If homosexual mates haven't "come out" and stabilized their identities and relationships with family, friends, and co-workers, doing so after re/commitment adds a major emotional task to other stepfamily-adjustment projects (http://sfhelp.org/ 09/sf-task1.htm and ..09/merge.htm). Not coming out, and prolonging the "family secret," promotes shame, anxiety, distrust, avoidances, doubt, guilt, and false-self dominance. A healthy committed partnership can help a co-parent to publicly claim (this part of) their human identity and dignity.

The emotional, financial, and logistic complexity of a public commitment ceremony can inhibit the start of the new stepfamily. **Re/wedding ceremonies are complex** enough for heterosexual couples! See ..Rx/spl/wedding1.htm and the suggestions below.

Misunderstanding, hostility, and rejection from stepkids' other parent/s, relatives, and society, including schools and churches, _ **add multiple stresses** to a homosexual home and nuclear stepfamily, and _ limit effective supports. Local and Internet gay and lesbian communities, and sympathetic lay and professional supporters may offset this. See ..11/project11.htm for ideas on forming a support network.

The **chances for strife between stepkids' bioparents and their relatives is higher** than for heterosexual couples. For many reasons, that's likely to reduce the nurturance level of your home, which raises the odds of significant inner wounds in you and your visiting or custodial kids. The seven Project-2 skills are even more important to typical homosexual partners.

The **chance for expensive, emotionally-draining legal custody battles** and extended-stepfamily polarizations **is higher**, because of our ancestral religion-inspired bias against homosexual parents. These may lower the nurturance levels of your homes and relationships.

Kids are more apt to feel social confusion, embarrassment, and guilt if they have to say one of their parents is in love with a same-gender partner. Kids' peers can scorn or shun such a child, prompting evasiveness, isolation, and lying. Those cause (added) shame, anxiety, and guilt, specially if kids don't feel safe in confiding with their main caregivers. All of these can amplify or promote false-self wounds, which ripple and add problems at home, which stresses partners' hopes, resilience, and commitments.

More *Cons* in typical homosexual-couple re/commitment decisions . . .

Regardless of whom they live with, **minor kids with homosexual co-parents probably face extra adjustment needs** on top of the dozens on p. 454. That adds to the odds they'll "act out," and raises the complexity and difficulty of forming an effective, informed co-parenting team (Projects 6 and 10). That may lower the cohesion and nurturance level of your nuclear stepfamily (Chapter 3).

Depending on your state's laws, **the odds are lower that a same-gender co-parent can legally adopt their stepchild.** That may hinder household cohesion and loyalty, and promote fragmented stepfamily identity. Most heterosexual American stepparents don't adopt their stepkids.

If homosexual mates want an "ours" child, making that happen via adoption or insemination is far more complicated, expensive, and stressful than for heterosexual peers. The reasons and implications are too complex to summarize here.

Intra-home and inter-home **anxieties and conflicts can erupt when a stepchild enters puberty**, and relatives and neighbors acknowledge they're a sexual person. The sexual preference of the co-parents can (re)cause or resurrect intense loyalty conflicts and relationship triangles. This is specially likely in low-nurturance families where ethnic and/or religious traditions c/overtly fear, reject, and revile homosexuals.

The high majority of TV, movie, educational, and print-media portrayals of stepfamilies are of heterosexual partners and their kids and kin. This can promote **extra social alienation and isolation** in homosexual co-parenting homes and relationships. Shame-based homosexual stepfamily adults and kids are at double-risk of covertly feeling *weird, unnatural,* and *abnormal.* This can hinder personal recoveries from false-self dominance, which lowers home and stepfamily nurturance levels.

The chance for **conflicts from a stepchild's heterosexual bioparent re/marrying and/or conceiving a child are higher**. The new heterosexual stepparent and their kin and friends may be biased, ignorant, critical, anxious, and rejecting of their stepchild's same-gender co-parents. This generates complex loyalty conflicts and relationship triangles for everyone. This is specially likely if the co-parents are controlled by false selves, and/or aren't fluent in the seven communication skills in Project 2.

Periodic **stress over school conferences and family-oriented events** (e.g. Mother's and Father's Days, Thanksgiving, Easter, birthdays, and school graduations) **is likely to be greater** than with heterosexual couples. The need to invent meaningful new rituals and holidays that fill everyone's needs to celebrate with joy, vs. shame, ambivalence, avoidances, and guilt, is higher.

Homosexuals are at greater risk of occupational bias, job loss, and unemployment, than typical heterosexual peers. That can mean greater partnership and household financial anxiety and stress at times, on top of other stressors and adjustment tasks. It can also promote conflicts with ex mates over child support.

Each same-gender couple and stepfamily will have different mixes of these pros and cons, and other unique factors. **The bottom line: evolving high-nurturance stepfamilies is a** complex, long-term challenge. For typical same-gender couples and prior kids and ex mates, **it's significantly *more* complex and risky**. That's not a reason to deny committed, informed love. It's *more* reason to work patiently and courageously at these seven evaluation projects and the relevant tasks above. See this three-part Web article for more perspective: ..Rx/mates/gender.htm.

If you and your beloved are racially different, what's unique for you?

Bi-racial Couples' Pros and Cons

Most of the standard and extra *Pro* re/marriage factors above also pertain to racially-mixed suitors and their kids. A major plus here is the chance to have members of both extended biofamilies enriched via learning and sharing in the cultural traditions, rituals, beliefs, and cuisine of the other race. This is also true for courting couples from different religious beliefs, traditions, and ancestries.

The re/marital *Cons* are similar, and differ in some key ways.

Re/marital Cons

The main extra re/marital variable is how genuinely stepfamily members can respect and accept each other's nuclear and extended biofamilies as co-equal, dignified human beings. People from low-nurturance childhoods are more apt to hold and deny **conscious and unconscious racial (or religious) prejudices**. These usually promote minor to major c/overt disrespects, distrusts, conflicts, rejections, hurts, and resentments. *These* promote escalating guilt, shame, and anxieties in bi-racial stepfamily homes and relationships, specially if adults aren't fluent in the seven Project-2 skills.

Each partner may have to resolve a **more** potent emotional brew of **shame, guilt, uncertainty, and anxiety** about publicly loving and desiring a person from another race than same-race mates. This is specially likely if the suitor has one or more dependent custodial or visiting kids.

The **odds of culturally-based misunderstandings, biases, and conflicts** over stepfamily identity, membership, values, rituals, roles, rules, and priorities (loyalties), **are generally higher** than with same-race couples. This reality raises the value of partners working together at evolving effective communication skills (Project 2) *before* deciding whether to re/wed.

The **decisions to adopt a stepchild and/or to have an "ours" child are more complex**, so the chances of deciding "wrong" (viewed years later) are higher for than same-race peers. Relatives' reactions and influences are more likely to be polarized and divisive, also, which implies less support for the couple.

Bonding between stepkids, stepparents, stepsiblings and step-kin **may be slower or not happen**, because of racial biases, confusions, ambivalences, and social pressures. Key re/

marital factors are _ how clear each partner is on, and how proud of, their personal and racial/ethnic identities; and _ how bi-racial stepparents and custodial and/or visiting stepkids relate, over time. Ex mates' biases can either amplify or reduce stepkids' confusions and reactions to having a stepparent (and stepsibs) of another race and culture.

Bi-racial couples **may have a significantly harder time finding unbiased, informed stepfamily support** (friends, clinicians, clergy, support groups) for themselves and their kids than same-race peers.

(Add your own Cons)

Bottom line: homosexual, bi-racial, bi-religious, and some widow/er couples have **higher vulnerabilities to the five stepfamily re/marriage hazards**, and a proportionately higher need to do the seven courtship projects to raise their odds for long-term happiness and contentments. See <u>Rx/mates/ prejudice.htm</u> for more perspective.

Recap

This seventh stepfamily-courtship project is each of you partners using the knowledge you've gained from the first six projects to pick the right *people* to re/wed, for the right *reasons*, at the right *time*. This chapter proposes 10 options toward making wise re/marital choices. The long-term value you'll all receive from this project is directly proportional to the time and effort you and your co-parenting partner/s have invested together in the first six projects.

Ideally, all three or more of your co-parents now have accurate stepfamily-ocean and star charts, weather information, navigation guides and tools, a sailboat-owners' manual, and clear job descriptions; *and* you all agree on where you want to wind up with your kids and key supporters decades from now. Experience suggests that average stepfamily-ocean sailors like you all take four or more years to get their sea legs . . .

All seven multi-step projects (p. 122) aim to help you partners and your kids avoid the high *real* risk of stepfamily re/divorce. These projects build on each other.

This book is slanted toward co-parents considering re/wedding and their supporters. What if you've already decided, and your stepfamily yacht is in mid ocean?

If You're Already Re/married . . .

The first six projects can still be invaluable to you. They're really about living well and at your full potential, not just building a high nurturance stepfamily. If you do the projects honestly, you may discover that you and/or your mate have made some wrong re/marital decisions. The way stepfamilies are structured seems to force co-parents to confront who they *really* are (e.g. wounded survivors of low-nurturance childhoods), and what they and their kids need to heal. If your re/marriage is in major trouble, these projects may not be enough to restabilize and heal it. They will at least help you understand and validate what you all are experiencing.

Doing Project 1 well will either show you that your true Self is often in charge, or that a devoted, myopic false self has been trying to protect you. If so, your core choice is whether to free your true Self from custody, and harmonize your inner family. Do you see those as win-win outcomes? If you and/or your fine mate have some or all of the six psychological wounds, working on personal recovery will benefit you and any dependent kids in all cases.

Learning to use the seven effective-communication skills in Project 2 can improve all the relationships in your life. That includes the relationships among your inner family of subselves, if you elect to do some form of "parts work." Teaching these skills to your kids is a lifelong gift beyond value, re/married or not.

Projects 3 and 4 can grow your co-parents' clarity on who you *really* are (normal steppeople), and expose unrealistic stepfamily expectations that may be promoting stress inside and among you. Putting your true Selves in charge and using effective communication skills can help you adapt to more realistic role and relationship expectations, over time.

If you're significantly wounded and choose to recover, Project 5 can help thaw frozen grief you may have carried since childhood and/or since your prior family "broke up" (reorganized). It can also help you help minor kids and others with any frozen grief burdening them. Doing these can reduce vulnerability to "depressions" and some physical illnesses, and may extend your lives, re/married or not.

Do you know yet what you're on Earth to do? An option in the first half of Project 6 is evolving a *personal* mission statement. You and your mate each being clear on your personal life purposes promotes (your Selves) agreeing with clear-minds on your *re/marital* and *stepfamily* mission statements. It's never too late to clarify "Where do we want to go together?"

If you were clear on what your mission on Earth is, how would that affect your daily life? If you care about dependent kids, the second half of Project six (learning kids' needs, and cooperatively drafting co-parent job descriptions) can help you nurture them well. Average kids of divorce or death and parental re/marriage have a *lot* on their plates, and need all the informed adult help they can get!

I suspect that hectic daily life in America and your narrow-minded false self will urge you to put immediate life responsibilities and chores before doing these six projects. I encourage you to imagine your older (Future) self as you're dying in mind, as you decide your daily priorities. Each day of your life is like a brick. As you approach death, you'll review what you've built with the bricks of your days: a proud, useful, enduring structure, or scattered half-formed piles with no form or theme . . .

We're ready to start saying goodbye for now. Did you know that "good bye" comes from our English ancestors wishing each other "God be with you" and "(have a) good day"? The last Chapter in Part 2 offers some summary comments and ideas on "Now what?"

17) Summary and Next Steps

We're at the end of our journey in this book. You've studied your five re/marital hazards and seven antidote
projects. Your life path beckons. How (or will) you *use* these
ideas and resources to guide your life decisions? What are you
feeling and thinking now? This chapter adds . . .

+ Four major options for you partners to consider together.
+ A summary of five post-re/wedding projects.
+ Four key suggestions for your ceremony, if you choose
  to re/wed.
+ A summary and final status check on the key ideas in
  this book, and . . .
+ Closing comments and inspirations.

Your choosing to re/marry and form or join a stepfamily is
one of the most far-reaching decisions you'll ever make. This
is partly because there are one or more kids who are depending on you to research the choice well. It's also true because
you probably have half or less of your life remaining. This re/
marriage decision is harder than other complex choices because there is probably much relevant information that you
don't know you don't know. Unless you've been a re/married
co-parent before, your past life experience does *not* prepare
you to make a wise decision here.

I recall typical reactions among the several hundred courting couples in a re/marriage-preparation seminar I've co-led

for 15 years. At the end of a half-day overview of the five re/
marital hazards and the 12 co-parent projects, many said, "I
feel *overwhelmed*!" Others felt *discouraged, awakened, determined, empowered, enlightened, better informed, clearer, confused, scared,* and *more motivated.* Some were *angry* that I had
rained on their romantic parade. They were *sure* that re/divorce
was not a risk for them and their kids. A sure sign of needy
false selves at work!

Do any of these describe how you're feeling now? If not,
what *are* you feeling? If all these projects together seem daunting, take heart:

Each project is composed of smaller steps. You can clarify
and master these patiently, one at a time, like completing courses
leading to an educational degree or trade certificate.

You **are in charge** of your pace in doing these projects.
You don't have to please anyone else. Unlike a school curriculum, you can work, pause, rest, or do other things any time you
want.

These seven projects are best begun in order. They overlap. If you chose the order I've suggested, I believe progress
on the earlier ones will make the later ones easier. Your inner-
family leader/s may feel differently.

Edit each project to better fit your unique personality,
history, and circumstances. You don't have to follow the steps
as I've outlined them. If free to lead, your true Self knows how
to select among these steps and tailor them or add your own.
Armed with new knowledge in this book and related Web pages,
s/he knows how to make your best long-term re/marriage
choices.

**You have one or more co-parenting partners to do these
courtship projects with.** Ideally, if you're a divorced bioparent,
your ex mate will do them with you, whether s/he is single,
courting, or re/married. Your re/marriage choices (and your ex
mate's) will affect all your lives for decades to come!

Four Key Options

As you decide what to do with these challenging projects, notice where your thoughts and actions focus . . .

Who **are you focused on now:** one or more kids, yourself, your partner, both of you, someone else, God, or all of you? False selves are often unbalanced here. I suggest you focus steadily on filling *your* needs first, and then on those of any dependent kids.

What *time frame* **are you focused on:** the next weeks or months, or the rest of your life? Except for *Catastrophizer* subselves, typical false selves are relentlessly focused on *now* or the near-term future. I suggest you consciously choose a long-term time frame to help you make your re/marriage decisions. And . . .

What **are you and your partner focused on?** Whether the other *person* is the right one for you? Lowering your discomforts? Your potential re/wedding and honeymoon? How your kids and/or key others may be affected by your decisions? Rescuing your partner? Are you focused on sex? Money? Revenge? Security? "Normalcy"? Other things? What needs are your dominant subselves focused on filling? Among all these options, I urge you to focus overall on what choices are most likely to promote your inner-family healing and harmony, *long term.*

Finally, **note what you're** *not* **focused on.** Are your controlling subselves avoiding (denying) anything, as you mull whether to re/marry or not? How can you tell? One toxic avoidance is not keeping your kids and ex mates clearly informed of your adult relationship status, and considering re/marriage. Without exception, keeping these a secret is glaring evidence of false selves in control.

Another option you partners have is if and when to **share these stepfamily ideas and resources with other family members.** Ex mates and their kin, grandparents, adult siblings, and other relatives will be affected by your three re/marriage choices. Their knowledge, biases, agendas, and inner-family factors will affect your, your kids', and (perhaps) your partners' lives if you re/marry. Ideally, all of you can discuss the relevant parts of this series of books and Web articles together, to promote long-term extended-(step)family unity, teamwork, and harmony.

A third choice you two lovebirds have is to **learn and do these seven projects as a self-study course** together, or with a group of couples considering re/marriage. Based on 20 years' experience, all the materials for the course are on the Web at http://sfhelp.org/07/bhsf/intro.htm. It's free!

Finally, have you thought about widening your Project-7 perspective by **affirming your current stepfamily *strengths*?** You may be surprised at how many you have! To identify them try out the multi-part inventory at http://sfhelp.org/07/strnx-intro.htm. You can also use this detailed inventory as a way to measure your re/marriage research and stepfamily-building progress, over time.

In your unique situation, there are probably more useful options toward making three sound re/marriage decisions. The key here is self- and situational *awareness*, which is a core skill in Project 2.

If You *Do* Decide To Re/marry . . .

How can you effectively nurture and strengthen your inner and outer relationships over time, and *enjoy* them all together? Part of your re/marriage decision is whether you're each comfortable enough with continuing parts of the first six concurrent projects, and adding five *new* ones. Sound challenging? It is! Perhaps 30% of typical American stepfamily co-parents find ways to meet this rewarding challenge together, over time. *You can too*! The five new projects are . . .

Project 8) Nurture your re/marriage steadily, and keep it second only to your personal health, growth, and recovery. Do this without guilt, shame, and/or anxiety, no matter what other people say or imply. See (http://sfhelp.org/08/links08.htm). And . . .

Project 9) Merge and stabilize your three or more multi-generational biofamilies over four or more years. As you do, resolve *many* conflicts over assets, priorities, values, roles, membership, family identity, rules, and traditions (..09/ links09.htm). Do this while you do . . .

Project 10) Build on Project 6 to **keep developing an effective co-parenting team** and nurturing your minor kids (..10/ links10.htm); and . . .

Project 11) Evolve an effective **support** network for your three or more co-parents and your dependent kids (..11/ links11.htm).

And as you do all these many complex things, do . . .

Project 12) Daily, help each other **balance** all these projects, your careers, friendships, community obligations, social causes, personal growth, and local crises, **and** *enjoy the whole adventure!* (..12/links12.htm).

The fourth volume in this series, "Build a High-nurturance Stepfamily" outlines these five post-re/wedding projects and integrate all your 11 ongoing tasks.

That's the big picture as I see it, after 23 years' study and my personal stepfamily experience. I suggest that you're most likely to stay grounded if you two expect that learning the Part-1 basics and stabilizing all 11 of these projects well enough will take you four or more years *after* re/wedding (vs. co-habiting). Most of these projects have no real end point, and will require much less daily attention as you merge and stabilize.

If you choose to try the grand adventure, here are a few experience-based . . .

Suggestions for Your Re/Wedding

If an average first-wedding service is like planting a rose bush, then planning a typical stepfamily nuptial ceremony is like designing formal palace gardens. There is no social consensus for how to "do" a re/marriage service and honeymoon "correctly," yet. Compared to a "standard" first wedding, your re/commitment ceremony involves many more people, cultures, roles, and traditions to consider and balance. The odds are higher now that you, your new beloved, and your other co-parents come from different spiritual faiths and religious and ethnic traditions.

It's outside the scope of this book to go into much detail here. Your local library staff can guide you to magazine articles that offer ideas and suggestions about re/weddings. The Internet is another rich source: e.g. www.familymedallion.com and www.brideagain.com. Also consider "Weddings—A Family Affair: The new etiquette for second marriages and couples with divorced parents," by the president of the Stepfamily Association of America (SAA) stepmom Margorie Engel, Ph.D.

Here are four suggestions from my experience:

Choose a clergyperson who knows about stepfamily re/ marriages and dynamics to sanctify your ceremony. His or her private counsel and public leadership will help you and your kids and other co-parents get off to a *realistic* start together. If you can't find such a person (which is likely), ask the clergyperson you choose if they'll scan this book or equivalent before the ceremony. This can help them appreciate and validate some of the re/marital challenges you'll be encountering. Familiarity with either Prepare/Enrich MC or FOCCUS (p. 362) is a plus. If you know other co-parents, they may be able to suggest a stepfamily-aware pastor, minister, rabbi, or priest.

Secondly, if you partners haven't yet experienced serious loyalty conflicts (p. 186) and persecutor-victim-rescuer relationship triangles (..09/triangles.htm), planning and experiencing your stepfamily re/marriage ceremony and reception will surely cause them. If you partners and your key supporters _ know what these divisive clashes are, _ expect them, _ discuss generally how you want to handle them together, and _ prepare your kids for them, you lovebirds will take them in stride. If you haven't recently, read and discuss ..09/lc-intro.htm and ..02/a-bubble.htm on the Stepfamily inFormation Web site. An option: declare your shared priorities as part of your public vows. Again, my experience suggests for *long term* stepfamily

success, usually put your individual wholistic healths and integrities first, your re/marriage second, and all else (usually)
third. How does that feel to each of you?

Third, I encourage you to **use stepfamily language and
titles in your ceremony** and social celebrations. This is your
first chance to declare to all the important adults and kids in
your life that you all are not just "a (bio)family." In their wedding vows, some stepparents include a *co-parenting* declaration, and then present a gift or token to each of their stepkids
that symbolizes it. New stepparents may also elect to acknowledge their stepkids' relationship with their other bioparent/s,
and invite and pledge respectful co-operation.

Finally, **if you two drafted a mission statement** (Project
6), this is a rare chance to **affirm it verbally** together to all
your key supporters and stepfamily members. Option: include
a copy of your statement in your wedding invitations and/or
any printed program your guests receive at the ceremony or
reception. Recall the sample on p. 330.

For more ideas on your complex re/commitment ceremony,
see the Web pages at ..Rx/spl/wedding1.htm.

Postscript: your shared decision about taking a honeymoon
is probably a good indicator of how your re/marriage will go.
Decisions I've heard range from taking kids along, to deferring a honeymoon, to taking a Holiday Inn weekend in town,
to no honeymoon at all, because of finances, other commitments, and higher priorities (*red light!*).

Summing It All Up

Pause, breathe, and reflect: do you remember why you chose
this book? Were you seeking information? Perspective? Validation? Did you want direction and ideas on the complex question of whether to re/marry or not? Did someone you respect
say, "Read this"? Perhaps you aren't clear on your true needs.
Your needs may have shifted as you read.

Recall that when their Self is trusted to guide their inner
families, most people say some of these: "*Now I feel firm,*

grounded, clear, alive, alert, aware, balanced, focused, calm, purposeful, 'up,' positive, resilient, compassionate, present, and confident." Do you feel a mix of those right now?

Perhaps your greatest challenge here is deciding *"Who* is deciding what I do with these courtship projects: my Self, or some other personality parts?" **Project 1 is the keystone** to your ongoing life quality, productivity, and all your relationships and goals, not just to choosing whether to re/marry. If anxious Guardian and/or Vulnerable subselves are controlling your thoughts, feelings, and perceptions, I suspect they will try to sabotage or control your working at these projects. To get an initial sense of whether a false self is holding your Self in protective custody now, review the family nurturance traits you grew up with (Chapter 3), and thoughtfully fill out or review the worksheets describing false-self and co-dependence traits (pp. 401 and 413). Using all 12 Project-1 checklists is better.

> # **Final reality check**: Consider meditating or journaling on questions like these: (T = true, F = false, and ? means "I'm not sure.")
>
> + Now I solidly believe the five re/marriage hazards (Chapter 4) _ are credible, and _ apply to me and the people I most care about. (T F ?)
> + I accept without reservation that _ we adults and kids are now, and will be, a normal *stepfamily* [vs. "just a regular (bio)family"], _ which is *very* different than an intact biofamily. (T F ?)
> + If we choose to re/wed, I *really* accept that our kids' other co-parents will be full members of our multi-home stepfamily for decades to come. (T F ?)
> + After rereading them now, I honestly feel that none of the courtship danger signs on p. 10 apply to my kids and me now. (T F ?)
> + I come from a high-nurturance childhood (T F ?)
> + My partner clearly comes from a high-nurturance childhood (T F ?)
> + My and/or my partner's ex mate/s clearly come from a high-nurturance childhood. (T F ?)

+ I am not significantly controlled by a false self. (T F ?)
+ My partner is usually governed by her/his true Self. (T F ?)
+ _ My partner and _ I are well-motivated now to _ learn the main concepts in the Quiz on p. 83, and _ teach them to our kids and key others. (T F ?)
+ Nothing prevents my partner and me from beginning the seven re/marriage-evaluation projects now. (T F ?)
+ On a scale of 1 to 10, how motivated am I to work on these projects now?" (10 = *very* motivated) ___.
+ I feel totally comfortable now with my partner's knowledge of the _ hazards and _ projects, and with _ her or his genuine interest in working with me on our projects now. (T F ?)
+ What, if anything, is more important to me now than working on these re/marriage-evaluation projects?
+ Do I need a professional opinion on _ my conclusions here, and/or on _ what my next best actions are?"
+ Some people who would probably benefit from the ideas in this book are: (who?)
+ What are my main _ priorities and _ options now?
+ What are the most important awarenesses I've gained from reading this book and the related articles? (Option: jot these down thoughtfully inside the front or back cover, and reread them in the future.)
+ As I consider possible stepfamily re/marriage, what are my inner-family members feeling and thinking now?
+ What is my "still, small voice" saying right now? Do I trust it?

Become aware of how you react to these questions right now. Do you pause and meditate on them? Ignore them? Postpone them and continue reading? Something else?

I'll close with a true story of a loving, middle-class Midwestern couple considering remarriage. "Larry" (not his name) was the widowed dad of four minor kids, and had a Latino Catholic heritage. "Marcia" had divorced several years earlier, and had custody of three minor biochildren. Her people had middle-European roots and traditions.

These co-parents were college educated, in their 40s, and felt like soul mates. On a panel of stepfamily co-parents, they told their story. They had met five years before, and had been wrestling with all the issues you've read in these chapters. Marcia and Larry agonized over whether to re/marry and when, because they accepted that the odds were against them. They knew nothing of the five hazards and these seven projects, but had read some stepparenting (vs. re/marriage) books and articles.

With some humor, each partner reported liking some of their partner's kids, and disliking others. Some of their kids got along well, and others ranged from disinterested to hostile. Both partners had financial problems and were struggling to balance lives as single parents and employees. They had been engaged twice. First Larry, and then Marcia broke their relationship off as the wedding approached, for various reasons. A major one was a web of stressful loyalty conflicts that they couldn't resolve well enough. Another was that Larry said honestly that he had not really mourned the loss of his first wife well enough, nor had several of his kids.

The couple was miserable apart, and scared to commit to merging their and their exes' extended biofamilies. Three years before the panel, they brainstormed a compromise solution that illustrates how many options there are in complex stepfamily courtship. They decided to buy adjacent town homes and live as loving neighbors until the youngest of their kids left home. They had meals in each other's homes, shared holidays, took vacations together, and their kids got to know each other as neighbors and schoolmates. Several became best friends.

Occasionally they would go to each other's churches. Their relatives had many chances to meet each other. She and her ex Michael were working patiently on resolving some thorny divorce-related issues for their kids' sakes. Marcia and Larry maintained separate finances, and took their time discussing future asset and debt ownership. This grounded, honest couple did not describe their decision about sexual intimacy. What ever it was, they each seemed content enough.

As they sketched their saga, the reactions of other panelists and the co-parents in the audience ranged from disbelief to criticism to awe. In the hundreds of co-parent couples I've interviewed, I've never met another who chose a re/marriage compromise like this. I talked with them several times before and after the panel discussion, and sensed that neither partner was significantly dominated by a false self. If true, I suspect that's a major reason they were able to reach this compromise to their unique tangle of the five hazards.

Another reason was Larry and Marcia had each accepted their stepfamily identity early in their courtship. That motivated them to read and discuss a series of books about stepfamilies, which led to a healthy fear of being among the millions of re/divorced U.S. co-parents. They trusted their inner voices, which said that if they remarried at that time in all their lives, it probably wouldn't work.

You and your present or future partner are unique persons, from unique families and ancestries. How you (your governing subselves) decide to evaluate your re/marriage and co-parenting decisions will be unique, by definition. So free yourselves from relying on "what others do" as a reliable guide for your researching the right persons to re/wed, for the right reasons, at the right time!

One last time: after researching stepfamilies since 1979, I propose that five reasons that well over half of courting American co-parent couples *just like you* make three wrong decisions and re/divorce emotionally or legally are . . .

Unseen mixes of up to six psychological wounds in one or more of your three or more co-parents and some kids. The key wound is the loss of the wisdom, calmness, perspective, and leadership of the true Self. I believe these wounds come from low-nurturance early childhoods, passed on by unaware, wounded ancestors and an unaware society in denial; plus . . .

Co-parents' shared *unawareness* of _ high-nurturance family traits, _ dominant false-selves, _ effective communication skills, _ stepfamily myths and realities, _ stepkids' special adjustment tasks, _ healthy grieving principles, and _ their unawareness; plus . . .

Blocked grief in one or more stepfamily adults and/or kids. This follows major losses in _ childhood, _ biofamily breakup, _ single-parent family breakup, _ parental re/marriage, and _ stepfamily co-habiting. Blocked grief is a symptom of the two factors above. And . . .

Courtship neediness and romantic idealizations and hopes, based on unawarenesses and false-self reality distortions. Well-meaning, unaware supporters often amplify couples' courtship illusions. These include (some) stepfamily authors and human-service professionals (including clergy), who don't know what they don't know about stepfamily hazards, dynamics, adjustment tasks, and realities. When co-parents re/marry and start to have significant trouble because of these four factors, most of them find . . .

There is little or no *informed* **stepfamily help** for them and their kids in their community, church fellowship, local professionals, or the media.

Compare how you feel about these five hazards now vs. when you first read them. Has anything changed?

This book outlines seven effective ways you partners can evaluate these hazards in your situation, and to begin to correct or avoid them. Individually and together, the ways (projects) are complex. Some are alien, and all are challenging.

The odds of your mastering these interactive projects well enough soar if you partners' draft personal re/marital and stepfamily mission statements. Here again is the inspiring example from Stephen Covey's "Personal Leadership Application Workbook":

"The mission of our family is . . .
to create a nurturing place of order, truth, love, happiness,
and relaxation; and . . .
to provide opportunities for each person
to become responsibly independent,
and effectively interdependent, . . .
in order to achieve worthwhile purposes.
Our Family Mission
To *love* each other . . .
To *help* each other . . .
To *believe in* each other . . .
To wisely use our time, talents, and resources to bless others . . .
To worship together . . .
Forever."

If you partners haven't yet drafted one, imagine what it would be like to have a thoughtful declaration like this to guide you through tough stepfamily uncertainties and conflicts—starting with your six complex questions in Project 7 (p. 357). Also imagine having a guide like this for your *inner* family of personality subselves in confusing times! Finally, imagine helping each of the young people in your lives to build such a foundation for their inner teams and lives.

With the love you share, your Selves in charge, your blende visions and patience, and your versions of these seven projec as guides, you partners may choose to start building a wond fully satisfying re/marriage. That can be the rock-solid core merging your several biofamilies to build a high-nurtura fulfilling stepfamily for your present and any future kids yourselves.

After great study, deliberation, and discussion, your voices may also decide that committing to each other n ever) is probably not the best thing to do. To decide think *long range* and prepare as you would for a glob; sailboat cruise or other major expedition. The keys to sage are: _ take your time, _ learn to become true tear learn "the (stepfamily) ropes" and what supplies and sl need, and _ chart your course *before* you cast off with any kids from shore . . .

Consider using the books in this series and/or the related Web pages at http://sfhelp.org as guides, as your adventure unfolds. I welcome your feedback via the Web site or email to pilgrim27@aol.com.

Note to special readers: young and unborn Earthlings desperately need local and national legislators and media leaders to evaluate all that you have read here. If by chance you feel called to act on this need, there is *much* you can do to help banish unawareness (p. 83) and reduce epidemic low-nurturance caregiving, false-self wounding, and (re)divorce. For ideas and options, see http://sfhelp.org/prevent/lay1.htm.

Bon Voyage!

Part 3) Resources

A) Checklist: traits of false-self dominance.

B) Checklist: typical traits of co-dependence.

C) Comparing stepfamilies and intact biofamilies.

D) Priorities worksheet: what's important to us now?

E) Summary: what your minor (step)kids need.

F) Summary: three *right* re/marriage choices.

G) Glossary: key stepfamily words and terms.

H) Selected resources.

Index.

A) Traits of False-self Dominance

47 Common Personal Behaviors

This is one of three tools in this book to help you assess whether you or another person has some of the six psychological wounds (p. 142) from a low-nurturance childhood. The other tools are Chapter 3 and Resource B. See the full set of 12 self-assessment checklists on the Web at http://sfhelp.org/pop/assess.htm, and in the book *"Who's* Really *Running Your Life?"*

Premises

Young kids raised in low-nurturance homes (Chapter 3) don't get important needs met. To survive, they automatically adapt by developing a protective false self. Psycho-spiritually neglected kids develop an "inner family" of Regular, Vulnerable, and Guardian *subselves* or *parts*: a protective "false self" that regulates their perceptions and behaviors without their awareness. False-self dominance and wounding is *normal* and a silent epidemic in our society. It ranges from minor to significant to extreme. I believe many *character*, *mood*, and *personality disorders* are manifestations of false-self control.

Protective false selves lack the wide-angle, far-seeing wisdom of the true Self (capital "S") that every infant is endowed with at birth. These well-meaning, short-sighted subselves regularly make toxic choices, including marrying the wrong people, for the wrong reasons, at the wrong time. Significantly-wounded partners in denial risk *unconsciously* re-creating low-nurturance homes and promoting dominant false-selves in their kids as their unaware ancestors did.

Adults and kids dominated by false selves display characteristic behaviors that adults from high-nurturance childhoods usually don't. Since becoming aware of these traits in 1986, I have consistently found patterns of the behaviors below and those in Resource B in over 80% of my many hundreds of divorced and stepfamily therapy clients and students. Many report coming from low-nurturance early years (Chapter 3), and others (i.e. their false selves) deny or minimize that.

Once significantly-wounded people become aware of their false selves' control, they can intentionally empower their disabled Self to harmonize and safely direct their inner family, over time. Project 1 in this and the guidebook below is one way to do that. Generally, those who do this report that their health, relationships, productivity, spiritual awareness, zest, and serenity increase over time.

By itself, this inventory may not be a reliable indicator of whether or not you're significantly wounded and dominated by a false self. That's because the distrustful subselves controlling your inner family may need to distort your understanding of these items, and/or your response to them.

You can get a more accurate reading by doing all 12 checklists in *"Who's Really Running Your Life?"* or the Web site, and looking at their results all together. Doing this worksheet *honestly* can give you a useful overview of how average people from low-nurturance childhoods conduct themselves before getting into true (vs. pseudo) recovery from false-self control.

I've compiled the behaviors and traits below from over a dozen veteran mental-health authors who have written on co-dependence, Adult Children of Alcoholics, toxic childhoods, addictions, and recovery from childhood trauma. My own clinical and personal experiences consistently validate these traits and their origins.

Suggestions

To get the most from this resource . . .

+ Choose a non-distracted time and place to do this worksheet, and take care of any physical needs you have. Reserve at least 30".

+ Adopt the "mind of a student." Be curious and nonjudgmental, vs. anxious or skeptical. Try for a win-win attitude: anything you learn here is useful!

+ Pick an adult or child you wish to assess for false-self traits. If it's useful, pick a time frame: now or other. Then take your time, and thoughtfully check each item that feels solidly "true." The "__ __" symbols allow you to assess two people. I recommend assessing one person at a time, starting with *you*.

+ Consider journaling as you do this worksheet. Your thoughts, feelings, and awarenesses as you do this are as valuable as your checkmarks and blanks.

+ If there are others who might benefit from this checklist, copy it first. You can also copy it from the Web, at http://sfhelp.org/01/w1-gwctraits1.htm).

+ This is about discovery and potential recovery, not *blame*. These traits are not good or bad, they're symptoms of toxic false-self dominance.

+ Check each sub-trait before deciding to whether check the main trait. Option: use 1 to 5, instead of check or blank.

+ Asterisk or hilight any items you feel are specially important. Write margin notes or symbols to add emphasis.

+ When you feel some mix of *calm, centered, energized, light, focused, resilient, "up," grounded, relaxed, alert, aware, serene, purposeful,* and *clear*, your Self is probably leading your inner team of subselves. If you don't clearly feel a version of these now, other subselves are about to fill out this worksheet. To protect you (i.e. some young Vulnerable parts), they'll probably skew your results, so use the additional 11 worksheets to seek "the truth."

+ + +

__ __ **1)** S/He _ usually thinks in black/white *bi-polar* terms: i.e. s/he sees things as either right or wrong, good or bad, relevant or not, logical or "stupid," not somewhere between, or a mix. In internal or social conflicts, s/he tends to see only two options, and has trouble brainstorming. S/He's _ mildly to very uneasy with ambivalence, vagueness, or uncertainty.

__ __ **2)** S/He is _ often a compulsive perfectionist ("I can't help it"). Achieving perfection _ feels unremarkable and merits no praise, but achieving less is shameful. S/He _ has trouble enjoying her/his own achievements, and _ is often uncomfortable receiving merited acknowledgment and praise.

__ __ **3)** S/He is _ often rigid and inflexible. S/He _ thinks obsessively, and/or _ acts compulsively, even if personally unpleasant, unnecessary, or unhealthy; *or* _ s/he is often overly passive, cautious, and compliant, fearing to take personal, social, and occupational initiatives and risks.

__ __ **4)** S/He is usually _ serious, intellectual, and analytic, wanting to *understand* life and situations, and know in great detail why things are as they are. S/He _ may be interested in psychology and counseling, and/or _ analyze and discuss human behavior "endlessly."

__ __ **5)** S/He is often _ confused, disorganized, overwhelmed, dependent, and "helpless;" *or* s/he _ is fiercely independent, domineering, over-organized, and overcompetent. S/He _ depends excessively on, *or* _ stubbornly avoids, medical, psychological, social, and/or spiritual help.

__ __ **6)** S/He is _ uncomfortable being silly, spontaneous, or child-like ("doesn't know how to play"); *or* s/he _ is often silly, simplistic, playful, superficial, and joking.

__ __ **7)** S/He is either _ extremely responsible (over-willing to take charge, organize, and fix things, even if personally taxing); *or* s/he _ is frequently irresponsible and undependable. S/He probably _ denies, _ minimizes, and/or _ rationalizes (justifies and defends) either behavior.

___ ___ **8)** S/He often has trouble _ feeling and/or _ expressing strong emotions, and/or ___ tolerating them in others; specially anger, hurt, fear, and sadness. S/He _ often feels "nothing;" *or* s/he _ has unpredictable or inappropriate outbursts of rage, sadness, weeping, "depression," or anxiety. S/He may _ never apologize, *or* _ apologizes "all the time."

___ ___ **9)** S/He compulsively _ needs to control personal emotions, key relationships, and interpersonal situations. S/He is either _ overly aggressive, rigid, and domineering; *or* _ subtly, persistently manipulative (e.g. using guilt trips or a "helpless victim" stance) to "always" get her or his way. Where true, s/he probably _ denies, _ minimizes or jokes about, or _ rationalizes this ("I can't help it," or "I have to, because . . .").

___ ___ **10)** S/He has _ significant memory gaps about early childhood years and events, and one or both parents. S/He _ knows little about one or both parents' childhood experiences and feelings, and _ finds that unimportant or unremarkable.

___ ___ **11)** S/He's socially _ very shy *or* _ very charming, and _ has few or no real (intimate) friends. S/He has a history of relationship _ avoidances and/or _ "failures," including divorce/s. S/He demonstrates _ high discomfort with interpersonal commitment and/or intimacy, and _ consistently _ denies, _ minimizes, or _ rationalizes this.

___ ___ **12)** S/He _ may be sexually dysfunctional: e.g. impotent, frigid, or non-orgasmic; and/or _ compulsively avoids sexual contact; *or* _ s/he is overly seductive, voyeuristic, and/or promiscuous ("oversexed"). S/He may be secretly confused about, and/or ashamed of, her or his _ gender, _ body (parts), _ sexual feelings, _fantasies, and/or _ behaviors.

___ ___ **13)** S/He _ "never gets sick," *or* _ suffers chronic illnesses like migraines or other headaches, back, neck, or other muscle pain; insomnia or apnea; obesity; asthma; gastric, intestinal, or colon problems; anxiety attacks; phobias; allergies; or other emotional or physical maladies which may not respond to appropriate medications or therapies. S/He _ may rely on medications to provide daily rest, digestion, comfort, focus, and mood-stability.

___ ___ **14)** S/He is _ highly uncomfortable about revealing personal thoughts, feelings, and experiences (excessively distrustful); *or* s/he _ often discloses personal things inappropriately (naïvely over-trusting).

___ ___ **15)** S/He is _ uncomfortable giving, getting, and/or observing affectionate touching and hugging ("stiff" or "cold"); and/or _ touches others dutifully, awkwardly, or inappropriately.

___ ___ **16)** S/He _ often avoids personal conflicts with or between others by changing or controlling the conversation, getting intensely angry, "collapsing," or withdrawing physically and/or emotionally ("numbing"); *or* _ s/he seems to often *enjoy* triggering or experiencing conflicts with or between others.

___ ___ **17)** S/He is _ very opinionated and reactive about, and/or _ was or is compulsive about, one or more of these:
_ Ethyl alcohol in some form (liquor)
_ Prescription drugs or _ Illegal ("hard") drugs
_ Excitement and drama
_ A special hobby
_ Pain and/or death
_ Sugar, fats, and complex carbohydrates (junk foods)
_ Caffeine and/or nicotine, and attempts to "quit"
_ Another person (codependence)
_ Cleaning, neatness, lists, and/or organization
_ Food, dieting, and/or nutrition
_ Health, fitness, and/or exercising
_ Work, "busy-ness," and/or "being *productive*"
_ "Justice" and/or "fairness"
_ Protecting a child or social "underdogs"
_ A social "cause" like abortion and gun control
_ Material possessions (shopping and comparing)
_ Psychological "recovery" (e.g. Project 1 here)
_ Sex, masturbation, and/or pornography
_ God, worship, church, salvation, hell, and/or Satan
_ Lying, secrecy, truth, and/or honesty
_ Personal image, and/or others' opinions

_ Money, wealth, saving, spending, and/or gambling

__ __ **18)** S/He has _ children, _ relatives, and/or_ past or present partners, who _ excessively obsess about, or __ are or were addicted to, one or more of the above.

__ __ **19)** S/He has _ recurring depressions, apathy, and/or _ tiredness "for no reason." S/He may have periodic _ sleep disorders like insomnia, apnea, narcolepsy, and/or nightmares.

__ __ **20)** S/He often feels vaguely *empty*, "something's *missing* (in me)," or "I'm *different* than other people somehow . . .," without knowing why.

__ __ **21)** S/He is _ significantly uncomfortable being alone; *or* s/he _ prefers solitude to an unusual degree, and _ seems socially isolated.

__ __ **22)** S/He _ has consistently low self esteem; _ is often harshly self-critical; _ discounts her or his own successes and/or merited praise; _ is constantly apologetic or defensive; _consistently avoids making or keeping solid eye contact with some or most men / women / authorities / people. S/He _ commonly uses "you" or "we" rather than "I."

__ __ **23)** S/He _ often experiences mind-racing or *churning*: ceaseless "inner voices" (thought streams), which _ are frequently anxious, fearful, critical, self-doubting, argumentative, and/or chaotic. S/He may _ have marked trouble concentrating, and _ have been assessed as having "Attention Deficit Disorder" (ADD).

__ __ **24)** S/He is _ often anxiously alert to the present and expected future opinions, feelings, and actions of other people (hypervigilance). S/He tends to _ assume others' (usually stressful) beliefs or intentions, and _ often reacts to things that haven't happened yet as though they had. ("I *know* you'll have an affair!")

__ __ **25)** S/He often _ smiles and/or chuckles inappropriately when nervous, hurt, confused, scared, angry, or worried (i.e. often). If so, _ s/he is usually unaware of this habit; _can't explain it; and _ may minimize, intellectualize, defend, or joke about it to hide related anxiety.

__ __ **26)** S/He _ often feels vaguely or clearly victimized

by others or "fate", _ regularly avoids taking responsibility for
her or his own choices, and _ denies or _ endlessly rationalizes
doing so; *or* s/he _ assumes *too much* responsibility, and _
obsessively feels guilty and *bad* for things beyond her or his
control.

__ __ **27)** S/He is _ highly sensitive to real or imagined
criticism from others; and _ unnecessarily rationalizes, explains,
and/or defends his or her own actions and values. S/He is _
quick to blame others *or* _ often empathizes with "the other
guy's" situation, and defers to them.

__ __ **28)** S/He commonly _ fears, distrusts, is tense around,
and/or argues with people in authority roles. S/He either _ feels
very anxious without clear instructions, *or* _ compulsively resists them and acts independently, even if self-harmful.

__ __ **29)** S/He often _ fears saying "no" and setting appropriate limits (boundaries) with others. S/He _ feels guilty
about asserting her or his own _ needs, _ tolerances, and _
ideas; and may do so _ expecting others to discount, ridicule,
or ignore them.

__ __ **30)** S/He semi-consciously _ confuses pity with love,
and/or _ associates love with pain. S/He _ usually focuses on
others' needs first, and tends to _ rescue or "fix" them; *or* _ s/
he is overconcerned with her or his own needs ("self centered").
S/He _ avoids intimacy, or _ cyclically seeks, then runs from it:
i.e. s/he has a history of "approach-avoid" relationships.

__ __ **31)** S/He _ hangs on desperately to relationships
which repeatedly cause significant shame, anxiety, guilt, confusion, and pain. S/He _ may repeatedly cycle between intense
jealousy and guilt. Her or his _ major personal relationship-
choices are often largely based on fears of criticism, "being
wrong," rejection, and abandonment (See Resource B).

__ __ **32)** S/He _ feels bored, restless, or uneasy without
current personal or environmental crisis, drama, or excitement.
At times _ s/he seems to seek or *make* crises, and _ denies,
minimizes, jokes about, or justifies this.

__ __ **33)** Typically s/he _ is passive, timid, and reactive to
other people and situations; *or* s/he _ is often self-harmfully

impulsive, spontaneous, and aggressive. S/He may _ claim "I can't help it."

__ __ **34)** S/He often _ feels alone, disconnected, or lonely, even in a group or crowd. S/He _ rarely feels s/he really *belongs* anywhere, and may or may not disclose that to others.

__ __ **35)** S/He _ often seeks pleasure and gratification (comfort) *now* vs. later; S/He _ may defend or minimize this, _ rationalize by saying "I can't help it," or _ deflect from it by joking.

__ __ **36)** S/He prefers to work independently (e.g. as a consultant, craftsperson, or entrepreneur) and/or in a solitary setting. S/He either _ changes jobs often *or* _ stays at the same job for years. S/He _ works in a human-service occupation or avocation (nurse, doctor, teacher, counselor, mediator, lawyer, beautician, case worker, clergyperson, realtor, accountant, coach, nanny, day care worker, professional consultant, customer-service rep . . .)

__ __ **37)** S/He _ rarely *or* _ frantically initiates social activities. S/He habitually _ avoids *or* _ compulsively seeks being the center of social and/or occupational attention.

__ __ **38)** S/He is often _ self-centered, grandiose, and hyper health-conscious; *or* s/he is _ subtly or clearly self-abusive, self-deprecating, self-sabotaging, and self-neglectful (e.g. seeing a doctor, dentist, gynecologist, oculist, or therapist only in crises).

__ __ **39)** S/He _ habitually withholds, shades, or distorts the truth (lies), to avoid expected criticism, rejection, loss, or "hurting others." S/He _ denies doing this, and _ secretly feels righteous and justified and/or guilty and ashamed.

__ __ **40)** S/He is _ secretly or openly critical or ashamed of her or his "looks," appearance, or body. S/He may be _ extremely modest *or* _ very immodest. S/He consistently grooms and dresses either _ shabbily and drably *or* _ gaudily, over-formally, or perfectly.

__ __ **41)** S/He is _ notably pessimistic, skeptical, gloomy, cynical, and "negative;" *or* s/he is _ idealistic, unrealistically optimistic, relentlessly cheerful (including crises and traumas), and compulsively focuses on "the bright side" of things.

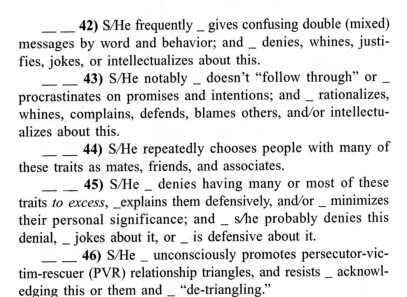

__ __ **42)** S/He frequently _ gives confusing double (mixed) messages by word and behavior; and _ denies, whines, justifies, jokes, or intellectualizes about this.

__ __ **43)** S/He notably _ doesn't "follow through" or _ procrastinates on promises and intentions; and _ rationalizes, whines, complains, defends, blames others, and/or intellectualizes about this.

__ __ **44)** S/He repeatedly chooses people with many of these traits as mates, friends, and associates.

__ __ **45)** S/He _ denies having many or most of these traits *to excess*, _explains them defensively, and/or _ minimizes their personal significance; and _ s/he probably denies this denial, _ jokes about it, or _ is defensive about it.

__ __ **46)** S/He _ unconsciously promotes persecutor-victim-rescuer (PVR) relationship triangles, and resists _ acknowledging this or them and _ "de-triangling."

__ __ **47)** Unless already in true wholistic recovery from false-self domination, s/he will _ discount, avoid, intellectualize, disparage, or distort Project 1 in this book (identify and recover from major inner wounds), and _ deny, justify, or trivialize that.

Because none of us grew up in perfect childhoods, *everyone* has mixes of these traits! Note how many of these 47 behaviors you checked about yourself here ___. There is no formal "scoring" key. **The more of these items you checked, the higher the odds** you're often controlled by personality subselves who don't know or trust your skilled inner leader, your Self.

Crosscheck your results by __ reviewing the 28 traits of high-nurturance families in Chapter 3, and __ the traits of co-dependence on p. 413. My clinical experience is that the fewer high-nurturance traits you grew up with, the more behavioral traits you'll check in this and related worksheets *unless* your false self promotes protective denial of them.

For a more thorough evaluation, fill out all 12 of the Project-1 self-assessment checklists. If you feel you *are* significantly dominated by a false self, read "Who's *Really* Running Your Life?" for suggestions on personal healing. If you feel your *partner* is significantly wounded, ask yourself why you (your false self) are devoted to her or him.

Option: focus on your main childhood caregivers one at a time, and judge (subjectively) how many of these traits they had. Non-organic personality fragmenting migrates unseen down the generations, until spotted and healed. Do you have kids?

Reality check: which of these do you feel are clearly true now?

__ 1) My childhood family had over 20 of the high-nurturance traits in Chapter 3.

__ 2) I can clearly name the emotions that suggest a person's true Self is currently leading their inner family of subselves.

__ 3) I'm _ significantly wounded, and _ I'm committed to learning more about personal recovery from false-self dominance now.

__ 4) I _ have few of these traits, and _ feel I don't need to focus on personal healing.

__ 5) I'm _ not clear whether I have significant false-self wounds or not, and _ I'll do the other self-assessment worksheets to get clearer.

__ 6) I believe _ my partner is clearly wounded; and I'm comfortable _ saying that openly, and _ asking him or her to choose personal healing.

__ 7) My partner _ has few of these traits, and _ often displays the symptoms of a true Self in charge (p. 141, http://sfhelp.org/01/false-self.htm, and Project 1).

__ 8) I feel sure my Self is answering these questions.

Right now I'm aware of . . .

B) Typical Traits of Co-dependence

This is another of the 12 self-assessment checklists in the companion volume on healing inner wounds "Who's *Really* Running Your Life?" Like Resource A or Chapter 3, having many of these traits doesn't *prove* a false self controls you or another person. The more of the traits below that you check, the more likely it is that the person you're rating has significant psychological wounds, and probably doesn't know it.

Background

This worksheet is from a *Codependents Anonymous* (CoDA) 12-step handout. It lists common traits of people with the emotional/spiritual condition of *co-dependence,* and may be reprinted from the pioneering book on co-dependence by Anne Wilson Schaef. This term evolved in the 1980's from *co-alcoholic,* which mental-health workers use to describe someone who is compulsively over-enmeshed with, and over-dependent on, someone addicted to ethyl alcohol. Co-dependents compulsively over-focus on the welfare and activities of another person (often another addict), and feel helpless to prevent losing sight of their own needs, abilities, feelings, and lives. They lose healthy me/you boundaries and their own authentic personal identity.

In my experience, people with this psychological condition (vs. "illness") are compulsively attracted to partners significantly controlled by false selves. If you're courting a co-dependent and/or you may be one yourself, *seriously* question why you're pursuing the relationship. If a false self controls you, you won't be able to do this until well into personal recovery. As with addictions to substances (including fat, sugar, and complex carbohydrates), activities, and emotional states, codependence promotes escalating physical health and relationship stresses over time, until the person dies prematurely, or chooses effective recovery (Project 1).

From social and psychiatric tradition, many human-service professionals view addiction (specially to a substance) as a *disease*. I strongly disagree, though some chemical addictions *are* amplified by genetic predispositions. Fifteen years' research and personal recovery lead me to believe that any addiction is powered by an instinctive false-self drive to self-medicate (distract, numb) from recurring emotional and spiritual discomfort. That's psychological *injury*, not *sickness*! I believe co-dependence is a surface symptom of a false self dominated by fear of abandonment + emotional-spiritual emptiness + excessive shame. Once admitted, these can be reduced over time via inner-family therapy or equivalent.

Kids trapped in significantly low-nurturance childhoods (Chapter 3) feel chronic inner discomforts: significant shame, guilt, anxiety or terror, emptiness, and/or confusion. They're at significant risk of becoming dependent on the temporary relief ("comfort") of one or more addictions, like co-dependence. Related false-self symptoms are addictions to "love" and/or "sex(ual stimulation and release)," i.e. *excitement.* These are common enough in America to have justified national 12-step programs like SA (Sexaholics Anonymous), SAA (Sex Addicts Anonymous), and SLAA (Sex and Love Addicts Anonymous).

As true addictions progress they generate *more* emotional pain, and so are self-reinforcing. Some *substance* addictions compound this by developing physical cravings or dependencies. Personal recovery from psycho-spiritual wounding (vs. from addiction, which is a prerequisite) provides new healthy comforts, and helps to permanently break false-self addiction-distortions and toxic dependencies.

Project 1 in this book and the companion volume "Who's *Really* Running Your Life?" suggests ways to assess for and heal the inner wounds and unawareness causing co-dependence. If a false self dominates you, your protective subselves will try to distort your judgment on the items in this worksheet and Resource A. To guard against that, do all 12 self-assessment checklists in the book above or on the related Web site at ..01/links01.htm. To show others this worksheet, refer them to ..01/co-dep.htm.

Am I or Is My Partner Co-dependent?

The more traits you check, the more likely that the person you're rating _ is significantly wounded and has the condition of co-dependence. *If either of you have many of the traits now, you and any dependent kids are at significant risk of making wrong re/marital choices, and eventual emotional or legal re/divorce.*

Suggestions . . .

+ Do this worksheet by yourself, to avoid unconsciously skewing the results to please another person.
+ Choose an quiet, safe setting to do this worksheet. Allow at least 30" or more, if you want to journal about the experience. Have extra paper handy for notes.
+ Put other concerns aside for now. Adopt the attitudes that . . .
_ This investigation is not about blaming anyone, including yourself.
_ This is a win-win experience: you'll either find you don't have many traits of co-dependence, or if you do, you've discovered a reason to break old denials and start healing. And . . .

_ Doing this worksheet thoughtfully and honestly will raise your odds of making healthy re/marriage choices.

+ Reassure yourself that co-dependence is a common symptom of personality wounding that can be reduced. It is *not* a sign of *craziness, badness, failure, weirdness,* or a *"character defect."* It *is* a significantly harmful condition that deserves focused attention and patient, corrective action. There is a lot of *effective* help available now!

+ Focus on your relationship with your present partner, a former partner, or another key adult like a parent, sibling, relative, child, co-worker, or friend. Then check each item below *honestly*. If you're unsure about an item, use "?" Ask yourself whether each trait usually or generally applies to you and/or the other person. You don't *have to* show these answers to anyone, and it may be helpful to do so.

+ As you do this worksheet, notice your thoughts, inner images, and feelings. These are your subselves' reactions to each item, and are helpful clues to the truth. They're as revealing as your checkmarks are.

+ If helpful, change the wording of an item, and/or add items. Use a hi-lighter and/or write margin notes, symbols, or questions as you go. The "__ __" allows you to check the traits another person has, if you wish.

+ Option: instead of checkmarks, rank each trait 1 through 5 (1 = "a little," or "occasionally").

+ Copy this worksheet, so you can re-do it in the future, and/or give it to someone you care about. Access a copy at http://sfhelp.org/01/co-dep.htm.

+ Keep your perspective: you're evaluating for significant psychological wounds (p. 142), not just co-dependence.

1) About our Relationship

__ __ **1)** My good feelings about who I am depend on being liked by you.

me/you

__ __ **2)** My good feelings about who I am depend on getting approval from you.

__ __ **3)** Your struggle affects my serenity. My mental attention focuses on solving your problems, or relieving your pain.

__ __ **4)** My mental attention is usually focused on _ pleasing you and _ protecting you.

__ __ **5)** My Self-esteem is bolstered by _ solving your problems, and _ relieving your pain.

__ __ **6)** My hobbies and interests are put aside. My time is spent sharing your hobbies and interests.

__ __ **7)** Your _ clothing, _ personal appearance, and _ behavior follow my desires, as I feel you are a reflection of me.

__ __ **8)** I'm seldom aware of how I feel; I'm mainly aware of how *you* feel.

__ __ **9)** I'm seldom aware of what I want; I ask or assume what *you* want.

__ __ **10)** My dreams of the future are mainly linked to you.

__ __ **11)** My fears of your _ rejection and _ anger strongly shape what I say and do.

__ __ **12)** I use giving as a key way of feeling safe in our relationship.

__ __ **13)** My own social circle diminishes as I involve myself with you.

__ __ **14)** I put many of my values aside in order to stay in relationship with you.

__ __ **15)** I value your opinions and ways of doing most things more than mine.

__ __ **16)** The quality of my life hinges largely on the quality of yours.

__ __ **17)**

__ __ **18)**

2) General Traits of Co-dependents

me/you

__ __ **1)** We automatically assume responsibility for others' feelings and/or behaviors.

__ __ **2)** We _ have trouble identifying our feelings; _ invalidate them; and/or often feel _ confused or _ guilty about, or _ ashamed of them.

__ __ **3)** We have trouble freely expressing feelings _ at all, or _ without anxiety: i.e. "I'm happy / sad / joyful / hurt / confused / enraged / scared / anxious / numb . . ."

__ __ **4)** We often fear or worry about how others may respond to our _ feelings and _ behaviors.

__ __ **5)** We _ can't firmly say "no," *or* we _ feel very guilty and anxious if we do.

__ __ **6)** We automatically equate love with pain, anxiety, fear, and/or pity.

__ __ **7)** We generally have trouble _ making and _ keeping close relationships.

__ __ **8)** We _ greatly fear being hurt and/or rejected by others, and _ often expect these despite all reassurances.

__ __ **9)** We often have trouble making firm decisions.

__ __ **10)** We often minimize, alter, and even deny how we really feel.

__ __ **11)** We typically *react* to others' actions and attitudes, rather than act on our own.

__ __ **12)** We usually put other people's needs and wants well before our own, automatically.

__ __ **13)** Our fear of others' feelings (e.g. anger, indifference, and disapproval) largely determines what we say and do.

__ __ **14)** We _ question or ignore our own values in order to be accepted and liked by significant others. We _ often value others' opinions more than ours.

__ __ **15)** We often feel _ empty, _ different, and _ depressed, "for no reason."

__ __ **16)** Our self-esteem is bolstered by events outside of us. We have great trouble acknowledging good things about ourselves.

___ ___ 17) Our serenity and mental attention is determined by how others are feeling or acting.

___ ___ 18) We tend to harshly judge everything we do, think, or say, by someone else's standards. Few things we do, say, or think are "good enough." Perfectionism feels normal to us.

___ ___ 19) We don't _ know or _ believe that being vulnerable and asking for help is OK and normal.

___ ___ 20) We _ don't know that it's OK to talk about personal problems outside the family; or _ that feelings just are, and _ that it's better to share them than to deny, minimize, or justify them.

___ ___ 21) We tend to put other people's wants and needs before our own.

___ ___ 22) We're steadfastly loyal, even when we're repeatedly discounted, shamed, neglected, or used.

___ ___ 23) We have to feel clearly and steadily *needed* to have an OK relationship with others.

___ ___ 24)

___ ___ 25)

As I finish, I'm aware of . . .

and I want to . . .

Options

Depending on who you rated, you have many choices. Breaking denials about having the false-self symptom of co-

dependence is the first step toward freeing your Self and harmonizing your inner family.

If you haven't yet, _ see how many of the high-nurturance
family traits in Chapter 3 you grew up with; and _ thoughtfully
fill out Resource A, common behavioral traits of significant
false-self dominance.

If you checked many of these traits for **yourself** . . .

Start or continue the steps in Project 1: assessing for in-
ner wounds and healing them (p. 142). If you haven't yet, read
"Who's *Really* Running Your Life?" (www.Xlibris.com), or see
http://sfhelp.org/01/links01.htm on the Web. I also recommend
"Embracing Each Other," by Hal Stone and Sidra Winkleman
Stone.

Learn more about co-dependence and recovery in print,
from knowledgeable others, and from the Internet. Because
there is much controversy about co-dependence, read several
authors' viewpoints. See the suggested readings and the *Recovery* or *Psychology* sections of your local or online book-
seller.

Get help from a professional trained and experienced in
working with relationship-addiction management. Expect your
false self to resist this.

Seek and listen to others recovering from this widespread
toxic condition. Attend one or more local Co-dependents
Anonymous ("CoDA") meetings to learn what they do, how,
and why. If you can't find a physical meeting, there are probably CoDA groups on the Internet.

Postpone any stepfamily commitments until you make unmistakable progress healing the _ toxic shame and _ abandonment fear (false-self dominance) underlying your compulsion.
Needy co-parents controlled by a false self are at high risk of
mistakenly expecting that (re)marrying and/or having a child
will provide the comforts they've been self-medicating for.
Guarantee: months or years will pass as you learn painfully
that they *won't*. _ Reality-check this with people in true (vs.

pseudo) recovery for five or more years. I've been recovering for 15 years. It works!

Begin to teach key others in your life what you're learning about co-dependence, what causes it, and what it *means*.

Be alert for recovery mentors and hero/ines. Watch and listen for stories of people who discovered co-dependence, have progressed at reducing it, and report positive life changes and experiences!

If you checked many traits for **your current partner** . . .

Show this worksheet to them, _ **talk** with them directly about it, and _ recommend these same actions to them. _ **Do Project 1 together!**

Beware feeling anxious about or *responsible for* their re-actions and decisions. The most effective way to help long-term is _ set a worthy (recovery) example for them, and _ com-passionately *help by not helping*. Don't take responsibility for what *they* must do for themselves — i.e. don't *enable* them.

If relevant in your situation, evaluate **getting couples-coun-seling** on managing co-dependence. Avoid doing this for your partner's sake (rescuing), no matter how seductive or kind it feels!

If you checked many traits for **someone else** . . .

Use your new awareness to **replace blame or scorn with compassion**. If you've resented their *behaviors* for past hurts and insults, _ keep your feelings, *and* _ consider seeing them as wounded people from low-nurturance childhoods, vs. *bad*. Some forgiveness may grow from such a view. That helps *you both, and any affected kids.*

If s/he's open to it, **consider making this worksheet** and related Project-1 materials **available** to the other person with-out expectations. *Beware trying to save or fix others who aren't seeking help. That's a classic co-dependent urge!*

Reality check: check which items feel true now. Use "?"

if you're not sure. Check each main item if you check all sub-items in it.

___ 1) My childhood family had over 20 of the high-nurturance traits in Chapter 3 (p. 48).

___ 2) I can clearly name the emotions that suggest a true Self is leading a person's inner family of subselves. (p. 154)

___ 3) I _ believe I have the false-self symptom of co-dependence to a significant degree, and I _ feel very committed (vs. ambivalent) to learning more about personal recovery from false-self dominance (Project 1).

___ 4) I _ have few of these co-dependence traits, and _ feel I don't need to focus on personal healing now.

___ 5) I'm _ not clear whether I have "significant" co-dependence or not, and _ I'm going to do the other self-assessment checklists to get clearer. (http://sfhelp.org/pop/assess.htm)

___ 6) I believe _ my partner has clear symptoms of co-dependence. I'm comfortable _ saying that to them, and _ asking him or her to explore personal healing. I _ understand s/he must do this for herself/himself, not to please me.

___ 7) My partner _ has few of these traits, and _ often displays the symptoms of a true Self in charge.

___ 8) I'm _ not sure now if a false self dominates my partner, and _ I need to do more of the 11 checklists to widen my perspective.

___ 9) I feel sure my Self is answering these questions now. Right now I'm aware of . . .

Awarenesses . . .

C) Stepfamilies vs. Intact Biofamilies

72 Differences and Their Implications for Co-parents

We're about to dissolve a common re/maritally-toxic myth. It is held by many uninformed (vs. "dumb") co-parents like Jack and Sarah Tilmon (Chapter 7), and many untrained family-support professionals. The myth is "a family is just a family." A common version of this misperception is that "average stepfamilies are 'pretty much like' (typical intact) biofamilies." That's true and false.

Typical stepfamilies and intact biofamilies *do* have similarities. They also differ structurally and dynamically in over *70* ways. *If courting co-parents see only the similarities and minimize the differences, they're at high risk of unconsciously using unrealistic biofamily norms to assess whether to re/marry.* Often, what fills members' needs in an intact biofamily does *not* do so in a multi-home stepfamily. You may be an expert at driving a car, but you'd need extra training before flying a 747 jumbo jet with your whole family aboard . . .

Biofamilies and stepfamilies have been around since the earliest humans trod African soil, so they're both *normal.* Stepfamilies have probably been the historic norm until medical advances in the last 150 years. Because our grandparents' generation lacks historic perspective, they taught us that stepfamilies are *abnormal* and *unnatural*. Recall this premise from Chapter 3:

Families of procreation, re/marriage, foster care, and adoption exist to (1) produce wholistically-healthy, socially valuable, self-sufficient new adults, while (2) filling all members' core needs (p. 49) well enough as they and the Earth evolve.

Biofamilies and stepfamilies have the same potential to fill both these goals. **Neither type of family is inherently** *better,* they're just *very* different. At the end of this chapter, see if you agree with "very" . . .

To help you form realistic step-relationship expectations, we're about to compare traits of average multi-home stepfamilies with average intact, one-home nuclear biofamilies. To appreciate how different they are, we'll look at family structure, and then family-growth tasks. Then we'll summarize what all these differences *mean* to typical co-parents like you. First, let's summarize . . .

Similarities to Intact Biofamilies

When co-parents insist "A family is just a family," they're probably thinking that stepfamilies and intact biofamilies are "the same, because . . .

+ Both family types are composed of adults and kids living together part or all of the time, plus their biological and legal relatives (in-laws).

+ The adults _ are (usually) in charge of their homes, and _ do their best to guide, nurture, protect, teach, and prepare their dependent kids to leave, and live well-enough on their own.

+ All members of biofamilies and stepfamilies have daily needs to fill, developmental life tasks to master, and a range of daily responsibilities and activities like bathing, work or school, worship, socializing and play, meals, shopping, chores, and so on.

+ Both kinds of normal family evolve through a predictable, natural sequence of developmental stages, though
typical stepfamilies have extra stages.
+ Both stepfamilies and biofamilies periodically have **conflicts** _ between their members, _ with other people,
and with _ the environment. They use _ tangible **resources** (money, phones, cars, tools, appliances . . .)
and _ personal resources (like love, humor, time, intel-
ligence, patience . . .) to resolve their conflicts.
+ Steppeople and biopeople each have individual and
shared hopes, fears, goals, achievements, dreams, failures, joys, health concerns, celebrations, depressions,
identities, bodies, losses, etc . . .
+ Both family types naturally develop sets of personal and
group *values*; group *roles* (who does what) and *rules*
(when, how, and why); a *history*; an *identity*; and some
loyalty or bonding. And . . .
+ Biofamilies and stepfamilies both _ evolve within human and natural environments, and _ dynamically interact with each as contributors and consumers.

So when a stepfamily co-parent or relative says, "Hey, we're
just (like) a regular (bio)family!" they're absolutely right. Paradox: at the same time, there are at least . . .

72 Stepfamily-Biofamily *Differences*

Compared to intact biofamilies, typical multi-home
stepfamilies like the McLean-Tilmon-Cohen clan have very
different _ **structures** and _ developmental *tasks*. Using these
measures, stepfamilies vary more from average biofamilies than
typical foster, absent-parent, or adoptive families do. This has
some major implications for courting co-parents like you.

Note _ the individual differences below and _ the collective impact of *all* of them. This incomplete comparison covers
what I feel are the key differences. Because there are almost
100 structural types of stepfamily, yours probably won't have
all the differences noted below.

As you read, check each item you knew before reading this summary. Test my theory that typical people like you "don't know what they don't know" about stepfamily realities. Adopt "the mind of a student," and take your time with this . . .

Structural Differences

Structure refers to how a family is built, like foundation, walls, windows, plumbing, wiring, roofs, insulation, and landscaping comprise a house. "SF" below means, "Average multi-home nuclear stepfamilies." "BF" means "Typical intact one-home nuclear biofamilies." *Nuclear* means "minor kids and their main adult caregivers." Each numbered item is a structural feature.

1) Number of co-parenting homes in the nuclear family: **SF)** *One to three or more* custodial and non-custodial homes. If a childless adult marries a widow/er with kids, there is only one stepfamily home. This is true for about 10% of U.S. stepfamilies. **BF)** Normally *one* custodial home.

2) Number of biokids living at the time of the adults' commitment ceremony: **SF)** *One to six or more* (his, hers, and ours) kids, minor and/or grown. The average is two to four children. Most U.S. re/marriers have no initial kids together, and never co-conceive any. **BF)** *Normally none.* When children do exist, the marriers (usually) didn't plan them.

3) Number of co-parents in the nuclear family: **SF)** *Three or more*: typically up to four divorced bioparents, and one or two stepparents; **BF)** Usually *two* caregivers, alive or dead. There may be more, with live-in relatives or others.

4) Number of absent bioparents in the family: **SF)** *One or two*: his and/or her ex mates or dead spouses; **BF)** *None or one* (jail, military service, frequent travel . . .).

5) Number of co-parenting ex mates and their genetic and legal relatives: **SF)** *One or more* sets. They can collectively total dozens of people related to each stepchild. All become "step-relatives" at parental re/marriage. Since re/marriers are older than first marriers, the odds are higher that one or both of their parents and some senior relatives are dead when they re/wed. **BF)** *None.*

6) Number of living or dead **co-grandparents: SF)** *Six to 12* or more (bio + step); **BF)** *Four.*

7) *Half* **brothers and sisters: SF)** *Possible*; **BF)** *None* in the children's generation.

8) Number of minor kids living at home or away at school: **SF)** Typically *two to six* or more; **BF)** Typically *one to three* or more.

9) Physical and legal custody of dependent kids: **SF)** *More complex*: full, joint, or split. Custody is usually subject to legal decrees and parenting agreements which new stepparents had no part in drafting, but are bound by. **BF)** *Simpler*: shared full-time custody, with no legal decrees or parenting agreements to obey, enforce, or dispute.

10) Family variations: SF) *Almost 100 structural types*, considering mixes of partners' prior and current child conceptions, custodies, and prior divorces and/or mate-deaths. Members commonly feel "No one else is like *us*. We're unusual, abnormal, or non-traditional." This promotes co-parents and kids feeling *alien, weird*, and *alone*. This is specially uncomfortable to shame-based (psychologically wounded) co-parents and kids longing to feel *normal* and *OK*. About one of every six U.S. families is now a stepfamily, with regional variations. **BF)** *One* traditional family type: [mom + dad + biokids]. Members feel "Most other families are built like ours, so we're *normal* and *OK.*"

11) Adults' ages at (re)wedding (degree of life, marital, and parenting experience): **SF)** *Older and more experienced*: typically 30 to 50+. Stepfamily co-parents *may* be (vs. are) more mature. They also usually have more assets and/or debts. Women pick younger husbands more often than in first unions. **BF)** *Younger and less experienced*: typically 18-30. Typical partners are less mature and wealthy than re/married co-parents.

12) Mates' prior-family roles, rules, rituals, and traditions to merge after (re)wedding: **SF)** *More complex*: merge three or more sets of these: the two new mates' sets, + one or more ex mates' birthfamily + first-marriage family + (maybe) absent-parent family, after divorce or a partner's death. Re/marriers are more likely to come from different religions, ethnic backgrounds, and educational levels than first marriers. This promotes richness, and many merger values and priority conflicts. **BF)** *Simpler*: merge two sets of birthfamily values, roles, rules, rituals, and traditions.

13) Adults' and kids' _ mementos and memories of their prior marriage and intact biofamily, and _ inevitable better-worse comparisons: **SF)** *Many* tangible and abstract mementos. These may painfully and steadily remind step-parents "I'm not my mate's first co-parenting partner, and never will be." Comparing prior and new mates, homes, and families is normal. **BF)** *None*, though first-time spouses may have insecurities about mates' former intimate relationships.

14) Major tangible and invisible losses for kids, parents, and close relatives to mourn: **SF)** *Many* losses from death or divorce *and* re/marriage + cohabiting. Typical co-parents choose their losses, while most dependent stepkids' losses are forced. **BF)** *No equivalent losses*. All biofamily members do encounter other broken bonds over time.

15) Adults' parenting values, priorities, and styles: SF) *Pre-existing*. Co-parenting values and styles conflict more often, so more compromises are needed for re/marital and family harmony. **BF)** *Evolved together* over years; (usually) fewer parenting values-conflicts.

More *structural* differences between typical stepfamilies and intact biofamilies . . .

16) Mates' communication, negotiating, and conflict-resolving **styles** and effectiveness: **SF)** *Pre-existing*. There are more family members, more differing cultures, more post-wedding adjustment tasks (below), and more values conflicts to resolve. These combine to steeply raise the need for co-parents' verbal problem-solving effectiveness (Project 2). **BF)** *Evolved together* over years. The U.S. first-divorce rate suggests less than half of couples' communication styles are *effective*.

17) Possible household interference from "outsiders," and resulting conflicts: **SF)** *More likely*: Ex-spouses, their new mates (if any), ex and new in-laws, and possibly lawyers and courts, may interfere. **BF)** *Less likely*: mates' bioparents and/or relatives may interfere with co-parents' decisions, over time.

18) Prior traumatic family-reorganization experiences for adults and kids: **SF)** One or both co-parents and their biokids and kin did experience these from biofamily divorce or adult death. **BF)** *None*, though a spouse's bioparents may have divorced.

19) Co-parents' legal rights re minor kids' custody, school, health, etc.: **SF)** Stepparents have *few to no parental rights* without legal stepchild adoption. This varies by state statutes. **BF)** Bioparents share *more and clearer rights* and legal responsibilities.

20) Pre-nuptial legal contracts defining asset-ownership and disposition in case of (re)divorce: **SF)** *More common*, partly because new mates are wealthier. These contracts symbolize the real possibility of re/divorce and battles over marital property. Pre-nuptial agreements may cause distrust, resentments, and conflicts. **BF)** *Uncommon* except for wealthy couples.

21) Significant adult shame and guilt for divorcing ("failing") and inflicting pain and losses on their minor biokids and parents: **SF)** *Possible to probable* in one or more co-parents. Significant shame and guilt can powerfully corrode re/marital primacy and cause major loyalty conflicts and triangles until they're reduced. This is exaggerated in shame-based adults from low-nurturance childhoods. Minor kids may exploit this guilt and shame to test and/or to reduce their own anxieties. **BF)** *No equivalent feelings*.

22) Social status and common adjectives: SF) *Lower status*: typical social and media adjectives are "(Stepfamilies or steppeople) are *unreal, unnatural, abnormal, non-traditional, minority, and* stepmoms are *wicked.*" The Middle-English root prefix *stoep* means *deprived or orphaned*. Shame-based co-parents and kids can be extra uncomfortable with these, and try to minimize or deny their stepfamily status personally and socially.

BF) *Higher status*: biofamilies, bioparents, and biokids are described as *traditional, real, regular, normal, natural,* and *standard*. Adults and kids usually feel no great anxiety or confusion about their family identity unless living in a bigoted (ethnically or religiously conflictual) environment.

23) Mates' initial marital expectations, and motivation to succeed: **SF)** *More realistic* expectations, from experience; "We really might divorce." Higher adult re/marital motivations *may* include the intense need to avoid another divorce. Middle-age realities and anxieties can raise mates' motivation to "make it work this time." **BF)** Typically *more idealistic* and vulnerable to denials: "We'll *never* divorce!" First spouses have no personal divorce-pain experience to affect to their motivation and doubts. Adult children of divorced parents may be exceptions.

24) Incest taboo: the odds of inappropriate sexual attractions, actions, and abuses in family homes: **SF)** *Weaker*, so the odds of harmful stepparent-stepchild and step-sibs' sexual attractions and actions are higher. The chance for sexual abuse is higher in typical U.S. stepfamilies. **BF)** Usually *stronger*, because parents have lived with their kids since infancy. Even so, American sexual abuse is estimated at one of four girls, and one of seven boys is molested by their 18th birthday. This causes or amplifies *major* false-self wounding.

25) Nuclear family members' *last* **names: SF)** *Usually differ*. Without legal adoption or name changes, a re/married biomother and her minor kids, Half-siblings and stepsibs, and stepparents and stepkids last names differ. This can confuse personal and social identities, and hinder stepfamily bonding and loyalty. **BF)** Last names are *usually the same*. Depending on nurturance levels and ability to bond, this usually promotes clear personal identity ("I am a Martinez."), and (often) biofamily identity loyalty, and bonding: "We are the Swensons, and proud of it!"

26) Nuclear family members' *first* **names: SF)** *Duplicates and confusions are more likely.* Remarriers may each have a biochild with the same first name, and/or or a stepparent and stepchild's first names may match, and/or new and former mates may have the same first name. **BF)** Duplications and confusions are *rare* unless a son is "Jr."

27) Minor and grown children's impacts on the co-parents' relationship: **SF)** Typically *moderately to highly stressful* for years, with or without "ours" kids. Stepparents may feel "I love you (my mate), and I dislike your minor or grown child(ren)." Stressful loyalty conflicts and (persecutor-victim-rescuer) relationship triangles are much more likely in and between co-parental homes.

BF) Mutually-wanted children *usually strengthen* the mate's marital commitments and enrich their relationship. Kids can also cause divorce ambivalence and deferment, and bitter custody and co-parenting disputes. Loyalty conflicts and triangles are likely in low-nurturance co-parenting homes, but *feel* different than those in stepfamilies.

28) Adults' and kids' household and family *roles* ("who does what, here?") **and rules** ("How and when do they do their roles; what's right"?): **SF)** *30 possible family roles.* Half are unfamiliar (e.g. step cousin, non-custodial stepfather, visiting stepsister), and are learned slowly by experience. New rules must be evolved for each of these roles over many years.

There are few social norms now to guide steppeople in deciding, "Who is supposed to do what in our multi-home stepfamily; when, how, and for whom?" This justifies courtship Project 6: drafting re/marital and family mission statements, and co-parent job descriptions. The chance for significant role strain and confusion are higher for adults and kids.

BF) *15 possible family roles* (aunt, niece, son, sister . . .). There is much social tradition on how to do each family role "right," amplified by media portrayals. *Rules* for each role are usually learned from childhood and society.

29) Co-parents' permission and authority to discipline minor resident and visiting kids: **SF)** *Initially unequal.* Stepparents may or may not earn such authority over time. Stepkids' bioparents and/or bio-kin may undermine a new stepparent's attempts at child discipline, or give them too much responsibility too soon. Values conflicts over limit-setting and consequence-enforcements are more common and complex. **BF)** *Comfortably unequal, or co-equal* if both bioparents wish. Discipline co-equality is usually socially expected and accepted, depending on cultural and ancestral factors.

30) Adults' and kids' definitions of "Who belongs to my (extended) family?" **SF)** *Definitions usually differ widely* among various stepfamily members. Membership (inclusion) conflicts often cause resentments, hurts, confusion, loyalty conflicts, and relationship triangles. **BF)** *Definitions are usually similar.* Major differences over family membership are unusual, even if some members "aren't speaking." Exceptions occur in low-nurturance and divorced biofamilies.

31) Nuclear and extended-family bonding, identity, and loyalty: SF) *Initially, little or none.* These may be pretended for "politeness" and/or to avoid admitting *stepfamily* identity. Bonding, identity, and loyalty may *or may not* develop in and between co-parents' or all related homes, over time. The latter is a symptom of low ancestral and stepfamily nurturance. Like Jack Tilmon (Chapter 7), many stepfamily members may minimize or deny their identity as a stepfamily, and/or their stepfamily roles, from ignorance and semi-conscious shame and guilts. **BF)** *Usually stronger and clearer.* These primal attachments often transcend child neglects and abuses, if present.

32) Financial liabilities and assets, ownership, and allocation: SF) *Usually more assets* among three or more co-parents, *and more (potential) conflict* over asset ownership and allocation, including legal titles and wills. Both spouses are likely to earn higher wages than first-marrying peers, and have active careers and retirement funds.

"Assets" include insurance policies, real estate, vehicles, securities and other investments, IRAs and pension funds, jew-

elry and fine art, and retirement and savings accounts. Kids
may have assets (e.g. trusts and college funds) reserved in their
names. Low-nurturance stepfamilies are more likely to have
higher debts (e.g. credit card balances and kids' college loans),
and more conflicts over managing them.

BF) *Fewer assets and debts owned by fewer people.* Ownership is more apt to be joint and harmonious. Mates' individual or shared debts at re/wedding time are usually smaller
than re/marriers.

33) Nuclear-family nurturance level (Chapter 3): **SF)** *Probably lower*: evidence is the ~60% American (legal) re/divorce
rate. I assume psychological and legal divorce signify spouses'
disabled true Selves and unawarenesses (Chapter 5). Those
imply low extended-family nurturance and wholistic health for
all family members. Other evidence: typical stepfamilies have
more people, conflicts, and adjustment tasks; which can mean
more distractions from steadily attending personal, marital, and
kids' needs. Because everyone is older (except "ours" kids),
the profile of some family members' needs is different than in
younger families. **BF)** *Probably higher*, with local exceptions.

**34) Co-parents' wholistic healths and relationship suc-
cess**: **SF)** *Generally lower*. From 20 years' clinical experience,
I estimate that 80% or more of re/wedded co-parents come from
significantly low-nurturance childhoods. Their resulting psychological wounds promote repeated relationship conflicts and
breakups. Without Self-motivated, proactive recovery from these
wounds (Project 1), well over half of recent U.S. re/marriages
have failed psychologically or legally. Because re/marriers are
older, symptoms of their wounds like addictions, job losses,
depressions, divorces, bankruptcies, and health problems may
be more apparent than in wounded first-marriers.

BF) *Higher*. If divorce is a valid indicator, then the U.S. first-
divorce rate suggests at least half of the partners are wounded
survivors of significantly low-nurturance childhoods. The percentage of wounded *psychologically*-divorced partners is unknown.

35) Professionals' (counselors, clergy, lawyers, judges,
educators, doctors, etc.) **accurate knowledge** of family devel-

opmental phases, norms, and dynamics: **SF)** *Much lower*, partly because there is little call for informed training, and no insurance and certification (licensing) incentives to learn. Implication: there is much less *informed* education and effective help available to aid courting co-parents in evaluating re/marriage, and handling stepfamily problems with identity, membership, values, roles, and relationships. U.S. divorces, re/marriages, and re/divorces have surged since the 1950's. Sociologically, they're a new phenomenon.

BF) Professionals' knowledge is *much higher*, because intact biofamilies have been the social norm in recent generations.

Can you think of other *structural* stepfamily-biofamily differences? Pause and note your reactions now. Were your ruling subselves able to stay with this (pretty dry) comparison, or did you get bored or overwhelmed and jump here? How many of these 35 structural differences did you know already? Could you have written your version of all these items? If you're in a stepfamily, can your other adult members name most or all of these differences? There's no right or wrong here, only what *is*!

Many of these structural differences generate unique stepfamily adjustment tasks for adults and kids. Most of these tasks are concurrent, and recur across the years. These tasks are in addition to normal life challenges and changes that co-parents and kids must adapt to, like births, moves, retirements, and deaths. Typical re/marrying adults and many professionals aren't aware of or prepared for these unique stepfamily tasks. They don't know what they don't know (unawareness). **Here's an overview** of the tasks. As you read, check each task that you know already. If you know over 20 of these, you're *really* aware!

Different Adjustment Tasks

For more perspective and suggestions on many of these, see the Web articles at http://sfhelp.org/Rx/dx.htm. To show other people a summary of these tasks, invite them to read ..09/ sf-task1.htm. Ongoing or recurring tasks are asterisked (*):

1) Couples negotiate courtship with existing kids, ex mates, and ex in-laws in the picture: **SF)** *Required*. Logistics and emotions are often *far* more complex than typical first-marriage courtship. **BF)** Usually *no equivalent task*, so courtship is simpler, more focused, and more idealistic.

2*) All adults and kids **accept the new identity, "We are now all members of a multi-home *step*family."** Then _ members each decide "who belongs to (is included in) my stepfamily now?", and _ resolve major conflicts over this. **SF)** *Required* (Project 3). All three or more co-parents must learn and accept their shared stepfamily identity, and agree on who's included. Kids and adult often disagree on stepfamily-identity and membership definitions. This task recurs if another parent re/marries or re/divorces. **BF)** *No equivalent task*. Biofamily identity is usually clear to all. Family memberships (inclusions) are clear, and usually change only with births, weddings, legal adoptions, and deaths. Low-nurturance biofamilies may have conflicts here.

3*) Co-parents learn "What's *normal* in an average multi-home *step*family?" and teach the realities to key others: **SF)** *Required* (Project 4). Avoiding this greatly raises the odds of members' building conflictual *biofamily*-based role expectations of each other. This is ongoing as the stepfamily enters new developmental phases. **BF)** *No equivalent project*. Relatives, society, and the media have taught biofamily norms to caregivers since early childhood.

4a) All members identify and grieve prior tangible and invisible losses from _ divorce and/or death, and (later) _ re/marriage and _ co-habiting: **SF)** *Required* (Project 5). Prior grieving styles, values, and rules must be merged. Co-parents ignoring this vital project promote stepfamily conflict and eventual re/divorce. **BF)** *No equivalent task.* Biofamily members do have other losses to grieve.

4b) Help minor bio-kid/s' grieve (normal) fantasies and dreams of bioparent and birthfamily reunions: **SF)** *Very common.* If unmourned, this dream can block kids from accepting a stepparent, causing personal, household, and re/marital stresses. A bioparent's re/wedding *usually* shatters the dream . . . **BF)** *No equivalent task,* though kids in troubled low-nurturance biofamilies can dream about more family harmony until they lose hope.

4c) Bioparents, biokids, and often bio-grandparents really **resolve prior-divorce guilts and shames** (re "failures"): **SF)** *Required* unless the former mate died. Failure at this task can skew co-parenting priorities and cause divisive loyalty conflicts. This inevitably stresses their re/marriage over time. **BF)** *No equivalent task.*

5*) Family adults _ blend their styles of verbal communication, and _ **develop effective problem-solving skills together**: **SF)** *Required and more complex* (Project 2). Without progressing on this project *early,* all three or more co-parents are greatly hampered in accomplishing all other personal and family adjustment tasks in and between their homes. This project recurs if another ex mate re/marries. **BF)** *Required and simpler*: only two co-parents need to do this, not three or more. The U.S. first-divorce statistics suggest most first-marriers don't master this task well enough, because our society didn't prepare their parents well enough.

6) Courting adults each decide "Are these the right people to re/marry? Is this the right time? Am I re/marrying for the right reasons? **SF)** *Required, and far more complex* (Project 7). The U.S. stepfamily re/divorce epidemic implies that most couples don't research and evaluate these key questions well enough, and that our society condones this. **BF)** *Simpler.* Couples have no kids or ex mates to consider in answering these questions, and less life experience.

More stepfamily-biofamily adjustment-task differences . . .

7*) Co-parents make pre-nuptial-agreement decisions, and resolve any related family conflicts: **SF)** *More common.* Wealthier re/marriers often want to guard against possible re/divorce asset-conflicts and losses. Such legal contracts can breed distrust, hurt, anxieties, and resentments. This task may recur if assets change substantially. **BF)** *Unusual.* Most first-marriers aren't wealthy enough to worry about this, and don't believe divorce could happen to them. Over 50% are wrong in America 2000.

8) Re/marriers plan and hold a commitment ceremony for "the (step)family" and friends: **SF)** *More complex.* Who should come? Who should "stand up"? There are no social norms to guide engaged couples, their parents, and/or clergy here. Often, major loyalty conflicts and relationship triangles arise. **BF)** *Simpler.* Social norms and traditions are much clearer. There are usually no biokids, ex in-laws, and fewer legal relatives involved. See http://sfhelp.org/Rx/spl/wedding1.htm.

9) All family members adjust to kids', ex mate/s', and ex in-laws' reactions to co-parents re/marrying and merging homes: **SF)** *Required.* In some cases, kids, ex mates, and/or kin can become critical, hostile, rejecting, or intrusive. In other cases, most or all are supportive. **BF)** *No equivalent task* involving ex mates and living kids.

10*) Negotiate acceptable dwelling, furnishing, decorating, and space-allocation (e.g. bedroom) decisions. Merge physical and financial assets, ownerships, traditions, rituals, and values: **SF)** *Far more complex*: "Your home, mine, or a new one?" More people are affected, so these choices are usually more emotionally and logistically complex and conflictual for stepfamily members. Major concurrent values conflicts and relationship triangles are common. This task recurs each time the couple moves. **BF)** *Simpler.* The first dwelling is often new to both mates. There are far fewer belongings, assets, and rituals to choose among and blend.

11*) Members resolve name and family-role title confusions: "What should we call each other?" **SF)** *Required.* These confusions are often conflictual, stressful, and frustrating in and between linked homes, and with kin and friends. These can recur if kids change dwellings, new kids are born, and/or other co-parents or kin re/marry. **BF)** *No equivalent task.*

12*) Cope with a co-parenting ex mate and/or key relatives **who won't accept** their divorce, the re/marriage, and/or the new stepparent (i.e. hasn't grieved; see #4 above): **SF)** *Frequent.* When present, usually the ex felt abandoned and/or abused in their marriage, and has major denied childhood nurturance deprivations and related wounds (see # 28). Ex mate rejection and hostility can seem "endless" and insoluble. **BF)** *No equivalent task*

13*) Minor stepkids' key task: *test* to learn clearly _ "Am I safe in this family, or will it break up too?"; and _ "Who's really in charge of this home?" (See #16a): **SF)** *Required* if stepkids experienced prior parental divorce/s. Appropriate testing is often wrongly labeled "acting out," and the kids are shamed and punished. That promotes rebellion or apathy, and developing a false-self. This task can recur when the child's other bioparent re/marries, when either bioparent conceives a new child, and/or when a child changes custodial homes. **BF)** *No equivalent task*, but it can develop in a significantly low-nurturance biofamily home.

14a*) Non-custodial *bio*parent/s grieve and accept that _ they're missing much of their children's growing-up events, and that _ another adult with different values is co-raising their kid/s: **SF)** *Required* unless this other bioparent is dead or emotionally detached (wounded). This bioparent may fight such acceptance (denial), or accept and co-operate, or be indifferent and apathetic (false-self symptoms). This task is continuous, as each child grows through his or her developmental stages. **BF)** *No equivalent task.*

14b*) Non-custodial dual-role (bioparent + stepparent) **caregivers cope with frequent guilt, resentment, and sadness** that they're co-parenting others' child/ren instead of their own: **SF)** *Possible* if adult-child visitations and communications are infrequent, unsatisfying, and/or blocked by others. Stepparents without biokids don't face this. This task recurs as special milestones and events happen. **BF)** *No equivalent task.*

15*) New mates' make conception decisions: "Shall we have one or more 'ours' kids?" **SF)** *Probable* before and/or after re/wedding. Mates are older, and odds are higher that a bioparent says "No, I have enough kids." The decision is far more complex. If "Yes," new births often cause many multi-generational changes (losses) and loyalty conflicts. This task may occur more than once, and be triggered by a woman's aging. **BF)** *Simpler decision.* The co-parents are younger, have fewer financial issues and assets, and fewer other people (e.g. no existing stepkids, ex mates, ex in-laws) who are affected.

16a*) All co-parents _ learn and _ help dependent kids fill 15 to 30+ complex family-adjustment needs, in addition to their normal developmental needs (p. 457): **SF)** *Required.* Most co-parents can't name all these tasks (unawareness), which hinders their effectiveness and raises minor kids' distress. This task is ongoing, as each child matures. **BF)** *No equivalent task.* Bioparents strive to guide minor kids on many normal developmental (vs. divorce and stepfamily adjustment) tasks.

16b*) Co-parents agree on caregiving goals, plans, priorities, and responsibilities for each dependent child: **SF)** *Far more complex*: three or more co-parents and up to a dozen co-grandparents are involved, in two or more nuclear-stepfamily homes. Post-divorce hostilities and distrusts, ineffective communication skills, blocked grief, and adults' unawarenesses of step norms and unique stepchild tasks often interfere. This task continues as the stepfamily develops. **BF)** *Far simpler.* Only two co-parents and fewer relatives are involved, so the odds of conflict are lower. Bioparenting role-norms are clearer. There are fewer kids and tasks involved, and no parenting, visitation, financial support, and/or custody agreements to comply with and renegotiate.

More stepfamily-biofamily adjustment-*task* differences . . .

17*) All extended-family members **resolve a stream of values and priority (loyalty) conflicts** in and between their many linked homes: **SF)** *Required and much more complex.* Re/wedded bioparents must choose their mate "first" enough vs. biokids, kin, or work, or the stepparent grows resentful and eventually may re/divorce psychologically or legally. This on-going task can get easier *if* co-parents understand and admit these conflicts, and learn to use effective communication skills as teammates (Project 2). **BF)** *Uncommon and simpler*, unless the extended biofamily is significantly low-nurturance (Chapter 3). Often, biokids and parenting values are not the key marital conflict.

18*) Mates make enough quality couple-times to nourish their (re)marriage, discuss family goals and plans, problem-solve, and co-manage the family: **SF)** *Often much harder*, due to more homes, more people with busy schedules, more conflicting needs (responsibilities), and more simultaneous adult and child adjustment tasks. This is Project 8, which is ongoing. **BF)** *Easier,* unless one or both mates shun intimacy. There are far fewer people, relationships, needs, and tasks to consider.

19*) Resolve relationship problems between new and prior co-parenting mates, stepsibs, and/or step-kin and "ex" in-laws: **SF)** *Required.* Common conflicts: money; parenting values, responsibilities, and priorities; kids' education; religion; power and authority; time allocation; possessions; sexuality and privacy; health; and holidays. This is why Project 2 is vital. **BF)** *No equivalent tasks.* There *are* problems to resolve among far fewer people, with less old baggage, and fewer concurrent conflicts.

20a*) Financial decisions I: Shall I (a stepparent) include your kid/s in my will? In my health and/or life insurance? Shall I help pay for your kids' education and special needs? **SF)** *Required.* Stepparents' decisions here can cause gratitude, warmth, and bonding; or resentments, guilts, angers, and relationship triangles in and between extended-stepfamily homes. These decisions may recur as family membership, relationships, roles, and assets change. **BF)** *No equivalent tasks.*

20b*) Financial decisions II: all three or more co-parents agree enough on child-support amounts, timing, and allocations. Resolve conflicts co-operatively, without putting the minor kids in the middle: **SF)** *Required.* This is a complex, conflictual project requiring all co-parents' _ clear priorities, roles, and goals; _ forgivenesses of prior-family wounds; and _ shared effective negotiating skills (task # 5). This task is ongoing until the youngest child leaves home. **BF)** *No equivalent task.*

20c*) Financial decisions III: mates evolve a harmonious way of managing operating income and expenses, investments and savings plans; insurances, and deciding on asset titles (e.g. vehicle, securities, and real estate ownership). **SF)** *Required, and far more complex.* Common options: separate his, hers, and ours asset accounts, and/or one "common-pot" account; and separate or joint savings and investment accounts. This ongoing task requires mutual trust, time to talk, and effective verbal communication skills. **BF)** *Required, and far simpler.* The common bio-mate choices are *our* checking and savings accounts, investments, and shared asset-ownerships.

21) Decision: "Shall I legally adopt your child/ren?" SF) *Possible.* There are many emotional, financial, and legal complexities to this decision, including getting the absent bioparent's legal agreement to release parental rights and responsibilities. **BF)** No equivalent task.

22*) All co-parents manage regular and special child visitations between two or more co-parenting homes: **SF)** *Ongoing*, unless the other bioparent/s are dead or detached. This task often lasts until kids are late teens, and can be very conflictual in and between homes. **BF)** *No equivalent task.*

23*) Co-parents re/negotiate child-custody and legal parenting agreements as conditions change over time: **SF)** *Frequent*, unless the other bioparent/s are dead or all stepkids are living independently. Many causes for adjustment are possible. This task is often significantly conflictual without _ clear adult roles, _ prior losses well grieved, and _ effective adult problem-solving skills. This task can re-activate, depending on many factors. **BF)** *No equivalent task.*

24*) All family members adjust to minor children changing homes, schools, and custodial co-parents: **SF)** *Possible* (in ~30% of U.S. stepfamilies). Moving may be sudden and unexpected. It usually causes major concurrent financial, legal, space, privacy, priority, and role, and other changes (losses) and conflicts. This task can recur if co-parents move and/or adults and kids (e.g. teens) clash too much. **BF)** *No equivalent task*.

25*) _ Settle legal battles between divorced bioparents, and then _ heal the resulting related guilts, resentments, hurts, disrespects, and distrusts, over time: **SF)** *Common*. Typical conflict sources are child _ visitations, _ custody, and _ financial support; and _ enforcing or changing legal co-parenting agreements. Stepparents can add to or withdraw from the turmoil. This task recurs as kids' ages and expenses and co-parents' incomes change. Ex mate legal battles are *always* symptoms of false-self dominance, ineffective communication skills, and (often) blocked grief. **BF)** *No equivalent task*.

26*) Build stepparent < > stepchild *respect* (vs. love) **and** *trust* over time: **SF)** *Required* for minor and grown kids. Longterm success depends on many things, and is not assured. Low mutual respect cripples stepparent-stepchild discipline. That causes loyalty conflicts and relationship triangles, which stress re/marriages. **BF)** *No equivalent task*. Kids may lose respect for, and trust in, their bioparents in a low nurturance home.

27*) Nuclear-family members cope with social biases, misunderstandings, and related social isolation: SF) *Unavoidable*. Common biases are "Stepfamilies are second best, flawed, abnormal, not as good, and weird." Step-adults and kids may feel "We know no other (step)families like ours. We're *alone*." High-nurturance stepfamilies learn how to cope with this as they evolve. **BF)** *No equivalent task*, unless mates form a samegender, bi-racial, and/or mixed religio/ethnic biofamily.

28*) Co-parents break their denials of significant childhood nurturance deprivations, and steadily pursue personal recovery: **SF)** *Probable*. From 20 years' clinical experience, I estimate that about 80% or more of average divorced and stepfamily co-parents need to do this. *This is probably the single most important factor for long-term re/marriage and stepfamily success.* Recovery from the psychological wounds (p. 142) from nurturance deprivations (p. 48) is an ongoing adult process.

BF) From the U.S. first-divorce rate, I estimate that ~*50% of typical bioparents* need to do this. Most don't know of this task and don't *want* to know. This promotes first divorces, and unintentionally wounding future stepkids. **Implication**: when each re/wedding mate has been divorced before and isn't (yet) recovering from childhood wounds (Project 1), the odds are very high one or both will ignore the five hazards (Chapter 4), and make three *wrong* re/marriage choices (Project 7).

29*) Co-parents build and use a support network of informed relatives, friends, other co-parents, and professionals to help along the way: **SF)** *More vital than in a typical biofamily*, because of greater stepfamily complexity, tasks, hazards, conflicts, and "alienness." Kin often don't understand typical co-parenting tasks and issues. *Informed* classes and co-parent support groups are rare. **BF)** *Helpful, and less vital* because of the relative simplicity of typical biofamilies. *Effective* community and media co-parenting supports are usually far more available.

30*) Co-parents' _ sort, prioritize, balance, and co-manage all these tasks and normal life activities every day; and _ make enough time to play, relax, and *enjoy* their shared family process enough: **SF)** *Ongoing, and* far *more complex* (Project 12): There are more people, needs, and relationships; and more alien, concurrent tasks to balance. This raises the odds of repeated conflicts, and everyone feeling emotionally overwhelmed (inner family uproar). **BF)** *Ongoing and simpler.* There are fewer adjustment tasks and people to balance, so the odds of mates' feeling overwhelmed are generally lower.

31) Emotional or legal (re)divorce: All extended-family members _ resolve guilts, shames, angers, hurts, regrets, and fears over years, and _ grieve *many* complex losses: **SF)** *More likely:* over half of U.S. re/married co-parents (and their minor kids) re/divorce within 7-10 years of their commitment ceremony. Unknown millions elect to avoid legal re/divorce, and live in misery or numbness. Custodial and visiting minor kids are wounded either way. **BF)** *Less likely*: about 50% of U.S. first-marriage couples and their bio-kids now divorce legally.

+ + +

If you feel startled, anxious, and/or overwhelmed now, you're *normal*! That's how many co-parents increasingly feel after re/wedding, as they discover these many unexpected concurrent adjustment tasks over time. Recall that one of the five proposed re/marriage hazards is *unawareness*. How many courting co-parents and lay and professional supporters do you think could spontaneously describe even 20 of these 72 structural and task differences between stepfamilies and intact "traditional" biofamilies?

What do all these combined structural and task differences *mean* to typical co-parent couples like you?

Two Implications

Reading and discussing these structural and task differences in advance doesn't really prepare you partners for how confusing and alien these many adjustment tasks *feel*. Yet *not* studying and discussing the differences and stepfamily norms (p. 91 and Project 4) risks growing frustration, disillusionment, and stress for all stepfamily members. Does this make sense to you?

If you and your partner _ study and discuss these specific differences and tasks and _ accept a tailored set of them *before* deciding whether to re/wed, **you each are more apt to make three *right* nuptial decisions**. If you do re/marry, your awarenesses will help you form realistic role and relationship expectations of yourselves, each other, and your other stepfamily members. This builds an essential base for your doing effective inter and intra-home stepfamily problem-solving together, as you and your kids work at your complex overlapping projects.

The alternative is for one or more of your co-parents to deny that you're a stepfamily (i.e. avoid Project 3), or just pay lip service to that identity. That risks your *assuming* that "normal" (i.e. biological) family roles and norms are adequate to co-manage your related homes. Often, they *aren't*. Most of the hundreds of troubled co-parents I've met, like Sarah and Jack Tilmon, unconsciously follow this alternative. They do so mainly from denied psychological wounds, excessive neediness, and personal and social unawarenesses of their choices.

A second key implication of these *72* simultaneous step-bio differences **relates to the effectiveness of human-service professionals.** My experience is that very few counselors, clergy, teachers, lawyers, judges, and medical pros have ever seen a comparison like the one you've just studied.

Because of the five hazards, I believe you partners, ex mates, and kids have a greater need for *informed* professional help than your bio-peers. This is specially true _ in helping you decide whether or not to re/wed, and if you do, _ in the first several high-adjustment years. If you seek professional help, ask candidates their specific training in stepfamily tasks, structure, and dynamics. If they _ can't describe at least 20 of these 72 differences you've read about here (more is better), *look elsewhere.* Another criteria: See if they can _ spontaneously name *at least* 15 of the ~60 common stepfamily myths and realities summarized at http://sfhelp.org/04/myths.htm. Also ask if they _ can name many of the special needs typical stepkids have (p. 454). As a paying client, you have a *right* to ask. Your inner and physical kids and descendants need you to!

Step-adult and professional ignorance of these 72 differences and what they mean is part of the hazard of *unawareness.* Patiently studied and honestly discussed, Part 1 of this book and the related Web articles offer you lovebirds an antidote. It works best if you and your beloved are consistently led by your Selves and you're helping each other develop fluency with the seven communication skills in Project 2.

Pause and reflect on what you just learned. Breathe well from your belly. Notice what you feel and what thought streams your subselves are giving you. Take a few moments to identify the key things you want to remember about these structural and task step-bio differences and their implications.

Individual differences above may seem trivial. Note that

most of these tasks are concurrent and long-term. They're on top of your other life events and responsibilities. *Collectively* the alienness and sheer emotional complexity of kids' and co-parents adjustment tasks can be very stressful during the first several years of your stepfamily's evolution. Does that seem realistic?

If you, your partner, or someone important to either of you says, "Stepfamily, schmepfamily. C'mon, a family is just a family!" Acknowledge that from one perspective they're right (p. 424). From what you just studied, they couldn't be more mistaken! Keep this clearly in mind as you help each other do Projects 3 - 7 together!

Awarenesses . . .

D) Personal-priorities Worksheet

What's Most Important to You Partners Recently?

A key reason for widespread stepfamily discontent and re/divorce is that one partner wearies of feeling second (or fifth) best in their partner's demonstrated (vs. proclaimed) priorities. Read and mull the premises that follow. Then honestly rank your and your partner's recent priorities, based on your and their perceived *actions*. Then discuss the results together to affirm or problem-solve, vs. to blame, complain, or justify. Add the Web-page pointers (..**/***.htm) below to http://sfhelp.org/ to get the full Internet address of referenced articles.

Premises

If you don't agree with each of these, what *do* you believe?

1) Ongoing relationships exist to fill sets of *needs* in each partner (..02/needlevels.htm and ..02/a-bubble.htm.) A normal need in kids and adults is to feel noticed and valued enough by key other people, now and over time. Each partner needs the other to genuinely *want to* rank them and their relationship "high enough" in their life priorities. "Enough" is subjective. When the need to feel genuinely valued and appreciated isn't filled often enough in one or both partners, hurt, frustration, resentment, anxiety, and anger bloom. Without change, those eventually turn to indifference or hostility and distrust, and the relationship bond inexorably decays.

2) Each subself in your and your partner's inner family (personality) has its own relationship needs and priorities, so you each will feel "torn" (conflicted) at times. The subselves that govern your inner teams control your perceptions, feelings, and behaviors. If your relationship actions don't match your words or intentions, you're probably controlled by a protective false self (p. 139). That is, your true Self is disabled some or most of the time.

3) If you re/marry for the wrong reasons (Project 7), eventually one or both of you will begin to feel dissatisfied with your partner's priorities. This is specially likely if either of you depend heavily on strokes, attention, and primacy from your partner to maintain your self respect.

4) You and your partner each have the right to choose your own priorities, without guilt, shame, or anxiety. Neither of you has the right to *demand* that the other meet your needs for primacy. There are no "right" relationship priorities, only *real* ones. See ..02/rights.htm.

5) Your and your partner's *actions* over time **demonstrate your life priorities** more reliably than your words. Life priorities are based on emotional, spiritual, and physical needs, not logic. If a co-parent pretends relationship priorities to themselves or others because of duty, pity, guilt, shame, and/or fear, her or his actions will cause "double messages." ("You *say* you love me, but when your kids visit, I feel demoted to third best with you.") These suggest protective false-self dominance.

6) Hormones, habits, societal norms, old *shoulds*, physical comfort, and your unconscious mind all shape your dynamic mix of personal priorities. Through meditation, journaling, and honest discussions, you and your partner can each become clearer on your *real* priorities, as teammates. See if this helps you do that: ..02/dig-down.htm.

More premises about personal *priorities:*

7) To thrive, relationships need enough _ undistracted couple-time, _ effective problem solving, _ safe risks, and _ some willing (vs. dutiful) sacrifice of other activities and people by each partner. Partners usually need to feel their mate gives these things freely from love and respect, rather than from duty and/or anxiety about possible indifference, rejection, or abandonment.

8) Stepfamily re/marriages are steadily challenged because one or both mates care about minor or grown biokids and/or grandkids. That inevitably causes *loyalty conflicts* (p. 186), where the bioparent must demonstrate whose needs come first: their new mate's or their child's. Choosing not to choose ("You're *each* first with me!") is not an option. Unhealed divorce-related guilt and blocked mourning can skew a bioparents' priorities toward their biokids and away from their new mate. This inevitably causes *inner* and re/marital conflicts.

9) Your *courtship* priorities probably differ from those that will emerge if you re/wed. Each partner's mix and ranking of personal needs will change over time. So you both will be continually challenged to keep your relationship's priority high *enough* for each of you. This suggests value in mates periodically making reality checks: i.e. knowing and discussing your current priorities honestly together.

This worksheet provides a way to do that.

Suggestions

+ **Notice your feelings, needs, and expectations** now. Are you looking forward to this discovery experience? Anxious? Bored? Do you feel that filling out this worksheet and discussing the results with your partner will be useful?

+ **If you feel some mix of** *calm, centered, energized, light, focused, resilient, up, grounded, relaxed, alert, aware, serene, purposeful,* and *clear,* your true Self is probably leading your inner family of subselves. Note whether s/he's leading now, or some other subself is. (Who?)

+ **Scan the activity categories below**, and add any others you feel have been a significant part of your recent lives.

+ **Pick a recent time period**, like the last three months. Scan all the categories and then decide, "Generally where have I put the most and least of my daily energy in this period?" Take your time, and rank-order each of the categories (1, 2, 3 . . .). Option: pick the highest and lowest, then repeat with remaining categories until you run out. Ties are OK. Note any feelings or awarenesses that come up while you do this. *There is no right or wrong.*

+ **Think of someone who knows you well**, other than your partner. Would s/he basically agree with your ranking? Option: ask them.

+ **Repeat these steps for your partner's actions**. *Nonjudgmentally* rank how you see them generally having allocating their time and energy during the same period. This is about discovery, not blame! Again, note any feelings, thoughts, and questions that occur.

+ **Option: predict how your partner will rank** your and their own priorities, to see if you agree. Have some fun with this chance to learn!

+ When you're both done and undistracted, **compare and discuss what you each came up with**. See if this feels like *teammates* talking or something else (e.g. a competition or blame-defend match). Note objectively how each of you processes this: openly, anxiously, irritably, casually, humorously, defensively . . . What does that *mean* to you? Listen to your inner voices . . .

Where Our Time and Energy Go Recently . . .

The categories are in alphabetic order.

me/you

__ __ **Birthfamily relationships**: time with or for parents, siblings, and other key relatives.

__ __ **Communities**: neighborhood, church, town, regional, national, and/or global.

__ __ **Friendships**: socializing, entertaining, calling, supporting, and meeting new friends.

__ __ **Home and grounds**: selecting, furnishing, decorating, cleaning, maintaining, changing, planting, protecting . . .

__ __ **Leisure**: hobbies, travel, sports, reading, other media, pets, relaxing . . .

__ __ **Me** (personal time): eating, resting, exercising, meditating, worshipping and praying, counseling, grieving, journaling, hygiene, non-career education, personal growth, medical care, . . .

__ __ **Money, wealth, and financial security**: budgeting, spending, bill paying, investing, accounting, taxes, insurance policies, wills, saving, . . . (For earning, see "Work")

__ __ **Parenting** dependent and grown children and/or grandkids: enjoying, guiding, disciplining, supporting, playing, teaching, planning, protecting, problem-solving, communicating with other co-parent(s) and kin, financing . . .

__ __ **Possessions (material things)**: acquiring, installing, maintaining, protecting, using . . .

__ __ **Work and career**: commuting, job time, overtime, training, education, entertaining, resumes, searching, career counseling, discussing . . .

__ __ **You / Us (couple time)**: communicating, problem-solving or arguing, activities, intimacy, relationship-building, playing . . .

__ __ **Other:**

Options

With your results fresh in mind, decide whether your Self led your inner family in filling out this worksheet. If your partner filled the worksheet out, decide if his or her Self guided _ doing that and _ discussing it with you.

+ Review these premises about satisfying relationships, and discuss them with your partner: ..08/relationship.htm.

+ Mull how each of your childhood parents would have filled this worksheet out, and compare that profile to *your* current priorities.

+ Imagine filling this worksheet out 10 years from now. What do you think the results will be? What would you *like* the results to be? How does that relate to any personal and re/marital mission statements you drafted in Project 6?

+ If there is someone in your life who has strong opinions about your current life priorities, who is it? What effects, if any, does their opinion have on how you *feel* about your priorities (e.g. guilt, shame, anxiety, defensiveness, doubt, pride, apathy . . .)?

+ Review this sample Bill of Personal Rights, and see how that relates to your current priorities: ..02/rights.htm.

+ If you discover an inner-family or interpersonal conflict over your or your partner's life priorities, are you clear on what your options are? Do you know how to resolve *inner* conflicts and *values* conflicts? Do you partners have an effective strategy to help each other resolve these as teammates?

+ If you discover priority (*need*) conflicts, review Project 2 and these Web articles for perspective and options: ..09/lc-intro.htm, ..Rx/mates/loyalty.htm, ..09/triangles.htm, ..02/a-bubble.htm, and ..02/dig-down.htm.

Awarenesses . . .

E) What your Minor (Step)kids Need

~60 Concurrent Growth, Healing, and Adjustment
Tasks

P sychologist Judith Wallerstein has studied effects of divorce on a group of average California adults and children over many years. She concludes that dependent kids that are at special risk of developmental slowdown from parental divorce (and what led to it) are _ "latchkey" kids (no competent, supervising adults consistently home after school); _ kids supporting an overwhelmed (i.e. false-self dominated) custodial parent and/ or troubled younger siblings; _ kids caught in "endless" parental post-separation battles and court disputes over child custody, visitation, and/or financial support; and _ *kids of parental re/divorce.* If Wallerstein is right, this last group is specially sobering, since well over half of U.S. stepfamilies divorce psychologically or legally.

In their book "Second Chances," Dr. Wallerstein and Sandra Blakeslee propose that depending on many factors, *it may take an average minor child 10 to 15 years to fully master their overlapping biofamily-breakup adjustment tasks.* In making that estimate, they don't acknowledge false-self formation, what causes it, how it affects grieving, or the sets of tasks you're about to read about.

To prepare to use this checklist:

+ Focus on each minor and grown child in your life, and in your partner's life, one at a time. Write down each child's main current *needs* as you see them. List as many as you wish. Next . . .

+ Name the adults you feel are responsible for helping each child fill their mix of current and long-term needs (i.e. for *nurturing* them). Refresh your perspective by re-scanning the traits of high-nurturance families in Chapter 3. Then . . .

+ Read and discuss these http://sfhelp.org/ Web articles with your co-parenting partner/s: ..10/co-p-goals.htm, ..10/co-pinv1.htm, ..02/needlevels.htm, and ..02/a-bubble.htm.

Use this worksheet to help you partners discuss and draft knowledgeable "job descriptions" for each co-parent in your courtship or present stepfamily (..10/job1.htm, and Projects 6 and 10). You can also use it for school conferences and with any counselors or tutors you hire to help nurture your custodial or visiting kids.

Premises: stepfamily re/marriage implies that each mate takes on the role of *co-parent* (stepparent and/or bioparent) for someone's minor or grown child/ren. Co-parents want their custodial and visiting kids to grow into healthy, self-supporting, productive young adults. To achieve this, young kids in *any* family need adult help to fill ~25 developmental needs, over ~20 years. *Typical minor kids of divorce and parental re/marriage face two to five sets of family-adjustment needs* <u>on top of</u> *these 25!*

If co-parents, kin, and other supporters can name and describe their kids' _ developmental, _ healing, and _ adjustment needs, they're far better able to nurture their youngsters effectively toward healthy adult independence. Do you agree?

My experience as a stepfamily researcher and clinician since

1979 is that typical divorced and stepfamily co-parents and many clinicians can't name most of the adjustment needs that their minor kids have, or even some of their normal developmental needs. That implies that they can't accurately assess and effectively help their boys and girls to satisfy their mixes of *up to five dozen* simultaneous needs. That puts most minor kids at major risk of slowed or blocked development, and major inner wounds.

That implies that such kids _ will feel bewildered and overwhelmed, as they struggle for mastery of all these simultaneous challenges; so they _ may have major trouble succeeding as productive adults, and _ they're at significant risk of *unintentionally* creating new low-nurturance families (Chapter 3) as their parents did, _ passing on the six psychological wounds that they inherited (p. 142). See this sobering validation: ..01/ research.htm.

Average minor kids of re/marrying parents face two to five sets of adjustment tasks from . . .

1) Healing psychological wounds from an *unintended* low-nurturance childhood; plus . . .

2) Birthfamily reorganization from parental divorce, or death; and . . .

3) Extended-family reorganization when one of their bioparents re/marries, and . . .

4) Another wave of losses and role, relationship and family-ritual adjustments if their *other* bioparent re/marries and/or cohabits. Over half of these kids . . .

5) Must also adjust to their stepfamily breaking up within ten years after their parent's re/wedding.

These sets of tasks _ usually overlap each other and the kids' ~25 developmental needs (below), and _ require co-parental awareness, teamwork, and dedication for kids' real mastery. This happens while _ each of their two to four co-parents and up to eight co-grandparents are adjusting to their *own* versions of the same family-reorganization (divorce or death, and re/marriage) changes, compounded by the five hazards in Chapter 4. Not an uplifting picture, is it?

This chapter is a summary checklist of kids' normal developmental needs and three sets of adjustment needs. The children in your life depend on you adults to understand and help with these tasks (needs), so they can become healthy, responsible, independent adults, just as you depended on your caregivers. This checklist is suggestive, vs. "perfect," so edit it as you see fit. It's based on 64 years' life experience, and 23 years' clinical research and consulting experience with over 500 average Midwestern, Anglo divorced families and stepfamilies.

"An effective co-parent" may be defined as "an adult who _ understands each of these fours sets of tasks, and is _ skilled at, and _ motivated and _ able to provide consistently-effective guidance with them, so dependent kids _ master them well enough (in somebody's view) when they leave home."

Whew.

Alert: this list is intellectual, dry, complex, and may feel overwhelming. To get the most from this resource chapter, stay aware of your thoughts and feelings as you read. This list is as much about *you* as a child as about kids in your life now. If you get boggled, pace and refresh yourself. Consider taking notes as you read and react, to capture important awarenesses and questions real time. Take as much time as you need!

See if you agree with this attempt to describe . . .

Kids' Normal Developmental Needs

Edit this summary against your own experience, and any parenting experience so far. This checklist is not complete or prioritized. Satisfying some needs depends on previously filling some others. *Mastery* is a subjective concept. Option: try rank-ordering these tasks, and relating them to kids' age-zones (e.g. pre-school, middle school, high school). Gain perspective on these needs from Dr. Erik Erikson's timeless book "Childhood and Society." The second edition was published in 1963. Family therapy and the U.S. post-war divorce epidemic were blooming, and two decades would pass before brain multiplicity and personality splitting began to be understood.

+ + +

Reality check: as you read, reflect whether *you* had to fill each of these needs to succeed as an independent adult.

Each of your minor girls and boys needs to . . .

___ 1) Learn how to think critically, objectively, clearly, and independently, to make sense of the world and make effective daily decisions. This includes *many* subtasks, like mastering abstract concepts, growing fluent with a clear vocabulary, synthesizing unrelated ideas, discerning information patterns, staying focused, and logical induction and deduction. And . . .

___ 2) Learn how to _ be clearly aware of, to _ focus among, and to _ balance (prioritize), dynamic emotions, thoughts, hunches, intuitions, and current *needs*; in order to _ react to life challenges and opportunities in healthy, safe, and satisfying ways. And . . .

___ 3) Learn to monitor and shift their "bubble of empathic awareness" from focusing only on *their* current needs, feelings, and thoughts, or only on other people's ("Always think of the other guy!"), to automatically including themselves and selected other people. The ultimate phase of this developmental task is to develop an empathic awareness of all cellular and spiritual life forms on and beyond Earth. And your kids need to . . .

___ 4) Forge a realistic identity to credibly satisfy their core human questions "Who am I?", and "How am I like and different from _ my parents, _ other people, and _ others of my gender?" Part of this developmental task is _ developing and asserting personal *boundaries*: finding a stable, peaceful way to separate with minimal anxiety and guilt from _ caregivers' needs, and _ caregivers' visions of who *they* want the child to be. This includes kids' needing to evolve realistic understanding of _ their unique talents, and _ their personal limitations, _ without undue egotism, guilt, shame, and anxiety. And . . .

__ 5) **Forge genuine _ self-respect**, _ self-trust, and _ self-awareness as foundations for filling their daily and long-term personal and social needs well enough. This implies all their subselves' learning to trust and cooperate with their Self, other Regular subselves, and a benign Higher Power.

And your dependent kids also need to . . .

_ 6) **Learn how to communicate effectively** (p. 167) with peers, authorities, and strangers of any gender and race, in calm and conflictual situations. This includes learning how to _ identify and _ assert their current true needs, while _appreciating the needs of others. And . . .

__ 7) **Learn to understand**, appreciate, and care effectively for, their changing body, to promote ongoing wholistic health and healing. This includes kids' _ understanding, _ appreciating, and _ controlling their _ sensuality and sexuality. And kids also need to . . .

__ 8) **Learn _ how to form nourishing** (vs. toxic) emotional **attachments** to (bond with) selected people, ideas, visions, and principles; and _ learn how to grieve well when such (emotional - mental - spiritual) bonds break. And . . .

__ 9) **Learn to make balanced daily decisions** between . . .
_ short-term pleasure vs. long-term satisfaction;
_ pleasing others vs. themselves;
_ inner and environmental realities, vs. tempting illusions and distortions (like denials);
_ attitudes of pessimism, idealism, and realistic optimism ("glass half full"); and . . .
_ work, play, and rest.

And each of your kids needs to . . .

__ 10) **Learn effective social and relationship skills** like tact, empathy, intimacy, selective trust, assertion, cooperation, and respectful confrontation, to "get along well" with other people, including an eventual mate. Developing kids also need to . . .

__ 11) **Learn how to _ take responsibility for** the impacts of their actions, vs. denial, projection, repression, blaming others, numbing out, and "confusion;" while they learn to _ respectfully grant other people full responsibility for their own decisions, behaviors, feelings, health, and welfare. And also . . .

___ 12) **Learn _ how to learn**, evaluate, retain, sort, prioritize, and use (apply) new concrete and abstract information; and _ learn how and where to get needed information. Perhaps the hardest part of this task is _ learning how to *unlearn* old attitudes, beliefs, habits, and values that no longer fit current life reality and goals.

And you're probably helping your dependent kids to . . .

___ 13) **Evolve meaningful answers to** core life questions about spirituality and religion, life and cosmic origins, destiny, fate, good and evil, health and death; and _ learn to revere and develop the spiritual part of their nature in their life decisions. And . . .

___ 14) **Learn how to _ adjust to**, and *learn* from _ personal **mistakes and failures**, and to _ keep their wholistic (mental + spiritual + emotional + physical) balance. And growing kids need to . . .

___ 15) **Evolve** an authentic (vs. borrowed) framework of **ethics and morals**: discerning what's "right and wrong," and "good and bad," in any situation, and _ apply those judgments effectively toward filling daily and long-range personal and social needs; while they . . .

___ 16) **Learn _ how to earn and responsibly manage** money and debt, and _ respect and care for what money buys, including power and freedoms; as they . . .

___ 17) **Learn to make responsible, healthy decisions about** _ **sex** and _ child conception, and _ learn (these) fundamental ideas about child development and effective parenting; and . . .

___18) **Learn how to** understand, negotiate, and **balance the responsibilities and limits of key social roles** like child; grandchild; sibling; student; friend; sexual partner; parent; local, national, and global citizen; team and class member; neighbor; employee; taxpayer; consumer; spiritual being; debtor; and eventually independent wo/man. And ideally, kids learn to . . .

__ 19) **Acknowledge _ that they have a unique, worthy life mission**, or purpose, and _ and stay alert for "evidence" (thoughts, feelings, hunches, outside feedback), about what it is; while _ trying out as many "personalities" and roles as possible, as an explorer. That can help them . . .

__ 20) **Value and evolve a meaningful plan about where their life is going**. The alternative is living each day as a disconnected random experience, with no plan or life goal, and dying with regrets over a wasted life. And kids need to . . .

__ 21) **Learn how to ask for, and receive, needed human and spiritual help**, *without excessive guilt, shame, and anxiety*, when life becomes chaotic and overwhelming. And . . .

__ 22) **Learn _ to discern who and what to trust**; and _ how to adapt to people, ideas, and circumstances they *don't* trust enough. Part of this task involves _ learning to live comfortably enough with inevitable ambiguities and insecurities. And to gain independence, your kids need to . . .

__ 23) _ **Master basic life skills** like cooking, sanitation, hygiene, understanding contracts and laws, time management, and (usually) driving a vehicle; while they _ learn about the physical world, and _ to nurture the Earth, vs. deplete it.

__ 24) The master childhood-developmental task is to **promote inner-family (personality) leadership by their wise, competent true Self**. The alternative is a fragmented personality dominated by a well-meaning group of short-sighted subselves—a false self. Mastery of this keystone task in childhood is unlikely if false selves control one or more of your child's primary caregivers. It then becomes an adult "recovery" task.

__ 25) Mastering all these tasks well *enough* helps a developing child to _ **feel, _ spontaneously express, and _ receive real *love***, including _ non-narcissistic self-love.

__ (add your own developmental tasks . . .)

Notice how you feel now, and where your thoughts go. Did you get enough help with these basic child-development needs, before you tried independent living? Did each of your early caregivers fill these developmental needs as kids? In future years, do you think your kids will thoughtfully answer that question "Yes"? This is about *awareness*, not blame!

I propose that all kids instinctively struggle to master concurrent "growing up" tasks like these, regardless of their family, ancestry, and social environment. **On top of these tasks**, children who grow up in low nurturance homes and families must (eventually) find an effective way to *also* . . .

2) Admit and Heal Psychological Wounds

About 90% of typical U.S. stepfamilies now form after the divorce of one or both re/marrying mates. I propose that parental separation and divorce is a sign of significantly low psycho-spiritual nurturance in one or both mates' childhood years (Chapter 3). I believe that typical kids like Patty McLean (Chapter 7) growing up in significantly low-nurturance environments adapt automatically by developing a protective, short-sighted false self. In extreme cases of parental neglect and abuse, this becomes "Multiple Personality Disorder," now called "Dissociative Identity Disorder."

This instinctive neurological response is powered by the primal instinct to *survive* now, vs. grow (fill the developmental needs above). It results in the child's decisions, attitudes, and perceptions being significantly governed by a protective false self (p. 139). Over time, the child's experiential view of "normal" forms around this false self's perception of life, and how the environment reacts to its decisions and actions.

Bottom line: I believe most parents who separate or divorce, or avoid intimacy and true relationship commitment, are wounded and dominated by a survival-oriented false self. Until they _ understand the effects of this via Project 1 or equivalent, and _ work to restore or empower their true Self to manage their *inner* family of subselves (personality), they'll _ unconsciously cause their kids to grow false selves too, just as their unaware ancestors and society did.

So typical kids of parental divorce must fill some mix of the psychological-healing needs below, *on top of their normal developmental needs.* These new needs are all about unlearning toxic prior attempts to master these developmental tasks. Recognizing and mastering these healing tasks is a life-long process. It usually starts in middle age after "hitting bottom." The other family-adjustment needs below are usually encountered before this personal healing begins. That makes healing harder to acknowledge and master.

My experience is that tragically, our media and educational systems ignore this concept, so most fragmented people never perceive their or their kid's six psychological wounds. Caregivers are at high risk of mis-diagnosing or minimizing what their troubled kids *really* need. Fortunately, the 1980s "Adult Child" and "Inner Child" movements, facilitated by the Internet, are combating this.

Numbering continues from above, because all these tasks overlap. Numbers in parentheses refer to developmental needs above. The psychological-healing needs you're about to read are not ranked in importance. Together, they summarize what Project-1 *recovery* aims for. Each survivor of low childhood nurturance has a unique mix of healing tasks like these:

__ **26) Break protective denials that they _came from a low-nurturance childhood** and _ developed a protective false-self to survive, which _ is significantly stressing them and the people around them (24). In my experience since 1981, most significantly-wounded adults aren't aware of this task, or these:

__ **27) _ Take responsibility for their life and wholistic health**, and evolve an effective way to _ enable their Self, _ acknowledge a meaningful Higher Power, and _ grow inner-family harmony. Restated: this keystone task is _ recognizing that task 24 above was never done, and _ choosing to master it as a self-responsible adult. Related tasks are:

___ **28)** Heal toxic shame: **intentionally _ reverse low self-esteem and self-respect** over time, and _ develop unconditional love of Self and selected (or all) others (5). A parallel task is to . . .

___ **29) Change reflexive self-neglect** (self-abandonment) **to authentic** (vs. dutiful or fearful) **self-care** and self-nurturance. (7)

___ **30) Replace fear** and "irrational" expectation of abandonment by key caregivers, **with steady faith in** a loving and reliable Higher Power, key others, and true-Self reliability. Parallel tasks are reducing excessive fears of _ the unknown, _ normal interpersonal conflict, and _ overwhelm from intense emotions. (5, 22, 24)

___ **31) Convert vague or distorted senses of Self** (personal identity) including gender identity, to clear, healthy, and appropriate senses of true Self. This includes developing and accepting a realistic body image. (4, 5)

___ **32) Reverse distrusts** of _ personal perceptions and judgment ("self doubt"), and of _ the dependability and good intentions of most caregivers and adult authorities (22). A related task is to improve discernment of who deserves to be trusted.

___ **33)** Learn that _ there are no "negative" emotions, and _ **develop** the anxiety and guilt-free **abilities to _ fully feel and express** *all* **emotions within safe limits.** Also learn _ to be comfortable enough with others doing the same, specially with anger, sadness, confusion, despair, and fear. Failure to master these will seriously inhibit the wounded person's ability to grieve, communicate, and manage inner and interpersonal conflict well. (2)

___ **34) Develop the ability to usually tolerate _** change; _ uncertainty; _ inner-personal and interpersonal conflict; _ imperfection; and _ selective, healthy intimacies. This depends partly on learning to _ discern and _ accept what can be affected, vs. what is beyond the person's control (24, 25, and others). Typical false selves usually can't do some or all these well and consistently.

__ 35) **Replace self-harmful (toxic) ways** of self-soothing and self-comforting (e.g. addictions, reality distortions, and avoidances) **with self-nurturing habits** and healthy sources of comfort and reassurance. (7, 21, 23)

__ 36) **Strengthen their ability to** _ form and _ maintain genuine (vs. faked or strategic), emotional attachments to (**bond with**) high-nurturance people and goals. This is one essential for real social intimacy and effective re/marriage and co-parenting. (8 and others)

A final over-arching adjustment task for kids raised with too little emotional nurturance is to . . .

__ 37) **Become firmly convinced that their lives have intrinsic worth**, promise, and real meaning, vs. old nihilism ("nothing matters"), worthlessness, and inner emptiness. (5, 19, 20)

__ (add your own healing tasks)

Minor kids have little chance to recognize and master these healing tasks if their principle caregivers don't see them, and are denying their own inner wounds. Again: I propose that first divorce is a strong suggestion that one or both mates _ came from a significantly low-nurturance childhood, _ weren't able to master enough of their own developmental tasks, and _ were unaware of their inner wounds, or _ didn't know how to heal them. Most U.S. re/marriages follow the divorce of one or both partners . . .

How are you doing? This is pretty heavy going, isn't it? Do your subselves need a body or mind-break? When you're ready, refocus on the key kids in your life again. If and when their biofamily reorganizes (vs. "breaks up"), they're *also* confronted with some mix of this third group of personal tasks (needs) . . .

3) Adjustments to Parental Separation and Divorce, or Death

Many American kids are under 20 when their birthfamily reorganizes from the divorce, or desertion of a parent. The complex emotional, financial, and legal process and event of divorce adds stress to _ their years of inadequate emotional/spiritual nurturance, and _ the complex web of physical and emotional changes (losses) which precede and result from their family reorganizing. Often, a parent leaving or being ejected from home breaks kids' protective denial of "family trouble," and their personal stress soars. Other kids' stress soars because it's *not* safe to break their denials. Both amplify false-self dominance, which hinders satisfying all three sets of needs.

Many factors shape each child's reactions to birthfamily restructuring from parental death or separation, like age, gender, birth-order, extended-family presence and coherence, ethnicity, finances, education, local social conditions (support), and so on. Generally, the lower the child's emotional nurturance has been before parental separation or death, the more trouble s/he will have in filling developmental and personality healing needs (above), and the family-change adjustment needs below. Does that make sense to you?

Note that these adjustment tasks are concurrent with any incomplete developmental and personality-healing tasks. Depending on many factors, it may take an average minor child 5 to15 years to *stabilize*, vs. *fill*, their set of needs below. Kids who have adjusted and begun bonding in a stepfamily must do these tasks a second time if the stepfamily breaks up.

Again, numbering continues from above. Reflect on which of the needs above would need to be filled in order to master each one of these new ones:

+ + +

__ **38) Make stable sense out of why one parent left** them, and why their biofamily came apart. Progress with this task is greatly shaped by whether each bioparent is _ guided by their Self or not, and honest with _ themselves, _ their ex mate, and _ with the child. If a protective false self controls the child, parental honestly about their family's break-up may not be received clearly or at all because of excessive shame and guilt, distrusts, and reality distortions.

__ **39) _ Accept that *they* didn't cause their biofamily's reorganization,** and _ clarify and accept that someone else is responsible without anxiety. And . . .

__ **40) Grieve *many* concrete and abstract losses** (broken emotional bonds), over years. Parental dwelling moves, and visitations may cause waves of losses for adults and children alike. And . . .

__ **41) Change their views of one or both parents** from hero/ine to "flawed and still lovable" special adults. Filling this need depends on _ personal and family grieving progress; may include _ *forgiving* one or both parents; and is shaped by _ the post-divorce relationship between ex mates, and _ their abilities to think clearly and communicate effectively (Project 2). And . . .

__ **42) Heal _ unwarranted guilts** ("I did bad things that made them divorce") **and new _ shame** ["I'm unlovable and *bad* (worthless), so Dad (Mom) left me / us."]. And also . . .

__ **43) Draw clear new personal boundaries**: _ separate themselves from their parents' and relatives anxiety, needs, and conflicts, _ *without undue guilt, anxiety, and shame.* And . . .

__ **44) Re/build trust** that adult caregivers and authorities will not reject or abandon them, despite the child's major problems and self-perceived "flaws." And . . .

__ **45) Build new trust** that living bioparents and key sibs and relatives are safe, healthy, and happy enough after the separation and divorce/s. And . . .

__ **46) Adjust to many new _ roles, _ rules, and _ living conditions**, including _ (eventual) parental dating, and _ new post-separation responsibilities like taking more care of their home, themselves, younger sibs, and/or an overwhelmed bioparent.

This task often is compounded by learning new and sometimes clashing roles and rules in two bioparental homes, plus inter-home visitation rituals. *If a child came from a significantly low-nurturance biofamily, s/he will probably shuttle between* two *low-nurturance homes after parental separation.* There are exceptions. And many kids of birthfamily reorganization need to . . .

___ **47) Cope with one or both bioparents using them** as a weapon, spy, lure, confidant, or courier in ongoing relations with their other bioparent, and/or key relatives. This is specially likely when _ parents battle in court over child support, custody, and/or visitations; and when _ one or both bioparents verbally attack or revile the other parent in front of the child. Typical kids of parental divorce or death also must . . .

___ **48) Adjust their personal and family identities** over time to "*OK* divorced (or bereaved) (boy / son / brother / relative) or (girl / daughter / sister / relative)." And . . .

___ **49) Find and accept surrogate nurturance,** if biofamily parenting is inadequate. This is specially vital if their custodial caregiver/s are overwhelmed and regressed (dominated by a false self). A related task is to _ adjust well enough to any guilt, shame, or anxiety over _ seeking and _ receiving surrogate caregiving.

And over time, minor kids of birthfamily reorganization need to . . .

___ **50) Re/build authentic feelings** of personal security, confidence, optimism, and hope for their future _ as a whole, and as a competent _ adult, _ spouse, _ wage-earner, and _ (potential) parent.

How long do you think the average child of parental divorce or death would take to fill their set of these 13 adjustment needs, while progressing on their 26 developmental needs, burdened by major psychological injuries? If their custodial parent cohabits and/or re/marries before the child (or each bioparent) has progressed well on their key existing tasks above, the youngster now experiences their absent-parent family "breaking up" and . . .

4) Typical *Stepfamily* Adjustment Needs

The nature, mix, and complexity of stepfamily-adjustment tasks for a given child again depends on their age, sex, relations with each bioparent, understanding of parental divorce, and many other factors. Key factors are _ the degree of emotional/spiritual nurturance in their pre and post-divorce homes, schools, churches, and neighborhoods (Chapter 3). These depend largely on _ the degree to which true Selves lead the child's main and secondary caregivers.

Numbering continues from above. Note that these new needs extend or repeat some of those above. Generally, the more *developmental needs* your child has made major progress on, the more apt they are to adjust and stabilize to these new needs:

__ **51) Mourn and accept less (custodial) bioparental attention** and accessibility. This may coincide with teens' growing focus on socializing with friends and striving for independence.

__ **52) (Again) redefine _ personal and _ family identity,** and _ decide clearly "Who comprises my family now?" This is often in the face of co-parents' and relatives' confusions over their version of this task.

__ **53) Negotiate and stabilize several to many** "forced" (unchosen) **stepfamily _ roles and _ relationships,** like custodial or visiting stepchild and step-sibling, step-cousin, step-grandchild, half-sibling, etc. Typical biofamilies have 15 common roles; multi-home stepfamilies have ~30+. Co-parents often are as confused and conflicted about these as their kids.

__ **54)** _ **Adjust to new** _ **privacy and** __ **sexual norms and conditions** in their home/s.

__ **55) Continue grieving** prior losses, and __ start mourning a complex set of new abstract and concrete losses from the ending of their prior living situation.

__ **56) Form and act from clear personal boundaries** without guilt or anxiety, in case key relatives' or friends' disapprove of their bioparent's _ divorce, _ re/marriage, and/or _ cohabiting.

__ **57)** _ **Test for,** _ **learn clearly, and** _ **accept:**

+ What are the _ rules and _ consequences in my _ two co-parenting homes and _ complex new extended stepfamily?

+ Who's *really* in charge at each of my co-parenting homes? Who _ makes and _ enforces the rules, if anyone?

+ What's my _ rank (importance), and _ how much power do I have now to get others to fill my needs in each home?

+ How do I handle the (inevitable) differences in the _ values (preferences and priorities), _ rules, _ roles, and _ consequences between my several step homes?

And typical minor kids in new stepfamilies must . . .

__ **58) Build trust that "This home and family are safe** to belong to and bond with, because they won't break up like my *all* my other ones did."

__ **59) Adapt to feeling alone, confused, and weird** because most of the child's relatives, teachers, and some friends don't really understand what it's like to live in a stepfamily like theirs. And . . .

__ **60) Adjust their** _ **identity,** _ **power,** _ **loyalties, and** _ **"rank"** in their _ home/s and _stepfamily each time their co-parents have a new child (i.e. a half-sib); or a bio or stepsib moves in or out of their home; or a key person dies, moves away, re/marries, or re/divorces.

__ **61) Re-do most of these tasks** (with more experience and knowledge) **if their other bioparent re/marries *or re/di-***

vorces. Average stepkids may have four co-parents, eight co-grandparents, and dozens of co-relatives.

__ **62)** The Stepfamily Association of America guesstimates that over 60% of typical U.S. stepfamilies re/divorce within 10 years of the nuptials. That suggests that **a high percentage of the (usually teenaged) kids in them must master a** *fifth* **set of adjustments***:* re-doing many of tasks 38-50 above, concurrent with any unfinished prior tasks.

Typical stepfamily co-parents have their own version of most of these adjustment tasks (p. 435 and http://sfhelp.org/09/sf-task1.htm). Stepfamily literature suggests that it commonly takes co-parents and kids four or more years to stabilize (vs. satisfy) all these stepfamily-adjustment needs well enough. In two decades of stepfamily research, I've never seen any acknowledgement of these five overlapping sets of typical kids' developmental, healing, and family-adjustment needs. Have you?

Note what you're thinking and feeling. How many of these tasks could you have named before you read this? Think of the minor kids in your life: do you know which of these needs they've filled, and which they currently need help with? What kind of help do they need? From whom? What kind of help do *you* partners need to help *them*?

Now what?

Options

+ If _ *you* and/or _ your current partner are survivors of low-birthfamily nurturance (Chapter 3) and/or of biofamily breakup, **use the checklist above to assess yourselves.** How are each of *you* doing with your version of these needs? _ Do the same for your ex mates, and any new partners of theirs. _ Discuss this with appropriate members of your family. _ Review your life priorities, and decide if you want to act.

+ **Give a copy of this summary to each caregiver** whose behavior affects each minor child in your life, includ-

ing ex mates, concerned kin, teachers, tutors, and counselors. Tailor this list to suit each individual child.

+ **Agree with your partner** to use this summary to _ identify which needs each of your minor kids need help
with, and then _ evolve co-parent job descriptions in
Project 6 if you're courting, and Project 10 if you're re/
married.

+ **If you're contemplating re/marriage** _ to a bioparent
whose custodial or noncustodial biokid/s haven't progressed well on "too many" of these tasks (in your opinion), or if _ your partner isn't aware of these needs, or _
seems to minimize their relevance or importance, then
_ seriously question the wisdom of re/marrying them
(all). Your partner has the same option.

To help you partners evaluate your minor kids' status with
these tasks, here are some . . .

Options for Assessing Your Kids' Needs-status

You've just read a summary of *62* developmental, healing,
and family-adjustment tasks that typical minor kids of divorced
and re/married parents often face. Kids whose parent died have
most of the same needs. Depending on many factors, most of
the tasks will overlap. Seen all at once, they can easily overwhelm the staunchest co-parent or supporter, let alone a boy or
girl!

How can you partners realistically gauge where each of
your minor kids stand with their mix of these developmental,
healing, and adjustment needs?

Basics

An early goal in Projects 6 and 10 is to "learn what your
dependent kids need." That's a simple phrase for a *very* important, complex effort, partly because it challenges you to realistically evaluate some abstract, psychological aspects of your
custodial and visiting kids. An advantage you may have is that

typical stepparents may be more objective about this assessment than biomoms and dads.

If you re/marry, a future Project 10 goal is "build an effective co-parenting *team* over time, to help fill your and your kids' (many) needs." Success at this depends on your progressing on all seven courtship projects "well enough." For perspective on project 10, see Chapter 8, and/or read ..10/ project10.htm.

As a fledgling engineer, I learned to start a complex design project by defining the desired outcome clearly, and working backwards to see what was needed to achieve it. In "stepfamily engineering," that becomes "Define _ the questions about each child you want credible answers to, and _ how you co-parents want to *feel* about _ yourselves and _ your research process, when you're done. Then work backwards to see how you two or more co-parents and concerned kin can do those together."

Because typical divorced families and stepfamilies are emotionally volatile, I suggest you start with "How do we want everyone to feel as our child research progresses?" Compare my proposed answer with yours:

"We want _ our co-parents and kids to each feel respected, aware, harmonious, and hopeful; and to feel _ united and motivated on a common, worthy project."

If you co-parents ignore getting clear on this question together, you risk unrealistic results from Project 6: drafting co-parent job descriptions. *How* and *when* you co-parents approach Projects 6 and 10 are just as important as what they yield and what you do with the results!

<u>First Steps Toward Assessing Your Kids' Status</u>

Parts of what follows are available at http://sfhelp.org/10/ kid-dx.htm. To begin, you co-parents will need clear, *consensual* answers to . . .

"When should we do this child needs assessment?"

"Who will participate, and who will lead?"

"Which kids, specifically, are we going to assess?"

"What preparation do we need?"
"What specific questions are we trying to answer?"
"Who's responsible for acting on our results?"
"How will we resolve disputes among us?" And . . .
"How can we optimize our efforts together, over time?"
Suggestions . . .

"When Should We Do This Child-needs Assessment?"

Ideally, well *before* making any re/marriage decision, as the first part of Project 6. Whether you're courting, newly re/ wedded, or reading about this years after re/marriage, your young and grown kids need you co-parents to begin this needs-assessment *now*! Every day that passes without you adults (including co-grandparents) learning your kids' status on their overwhelming four sets of simultaneous tasks increases their risk of suffering false-self domination, stepfamily stress, and possible re/divorce.

"Who Will Participate and Lead?"

Ideally your _ three or more co-parents, and _ any concerned blood and legal relatives of the kids in your divorced or remarried family will take part. Many factors can prevent this. Your option is to accept that, and say "Starting with our bioparents and stepparents, how many of our extended-(step)family adults are genuinely interested in helping with this important needs-assessment, once they understand it?

If some adults are blocked from supporting your kids by old distrust, hurt, anger, crises, disrespect, guilt, and/or disinterest, your options include _ ignoring them; _ appealing for their help, for the kids' sakes; _ scorn and ridicule them; or _ use the Serenity Prayer and a long-term view, and keep them respectfully informed of what you're trying to do, why, and what's happening as you progress.

Someone has to take responsibility for planning and facilitating this project or it won't get done. Do you have a leader (or co-leaders) yet? If not, what or who is in the way? If so, what do you know of this leader's true needs and motives? How does this project rank in their current priorities? See p. 447.

How does the *style* of this family leader (authoritarian, democratic, decisive, inconsistent, empathic . . .) affect the motivation and cooperation of your other caregiving adults? Does s/he acknowledge being the leader? Is s/he comfortable with that role? What help does s/he need from the rest of you? From knowledgeable outsiders?

"Which Kids Will We Assess?"

I suggest "Each minor *and grown* child of each of our two or more related co-parents." Beware of *assuming* that an apparently happy, "well-adjusted" child has filled all four sets of needs! False selves are experts at protectively camouflaging pain and unmet needs from _ their host person _ and key people around them.

Popular false-self strategies are denials (of needs and inner anguish); emotional numbing; unconscious distraction (by substances or "busyness"); chronic "illness" and/or "depression;" procrastinating; lying; intellectualizing; isolating; and repression. Adults and kids of death or divorce and re/marriage have a *lot* of losses to mourn, questions to clarify, adjustments to make, and at least six emotional wounds to heal (Project 1)!

"What Training and Preparation Do We All Need?"

If you're courting, your best preparation is to _ get familiar with the seven projects in Part 2. Then _ make major progress over some months on the first five projects, and the first half of Project 6 (draft a mission statement). Then finish this chapter, and fill out this checklist thoughtfully with your partner and other willing co-parents.

If you're already remarried, _ continue Projects 1 through 6, _ start making stable progress on projects 8 and 9 together, and _ see the outline for Project 10 (http://sfhelp.org/10/

project10.htm) for requisites, options, resources, and direction. All of these are moving targets, and works in progress.

"What Specific Questions Are We Trying to Answer?"

Have all your active co-parents and caregivers _ review copies of this checklist. _ Discuss and edit the list to fit your values and situation, and _ evolve a set of specific child-needs that you all believe are important. Try to avoid black/white (either-or) thinking, and _ be alert for normal values differences, loyalty conflicts, and divisive persecutor-victim-rescuer (PVR) relationship triangles. The basic question is: which of these 62 needs does each of your dependent kids require your help with?

"Who's Responsible for Acting on Our Results?"

Your co-parenting team will probably judge that each of your kids is "OK enough" with some items in each of their four sets of needs. Each young person will be judged "not OK enough" with other tasks, and *"maybe* OK enough for now" on others. Once you all assess these, who will act on your results, how, and when?

Ideally, your research process here will have helped you caregivers progress on building a caregiving team. Optionally, it will have hilighted what or who blocks such team building.

You adults will have differing priorities on which kids you want to support, how often, and to what extent. That's *normal* in typical stepfamilies! I recommend that you all patiently negotiate who's responsible for helping which child with what needs via a series of discussions. Then for your kids' sakes if not your own, help each other evolve meaningful "job (role) descriptions" to clarify and document your chosen responsibilities and targets.

You've probably never seen bioparents use child-care job descriptions. This is likely because there are _ only one or two primary caregivers, not three or more; _ probably fewer kids than you all have; and _ the kids only have one set of (developmental) needs to fill, not three to five simultaneous sets!

How to help your kids with selected tasks would fill another book. See the *Solutions* series of articles at http://sfhelp.org/Rx/dx.htm, and books and Websites in Resource H for ideas. Also read about picking a qualified stepfamily clinician (http://sfhelp.org/11/counsel.htm), and periodically discuss whether professional help with some or all of these needs is warranted.

Members of typical divorced families and stepfamilies need more outside help than peers in intact biofamilies. Seeking and using professional help in a divorced or re/married family is a sign if wisdom and *strength*! See task 21 above. Exception: using lawyers and legal power to substitute for effective co-parental communication and problem-solving *guarantees* that false selves are running your show.

"How Will We Resolve Disputes Among Us?"

Your child task-status research *will* be hindered by values and loyalty conflicts, *inner* family conflicts, and PVR relationship triangles. If each of your co-parents have _ progressed on Projects 1 and 2, and _ read and discussed the Web articles at the start of this chapter, you co-parents *can* evolve effective ways of resolving these hindrances together. Two basics: each of your co-parents _ adopt an ("=/=") attitude of self and mutual respect, and then _ agree that your minor kids depend on you *all* to heal any personal and relationship barriers to form a caregiving team.

When these conflicts, communication blocks, and triangles occur, _ acknowledge them, and _ refocus your team on resolving them one at a time. Seductive alternatives are ignoring, minimizing, or postponing them; or falling into unproductive blame > defend > counterblame cycles. You are the only people on our planet who can nurture your kids as they struggle to master their complex mixes of the tasks above.

Option: Use the worksheets and resources at ..02/

links02.htm or in "*Satisfactions*—Seven Relationship Skills You Need to Know," to help you all resolve these team-building and research barriers. Give everyone a copy of this summary of common communication blocks: ..02/evc-blox.htm, and use it to promote *cooperative* problem solving.

"How Can We Optimize Our Efforts Together?"

I believe you co-parents will be far more apt to share old-age satisfaction and contentment if you help each other . . .

Learn _ how to tell if your Selves are leading your respective inner families, and _ what to do if they aren't (Project 1). Make true-Self empowerment a high *family* priority.

Focus steadily on how you adults want to promote the high-nurturance traits in Chapter 3 *long-range*, via acting from your family mission statement/s and job descriptions (Project 6).

Evolve and *use* a shared definition of "effective co-parenting" (p. 457) based on understanding each of your kids' developmental and adjustment needs. Resources: *Build a High-nurturance Stepfamily* (xlibris.com) and ..10/co-p-goals.htm.

Adopt the attitudes that . . .

+ mastering "co-parenting" together is a priceless adventure and opportunity, vs. an ego-contest, power struggle, or an onerous obligation and chore.

+ each of your kids' needs and spirits, and each of your co-parents' needs and spirits, are of equal importance to you all; and that . . .

+ each of you adults are *students* in a new, challenging stepfamily environment, so helping each other *learn* (e.g. Chapters 5 and 6, and Project 4) is a priceless gift to you and your future generations.

Keep your perspective: Projects 6 and 10 are two of 12 simultaneous co-parent tasks (Chapter 8). They all overlap, and contribute toward building a high-nurturance stepfamily, over many years. Help each other patiently progress on all of these, and recall: *"Progress, not Perfection!"*

Recap

Parenting is the decades-long process of intentionally filling growing kids' kaleidoscope of mental, emotional, spiritual, and physical needs, while filling your own: i.e. *nurturing.* Long-term stepfamily co-parenting success is *far* more complex and difficult than rearing kids in intact high-nurturance biofamilies. Project 6 is a series of initial steps for all your kids' co-parents to take together toward such success.

The first half of this chapter proposes four sets of concurrent, interactive tasks that each of your minor kids needs *informed* adult help with. The second half suggests how you co-parents can assess how well each of your minor and grown kids is doing at filling their mix of these needs. No matter how competent or stable they appear, your kids *really* need your wisdom, heart, patience, and humor here!

If you're considering stepfamily re/marriage (or you may), use this chapter as a resource to help you complete Project 6 with your beloved. Unawareness is one of five roots of re/divorce. Part of what you caregivers need to know is specifically what each of your dependent kids needs.

If you're already re/married, use this chapter as a resource for Project 10: building an effective co-parenting team, and nurturing you all and your great future fan of descendents.

If you're a professional supporter of troubled, divorced, and re/married families, specially if you're a clergyperson, therapist, or family-law attorney, weave what feels credible and important to you from this chapter (and book) into your work, and alert your colleagues and employers.

 # Reality check: once again we've covered a *lot* of ideas. Relax from the details, breathe well, stretch, and see where you stand now. T = true, F = false, and "?" means "I 'm not sure."

1) I could name over 30 of these needs before I read this chapter. (T F ?)

2) I believe this is a reasonably accurate summary of the normal developmental and family-adjustment needs that aver-

age minor kids of parental divorce and re/marriage have. _ If I don't think so, I know how to improve this summary. (T F ?)

3) For each minor and grown child I care about, I'm clearly aware of their status with these needs. (T F ?)

4) I'm clear enough now on _ my and _ my partner's (adult) status with each of these needs. (T F ?)

5) I see significant value in using the ideas in this chapter now to help meet the needs of _ me, _ my co-parenting partner/s (if any), and _ each custodial or visiting child that depend on me or us. (T F ?)

6) I can clearly describe _ co-parent Project 6 (and if you're re/married, _ Project 10) to an interested stranger now; and _ I genuinely want to work at our version of these projects *now*, vs. "soon" or "sometime." (T F ?)

7) I feel comfortable enough discussing the ideas and suggestions in this chapter now with _ my adult partner/s, _ other family members, and _ any professional supporters. If not, I know _ why, and _ what to do about this. (T F ?)

8) I fully accept that without informed help from me and my caregiving partners, _ the minor kids that depend on us may not fill their set of these many needs; and that _ my and my partners' acceptance of this amounts to child neglect. (If you don't agree, what would you call it?)

9) I accept without ambivalence that if I choose to re/marry, I share ongoing responsibility to help each minor child in our stepfamily satisfy their set of these needs over many years.

10) I'm clear that my true Self has answered these questions. (T F ?)

Awarenesses . . .

F) Summary: Three Right Re/marriage Choices

Pick the right people to re/wed,

for the right reasons, at the right time

The Stepfamily Association of America estimates that 60% of couples re/divorce. The rate is higher if you include couples that re/divorce psychologically but not legally. The implication is that most couples *like you* are overcome by the five hazards in Chapter 4, and make up to three wrong re/ marital choices.

This chapter offers a framework of experience-based criteria to help you partners make the three best long-term re/ marriage decisions you can for you and your descendents. The framework is based on all the information in and related to Parts 1 and 2 of this book.

This chapter summarizes the three full right-choice worksheets you'll find at ..07/links07.htm. I recommend that you use this summary to raise your and your partner's awareness, and use the Web worksheets to answer the six questions posed in Project 7. Using the worksheets alone vs. with your partner raises the odds you'll make unbiased re/marriage decisions.

As you work through this framework, notice which items cause you the most unease. Use a hi-lighter, jot margin notes, add criteria that occur to you, and possibly journal your thoughts and feelings as you go. Keep "the mind of a student," and take your time with this.

Option: reread _ the "Courtship Danger" items on p. 10 (http://sfhelp.org/07/danger.htm) and _ the five re/marriage hazards on p. 69 to sharpen your perspective on what you're about to do here.

Is your Self in charge right now? If you're not sure or you say "No," your responses below will probably be skewed. The stakes for you and dependent kids are very high.

Who Are the Right *People* To Re/wed?

To enjoy your re/marriage and build a high-nurturance stepfamily together over time, I believe each courting co-parent needs to soberly evaluate some key personal traits of each of their _ two or more potential co-parenting partners; _ minor and grown potential stepkids; and _ relatives who matter to your prospective mate and to each prospective minor and grown stepchild.

Here's a general profile of the right co-parents to re/wed, starting with you and your beloved. I suggest you don't check an item as true unless you can confidently check each sub-item in it. Hedging on these suggests false-self control, and raises the odds you'll make wrong re/marital choices. Option: use a range of 1 to 5 on some of these, rather than a checkmark.

The Right *Co-parents* (Including *You*) . . .

This section summarizes two full checklists: the right *partner* to commit to (http://sfhelp.org/07/rt-partner.htm) and the right related ex mates and their new mates, if any (..07/rt-co-p.htm). **These right co-parent factors are *in addition to* the normal considerations** that suitors mull in deciding whether to commit to each other for life.

Each co-parent . . .

___ **1)** is from a reasonably high-nurturance childhood, per Chapter 3; *or _ each co-parent is clearly in effective true re-*

covery from false-self control (p. 151); *or* each is at least _ genuinely interested _ in learning more about how to identify and heal the six psychological wounds (p. 142) and _ avoid passing them on to your minor kids. Option: use Resources A (p. 401) and B (p. 413) to help evaluate this.

___ **2)** Each can clearly describe many of the specific traits of _ a high-nurturance family (p. 48), _ a healthy relationship (..08/relationship.htm), and _ an effective co-parent (p. 457); and _ each of our co-parents values each of these highly. Actions are better indicators than words here.

___ **3)** Each co-parent solidly accepts that in stepfamily conflicts without viable compromises, co-parents usually need to put their personal integrity and wholistic health first, their re/marriage second, and all else third, without anxiety or guilt. If a co-parent says, "I accept this," _ her or his actions and words match. *Caution*: some wounded bioparents change their minds on this after re/wedding, and loyalty conflicts bloom.

___ **4)** Each adult is steadily _ clarifying the purpose/s of his or her own life, and _ can realistically name their major personal _ skills, talents, and _ limitations.

___ **5)** Each co-parent can _ name and _ describe when to best use the seven communication skills that promote effective inner and interpersonal conflict resolution; and _ often models these skills now. (Project 2)

And for long-term successful stepfamily re/marriage, each of your three or more *right* co-parents . . .

___ **6)** Will _ clearly accept your (prospective) identity as a normal, two or three-home nuclear stepfamily; and _ agree on who belongs to it (Project 3). Each co-parent _ clearly accepts that both bioparents of each stepchild are full members of your potential stepfamily; and each adult *wants* to learn _ the main differences between stepfamilies and biofamilies (p. 425) and _ the 60 realities at ..04/60expect1.htm, to help us all build realistic stepfamily relationship and role expectations (Project 4).

___ **7)** Each co-parent _ knows good-grief basics (p. 248 or ..05/grief-quiz.htm), _ can name most of the symptoms of blocked grief (p. 303 or ..05/grief-symptoms.htm), and _ can clearly describe the traits of a pro-grief relationship, home, and family (Project 5). If any co-parent can't, _ s/he is clearly self-motivated to learn these now.

___ 8) Each *right* co-parent can respectfully _ negotiate and _ keep clear, stable emotional boundaries around their respective marriages and homes. (Can you describe what an "emotional boundary" is?)

___ 9) Each of our co-parents is _ genuinely interested in doing some version of the 12 co-parent projects in Chapter 8 over four or more years _ as teammates (vs. friends), for the sakes of themselves and our minor and grown kids and their descendents.

___ 10) Each prospective right co-parent _ can name many of the ~60 developmental and special adjustment needs that average stepkids must fill (p. 454). Each _ *wants* to assess the need-status of each child involved, and _ to patiently assist her or him within their limits. Each co-parent _ is clearly motivated to _ form a co-parenting team and _ draft co-parenting "job descriptions" for each minor child.

___ 11) Each divorced co-parent is proactively working toward _ healing any significant prior _ disrespects, _ hurts, _ distrusts, _ guilts, and _ resentments; and _ settling any related financial debts, with their ex mate/s. (..Rx/dx.htm).

___ 12) Each co-parent is firmly opposed to using lawyers and the legal system to force resolution of co-parenting conflicts over child custody, visitation, and financial support. See ..Rx/ex/legal.htm.

And the *right* co-parents to commit to . . .

___ 13) Are each open to _ using stepfamily-informed professionals (clergy, clinicians, educators) along the way, and to _ exchanging ideas and encouragements with other stepfamily co-parents in person and/or on the Internet. (Project 11)

___ 14) The right *partner* to commit to and I have clearly and honestly discussed our respective ideas and needs on _ child conception; _ stepchild adoption; _ co-parenting expenses, insurance, and wills; _ key parenting values and priorities; and

_ why we each want to re/marry and form a complex, risky stepfamily. _ S/He and _ I feel compatible enough on all these, *or* _ we're working effectively towards that.

___ 15) My partner _ genuinely wants to discuss all these stepfamily factors with me, rather than avoiding, denying, postponing, arguing, demanding, threatening, minimizing, controlling, or manipulating.

___ 16) Clearly, none of our co-parents are _ overusing or addicted to _ any substance (including fat and sugar); _ an activity, like work, gambling, TV, spending, or exercise; _ another person (p. 413); and/or _ a mood state like excitement, anger, or sexual arousal.

If you feel *sure* that you and your two or more prospective co-parenting teammates have enough of these factors, then each of you lovebirds evaluate whether you're committing yourself and any biokids to the right *stepkids*. Who are they? Numbering continues from above.

The Right Stepchild/ren

This condenses the full worksheet at http://sfhelp.org/07/rt-stepkid.htm. **Each prospective minor or grown stepchild in my situation . . .**

___ 17) is _ friendly and _ respectful enough with _ me and _ each of my biokids. I and each child _ have no significant "bad chemistry" (i.e. dislike, disrespect, distrust, disinterest, anxiety, or sexual tension) with each other. _ People who know us well would agree with this.

___ 18) isn't _caught in the middle of warring bioparents, _ siding with one against the other, _ refusing contact with one or both, or _ caretaking a wounded bioparent and/or troubled siblings.

___ 19) is progressing well enough, in my view, with _ their normal developmental tasks, _ their healing tasks from childhood deprivations (if any), and _ adjustment tasks from their biofamily reorganizing. Answering this implies that you know what those needs are (p. 454).

___ **20)** Each potential *right* stepchild _ can accurately described why their parents divorced in age-appropriate terms; and _ has been honestly assessed by me and one or both bioparents for signs of significant blocked grief. _ We all agree that each child has few or none of these signs; *or* if any child does, _ relevant co-parents and kin are co-operating effectively to help free up normal mourning now (Project 5). And each *right* stepchild . . .

___ **21)** is clearly not overusing or addicted to _ any substance (including fat and sugar); an activity, like work, gambling, TV, spending, or exercise; _ another person (p. 413); and/or _ a mood state like excitement, anger, or sexual arousal. And . . .

___ **22)** Each *right* minor and grown stepchild is _ clearly aware that I and their bioparent are considering stepfamily re/marriage. Each child has been able to _ vent their true feelings about this, and to _ ask us adults honest questions about what changes stepfamily cohabiting would bring to them and the people, pets, and things they care most about. Minimizing or hiding romantic courtship from biokids, ex mates, and/or key relatives is a *clear* sign of false-self control, no matter what the reason.

Notice what you're thinking and feeling. Do you need a break? The final aspect of picking the right *people* to re/wed is committing to . . .

The Right Relatives

In evaluating these factors, consider each relative who is emotionally significant to _ each of your co-parents and _ each minor or grown (step)child. Give special focus to siblings and grandparents. Consider including dead relatives whose memory or bequests currently influence any co-parent or child. Highlights: **For long-range re/marital success, the right in-laws to commit to ...**

___ **23)** are _ clearly guided by their true Self, *or* _ are surely in effective recovery from any significant false-self dominance, *or* _ seem motivated to study Project 1 now, and to _ self-assess for the six wounds (p. 142). And ...

___ **24)** Each active relative _ clearly accepts that your re/marriage will make them part of a normal extended *step*family; and _ they want to _ agree on who comprises this stepfamily and _ learn and discuss stepfamily norms (p. 91 and ..04/myths.htm) and uniquenesses (p. 425). Restated: each key relative is *interested* in _ doing versions of Projects 3 and 4 now, and _ discussing them with our other members. And ...

___ **25)** Each has largely resolved any significant _ guilt, _ anger, _ sorrow, and/or _ worry (anxiety) related to a child's or relative's death, divorce, or other trauma. And ...

___ **26)** Each key relative has stable _ interests, _ boundaries, _ friends, and _ life-goals of their own, vs. being overly enmeshed with or dependent on their child/ren and any grandkids, nephews, and/or nieces.

___ **27)** Each key relative is clearly not overusing or addicted to _ any *substance*, including fat and sugar; _ an *activity*, like work, gambling, TV, spending, or exercise; _ another *person* (p. 413); and/or _ a *mood state* like excitement, anger, or sexual arousal; and ...

___ **28)** Each _ bio- and _ step-grandparent has appropriate _ boundaries and _ relationships with their former sons and daughters-in-law. Each grandparent is clearly _ open to including and building warm relationships with _ their grandkids' prospective new stepparent and _ any step-grandkids. I see no significant signs of _ bio-family favoritism and/or _ re/marital disapproval in any senior adult in our several extended biofamilies.

+ + +

This is the *short* list of traits of the right *people* to re/ marry: co-parents + stepkids + key relatives. Note that first-marriage fiancés aren't faced with most of these questions.

If your Self feels your prospective stepfamily members have enough of these traits, then take an honest look at *why* you're considering commitment to all of them. If you and/or your partner are carrying low-nurturance wounds like Sarah and Jack Tilmon and millions of your peers, your false selves will probably distort your answers to fit key *unconscious* needs, and deny doing that. Is your Self answering these questions? Again, the numbering of these re/marriage-decision criteria continues from above.

Some Key Right *Reasons* To Re/wed

You may have found the right partner, co-parents, stepkids, and relatives to commit to, but have the wrong reasons for pledging your troth (true fidelity). What are common right *reasons*? Add your own to these . . .

___ **29)** To lovingly help each other heal, grow, and fulfill our respective life purposes as unique, worthy persons.

___ **30)** To share the challenges, heartaches, and joys of responsibly conceiving and/or raising one or more kids together.

___ **31)** To provide a stable, safe, high nurturance home for our existing dependent child/ren. (Chapter 3)

___ **32)** To cause, share, and enjoy life experiences together as loving, mutually-respectful companions.

And we want to re/marry . . .

___ **33)** To fulfill our Higher Power's plan and dream for each of us and the world.

In contrast, http://sfhelp.org/07/rt-reasons.htm offers *30* common unhealthy reasons that typical lonely, weary, lusty, anxious, spiritually empty, wounded co-parent suitors (i.e. their false selves) use to re/marry. Their excessive shame, guilts, fears, and reality distortions (like denial) magically make their set of *wrong* reasons to re/wed seem perfectly sane and logical, despite all inner and outer warnings. This complex re/marriage and co-parenting decision is often influenced by uninformed and significantly wounded well-wishers.

If _ your prospective stepfamily members are the right *people*, and _ you partners wanting to re/marry for the right *reasons*, you may still harvest long-term heartache for you and your kids by _ re/wedding too soon. The four worksheets starting with http://sfhelp.org/07/rt-time.htm can help assess your timing together. Here's a summary:

When Is the Right *Time* To Re/wed?

___ 34) If either of you partners was previously married, _ your biofamily separation (vs. "divorce") or your mate's death was at least 24 months ago; and _ you courting partners have known each other and any related kids for at least 24 months. Longer is safer in both cases.

___ 35) You courting partners (or ideally all three or more of your prospective co-parents) have worked seriously at Projects 1-6 together for at least nine months. Can you name them now? As a result, you each . . .

___ 36) Can define _ *inner family (personality), subself, false-self wounds, real* and *pseudo recovery,* and *true Self traits;* and _ the emotional symptoms of having a true Self guiding other subselves.

___ 37 Can accurately _ name and _ describe the five stepfamily re/divorce hazards (p, 69), and _ the 12 related co-parent projects in Chapter 8.

___ 38) You all can name at least 15 of the traits of high nurturance families on p. 48, and _ the six inner wounds that usually result from low childhood nurturance. (p. 142).

___ 39) You co-parents all can clearly describe _ the difference between real and pseudo recovery (p. 157) from the six wounds, and _ are clearly each well along in any needed personal recovery. (Project 1) Take your time with this one!

___ 40) You each can now spontaneously name at least 30 of the 60 differences between typical biofamilies and multi-home stepfamilies (p. 425).

__ **41)** Each of your co-parents can _ name at least 20 of the 60 common myths about stepfamily life, and _ the corresponding realities (http://sfhelp.org/04/myths.htm). More is better.

__ **42)** You each can _ name and _ describe each of the seven communication skills in Project 2, and are _ reasonably fluent at *using* them now to resolve recent _ inner-family and _ interpersonal conflicts.

And if it's the right time to re/marry, you, your partner, and your related co-parents . . .

__ **43)** Can each _ name at least 30 of the 60+ developmental and adjustment needs that typical minor and grown stepkids must fill (p. 454), and can describe _ how to assess your kids' status with their needs, and _ some practical ideas for how to help do this effectively. And . . .

__ **44)** You all can name at least 20 of the ~40 common environmental differences between "stepparenting" and traditional bioparenting roles (..10/co-p-dfrnces.htm), and _ what these differences *mean* in your situation.

__ **45)** You all _ have discussed, and _ are in general agreement on, which of your three or more co-parents is responsible for what, _ emotionally, _ financially, and _ legally, for each minor stepfamily child. (Project 6, ..10/co-pinv1.htm, and ..10/job1.htm)

__ **46)** You three or more co-parents have all _ honestly discussed stepchild legal adoptions; _ "ours" child conceptions; _ pre-nuptial agreements, and _ stepparents' estate plans (legal wills); _ major asset ownership and management (e.g. vehicle, savings and investment accounts, and real estate titles); _ incomes and expenses; and _ respective child-discipline values and practices; and _ you all are in general agreement on each of these *or* _ you're negotiating mutually-respectful compromises.

__ **47)** All your co-parents and kids are _ well along in grieving your respective prior losses, and _ are expecting and _ prepared to grieve the _ tangible and _ invisible losses that stepfamily re/marriage and cohabiting will inevitably bring (as well as enjoy the gains!).

And it's the right time to re/marry if . . .

__ **48)** Each _ prospective stepparent and _ each minor or grown biochild has had _ many shared experiences with each prospective stepchild and stepsibling, like meals, vacations, birthdays, and holidays. _ Everyone has had a chance to experience the "chemistry" among you all, and _ discuss it honestly. And . . .

__ **49)** Each divorced bioparent among you has clearly resolved their main core _ guilts, and _ inner and _ interpersonal conflicts about divorce _ causes and _ impacts; _ child custody, _ visitations, _ financial support, and _ co-parenting; and _ any related legal battles and _ extended-family conflicts. And . . .

__ **50)** You prospective partners can clearly describe _ what you want your re/marriage and your multi-home stepfamily to accomplish, long-range, and you have _ rough-drafted and _ discussed a meaningful mission statement together (Project 6). And . . .

__ **51)** You feel _ your true Self solidly believes that _ you had "enough" of the right *people* and right *reason* factors above, now; and that _ that your beloved's true Self feels the same way.

You've just read a *summary* of key traits that I believe generally define the right *people* to re/wed, the right *reasons* to re/marry into a stepfamily, and the right *time* to re/commit. The full right-choice checklists come from my 23-year quest to understand why most Americans re/divorce. What are you feeling? Normal reactions for Cupid-controlled co-parents are *overwhelmed, startled, skeptical,* and *uneasy* or *anxious.* Others feel irritated or *angry!*

Together, these 51 requirements are pretty overwhelming. The three full worksheets for Project 7 are even more daunting. *So is the trauma for partners and kids that precedes and fol-*

lows stepfamily separation and re/divorce. Does the statement "most stepfamily re/marriages break up" make more sense to you now? Stepfamilies are not for the faint-hearted!

I hope you draw **two main things** from studying this Project-7 summary resource:

> \+ Stepfamily re/marriage and co-parenting is more complex and stressful than in intact biofamilies, so prior marital and parenting experience alone is *not* a valid guide to long-term success; and . . .
>
> \+ **Stepfamily re/marriage can thrive** *if* both partners _ are well informed in advance of what they and their kids will probably encounter, _ patiently research three *right* re/marital choices, and _ agree on how to prepare well together.

This and the prior two books in the series aim to help you understand *why* you should prepare, and to give you partners a viable framework for doing so together. If you re/marry, *Build a High-nurturance Stepfamily* (xlibris.com) adds five more projects to help you build a high-nurturance stepfamily together. (p. 126).

Reminder: **see the full right-choice worksheets** starting with http://sfhelp.org/07/rt-partner.htm. Also consider taking the **free** re/marriage preparation **course** at http://sfhelp.org/07/bhsf/intro.htm.

G) Stepfamily Relationship Terms

My experience is that average divorced and/or re/married co-parents like Jack and Sarah Tilmon often have under-developed family and relationship vocabularies, and don't know it. They're unclear or mistaken on what key terms mean, and use them in ways that *increase* stress. Words are the basic tools you depend on to describe and fill your social needs, and nurture healthy relationships.

To promote clearer thinking, talking, and problem solving, this chapter defines selected family-relationship terms. Many will differ from what you're used to because they refer to the false-self wounding that (I believe) is common to divorced families and stepfamilies. Experiment: before reading each definition below, review yours. For a relationship and *communication* glossary based on inner-family premises, see "*Satisfactions*—7 Relationship Skills You Need to Know" (www.Xlibris.com). The abbreviation "q.v." below means the Latin "quod videt," meaning "which see."

These definitions are in alphabetical order:

Abandonment is unintentionally or consciously neglecting _ the true needs of a dependent person, and/or _ ignoring the responsibilities of an accepted social or family role. For a young child, emotional and/or physical abandonment by primary caregivers causes *terror* and a pervasive sense of worth-lessness and unlovability: *shame* ("low self esteem").

Terror and shame automatically promote adaptive false-self formation, and are carried unconsciously into adulthood by young (Vulnerable) subselves. Until recognized and healed via personal recovery, excessive shame and fear of abandon-ment promote co-dependence or isolation, (re)divorce, illness via self-neglect (*self* abandonment), and premature death. If not identified, they usually pass on *unintentionally* to any mi-nor kids who depend on the wounded adult. See *Family, Love, Neglect, Nurture, Recovery,* Chapter 6 in Part 1, and Project 1.

Absent parent: (1) a caregiver who has little or no nurtur-ing impact on a dependent child; and (2) a geographically-distant caregiver who has a significant psychological and/or genetic effect on a child. The caregiver may be a genetic, psy-chological, or legal parent, like a non-custodial stepparent. In a divorced-family or stepfamily context, casual use of this term can unconsciously minimize full family membership of an in-active, dead, or non-custodial co-parent. From a child's view, their "other (noncustodial or dead) parent" is emotionally, fi-nancially, and genetically very influential, whether active or absent. See *Co-parent, Parent, Single parent,* and *Stepparent.*

Abuse, Abusive, Abuser: I've often seen these provocative words harmfully misused by co-parents, clinicians, lawyers, and authors. Using them appropriately is vital in healing child-hood-neglect and divorce-related wounds. For behavior in a two-person relationship to be *abuse*, three things must be clearly true. If they're not all present, the behavior is *aggression.* "You were aggressive with me" is far less shaming and inflamma-tory than "You *abused* me."

The three conditions are . . .

__ *One person must have some power over the other.* S/He must control and provide something that the other person de-pends on, and can't provide easily or at all for himself or her-self. In *child* or *elder abuse,* this manifests as a person being significantly dependent on their caregiver/s for shelter, food, clothing, health care, companionship, and other necessities.

__ *The "power person" must _ willfully gratify some personal need/s* by using the dependent person _ in a way that significantly harms the latter psychologically, physically, and/or spiritually. What constitutes "significant harm" is subjective. Gratifying sexual needs against a dependent person's will or knowledge causes massive trauma in all three domains.

__ *The dependent person must be unable (vs. unwilling) to safely _ defend themselves or _ withdraw* from the power-person's toxic behavior. Co-parents with the psychological wounds of excessive shame, fear, and reality distortion may believe they can't defend or leave an abusive relationship safely, so they endure harmful aggression they really could avoid— i.e. they accept the *Victim* role in a PVR relationship triangle. See Project 1.

Note the implications of this three-factor definition: if an enraged adult yells obscenities, threats, or shaming insults at a dependent child (*verbal* abuse); or whips, burns, starves, or locks them up (*physical* abuse), that is *clearly* "child *abuse.*" So is an adult intentionally scaring a gullible child with vivid forecasts of an all-powerful, wrathful God punishing them for being "bad" by forcing them to "burn forever in hell" (*spiritual* abuse).

I propose that caregiver abandonment (neglect), and chronic aggression and abuse, all promote significant false-self wounds in young kids. See *Bonding, Shame,* and *Toxic.*

"Act out" is slang for defiant, conflictual, or self-harmful behavior, usually associated with kids and "childish" adults. In my experience, "acting out" is _ a cry for help; _ a signal that the person's family is low nurturance; and _ the family's leaders are psychologically injured, and don't know it or what to do about it. A teen's "acting out" may be their way of moving toward appropriate or self-protective independence.

A common misconception is that when stepkids act out, they're being rebellious, disrespectful, and selfish. I believe what they're usually doing is necessary *testing* to see _ what the rules are in their complex new stepfamily, _ who's in charge, _ who sides with who, and _ how much power the child has.

Their legitimate goals are to build trust that _ their custodial parent won't abandon them, and that _ *this* family won't disintegrate like prior ones did. Another possibility is that the "acting out" a child of divorce or parental re/marriage is an expression of grief anger over their many losses. If so, it may mean their caregivers haven't made it safe to express anger in a less disruptive way. A third possibility is that the child is dominated by young hurt and angry subselves which block them from progress on filling their developmental needs (p. 457).

Adult "acting out" probably indicates dominance of a false self that doesn't know how else to get their needs met. See *Aggression, Passive-aggressive,* and Projects 1, 2, and 5.

Addict, Addicted, Addiction: Like *abuse* and *rape*, these are provocative words that are often misunderstood and misused. A true addiction is a compulsive behavior that . . .

+ Emotionally, physically, and/or spiritually harms the addict, associates, and dependents;
+ Is self-reinforcing and progressive;
+ Has predictable stages and symptoms (like denial); and . . .
+ Can't be stopped by logic or "will power" alone.

Compulsive harmful behavior that doesn't meet all four of these criteria can be called "self-neglect" or "self-abuse."

The four types of addiction all temporarily numb or distract from great inner discomfort like shame, guilt, fear, emptiness, despair, and confusion. The four are:

+ *chemicals*, including fat, sugar, and complex carbohydrates (junk food);
+ *relationships* (co-dependence),
+ excessive *activities* like work, gambling, shopping, eating, sex, fitness, Internet surfing, cleaning . . .); and . . .
+ *emotional states* like rage, excitement, and sexual arousal and release.

Some chemical addictions like ethyl alcohol, nicotine, and some hard drugs, promote physical (cellular) cravings that amplify the compulsive need for psychological numbing or distraction.

I believe true addictions *always* indicate that the addict:

_ had a low-nurturance childhood, and _ has significant psychological wounds.

_ will steadily prefer other wounded people for companionship and intimacy, despite logical reasons not to.

_ has high odds of lowering the nurturance level in their current personal and work settings, which causes interpersonal stress and woundings over time.

_ may arrest (vs. cure) their addiction by committing to a version of the 12-step Alcoholics Anonymous philosophy. This usually does *not* heal the underlying false-self dominance. And a true addict . . .

_ may "quit" one addiction, and their false self will covertly compensate by starting another one (cross addiction). And s/he . . .

_ can permanently reduce her or his compulsive behaviors by some form of *inner* family therapy which empowers their true Self.

Perhaps 70% of the ~1,000 typical divorced and stepfamily adults I've worked with since 1981 have reported personal addiction, addicted partners, and/or addicted childhood caregivers and ancestors. Both my parents were functional alcoholics in full denial. I have been in personal "ACoA" recovery from the childhood effects of this since 1986. Are there people in your family, key relationships, and/or ancestry who may be or are true addicts? See *Toxic* and Project 1.

Bio- (prefix): shorthand for *biological* (genetic), as in *bioparent, biomother, biofather, biosister, biobrother, bio-grandparent, biochild,* and *bio-kin*. The prefix is useful because intact-biofamily roles, tasks, and dynamics are often very different from their post-divorce and stepfamily counterparts. Biofamilies and biofamily roles are often thought of as normal, natural, and traditional. This can invoke shame, by implying that *step-* equivalents are *abnormal, unnatural, and nontraditional*. See *Co- (prefix)* and *Step- (prefix)*.

Bioparent: see *Parent*

Blended (step)family: the false selves of co-parents and professionals who dislike the unpleasant associations of *stepfamily* may use the more palatable title "blended family." I feel that this is an understandable, potentially *harmful* example of unconscious reality-distortion and avoidance. Technically, both co-parent partners in a blended or "complex" stepfamily home have conceived kids with earlier partners. So both caregivers in a true *blended* household are dual-role co-parents in a three-home nuclear stepfamily, unless a prior partner died. All blended families are stepfamilies, but not all stepfamilies are blended. Confusing, isn't it? See *Half sibling, "Ours child," Re/divorce, Re/marriage, and Stepsiblings.*

Bond (verb): the process of developing a one-way or mutual psycho-spiritual *attachment* (caring and need) between two living things. Adults and kids have the innate urge and capacity to form emotional/spiritual *attachments* to selected other people, pets, rituals, tangible and abstract things, sounds (e.g. music), places, concepts, and causes. Noun: a *bond* is the psycho-spiritual "connection" (spontaneous interest and caring) between a person and any of these, as in "Jeremy and his Mom had a strong bond."

This term is specially relevant in divorced and stepfamilies because many members are confronted with the needs to repair old bonds and forge new ones. Typical stepparents want to bond with their stepkids and stepkin, and feel "like a real (bonded bio-) family." Infants and unwounded parents follow a primal wired-in neural program to bond. For other people, the typical semi-conscious needs causing the urge to *bond* are to . . .

+ feel the pleasure of altruism: selfless concern for others;
+ feel valued, understood, and respected by another person;
+ avoid the terror, despair, and emptiness of feeling alone and helpless;
+ feel emotional stimulation, support, comfort, and companionship, and to . . .
+ feel personally normal and socially acceptable.

Stepfamily adults and some supporters who minimize or avoid their stepfamily identity are often stressed by unrealistic (bio-based) expectations about how fast, and how intense, stepfamily-members should bond with each other. Some stepfamily members *never* bond. They may or may not pretend to care because of social "obligation", ignorance, guilt, anxiety, and/or shame.

In troubled and divorced families and stepfamilies, co-parents and kids from low-nurturance childhoods may have crippled or undeveloped abilities to bond. Without understanding this and why it's so, this weak bonding causes personal and family hurt, confusion, shame, guilt, anxiety, and anger. These combine to lower family nurturance, and promote psychological wounding. True recovery from false-self control can restore some ability to bond, over time. See *Loss, Love, Nurture, Splitting,* and Projects 1, 3, and 4.

Boundaries: See *Family system.*

Caregiver: a person of any age who is spontaneously or dutifully concerned about the needs and welfare of another living thing. S/He *wants* to, or feels s/he *has to* spend time, effort, and personal resources to fill the other's needs. A family *caregiver* is any adult or older child who focuses on filling the current and long-term needs of a dependent resident or distant family member.

High-nurturance relationships and families can't exist without one or more effective caregivers attending the needs of dependent members. A key factor is the *self*-care that such providers give themselves as they tend the needs of other members. Caregivers who overfocus on filling others' needs and neglect their own unconsciously foster low family nurturance. This is also true of families where caregivers are overfocused on their own needs ("I'm 1-up"), and neglect those of their dependents. Both situations suggest significant psychological wounding.

People have different standards and expectations about who is "supposed to" provide *what* care for *which* other family members, depending on the type and development-level of the family. Stepfamily members who expect the intensity and quality of caregiving in new stepparents and co-grandparents to match typical (or idealized) biofamily peers are usually frustrated, disappointed, and disillusioned, over time.

Do you see value in distinguishing between care*givers,* and care*takers*? See *Bond, Co-parent, Need, Nurturance, Parent, Psychological parent, Role,* and *Stepparent.*

Co- This prefix comes from the Latin root "com-," which meant *together.* Co- is a more emotionally neutral prefix for re/marriage-family roles and relationships than "step-" and "bio-". Our culture has inherited the bias that stepfamilies are less *normal* or *natural* than "regular" (intact bio) families. Our media unconsciously promotes this. To offset this bias, some people prefer *co-family, co-parent,* and *co-child,* because "co-" implies equality, as in *co-operate* and *co-chairperson.* Which would you rather be called: "step-" or "co-" (or neither)?

Shame-based adults and kids can feel *more* inferior if they're in a stepfamily. Their false selves can compensate by avoiding "step-" words and rejecting or minimizing their stepfamily identity. Jack Tilmon (Chapter 7) is a typical example. This avoidance (denial) promotes holding unrealistic biofamily-based expectations about themselves and other stepfamily members. See *Bio-, Co-parent, Step-,* and Project 3.

Co-dependence: is a generalization of the clinical term "co-alcoholic." It denotes a widespread form of toxic relationship addiction (q.v.) indicating _ serious inner wounds, excessive _ shame and _ fear of abandonment, and _ a low-nurturance childhood. See p. 413.

Communication: _ any perceived behavior that causes a physical, spiritual, mental, or emotional change in another person; or _ the exchange of behaviors between people trying to fill two or more of six current needs (p. 182). Can you name them? When all participants feel their true (vs. surface) needs are filled well enough, communications are *effective.* See *Conflict, Needs, Problem,* and Project 2.

Complex stepfamily is one in which each co-parent partner _ has prior children and _ both *bioparent* and *stepparent* roles. This implies that there are four related living or absent co-parents, and (usually) at least three co-parenting homes in the nuclear stepfamily. It is also called a *blended* stepfamily (q.v.). In a *simple* stepfamily only one co-parent has prior biokids. There are almost 100 structural types of complex and simple stepfamilies, considering combinations of child conception, child custody, and prior relationship status. See *Family structure,* and *Nuclear stepfamily.*

Conflict (noun and verb) means two or more opposing needs, perceptions, or values _ *inside* a person, and/or _ *between* two or more people. Unaware people often focus on *surface* needs in a conflict ("I think you're too harsh with your daughter.") rather than discerning the semi-conscious *true* needs (p. 49) underneath them ("I need to _ honor my own integrity, _ respect you as a co-parent, _ protect our relationship, and _ help my stepdaughter.") *Confusion, doubt,* and *anxiety* signal "I have an *inner* conflict among my subselves."

Typical stepfamilies have more people and conflicts than average intact biofamilies. This is specially so if co-parents and/or kids are controlled by false selves. Common conflicts unique to stepfamilies include _ family *identity* ("We're a *stepfamily.*" "Oh no we're not!"); _ *membership* ("My ex wife belongs to our stepfamily." "Oh no. I'll die before I accept that!"); _ *parenting values* and *methods*, _ cultural *traditions* and *values*, _ assets and debts, and _ disputes over child *visitations*, *custody*, and financial *support*, including insurance and wills.

Conflicts between people are often three concurrent clashes: within my inner family, within yours, and between our active subselves. Knowing this can greatly enhance your ability to permanently resolve conflicts, using "parts work" (Project 1) and the seven skills in Project 2. See *Needs* and *Problem.*

Co-parent is a bioparent, stepparent with or without biokids, or other family caregiver (q.v.). Divorced and stepfamily co-parents are either custodial or non-custodial. Some are both at once, if their several biokids live in different homes. People like Sarah and Jack Tilmon (Chapter 7) are *dual* co-parents because they each are nurturing one or more biokids and stepkids. Depending on your definition, Patty McLean's nuclear stepfamily has five or six co-parents living in three (or four) related homes with their five minor kids. See the "map" on p. 99.

Co-parent is emotionally neutral. It helps to offset our un-challenged cultural bias that bioparents are better or more *natural* or *normal* than (people in the role of) stepparents. See *Absent parent, Bond, Bio-, Caregiver, Co-, Nurture, Parent,* and *Step-.*

Counseling: see *Therapy*

Custody, Custodial (child, co-parent, home): these words come from Latin roots meaning "to guard." After a separation, divorce, or parental death, courts designate legal *primary, residential (physical), split (residential and parental), or joint* (shared) custody to caregiving co-parents or relatives. They do this to promote clear social and legal awareness of who is primarily responsible to guard the welfare of (nurture) dependent kids. In many cases, conflicted co-parents can't agree on these, so a court imposes its judgments based on the assessed "best interests of the minor child/ren."

Since 1981, my clinical experience with hundreds of divorced couples and stepfamilies has consistently been that . . .

+ Major custody disputes *always* indicate _ significant false-self dominance and wounds, _ a low-family-nurturance ancestry, _ ineffective communications skills, (often) _ blocked grief; and adult _ unawareness of these and _ their implications.

+ The best custody arrangement in any situation maximizes a stable, high-nurturance environment (p. 48) for all kids *and concerned co-parents.*

+ In deciding custody disputes, co-parents and supporters are usually unaware of _ what constitutes a high-nurturance family (Chapter 3); _ the kids' complex sets of concurrent special needs (p. 454), and _ the long-term value of encouraging wounded co-parents to heal their childhood and marital wounds, distrusts, disrespects, hurts, and resentments.

+ People tend to overfocus on surface custody conflicts, and minimize or ignore the underlying *family system* problems. That promotes recurring dissention and low home and family nurturance. These are *not* in the best interest of the minor kids involved.

+ The best custody choice may shift as circumstances change from mixes of _ parental death, re/marriage, and re/divorce; _ new child conceptions; _ stepfamily conflicts; _ financial and health issues, including addictions and recoveries; and _ kids maturing; and . . .

+ Few legal and health professionals involved in resolving custody disputes, including clergy, have adequate understanding of the five hazards (p. 69) and stepfamily realities (p. 91).

All these can promote well-intentioned but ineffective or toxic (wound-enhancing) custody decrees. See *Caregiver, Childhood, Divorce, Need, Nurture,* and *Toxic.*

Denial is a survival reflex which protects against conscious awareness of an uncomfortable reality. A classic symptom of true addiction is the person *denying* they have a toxic compulsion when it's obvious to others that they do. Denials and other reality distortions (repressing, minimizing, rationalizing, exaggerating, intellectualizing, fantasizing, idealizing, black/white thinking, and projecting) are strategies used by Guardian subselves to protect scared, shamed, overwhelmed, or guilty young Vulnerable subselves. Most (all?) denials suggest local or chronic false-self control. Two common toxic stepfamily denials are "We are *not* a stepfamily," and "(an ex mate) is *not* part of our (step)family!" Blocked grief is a form of denial. The master denial is of itself ("I'm *not* denying anything!"). People in denial are not *weak, irresponsible,* or *bad*; they're wounded, scared, and unaware of protective false-self dominance. See *Subself* and Project 1.

Divorce, re/divorce: these words have many meanings. At times, not distinguishing between the meanings can promote significant misunderstanding and stress. Most U.S. stepfamily re/marriages follow one or more divorces, and end in re/divorce. (The "/" notes it may be a stepparent's first). Divorce is simultaneously . . .

+ **The gradual pre-legal** *psychological* **process** in one mate and often their kids and kin, of losing _ respect, trust, and caring for a loved or esteemed person, _ emotional security, _ family identity and pride, _ hope, and _ motivation to improve. This process can extend far beyond granting a divorce decree, and may be amplified by legal-divorce conflicts and hostilities. And *divorce* is . . .

+ **The cause of shameful feelings** of personal "failure" in one or both mates, and perhaps their living bioparents. These feelings are specially powerful in shame-based adults and kids. And *divorce* includes . . .

+ **A change in the personal identity** of each mate. "Yesterday, I was a *wife* (*husband*). Today, I'm a single divorced wo/man." This invisible shift can significantly affect how each mate and special other people (like grandparents) feel about themselves and each other. And divorce is also . . .

+ **A powerful** *learning experience*, which shapes future choices of new mate (if any), and expectations about re/marriage. ("I no longer believe 'til death do us part,' and 'our love will see us through'"). And divorce is . . .

+ **The complex, painful** *social* **process** of reorganizing the relationships and rankings of family and friends, as two mates and any kids and bonded relatives separate emotionally, physically, and legally. This includes complex, stressful changes in the roles and relationships among all members of the extended biofamily or stepfamily, including name changes, wills, insurance, and identities. This multi-level reorganization causes a web of losses (broken bonds) in adults and kids that requires a pro-grief environment to heal, over time. And divorce is also . . .

+ **The** *legal* **process** resulting in formal dissolution of a socially-recognized marriage. In contested divorces, competing lawyers usually amplify the conflict between partners, which adds hurts and resentments that take years to heal. That _ lowers the nurturance level of their post-divorce family for years, _ increases psychological wounds in all concerned, and _ lowers the success odds of later re/marriages. This legal process also involves negotiating complex, conflictual changes in responsibilities and asset ownership, like home and car titles, savings accounts and debts, insurance coverages, and wills.

And *divorce* can also mean . . .

+ **The *courtroom event*** that ends this legal process, and results in a legal document decreeing that partners are no longer subject to local laws and responsibilities as married mates. If biokids are involved, the decree or a related *parenting agreement* often stipulates co-parenting responsibilities and behaviors. This decree often affects the roles and rights of new mates, who have little ability to amend that. In a re/divorce, step-parents usually have few or no legal rights or responsibilities to their stepkids, depending on state laws. And . . .

+ **Divorce is the *religious* and *spiritual* process** of reconciling these personal and social processes and events with a Higher Power, and formally recognizing that a spiritually-sanctioned union is dissolved. Divorcing Catholic couples must obtain a ruling from a tribunal affirming that there are acceptable reasons for dissolving their vows to each other and God. This formal *annulment* process is often long and arduous, increasing the agony of the overall divorce process. It can evoke intense guilt, shame, embarrassment, and anxiety in the partners and their religious relatives and friends. These can hinder personal and family mourning and recovery from inner wounds, promoting low family nurturance.

Finally, divorce and re/divorce are . . .

+ **Symptoms that one or both partners** picked the wrong *people* to commit to, at the wrong *time*, for the wrong *reasons.* The recent ~47% U.S. first-divorce rate and higher re/divorce rate implacably suggest widespread psychological wounding in our population and ancestors. This implies epidemic unawareness in our society, our family laws, and the programs that train our clergy, lawyers, judges, clinicians, and family-life educators.

A second or third divorce implies the person is *still* _ significantly dominated by a false self, and unaware of _ their wounds, _ key relationship skills (p. 83), and _ their unawarenesses.

I believe many researchers, clinicians, authors, and divorced people over-focus on the impacts of the legal divorce process and event, and minimize or ignore the psychological/spiritual wounds and ineffective communications that cause it. Many learned and lay studies, books, articles, and laws focus on the "effects of divorce," and completely overlook the significant psychological wounding that starts in the partners' childhoods. See Projects 1, 2 and 5.

Dysfunction: see *Family functioning, Needs, Nurturance, Toxic*, and p. 48.

Emotion is any of a range of primal, reflexive neorochemical and hormonal reactions to perceived changes in our inner and/or outer environments. Caregivers and our media cause major stress in families and relationships by thoughtlessly labeling some emotions as *positive* (love, joy, happiness, compassion . . .) and others as *negative* (rage, hate, terror, shame, guilt, confusion, disgust . . .). I propose that *all* emotions are useful signals that we have important needs to fill. Unaware people judge the *effects* of impulsively reacting to or expressing emotions as harmful or negative. They also thoughtlessly rule that any discomfort is *negative* (vs. natural, inevitable, and useful), and comfort and pleasure are positive (better).

These unconscious biases can lower family and relationship nurturance levels. Thinking, saying, or implying that a child or spouse is *wrong* or *bad* for feeling or expressing normal emotions like sadness, fear, confusion, hurt (pain), or anger can cause surges of hurt, resentment, anger, doubt, shame, guilt, and anxiety. Unless these are processed internally and socially, they amplify false-self dominance. High-nurturance families and relationships prize *all* emotions, and encourage responsible expression of them. Notice what your subselves are saying now. See *Despair, Fear, Empathy, Love, Joy, Happiness, Shame,* and Project 1.

Empathy is ability to accurately understand and *feel* what another person is feeling, thinking and needing, without judging or losing inner-family stability. *Sympathy* is understanding another person's situation without accurately feeling what they feel.

Kids and adults range from unempathic to over-empathic (enmeshed). People controlled by false self often feel too little or too much empathy, which unbalances their me-you awareness "bubble" (..02/a-bubble.htm) and their relationships. Low empathy in (step)family relationships promotes conflict, hurt, misunderstanding, distrust, disrespect, and disinterest: low nurturance. I believe high-nurturance families usually promote development and expression of balanced self and mutual empathy in all their members. What do you think? Balanced empathy is a requisite for effective listening. See *Emotion* and Projects 1 and 2

Enabling: traditionally this word means to empower a person or group to do something ("A college degree will enable you to earn more.") A second meaning has emerged since the 1980s: to promote a self-harmful attitude or behavior in a person by not confronting them on it clearly, firmly, and respectfully. Avoiding direct confrontation enables the person to keep thinking or doing the thing (like self-neglect or abuse, or an addiction) that harms them and others. In my experience, enabling suggests co-dependence (self-medication via relationship addiction), and is a *sure* symptom of significant false-self dominance and wounds. See *Addiction, Denial* and *Conflict.*

Extended family: includes all living *and dead* genetic and legal relatives of emotional or genetic importance to a child or adult. Usually a child's extended family spans three living generations. It includes two bioparents, four genetic grandparents, and siblings, aunts, uncles, and cousins, connected by genes, marriages, and adoptions; plus special bondings with nannies and best friends. Who comprises your and your kids' extended families now? See *Family* and *Family system.*

Extended *step*family: all living and dead members of three or more related co-parents' extended biofamilies. At holidays and major events like weddings, Christenings, Bar and Bas Mitzvahs, graduations, and funerals, ancestral custom urges co-parents to invite "the whole family." In a stepfamily, who does that include? Typical extended stepfamilies like the McLean-Tilmon-Cohen clan (Chapter 7) can include 60 to 100 members or more, living in many related homes all over the continent. Most don't know each other well or at all. See the genogram on p. 96 to get a visual impact of this.

How many of your (step)family adults and key supporters would agree with this definition? Often many people in an extended stepfamily don't identify as belonging to a *step*family, let alone an "*extended* stepfamily." This promotes unrealistic expectations, disappointments, misunderstandings, confusion, and conflict. Co-parent Projects 3 and 4 aim to reduce these over time. See *Blended family, Family, Family map, Family system, Nuclear stepfamily*, and Project 3.

False self: one or more personality subselves, usually Guardians and/or young Vulnerables, who have blended with (disabled) the resident true Self (q.v.). See p. 139, *Inner family, Personality, Subself,* and Project 1.

Family: two or more people who steadily feel bonded together by some combination of emotions, commitments, history, genes, legal contracts (like "marriage"), last names, memories, customs, and ongoing dependencies (needs).

Families exist in every culture and era because they fill some core child and adult needs better than any other human grouping. Can you name these specific core needs? Would each of your members say their current family fills all their core needs (p. 49) well enough? Any family can be judged somewhere on a scale between low to high nurturance, depending on how well each member's (including adults) core needs usually get filled. Would you say the nurturance level of your family is high *enough*? Who determines that level?

There are many kinds of human family: biological or birth family; absent-parent ("single parent"); foster; bi-racial; multi-cultural; adoptive; communal; childless; step; homosexual; and psychological (no common genes). Each of these _ is *normal* (has existed across human history), and has _ some things in common with all others and _ some facets that are different (vs. *better*). As global human health has greatly improved in the last century, two-parent biofamilies have become the social norm in most developed nations. Typical stepfamilies differ in more ways from traditional intact biofamilies than any other family type. See *Family map, Family structure, Family system, Nuclear family, Nurturance, Stepfamily,* Chapter 6, and p. 425.

Family functioning: how often and how well all family members get their core needs met over time determines how well the family *functions* or "works." Most of these needs can be filled outside a family, but they can't all be filled together in the same way.

Dysfunctional family has become a vague pop-psychology buzzword since the 1980's. I believe Jack, Sarah, and Ted (Chapter 7) each came from very dysfunctional (low nurturance) families, and were *unintentionally* creating a new one for 13-year-old Patty McLean. See *Family, Family system, Needs, Neglect, Nurturance, Wholistic health,* and Chapter 3.

Family identity: the history, boundaries, goals, values, and collective traits that distinguish one family from another. An obvious trait is member's last names. Less obvious factors are genetic, ethnic, cultural, and religious inheritances and traditions, ("We always have salmon for the December Holiday."), and family history ("I come from a long line of military men.")

One of many stepfamily-merger tasks in Project 9 is to gradually combine the identities of each co-parent's extended biofamily, and forge a new, stable *stepfamily* identity. That takes _ all members' accepting that they are forming a *step*family (Project 3); _ resolving many inevitable conflicts (Projects 2 and 9); _ years of sharing new experiences (vacations, holidays, celebrations, meals, crises) and building new traditions; and _ a conceptual shift from "our family and yours" to "our stepfamily." This complex process works best if all co-parents agree *early* to evolve and use a mission statement to guide it (Project 6). Many factors can hinder or block this evolution.

Ideally, courting co-parents recognize this long-term identity-forging project before re/wedding. If they do, they can help their stepfamily members to feel growing senses of "we-ness" (belonging), loyalty, and pride. Re/divorce statistics imply this happens in under half of typical U.S. stepfamilies. Are you clear on *your* family and personal identities? See Projects 1, 3, 4, and 6.

Family map or *genogram* shows how members of a multi-generation family relate to each other, and some key facts about each person and couple. These maps can help courting and re/ married couples discover and resolve stepfamily identity and membership conflicts (Project 3). The Web article at http:// sfhelp.org/03/geno1.htm explains how to make a family map, and suggests ways to use it together. See the samples on pp. 96 and 99, and *Structural map*, Chapter 4, and Project 3.

Family roles: A *role* (like *stepmother* and *husband*) is a chosen or imposed set of values, goals, and responsibilities that a family member values and acts on or doesn't. A family role description is like an occupational job description. It specifies responsibilities in the home and extended family, and may prioritize them. Family roles can be _ *dictated* by someone or society, and accepted or rejected; _ *assigned* by one or more people without negotiation ("older kids should watch out for younger ones"); or _ *negotiated co-operatively* by all family members to fill their respective needs. Most families form family role descriptions unconsciously from childhood imprinting, personal experience, local society, and the media.

In high-nurturance families, all members are _ clear enough on their different roles and _ agree enough on them. Jack and Sarah Tilmon's stepfamily home (Chapter 7) was rarely harmonious. This was because Jack was aggressively dictating the roles of his wife and stepdaughter, rather than respectfully negotiating them based on his *and* their needs and values. His rigid (fear-based) justification was that he was following God's Biblical instructions to be the loving, strong male head of the household. That put him beyond negotiation or discussion, and was killing his second marriage and wounding his stepdaughter.

Family roles usually come in pairs: parent-child; husband-wife; brother-sister; uncle-nephew; and so on. We label our roles to help identify and discuss our expectations of how each person is "supposed to" act toward the others in their family. For example, co-parents like Sarah and Jack are "supposed to" guide, nurture, and protect Patty and her two step-sibs to help prepare them for successful independence and social contribution.

At age 13, no one expected Patty to guide, nurture, and protect her co-parents. But because her caregivers were significantly wounded, she often *gave herself* the covert role of supporting her troubled mother with her stepfather's disapproval, rages, and shaming lectures. Her mother's false self encouraged this, and overruled her *Good Mom* subself's deploring it. This hindered Patty in filling her many psycho-spiritual needs (p. 454) and fill her other roles (*student* and *developing adolescent girl*), but she and her mother saw no options.

Typical extended biofamilies like yours have up to 15 different roles, like father, aunt, nephew, sister, and grandfather. Typical extended *step*families have these 15 and up to 15 *more* roles, like step-grandfather; half-sister; step-cousin; non-custodial biofather; and visiting stepbrother. Stepfamily members and supporters are often unclear on each of these strange new family "jobs," and how to "do" the roles *right*. Part of Projects 6 and 9 is co-parents intentionally helping all members clarify these responsibilities, and what to *title* each role ("You're not Marian's *real* sister, you're just her *half*-sister."). This is no small task, specially if stepfamily members are distracted or wounded and don't learn to negotiate effectively [Project 2]!

Psychologists observe that a significant stressor for some people is "role confusion" or "role strain." This occurs when a person feels _ unclear on their key responsibilities and/or _ inadequate to do them competently, and/or _ has simultaneous roles that clash and/or are _ collectively overwhelming.

I suspect that many custodial co-parents in absent-parent families and stepfamilies suffer role strain, amplified by their unseen psychological wounds. Antidotes are to _ work at Project 1, _ clarify your personal and family mission, then _ define its current roles, and to _ learn to set personal limits ["No, I can't (or won't) do that.]" without major guilt and anxiety. See *Family functioning, Family system, Stress, Structural map* and Project 6.

Family rules: A personal or family *rule* is a *should (not), ought (not), must (not), have to, can (not), or do (not).* Every human personality (inner family), relationship, home, group, and community evolves hundreds of primary and lesser rules. We do this consciously and unconsciously to fill our primal needs for "order" (security). Rules have little impact unless they include _ meaningful consequences that are _ predictably and consistently enforced. Do you agree? If so, is this true in your home?

All households and extended families inherit, generate, and bequeath hundreds (thousands?) of general and special rules. Some are silent and others are earsplitting. "In this house, we (*should*) eat with our mouths closed!"; "(You *must*) look at me when I'm talking!"; "Stepsiblings *must not* act on sexual feelings for each other (or feel any);" and "(Co)parents *must* act responsibly and morally!" (by someone's definition) are examples. Parental discipline is an evolved set of behavioral rules and (maybe) consequences for minor kids.

Homes and inner and physical families with inconsistent or few enforced rules are chaotic. Their main demonstrated rule is "We will accept or enforce few rules, and will endure the results." Families and households with too many rules, and/or inflexible rules, are *rigid*. Jack Tilmon's excessive need for control, order, and moral "rightness," and Sarah's shame and fear of setting assertive limits with him, created a home with rigid, shaming rules for Patty McLean. Jack's false self switched to another set of rules when his biokids Annie and Roger visited. He vehemently denied that (reality distortion), because of rigid belief (rule) that "A Christian father *must* (want to) be scrupulously fair and loving to all."

Nuclear stepfamily homes usually have two sets of rules: "kids here" and "kids away." A challenge for most minor stepkids is to adapt to two different sets of rules that they didn't choose, may not understand, and often can't easily affect. Co-parents governed by false selves often generate conflictual, vague, unrealistic (biofamily-based), or unenforced home and family rules, and deny or justify that.

A primary adjustment task for every new stepchild is to persistently *test* the key rules in each of their co-parenting and relatives' homes to learn if they're really *safe* there. Unaware or overstressed co-parents may mis-label this instinctive testing as being *uncooperative, defiant, rebelling,* or *acting out* (q.v.). Step-teens need to test *and* experiment with their independence.

Co-parents in a new stepfamily must acknowledge and resolve legions of family-rule conflicts in and between their related homes. Their success at this strongly shapes whether solid extended-stepfamily bonding develops over time. Household and extended-family role, rule, and consequence negotiation, enforcement, and stabilization are a large part of co-parents' post-re/wedding Projects 9 and 10. Does this sound like fun? See *Conflict, Family structure,* and *Family roles.*

Family strengths are the mental, emotional, spiritual, physical, and tangible assets that promote a family's stability, function, health, and nurturance level. Each family member contributes personal talents and strengths, needs, and limitations. To merge successfully and "work" well over time, typical stepfamilies need special strengths: co-parents' _ wholistic health and _ knowledge (p. 83 and 91); abilities to bond and exchange love; effective grieving and communications (projects 2 and 5); patience; humor; creativity; flexibility; commitment; the open "mind of a student;" and informed help (Project 11). All families depend on each adult's *inner* family strengths. To help you affirm and develop your stepfamily's strengths, see the worksheets beginning at http://sfhelp.org/07/strnx-intro.htm. See *Family functioning, Family identity, Needs,* and *Nurturance.*

Family structure: all the components that make up a family. A building's structure is the foundation, wall and joist framing, and roof; electrical, temperature, and plumbing systems; and windows, doors, floors, and furnishings. In the same way, a family is "built" from people, values, roles, rules, history, customs, rituals, goals, assets, and boundaries. Families that have compatible, stable structures tend to yield higher nurturance than families with weak, damaged, or unplanned structures.

If the ***inner*-family structure** of each co-parent is harmonized and led by a true Self who has clear local and life goals, the structure of the physical family they co-create and manage is likely to be highly nurturing and resilient. The same is true for multi-generational extended families and other human organizations, including church congregations, cities, and nations. For a way to see (diagram) the structure of any inner or outer family, see ..09/map-str1.htm. See *Family function, Family map, Family system,* and *Structural map.*

Family system means the combination of . . .

+ all the emotionally, spiritually, legally, and genetically-important _ *people* comprising a nuclear or extended family. Each person is also a system of systems. Plus . . .

+ the _ needs, _ values, and resulting relationship _ *roles* and _ *rules* that govern how these people behave together _ normally, and _ in conflicts and crises. These may or may not include _ clear, long-term family goals (a *mission*); plus . . .

+ the _ tangible *assets* of the family, like dwellings, vehicles, money, tools, appliances, and clothing; and . . .

+ the _ physical and invisible boundaries that separate this system from other systems like neighboring families, the city, their church community, the nation, and the local and global ecosystems. Closed doors, clothing, "personal space," and words like "no" and "yes" are basic tools we use to define the physical and psychological boundaries between our human systems. Boundaries range from *closed* (other people and ideas are not allowed in, and family secrets and taboos are sternly enforced); to *open* (most people, ideas, objects, and information are allowed in and out); to *non-existent* (no restrictions at all).

Understanding and discussing how these facets of your complex, dynamic stepfamily system interact can help all your members see how a change in one part of the system (like a birth, divorce, graduation, geographic move, death, injury, and financial change) affects *all* stepfamily members, roles, rules, and sometimes the boundaries of your system. Understanding systemic changes and their impacts on family members and relationships can help co-parents' promote healthy grief and high nurturance in your homes.

Your family *structure* (how it's built) is static, like a parked car. Your family *system* is dynamic (the parts of the moving car interacting), as the members, roles, rules, and the outer environment constantly change.

All natural and man-made systems are composed of cascades of smaller sub-systems, down to molecules and sub-atomic particles. Each organ in the system of your body is a sub-system composed of smaller systems. Each household of kids and adults is a sub-system of your larger multi-generational extended-family system. Each re/marriage home has (hopefully) a sub-system of adults with effective boundaries, and other sub-systems of live-in and visiting kids.

Typical multi-home stepfamilies take four to 12 years to stabilize (see Papernow, p. 541) after a re/marriage and cohabiting, because of the complexity of merging co-parents' three or more extended-family systems into a larger *meta*-system: a system of systems with its own rules. For more on this long-term merger project, see "Build a High-nurturance Stepfamily" (Xlibris.com, 2001); and the Web articles at ..09/project09.htm and ..09/merge.htm.

Fear is a primitive neuro-chemical *survival* reflex that subselves use to signal alarm that they and/or their host person are at risk of major discomfort or injury. Depending on which subselves have displaced the Self (if any), fear ranges from *vague unease* > *uneasy* > *anxious* or *worried* > *scared* > *terri-fied* > *panicked* > *hysterical*. Each personality subself, including your Self, can experience different levels of fear at any given moment. Fear comes from interpreting current or imagined inner and outer events. Alternative emotional states are *confidence, serenity,* and *numbness.* See *Emotions, Stress,* Project 1, and ..01/fears.htm.

Fear-based personality: an adult or child whose inner family is often or always ruled by fearful Vulnerable and/or Guardian subselves. Members of low-nurturance groups are often (fear + shame) based, until choosing true _ recovery from inner wounds and _ higher-nurturance environments. See *Childish, Emotion, False self, Shame-based, Splitting,* and Project 1.

Grief, grieving, mourning: the natural emotional + mental + spiritual process that leads to accepting broken emotional/ spiritual bonds and forming new ones. Blocked grief is a major stressor in many troubled people, families, and groups. It's usually based on false-self dominance, adult unawareness of grieving basics (p. 248), and missing inner and outer permissions to mourn. See *Bond, Loss,* and Project 5.

Half brother or sister: Jack Tilmon's first wife Karen re-married and co-conceived an *ours* baby (Sharon) with her new husband Rick Cohen. Sharon Cohen had her mother's half of Roger and Annie Tilmon's genes, and her father's half of Nick Cohen's genes, so she was the "half sister" of the other three kids. Paradoxically, Sharon is not a stepchild (has no stepparent), though she belongs to a three-home stepfamily (p. 99).

Do half siblings feel the same kind of dignity, family bonds, status, and worth that full siblings do? Would you feel good about being a "half" anything? Because half sibs are a small minority in our population, they can feel semi-consciously *inferior, odd,* or *abnormal,* even if they're consistently treated as having equal dignity and value. Their co-parents (false selves) may leak unconscious beliefs that half siblings are vaguely sub-

standard, or are deprived of *normalcy*. Without adult awareness and effective nurturing, such leaked beliefs can lower an
"ours" child's self esteem, degrading their stepfamily and other
relationships. This is specially likely if one or both parents come
from low-nurturance childhoods. See *Family map, Family structure, Family system, Nuclear stepfamily, "Ours" child, Shame,*
and Project 3.

Happiness is the elusive experience of having most or all
of our current cellular, spiritual, and subself (psychological)
needs satisfied well enough. Shifting from unhappiness to toward happiness is called *comforting*. Feeling *secure* may or
may not cause *happiness*. *Joy* is transitory peak happiness. *Hope*
is the vision of future happiness. Happiness is most likely when
_ your true Self is trusted and willingly followed by other
subselves, and you're _ in at least one high-nurturance (loving) relationship. *Satisfaction* is filling some current needs (reducing *frustration*), and may fall short of *happiness*. Courtship
is often motivated by the idealistic dream of happiness. See
Love, Recovery, and *Wholistic health.*

***Inner* family:** the group of Regular, Vulnerable, and Guard-
ian subselves or "parts" that comprise your personality and
shape your identity, perceptions, needs, health, and behavior.
They have goals, roles ("jobs"), rules, rituals, relationships, and
behave just like your physical family. They may be led locally
or chronically by a true Self, or other subselves (a false self).
See *False self, Family, Family functioning, Family system, Happiness, Personality, Splitting,* Project 1, and my book "Who's
Really Running Your Life?"

Loss: a broken emotional-spiritual *attachment* to a person,
pet, object, freedom, idea, dream, fantasy, cause, identity, status, ability, or feeling (e.g. security, health, youth . . .). Childhood neglect, parental death, divorce and re/marriage, aging,
and Natural change, cause complex webs of tangible and invisible losses. So _ a pro-grief family and _ personal *inner*
permissions to allow healthy three-level grief are priceless assets. See *Bond, Emotions, Grief,* Chapter 7, and Project 5.

Love is the powerful emotional-spiritual-cellular *feeling* and

mind-state that wholistically-healthy, well-bonded people develop for each other, themselves, and a benign Higher Power.
Love is a shorthand word-symbol for a complex mix of primal
feelings like (respect + compassion + empathy + interest + trust
+ concern + stimulation + admiration + *need*). Healthy caregiver
and friendship love omit the sexual desire that's part of normal
love between mates. Young kids raised in very low-nurturance
families (with "emotionally unavailable" or abusive caregivers)
often have stunted or undeveloped abilities to bond, need, and
feel, express, and/or receive love. *Sociopaths, hermits,* and
Narcissists are tragic examples.

Such deprived kids grow up surrounded by ceaseless media and social emphases on a mental-emotional-spiritual state
they don't feel and can only guess at. When such wounded
people say "I love you," they mean some mix of "I (need / pity
/ desire / feel obliged to / depend on / fear losing / want to
control) you." A symptom of this wound is when partners, children, or friends don't *feel* loved. This can also mean the other
person is _ psychologically shamed and numbed, _ doesn't
really love themselves, and _ and can't receive (experience)
genuine love themselves.

Romantic love has the special sparkle and excitement of
discovering and exchanging these ingredients, deliciously flavored with sexual desire and fantasies. This altered mind state
is not famous for calm, rational decision-making, like whether
or not to re/marry. This is specially true for suitors controlled
by needy false selves. I believe inevitable romantic-love distortions combined with four other hazards (p. 69) cause most
marriers to choose the wrong *people* to (re)wed, for the wrong
reasons, at the wrong *time*. See *Abandonment, Bond, Emotion,
Need,* Chapter 7 (Part 1), and Project 7.

Marriage and re/marriage can mean many things . . .

+ A fluctuating state of mind ("I feel *married*.")
+ A conscious personal commitment to a primary adult re-
  lationship above all others.
+ The spiritual union of two compatible souls.

+ A civil and/or religious ceremony and exchange of commitment vows and intentions.

+ An ongoing relationship between adult partners, with
unique expectations, responsibilities (*wife, husband,* or
mate roles), rules, and social status. The relationship
usually implies both partners like, love, respect, and
enjoy each other, and share common interests and goals.

+ A personal, social, religious, and legal sanction for adult
sexual intercourse, and the conception and raising of
children.

And *marriage* is . . .

+ An adult relationship model and template for minor kids
to learn from;

+ The "glue" that holds intact families and societies together, or doesn't;

+ Personal, legal, and spiritual contracts bound by inner,
civil, and religious laws; and . . .

+ A measure of _ social normalcy and _ adult maturity.
Never-married and divorced adults have lower social
status, since _ most ancestors marry at least once and _
divorce is a Christian "sin." Single adults may feel significant shame and guilt over these, specially if they
come from a low-nurturance childhood.

In discussing (re)marriage questions, goals, and conflicts,
it may help to identify which of these many meanings you're
referring to. *Re/*marriage is all of these, plus the ~20 emotional
and environmental differences summarized on p. 354. See *Bond,
Co-dependence, Divorce, Intimacy, Love, Needs, Nurturance,*
and *Relationship.*

Mental health and "illness": *Mental* refers to your conscious *thinking* domain ("mind"). Most people using *mental
health* and *illness* are really referring to mental + emotional +
spiritual + physical (wholistic) health. I propose that *health* in
these four domains means, "fully functioning the way humans
are designed to function." Full definitions are beyond our scope
here.

I suggest using *inner-family harmony* or *chaos* instead of these terms. Most people dislike feeling they're *ill*. *Mental illness* carries semi-conscious associations with *impaired, crazy, sick, abnormal,* and *bad*. These can evoke anxiety, shame, and avoidance (denials), specially in unrecovering co-parents and kids from low-nurturance childhoods. Mental illness is a relic of the "medical model" of human functioning, because much of our pioneering clinical theory was proposed by psychiatrists (MDs) like Sigmund Freud and followers. See *Happiness, Personality, Wholistic health,* Chapter 6, and Project 1.

   Needs are emotional, physical and/or spiritual discomforts (tensions) that shape human perceptions and behavior. Your needs can be . . .

   + Conscious, semi-conscious, or unconscious;
   + Trivial to intense;
   + Surface ("I need the car") or true ("I need a reliable way to get to the dentist on time, and return home safely and easily.");
   + Immediate to long-range;
   + Felt by one of your subselves ("I need to raise champion poodles."), several, or all of them ("We need enough oxygen, and to be able to breathe and use it.");
   + In synch with your partners' needs, or in mild to major conflict with them ["You want to go to Tanzania, and I want (need) to stay home."]; and your needs can be . . .
   + Judged by _ your subselves (e.g. your *Inner Critic*) and/ or _ other people as normal, legitimate, and valid, or ridiculous, childish, selfish, weird or sick, unreasonable, or incomprehensible.

   Family and relationship *nurturance* is a measure of how well people help each other to fill their mix of current and long-term true needs. *All* animal (cellular?) communication is instinctively driven by impulses and strategies to express and fill current true needs. A purist would say, *"Needs* make the world go 'round, not *love."* People (re)marry, raise kids, and (re)divorce to fill complex sets of surface and true needs. The more aware and respectful they are of their and each other's needs (empathy), the more likely they are to help each other fill them well enough *if their Self leads their inner families*. For perspective, see the Web articles at http://sfhelp.org/02/ ..a-bubble.htm, ..dig-down.htm and ..needlevels.htm.

   Neglect is ignoring or trivializing _ the needs and welfare of a dependent person, and/or _ the responsibilities of a chosen or imposed role. Neglect can occur from _ ignorance (a parent not knowing what their child needs), _ distraction (inner-family chaos), and/or _ indifference (blocked bonding). Partners who conceive or adopt children and fail to _ learn the youngsters' *true* needs and/or to _ fill them adequately, are *neglectful*, not *bad*. Most shame-based survivors of low-nurturance childhoods are routinely *self* neglectful, until committing to true (vs. pseudo) recovery. They're also apt to have high semi-conscious fears of abandonment, because they *felt* abandoned in their earliest years.

   If a child or co-parent is significantly wounded, one or more of their early caregivers were emotionally and spiritually neglectful and neglected themselves. The opposite of caregiver neglect is *nurturance* (q.v.): caregivers knowing and intentionally, consistently filling dependent kids' key health and growth needs. See *Bond, Abandonment, Family functioning, Love, Needs, Relationship*, Project 1, and p. 454.

   Nuclear family: A *nucleus* is the central core of something, like an egg yolk or the sun in our galaxy. Traditionally, the nucleus of a multi-generational *biofamily* is both bioparents + all emotionally-dependent kids. More broadly, a nuclear family refers to all people living regularly in the primary home of a minor child. Use *nuclear* (step)family when you want to focus on co-parents and dependent kids, rather than the larger multi-generational group of all their relatives: their *extended* stepfamily. Some people call stepfamilies *bi-nuclear*, because they're based on two linked co-parental homes. See *Family identity, Family map, Family structure*, and Project 3.

   Normal or Natural family: *Normal* means _ a quality, state, or thing that occurs frequently or permanently in a natural environment; or _ an event or reaction that follows a Nature law like gravity or the cellular pain-avoidance reflex. *Natural* means "not made by humans."

People comparing biofamilies and stepfamilies usually refer to the former as *natural* or *normal*. The same is true comparing bioparents and biokids to (the roles of) stepparents and stepchildren. These innocent adjectives imply that stepfamilies, steppeople, and step-roles are *abnormal* and *unnatural*, which isn't true. These implications can activate the excessive shame that co-parents and kids from low-nurturance childhoods carry until in true recovery. This causes semi-conscious minimizing or rejection of *step*family identity, which promotes unrealistic expectations, personal and relationship stress, and re/divorce.

Stepfamilies have probably been the norm throughout human history, until recent advances in human health lengthened the lives of bioparents. In our era, they are *nontraditional,* **not** *abnormal* or *unnatural*. The point: *adjectives count* in stepfamily and clinical relationships, and the media! See *Bio-, Co-, Step-,* and Projects 3 and 4.

Nuclear stepfamily means all legally, emotionally, genetically, and financially related bioparents, stepparents and custodial and noncustodial minor children. Before their divorce, Jack, Karen, Annie, and Roger Tilmon (Chapter 7) formed an intact, one-home nuclear biofamily. After they separated, Karen and the kids lived in one home, and their father lived in another: they formed a two-home, two-co-parent nuclear *absent-parent* family. When Karen and Jack each remarried, they, their new and ex mates, and their minor kids formed a 4-home, 6-co-parent, 5-child nuclear *stepfamily*. See their family map on p. 99.

Ask a stepfamily adult or child "Who's your family?" They'll usually name the people regularly living in or visiting their residence. Stepfamilies work best when all members value the needs, opinions, and feelings of people in *all* their related co-parenting homes. See *Extended stepfamily, Family, Family function, Family identity, Family map, Family structure, Family system, Nuclear family*, and Project 3.

Nurture, nurturance: _ learning the emotional, physical, spiritual, and mental needs of a dependent person, including yourself, and _ steadily *wanting* to invest time, energy, and other resources to fill them. Inner and physical families and relationships range from low-nurturance to high nurturance.

Caregivers in low-nurturance families may want to fill each other's needs, but not know what they all are. Can you and your partners name most of the 28 traits of a high nurturance family or relationship on p. 48? If not, you risk unintentionally neglecting core needs of people you care about, including yourself. That promotes six significant psychological wounds, stressful relationships, impaired health, and re/divorce. See *Abandonment, Caregiver, Love, Neglect, Parent, Relationship, Splitting,* Chapter 6, and Project 1.

"Ours" child: Unlike traditional biofamilies, stepfamilies can have minor and/or grown his, hers, and *ours* kids. A previously childless stepparent who co-conceives an "ours" baby can instinctually favor their child over their stepkid/s, despite trying not to. In a stepfamily crisis, blood usually *is* thicker than water when divorce-related guilt is unhealed. Kids of divorced parents like Patty, Annie, and Roger (Chapter 7) are often extra sensitive to potential caregiver favoritism. They'll instinctive test their adults' priorities until they feel secure and valued enough.

Imagined or actual co-parent favoritism usually generates significant loyalty conflicts (p. 186) and relationship "triangles" (http://sfhelp.org/09/triangles.htm). Without co-parental awareness and effective communication skills (Project 2), these cause nuclear-stepfamily tension and escalating re/marital strife.

One courting co-parent may want an *ours* child, and the other, often a veteran bioparent, is ambivalent or really doesn't. Couples that avoid discussing this honestly before exchanging vows risk *major* future heartache and conflict. This is specially likely if one (shame-based, needy) suitor is unaware of wanting to rescue or please their beloved, without valuing their own needs and priorities equally. Your unborn and living children totally depend on your honesty with yourselves and each other on future conceptions.

Each new baby sends emotional, financial, structural, and legal shockwaves throughout the extended stepfamily. These can undo biofamily-merger progress and take many months to subside. One of ~60 stepfamily common myths is that having an *ours* baby will nourish a troubled re/marriage, and calm a conflicted co-parenting home. Very often the reverse is true. See *Half brother / sister*, ..Rx/spl/ourschild.htm, and Chapter 3.

Parent (noun) is a person who contributes genes to a minor or grown child. "I am (not) a (bio)parent (or grandparent)" is part of an adult's personal and social identity. The verb *to parent* generically means, "I know and want to fill the emotional, spiritual, physical, and mental needs of (to nurture) a child." Many divorced bioparents and their re/marriage partners can't name the *many* concurrent developmental and special adjustment needs of their minor kids. (p. 454). Such parents *unintentionally* provide only partial nurturance, which is likely to promote or prolong psychological wounds in their kids.

Can you define *effective* parenting clearly? Bioparents and stepparents with unclear or conflicting definitions risk lowering the nurturance level in their homes and multi-home family. See p. 457, *Caregiver, Co-parent, Family, Needs, Nurture, Psychological parent, Roles, Stepparent,* Chapter 3, and Project 6.

Parent Alienation Syndrome (PAS) is a recent grass-roots term used to describe a bioparent who seems maliciously intent on disparaging and separating their child/ren from their other parent. This usually follows a bitter separation or divorce. I believe PAS is real, and *always* means one or both bioparents _ survived major childhoods abuse and neglect, _ are controlled by a false self and very wounded, and _ lack effective communication skills. They may also be burdened with blocked grief. An ex mate or partner exhibiting PAS behaviors should be a *glaring red courtship light* for a potential stepparent. See *Splitting,* http://sfhelp.org/Rx/ex/split.htm, and Projects 1, 2, 5, and 7 in Part 2.

Personality: the set of beliefs, associations, memories, talents, limitations, reflexes, attitudes, values, preferences, and priorities that distinguishes a person like you from all others.

Some researchers feel the basic (neuro-chemical) "structure" of a personality is set by age four or five. This series of books is based on the idea that your personality is the dynamic mix of a group of *subselves* who form in response to early-childhood nurturance levels. See Project 1 (p. 137).

Personality splitting: Radiology imaging and computer advances in the last generation reveal living brains at work. Images show that "thinking" involves many regions of the brain interchanging signals at once. That strongly suggests that our *personalities* are naturally composed of a group of semi-independent *subselves* (brain modules). As lay and professional awareness and understanding of this neural reality grows, it's becoming known as *multiplicity*.

Studies suggest that pre-birth and early childhood trauma strongly affect how an infant's brain neurons and synapses grow, die, connect, and function. Research on Dissociative Identity Disorder (previously Multiple Personality Disorder, or MPD) consistently shows sufferers to come from massive early trauma. D.I.D. is the extreme form of personality splitting, which is estimated to affect about 5% of living Americans. Researchers estimate it's lower in other countries. By definition, low-nurturance families leave young kids' needs unfilled. This is an ongoing daily trauma vs. a discrete one, so many survivors can't remember it. Protective amnesia may be a primal false-self strategy to prevent re-traumatizing from agonizing early-childhood memories.

Increasing evidence suggests that traumatized young children automatically "split" their personalities into *parts* to survive inadequate psycho-spiritual nurturance. All their (your) personality parts together act like a team or family, which ranges from harmonious (integrated) to chaotic (dis-integrated). A major implication is that low-nurturance kids grow up with a chaotic inner family among adults who are similarly split, and they all judge that as *normal*. That inhibits recovery.

Co-parenting Project 1 in this book focuses on identifying significant splitting in any of your family members, and starting to reduce it. See *Caregiving, Fear-based, Needs, Neglect,*

Nurture, Psychological parent, Psychological wound, Chapters 6 and 7, Project 1, and the book "Who's *Really* Running Your Life?—Free Your Self From Custody, and Guard Your Kids" (Xlibris.com).

Problem is a fuzzy word like "issue" for any internal or interpersonal clash of values, needs, opinions, beliefs, preferences and/or perceptions. Typical divorced families and stepfamilies have many more people, and more significant, complex inner-personal and interpersonal *problems*, more often, than average intact biofamilies. That's why starting co-parent Project 2 (learn to use seven problem-solving skills) *before* deciding to re/wed or not is so vital.

Most of the ~1,000 divorced, courting, and re/married co-parents I've met since 1981 aren't aware that most of the problems they're trying to resolve are *surface* **problems**. Using the mental/verbal skills of *awareness, clear thinking, digging down,* and *metatalk* reveals the true problems (needs) underneath these (p. 49), and who's responsible for resolving them. Then *assertion, empathic listening,* and *problem solving* skills help to identify, rank, and fill these core needs. Are you using these seven powerful skills with your partner and any kids? See *Conflict, Needs,* Project 2, ..02/dig-down.htm, and the book "*Satisfactions*—7 Relationship Skills You Need to Know" (xlibris.com).

Psychological parent: someone who wants to or has to nurture a child they didn't co-conceive. Examples are foster and adoptive parents, day-care providers, au pairs, babysitters, mentors, coaches, and stepparents. Older siblings nurture and protect younger kids in many low-nurturance families. Wholistically-healthy bioparents instinctively feel a fierce primal bond with their own kids, which psychological (non-genetic) parents may approach. The latter bond is often stronger with very young kids, and weak with teens. Minor stepkids have two bioparents and at least one psychological (step) parent. See *Bond, Caregiving, Co-parent, Needs, Nurture, Parent, Relationship,* and Project 6.

Psychological (inner) wound: a neural (brain) adaptation to lack of psycho-spiritual nurturance in early childhood. Unhealed, the condition promotes low-nurturance lifestyles, relationships, and families, and degrades personal wholistic health and longevity. Six common inner wounds are:

+ **Development of a** dominant reactive, short-sighted **false self.** This promotes . . .

+ Excessive **shame** ("I'm worthless, disgusting, and unlovable") and **guilts** ("I break key rules.");

+ Excessive **fears** of abandonment, emotional overwhelm (and hence of conflict and healthy grief), failure, success, and the unknown (change);

+ Protective **reality distortions**, like denials, repressions, exaggerations, minimizations, projections, psychoses, neuroses, and delusions. False selves usually deny their denials.

+ **Trust distortions:** compulsively _ trusting unsafe people and situations, or _ distrusting safe people and situations. This includes distrust of _ one's own judgment, and of _ the benign influence of a Higher Power. These five wounds combine to promote . . .

+ A **crippled ability to form** healthy emotional/spiritual attachments (**bonds**) with selected or all living things.

Combined, these wounds hinder self-awareness, effective communications, healthy grieving, and forming a personal identity, effective boundaries, and a life purpose. **These wounds tend to pass on the next generation** unless they're seen and intentionally healed over time. In my experience, over 80% of typical U.S. divorced and stepfamily co-parents are significantly wounded and unaware of it. Co-parent Project 1 focuses on identifying these wounds in co-parents and kids, and evolving an effective healing plan (recovery.) See *Abuse, Bond, Childhood, Neglect, Nurturance, Personality splitting*, *Recovery, Toxic,* and Project 1.

Recovery: intentionally working to _ reduce false-self (q.v.) personality dominance and five related psychological wounds (q.v.), _ empower true-Self leadership of your inner family of subselves, and _ grow inner-family purpose, trust, harmony, and contentment, over time. One way of achieving these is via informed *inner*-family therapy. Project 1 in this series of books focuses on identifying and recovering from crippling false-self dominance. Stable recovery from addiction (q.v.) is the gateway to full inner-family recovery. By definition, true recovery is a second-order change (p. 159). The alternatives are denial (of inner wounds and their impacts) and pseudo recovery (p. 157). See p. 153, *Nurturance, Psychological wounds,* and *Wholistic Health*

Relationship: refers to _ the behavior inside and between two people over time, and _ how the perceived behaviors of each partner *relate* to filling the key emotional + physical + spiritual + mental (wholistic) needs of both people. Restated: people have a relationship when the wholistic health of one or both *significantly* depends on the behaviors of the other, according to someone. How does this compare to your definition?

From this, a **high-nurturance** (healthy or functional) relationship is one that helps to fill each partner's true wholistic needs well enough, over some period. A **toxic** relationship hinders filling partners' true needs and promotes inner-family upset. Divorce is a sign that one or both partners' true (vs. surface) needs weren't filled well enough. The nurturance level of any relationship can be judged by at least three people: each partner, and an outside judge. Their opinions may match or clash, depending on their definitions and rankings of "true wholistic needs."

Besides low to high nurturance, your past and current **relationships can be judged as** *casual* to *serious*; *committed* to *uncommitted*; dependent, interdependent, or independent; platonic to romantic/sexual; stable to unstable; primary to minor; new to mature; static to dynamic; covert to overt; enmeshed (no boundaries) to emotionally close, to detached; and so on. Fluency with _ these terms and _ communication terms (metatalk skill, Project 2) can help you define and discuss your relationship goals, status, quality, and problems effectively.

I propose that your and your partner's shared clarity on what "high-nurturance relationship" means is essential for you to master all seven re/marriage-evaluation projects in this book.

Are you clear yet? Project 1 is about your developing high-nurturance *internal* relationships between your personality subselves. See *Family, Marriage, Need, Nurture, Parent, Roles, Stepparent, Toxic,* Project 7 in Part 2, and ..08/relationship.htm.

Shame is the crippling belief and feeling that "I am a worthless, unlovable, *bad* person." Excessive shame is one of six common personality wounds that shape the lives of kids and adults in and from low-nurturance childhoods. Recovery from false-self dominance includes converting this to "I am a worthy, lovable, important, unique person, and I always have been."—i.e. to serene self respect and self love. Shame-based people seem to unconsciously prefer each other as mates, which makes high-nurturance relationships difficult or impossible. Unaware shame-based caregivers tend to pass this wound on to their kids by unconsciously re-creating and tolerating low-nurturance environments as their ancestors and society did. See *Love,* Project 1, and ..01/shame.htm.

Shame-based (personality) is having an inner family dominated by shamed Vulnerable and protective Guardian subselves. Such people may also be *fear based* (q.v.), depending on how low their childhood nurturance level was (p. 48). In my experience, a high percentage of American divorcees and stepfamily co-parents are significantly shame and fear-based. They don't (want to) know that, and don't know what to do about it. Project 1 focuses on identifying and healing these crippling, self-perpetuating wounds over time.

Single-parent family commonly refers to the custodial parent and their minor kids after parental separation, desertion, or death. Casually used, this term minimizes or ignores the existence, needs, and welfare of the kids' other bioparent, their biorelatives, and any new partner and stepkids. These can unintentionally lower the nurturance level of the two-home nuclear family in many ways. If a single parent re/marries and they and/or their ex mate reject or ignore their identity as a multi-home stepfamily ("I'm a single parent, and my ex is re/married"), that promotes . . .

+ Stepfamily unawareness (Chapter 3),

+ Unrealistic role and relationship expectations, and . . .
+ Compounding household and inter-home conflicts over family identity, membership, names and role titles, roles, and loyalties. These lower home and nuclear-stepfamily nurturance levels, and promote psychological wounds in everyone.

I suggest describing a post-divorce or post-death family as an *absent*-parent family, vs. single-parent. There is always a second genetic bioparent, living in Tibet or across the street, or "dead but not forgotten." Your acknowledging their existence, genes, history, relatives, and needs, can reduce current and future conflicts. This is vital for wise re/marriage decisions. Do you agree? Strong resistance to this acknowledgment may indicate significant false-self reality distortion. See *Co-parent, Family identity, Family map, Family structure, Family system,* and Project 3.

Splitting (personality): See *Personality splitting.*

Step-: This prefix comes from the thousand-year-old English root *stoep-,* which meant *deprived* or *orphaned.* Orphans were common in William the Conqueror's world and ancestry, due to unprotected intercourse, disease, and malnutrition. Like "bio-," this prefix denotes a group of social relationships and family roles, like *stepfamily, stepparent, stepmother, step-grand-father, stepsister, step great-aunt, step-cousin,* and many more. If the relationships, adjustment tasks, and developmental stages in typical stepfamilies were the same as in average intact biofamilies, we wouldn't need these many terms and titles.

Words beginning with "step-" usually carry a faint or pungent semi-conscious emotional aroma of *second best, abnormal, unnatural, inferior, failure, weird,* and/or *strange.* These associations are constant reminders of prior divorce or death losses and pain. They start innocently in childhood, with ancestral folktales like Cinderella. Media journalists and commentators unconsciously promote this bias. Shame-based co-parents and kids react to this bias, and protectively minimize, ignore, or reject their step-hood. This promotes unwise re/marital choices, and ultimate re/divorce.

Lay people and clinicians use a wonderfully creative set of adjectives and terms to avoid the unpleasant taint of *stepfamily*. These include *bi-nuclear, rem(arriage), combined, reconstituted, merged, blended, reconstructed, serial, second, bonus family,* and *co-family*. Though well meant, I believe such terms promote stepfamily denials, myths, and ignorance. That fosters wrong re/marital choices, years of low-nurturance stress, and eventual re/divorce. See *Bio-, Co-,* and *Normal Family*.

Stepfamily: many co-parents and professionals I've met misunderstand this word. A stepfamily is any psychological and/or legal family including at least one adult in a stepparent (q.v.) role, and one minor *or grown*, custodial or visiting stepchild. Stepfamily roles, rules, and rituals begin to form well before being legalized by co-parents' commitment ceremony.

Depending on co-parents' prior divorce or death, ex-mate remarriage, child custody, stepchild adoption, and "ours" kid, combinations, there are almost 100 structural kinds of nuclear stepfamily. Unlike traditional (intact) biofamilies, this diversity guarantees that stepfamily adults and kids will rarely or never meet a family "like ours." This amplifies feeling isolated, weird, and alone in insecure (fear-based) kids and co-parents. This isolation adds to the justification for Project 11: co-parents' intentionally building and using a viable stepfamily support network. (..11/links11.htm).

Paradoxically, typical stepfamilies are the same as and *radically* different from traditional intact biofamilies (p. 425). Knowledge of these differences and what they *mean* during courtship can steeply increase your odds of re/wedding wisely and well. See *Bio-, Family, Family identity, Step-,* Chapter 3, Project 4.

Stepchild, stepson, and stepdaughter are three of an extended stepfamily's ~30 role-titles. A stepchild is any minor or grown, biological or adopted, custodial or non-custodial, daughter or son of a bioparent with a new adult partner. Serious re/marital courtship creates emotional (pre-legal) stepchild-stepparent *roles*. The co-parents' re/wedding ceremony and marriage license adds legal responsibilities to these roles. *A step-*

child is not a person, it's a *role* that a young or grown person is required to learn and clarify by trial and error. Often this role feels unwelcome, confusing, and stressful, and has few direct benefits.

A stepchild's bioparents may be widowed, divorced, or separated. A stepchild may or may not be legally adopted by a stepparent. Most aren't. They may or may not have stepsiblings and/or half-siblings. Roughly 20% of the students in American schoolrooms are stepkids, with regional variations. Roughly another 20% now live in absent-parent homes. Most will be visiting or custodial stepchildren before they register to vote.

Stepkids like Patty McLean, and Annie and Roger Tilmon (Chapter 7), can be influenced by four or more co-parents in two or more related homes. They're siblings in the same stepfamily, but have different last names which may differ from their biomom's. Stepkids can be nurtured, ignored, or wounded by eight or more co-grandparents.

All their step-relatives together would fill a small hall. They'll never meet many of them. Could sorting out, clarifying, and stabilizing this dynamic web of strange step-relationships boggle an average minor child trying to negotiate middle school, puberty, the millennium, and high school? Ask your nearest stepchild.

Typical minor stepkids face three or four concurrent sets of developmental and adjustment needs that _ they can't describe, name, or ask for help with; and _ typical co-parents, relatives, counselors, and teachers can't name these tasks either. These realities promote kids' inner-family dysfunction (wounding) and "acting out." Project 6 invites co-parents and supporters to _ learn about these needs (p. 454), and _ evolve co-operative plans to help kids with them. If courting co-parents do re/marry, Project 10 continues this vital work. See *Childhood, Family system, Need, Nurturance, Parent, Splitting, and Psychological parent.*

Stepparent, stepmother, and stepfather are three more of a stepfamily's 30 role-titles. Imagine trying to describe this term to a space alien. How about: "A *stepparent* is a grown human who is _ emotionally committed to a bioparent (Alien: "Uh, and *committed* means . . ."?), and _ chooses to fill the part-time or full-time *role* of co-nurturer, guide, and supporter to one or more of their partner's children from a prior union." Note what this definition implies: *"stepparent" is a family role, not the person filling the role.* If you feel that a stepparent *role* is inferior or abnormal, grant that the woman or man filling that role is not an inferior *person*!

A *stepmother* or *stepfather* can be courting, re/married, or re/divorced; custodial or not; a bioparent or not; and a different nationality, race, gender, culture, and/or religion than their mate or stepkids. Research shows that typical first-marriage mates are much more alike in these factors ("homogeneous") than average American re/married couples. Wider age gaps and older wives are also more common in re/marriages. This implies that there are more apt to be values' conflicts in stepfamily relationships than in typical biofamilies.

Note also that an adult may love (q.v.) a bioparent, and not really *want to* nurture their mate's prior kids. If the stepparent does nurture, their motives are duty, guilt, or fear of something. This lose-lose-lose scenario can occur when a minor biochild unexpectedly moves (or is forced to move) to live in their other bioparent's home. Another of the ~60 stepfamily myths is: "Your (or my) biochild/ren will always live with their other bioparent." Another is: "Your *grown* child will never come to live with us." Over time, the first of these expectations proves false in ~30% of U.S. bi-nuclear stepfamilies.

The goals of typical self-motivated stepparents are similar to those of healthy bioparents: nurture, guide, and protect needy stepkids. However, the personal, household, family, social and legal environments around adults in stepparent roles differ in ~*40* ways (..10/co-p-dfrnces.htm). This makes defining and filling the responsibilities of the stepparenting role *effectively* a real challenge. This is equally true for most co-grandparents, aunts, and uncles!

Co-parent Project 6 invites courting couples to _ earn

the special needs of each potential stepchild, and _ outline the related responsibilities of each bioparent and stepparent in their several co-parenting homes. See *Caregiver, Family map, Family roles, Family rules, Family structure, Family system, Needs, Nurturing, Psychological parent, Step-, Stepchild,* and Chapter 3. If you're re/married, also see ..10/ project10.htm.

Structural (family) map: a diagram of how members of a one-home or multi-home nuclear family relate to each other relative to rank, responsibility, power, and communications. Such diagrams can help you *see* and resolve structural problems. See *Family map, Family structure,* and http://sfhelp.org/ 09/map-str1.htm for perspective and map examples.

Subself: a semi-independent functional "part" of a personality, like a member of an orchestra or sports team. All kids and adults seem to have *Regular, Vulnerable, Guardian,* and probably *Higher* (spiritual) subselves who comprise their *inner* family (personality). They constantly interact with the environment and each other to cause "inner voices" (thought streams), images, memories, urges, hunches, emotions, dreams, and some bodily sensations. Most personal and social discord (including re/divorce) comes from subselves ignoring or distrusting their skilled leader, the Self (p. 139). See *False self, Multiplicity, Personality, Splitting,* Project 1, and the book "Who's *Really* Running Your Life?" (Xlibris.com).

Therapy is a voluntary or forced, focused experiential (mental + spiritual + emotional) process aiming to reduce current or chronic discomfort in a troubled person, relationship, household, or family. Therapy can be _ individual (child, teen, or adult), _ marital (couples), _ family, or _ groups of individuals, couples, or families. Therapy may be provided by one therapist, co-therapists, or a multi-disciplinary team. It can be inpatient (e.g. in a mental ward or hospital), outpatient (connected to an in-patient facility), or independent. I believe most therapy (vs. counseling) clients are currently or chronically dominated by false selves, and don't know it.

It's estimated that there are over 300 *types* of "talk" and other therapies, like Gestalt, cognitive, object relations, transpersonal, behavioral, short-term (brief), confrontational, psychodrama, psycho-synthesis, insight, family systems, grief, massage, hypnotherapy, bibliotherapy, rational-emotive, inner-family, pastoral, psychoanalysis, Theophostic, addiction, Jungian, EMDR, dance-and-movement, art, voice dialog, aroma, pre-marital, problem-focused, client-focused, paradoxical, wholistic, systemic, and transactional. This demonstrates our wonderful, vexing human complexity, and the wide range of evolving ideas about how to promote constructive change and comfort.

Therapy usually involves a mix of teaching, clarifying, confronting, venting, affirming, and problem solving. Many types include emotional "catharsis," or release (crying, intense venting, and/or raging). *Counseling* may include some or most of these, but focuses more on information exchange than on emotions or personality restructuring. Many people use *therapy* and *counseling* interchangeably.

Commonly, therapy is offered by licensed professional counselors (LPCs), licensed clinical social workers (LCSW), licensed marriage and family therapists, (LMFT), clergy with special training (pastoral counseling), clinical psychologists (MS, MSEd, and MC), and psychiatrists (MDs). Each has her or his unique knowledge bases, theoretical models, and preferred way of diagnosing and intervening. To my knowledge, few such professionals get any informed training on what you're reading in this series of books. For help in picking an effective stepfamily counselor, see ..11/counsel.htm.

Toxic relationship. A *toxin* is a cellular poison. A toxic relationship is one between subselves or people that consistently impedes filling someone's key true (vs. surface) needs (p. 49), including healing psychological wounds. Symptoms of a toxic relationship are someone often feeling a mix of anxiety or fear, shame, guilt, hurt or emotional numbness, frustration, sadness, and anger. A glaring symptom and cause is one or both partners often being controlled by a protective false self.

By definition, people in toxic relationships have chaotic *inner* families which usually mirror the dynamics and low-nurturance level of their childhood families. People who have rarely or never experienced a high-nurturance relationship or human setting are likely to equate low-nurturance with *normal*, and accept, complain, or endure it. See *Love, Marriage, Need, Nurture, Parent, Relationship, Wholistic health,* and Projects 6 and 7.

True Self (capital "S") is the part of a personality whose natural talent is to be an effective inner-family leader. As life experience and knowledge accumulate, your Self makes increasingly wise, wide-angle, long-range decisions *if allowed to by other subselves.* When their Self is steadily in charge in calm times and crises, people report feeling combinations of *centered, grounded, focused, light, calm, resilient, optimistic, sure, confident, alert, alive, aware, energized, serene, purposeful, motivated, clear, and balanced.* Selves can be disabled by other distrustful personality parts, causing unhealthy, harmful, or ineffective decisions. (Re)divorce suggests one or both mates are dominated by false selves (q.v.). *Inner* family therapy is one way to empower disabled true Selves. See *Happiness, Inner family, Personality, Splitting, Subself,* and Project 1.

Wholistic health: wholistic (usually spelled *holistic*) means (mental + spiritual + emotional + physical). *Health* means "functioning and growing at maximum human potential." Jack and Sarah Tilmon (Chapter 7) were each physically healthy, but (I believe) their personalities and emotional balances had been significantly impaired since early childhood. Hence their respective *wholistic* healths were low.

Because their lifestyles were all they knew, impaired wholistic health felt *normal* to Jack and Sarah. I suspect young Patty McLean's wholistic health was declining because of the *unintended* emotional-spiritual deprivations (low nurturance levels) in her two homes. This continued deprivations preceding her parents' separating. The relative personal and family nurturance levels of Karen and Rick Cohen and their kids seemed significantly higher to me.

The *spiritual* health of persons, couples, and families is controversial, hard to assess impartially, and (I believe) vital to wholistic health. Psychologically-wounded people minimize spirituality, become obsessed with it, and/or mistake *religion* for it. I believe many *religious* kids and adults like Jack Tilmon are trapped in fear and shame-promoting belief systems taught them in early impressionable years. Such rigid, judgmental belief systems diminish wholistic health, and promote false-self dominance and denial of it. For perspective on this, read "When God Becomes a Drug," by recovering Episcopalian priest Fr. Leo Booth. Nurturing (vs. toxic) spiritual beliefs and practices enhance personal wholistic health and family nurturance levels, beyond any question.

I believe that a family's (or any group's) degree of wholistic health is directly proportional to the nurturance level of each adult's *inner* family. That in turn is proportional to how often the person's true Self leads the other subselves. What's your view? How high-nurturance are the leaders in *your* family? In your childhood family? What would a knowledgeable, objective observer say? See *Caregiving, Family functioning, Family system, Need, Nurture, Neglect, Personality splitting, Psychological parent, Recovery, Toxic,* and Projects 1 and 5.

Your Own Definitions . . .

H) Selected Resources

Two of the five major hazards that promote stepfamily conflict, heartache, and eventual re/divorce are *unawareness*, and lack of *informed* stepfamily support. The resources below can help you combat both of these. Using resources like these can raise the odds you'll make three wise re/marriage choices together *if* your true Selves are doing the choosing.

These resources are just as useful if you're already re/married. They're organized by . . .

- Recommended books, by courtship project. Titles for professionals are shown at the end of the section.
- Selected websites and articles.
- Organizations.
- Newsletters.
- Family games, and . . .
- Co-parent support groups

Check the Web version of this chapter for updates: http://sfhelp.org/11/resources.htm.

Recommended Books, by Project

Some of these titles are out of print. Major booksellers can often locate and mail you copies for a reasonable cost. Try Amazon.com, Barnes and Noble (bn.com), and the Tattered Cover (www.tatteredcover.com). Larger public library systems have cross-indexing services that allow you to borrow books shelved in another location.

Project 1) Assess for Psychological Wounds

Who's _Really_ Running Your Life?—Free Your Self From Custody, and Guard Your Kids, by Peter Gerlach, MSW; Xlibris Corp., Philadelphia, PA; 2000. This is for people who want to assess themselves and past and present co-parenting partners for false-self dominance and related wounds. The book outlines a way to discover and recover from these, and protecting minor kids from them: inner-family therapy. Most of the book is available in the series of articles and worksheets at http://sfhelp.org/01/links01.htm. The book's bibliography and http://sfhelp.org/11/booklist.htm recommend other Project-1 titles.

Project 2) Build Effective Communication Skills

"_Satisfactions_—7 Relationship Skills You Need to Know," By Peter Gerlach, MSW; Xlibris, Corp; Philadelphia, PA, 2001. Based on 30 years' study and professional experience, this book proposes key attitudes and seven communication skills to resolve most internal and social conflicts _if_ your true Self is leading your inner family. Typical divorced families, foster families, and stepfamilies are riddled with both kinds of conflicts, and few of their co-parents know the skills. This book differs significantly from these, which are still helpful:

"Brain Sex—The Real Difference Between Men and Women,"** by Anne Moir, Ph.D., and David Jessel; Dell Publishing division of Bantam Doubleday, New York, New NY; 1989. An interesting, well-researched outline of why "male brains" and "female brains" experience the world and communicate _differently_.

"How to Talk so Kids Will Listen, and Listen So Kids Will Talk;" by Adele Faber and Elaine Mazlish; Avon Books, New York, NY: 1980. Clear, compassionate, and practical.

"If You Could Hear What I Cannot Say—Learning to Communicate With The Ones You Love,"** by Dr. Nathaniel Brandon; 1983. Bantam Books, New York, NY. A classic text and workbook.

"Fighting For Your Marriage—Positive Steps For Preventing Divorce and Preserving a Lasting Love," by Howard Markman, Scott Stanley, and Susan L. Blumberg; 1994. Jossey-Bass Publishers, San Francisco. A clear, well-grounded, well-illustrated guide to effective couples communication and methodical, co-operative problem solving.

"The Dance of Anger," by Harriet G. Lerner, Ph.D.; 1985. Harper and Rowe, Publishers, Inc., New York, NY. Though slanted toward women, this is an excellent book for anyone wishing to express and use anger constructively.

"Couple Communication I—Talking Together," by Sherod Miller, Elam Nunnally, and Daniel Wackman, ; 1979. Interpersonal Communications, Inc., Minneapolis, MN; Also available: a 1982 four-session workshop guide with two audiotapes, based on the book. Timeless.

"People Skills—How to assert yourself, listen to others, and resolve conflicts;" by Robert Bolton, Ph.D.; Prentice-Hall, Inc., Englewood Cliffs, NJ; 1979. Selected by the American Management Association, and totally applicable to couples and families. Bolton outlines five of the seven skills in Project 2, and omits some keys: inner-family harmony, digging down to true problems, awareness bubbles, and R(espect) messages.

"You Just Don't Understand—Women and Men in Conversation;" by Deborah Tannen, Ph.D., 1990. Ballentine Books, New York, NY. A readable, practical paperback on the differing communication styles of men and women, by a linguistics professor.

Projects 3 and 4: Books About Families and Stepfamilies

There have been scores of lay books published since 1976 on stepfamilies and stepparenting. Most of them are out of print because of low demand and (I think) narrow or off-target scope. Not one of them describes the five hazards or seven projects in this book. Many are autobiographical and/or aimed solely at stepmothers, despite stepfathers outnumbering them. Here are some classics, including books for co-parents in psychological recovery. See the Stepfamily Association of America's online catalog of lay adult, child, and professional stepfamily titles at http://saafamilies.org. Also ask your public or school library staff for stepfamily books for kids. There are more titles below, for Project 6.

"7 Habits of Highly Effective Families—Building a Beautiful Family Culture in a Turbulent World;" by Stephen R. Covey; Golden Books Publishing Co. New York, NY; 1997. By the acclaimed author of "7 Habits of Highly Effective People," who is an ardent proponent of living on purpose and family mission statements.

"Becoming a Stepfamily: Patterns of Development in Remarried Families;" by Patricia L. Papernow Ph.D.; Gestalt Institute of Cleveland; 1998. Though somewhat clinical, this is a clear, insightful exposition of different kinds of stepfamilies and how they evolve. By a stepmom, researcher, and clinician endorsed by the Stepfamily Association of America.

"How to Win as A Stepfamily," by John and Emily Visher; Dembner Books, New York, NY; 1982. A classic, by the wise, dedicated founders of the Stepfamily Association of America.

"Money Advice for Your Successful Remarriage—Handling Delicate Financial Issues With Love and Understanding;" by Patricia Schiff Estess. Betterway Publications, 2nd ed.; 1996. By the remarried founding editor of Sylvia Porter's Personal Finance Magazine.

"Second Chances," by Judith Wallerstein and Sandra Blakeslee; Ticknor & Fields, New York, NY. 1989 (follow-on to "Surviving the Breakup" below). A controversial description on how a group of typical California divorced families fared fifteen years after their family separation. While helpful, this book (like most in its class) omits any significant assessment of the impact of pre-separation and co-parent-childhood emotional neglects and the psychological wounds they promote.

* **"Stepfamily Realities**—How to Overcome Difficulties and Have A Happy Family;" by Margaret Newman; New

Harbinger, 1994. By a veteran Australian stepmother, therapist, and educator, this is one of the two best stepfamily
books I have read in 20 years of research. The other is
Papernow (above).

"Stepfamilies—Love, Marriage, and Parenting in the First
Decade;" by Dr. James H. Bray and John Kelly; Broadway
Books, New York, NY; 1998. A clear summary of the findings
of a multi-year study of typical stepfamilies.

"The Stepfamily: Living, Loving, and Learning," by Elizabeth Einstein; Macmillan Publishing Co., Inc., New York, NY;
1982. Many good ideas by a veteran stepfamily supporter.

Project 5: Spot and Free Up Blocked Grief

Many writings about grieving focus only healing bonds
broken by death. The help that books like those below offers
us "losers" applies to healing *all* our life-long losses.

"A Time To Grieve," by Bertha G. Simos; Family Service
Association, New York, NY; 1979. A therapist for 30 years,
Ms. Simos offers her timeless learnings about loss and griev-
ing in this paperback.

"The Courage To Grieve," by Judy Tatelbaum; Harper
and Rowe Publishers, New York, NY; 1980. A positive, upbeat,
realistic approach to accepting and moving beyond major losses,
by a therapist specializing in grief-work. See also **You Don't
Have to Suffer** (1989) by Ms. Tatelbaum.

"The Dance of Anger—A Woman's Guide to Changing
the Patterns of Intimate Relationships;" by Harriet G. Lerner,
Ph.D.; Harper and Rowe Publishers, New York, NY, 1985. Helpful for men, too, because many of us were taught to repress this
essential good-grief emotion, and/or to feel guilt, shame, and
anxiety if we express it.

"How It Feels When Parents Divorce," by Jill Krementz;
Alfred A. Knopf, New York, NY; 1984. Moving, honest com-
mentary from a score of kids from 7 to 16 on how parental
divorce affected them. Photos add to the impact of this hard-
back.

"Necessary Losses—The Loves, Illusions, Dependencies and Impossible Expectations That All of Us Have to Give Up in Order to Grow;" by Judith Viorst; Ballentine Books, New York, NY; 1986. A thoughtful, thorough exploration of the broken bonds we all experience, starting with separation from our mothers as infants. The authoress is a veteran Freudian clinician.

"Rebuilding—When Your Relationship Ends," by Bruce Fisher; Impact Publishers, San Louis Obispo, CA, 1987. A very reader-friendly, clear, realistic, helpful paperback for people grieving the loss of a love.

"Transitions—Making Sense Out of Life's Changes;" by William Bridges, Ph.D.; Addison-Wesley Publishing Co., New York, NY; 1996. A clear, thought-provoking acknowledgement of the constant changes in our lives, and our human need for healthy grieving.

"On Death and Dying," by Elisabeth Kubler-Ross; Macmillan Publishing Co., New York, NY; 1969. A classic on understanding and living well with *relationship* losses, including anticipating our own death.

Project 6) Mission Statements and Co-parenting

"The ACOA's Guide to Raising Healthy Children—A Parenting Hand book for Adult Children of Alcoholics;" by Dr. Jim Mastrich and Bill Birnes; Macmillan Publishing Co., New York, NY; 1988. This book applies to *all* wounded co-parents recovering from a low-nurturance childhood! So does this one:

"Breaking the Cycle of Addiction—A Parent's Guide To Raising Healthy Kids;" by Patricia O'Gorman and Philip Oliver-Diaz; Health Communications, Pompano Beach, Inc., FL; 1987. I suspect all addictions are a surface symptom of false-self dominance.

"Growing Up Divorced—Helping Your Child Through The Stages . . .;" by Linda Bird Franke; Linden Press, Simon & Schuster, Inc.; New York, NY; 1983.

"How to Develop A Family Mission Statement" (audio cassette—The 7 Habits Family Leadership Series), By Stephen

Covey (1996). I suspect there's a printed version among Covey's many writings. See his Web site for many useful resources.

"Making It As A Stepparent—New Roles, New Rules;" by Claire Berman; Harper & Row, New York, NY. 1986.

"Stepfather" (2nd Ed.), by Tony Gorman; Gentle Touch Publishers, Inc.; Boulder, CO; 1985. Though stepdads outnumber stepmoms, this is one of only a handful of books for the former. Real men *do* read books!

"Stepkids: a Survival Guide for Teenagers in Stepfamilies," by Ann Getzoff and Carolyn McClenahan; Walker & Co., New York, NY. 1984.

"Stepparenting—A Sympathetic Guide to Living With and Loving Other People's Children;" by Jean and Veryl Rosenbaum; E.P. Dutton, New York, NY; 1978. Notice how the title leaves out re/married *bioparents*. A brief, helpful book.

"The Good Stepmother—a Practical Guide," by Karen Savage and Patricia Adams; Crown Publishers, Inc., New York, NY; 1988. One of many titles for struggling stepmoms.

Project 7) Re/marriage and Adult Relationships

These are representative. There are many more!

"Co-dependent No More—How To Stop Controlling Others and Start Caring For Yourself," by Melodie Beattie; Harper & Row, Inc. New York, NY; 1987. A pioneering and still relevant introduction to the widespread condition of toxic relationship addiction.

"Embracing Each Other—Relationship as Teacher, Healer, & Guide;" by Hal Stone, Ph.D., and Sidra Winkelman, Ph.D.; New World Library, San Rafael, CA; 1989. An extension of their first book, examining how the selves within several people interact. This is what Hendrix (below) leaves out. A real eye opener!

"Fighting For Your Marriage—Positive Steps For Preventing Divorce and Preserving a Lasting Love"—see the entry under Project 2 above.

"Getting The Love You Want—A Guide for Couples," by

Harville Hendrix, Ph.D.; Harper Collins (Perennial Library); 1992. The title seems more fitting for singles (see below).

"Is It Love, Or Is It Addiction?;" By Brenda Schaeffer; Hazelden Educational Materials, Center City, MN; 1987. A clear introduction to the common false-self risk of confusing "love" with relationship addiction, by an empathic veteran therapist.

"Keeping The Love You Find—A Guide For Singles;" by Harville Hendrix, Ph.D.; Pocket Books, a division of Simon & Schuster, Inc.; New York, NY; 1992. A thought-provoking paperback that says without *awareness*, most marriage decisions are made by our unconscious minds. Hendrix posits that the aim of real marriage is to heal one's self by *intentionally* supporting your partner's recovery. "Healing" relates to a cascading series of psychological wounds many of us receive unintentionally in our first four to six years.

"Lifebalance—How To Simplify and Bring Harmony to Your Everyday Life," by Linda and Richard Eyre; A Fireside Book, published by Simon & Schuster, New York, NY; 1997. This is an enthusiastic, practical framework for couples who want to keep their priorities straight, and act on them intentionally to take charge of hectic lives. The Eyres promote weekly intentional balancings of personal, family, and professional goals and needs. A helpful guide for Project 12 in this series— doing 11 co-parent projects at once, plus "other life," without losing your balance (inner-family harmony).

"People Skills," by Robert Bolton, Ph.D.; See the entry under Project 2.

"The Good Marriage—How and Why Love Lasts;" by Judith Wallerstein, Ph.D., and Sandra Blakeslee; Warner Books, 1996; Also an audiotape. A helpful, practical study of the specific factors that 50 successful couples say keep them thriving. This may depress and/or intimidate aware, unrecovering survivors of childhood trauma because what it describes will probably seem alien or unattainable.

"The New Peoplemaking," by Virginia Satir; Science and Behavior Books, Inc., Palo Alto, CA; 1988. A paperback update of the classic on healthy personal and family relations.

The Struggle For Intimacy," by Janet G. Woititz; Health Communications, Inc.; Deerfield Beach, FL.; 1985. Brief, elegant, and instructive, for people recovering from childhood wounding. Janet's several other books are helpful too.

"Women Who Love Too Much," by Robin Norwood; Pocket Books, New York, NY; 1985. Widely read help for women in self-depleting co-dependent (addictive) relationships.

"Weddings, A Family Affair: The New Etiquette for Second Marriages and Couples with Divorced Parents," by Margorie Engel, Ph.D.; Wilshire Publications, 1998. Margorie is a veteran stepmom, educator, and the dedicated president of the Stepfamily Association of America.

Books For Professionals

"Becoming a Stepfamily", by Patricia Papernow. See the entry above.

"Divorced Families—A Multidisciplinary Developmental View;" by Constance R. Ahrons and Roy H. Rodgers; W.W. Norton, & Co., New York, NY; 1987. Traces the reorganization of typical biofamilies experiencing divorce separation and parental remarriage.

* **"Internal Family Systems Theory**," by Richard C. Schwartz, Ph.D.; The Guilford Press, New York, NY; 1995. This compassionate, seminal book applies family-systems principles to working therapeutically toward harmonizing individuals' *inner* families. Based on well over a decade of research and clinical experience, by an internationally recognized expert in healing dissociative (*inner* family) disorders.

"Old Loyalties, New Ties—Therapeutic Strategies with Stepfamilies;" by Emily B. Visher, Ph.D., and John S. Visher, M.D.; Brunner / Mazel Publishers, New York, NY; 1988. Adds experience and insight to their first book (below).

"Recycling the Family—Remarriage After Divorce (2nd edition)," by Frank F. Furstenberg, Jr., and Graham B. Spanier; SAGE Publications, Newbury Park, CA; 1987. Helpful sociological perspective.

"Remarriage & Stepparenting—Current Research and Theory;" edited by Kay Pasley and Marilyn Ihinger-Tallman; Guilford Press, New York, NY; 1987. The two-year findings of nine scholars focusing on the title subject. As usual, little is said about co-parents' childhood deprivations and wounds.

"Remarried Family Relationships," by Lawrence H. Ganong and Marilyn Coleman; SAGE Publications, Series on Close Relationships; Thousand Oaks, CA; 1994. Helpful findings and observations by two veteran stepfamily scholars.

"Stepfamilies—A Guide To Working With Stepparents and Stepchildren;" by Emily B. Visher, Ph.D., and John S. Visher, M.D.; Brunner / Mazel Publishers, New York, NY; 1979. The first of its genre, and still helpful.

"The Remarried Family—Challenge and Promise;" by Esther Wald; Family Service Association of America, New York, NY; 1981. A thorough Freudian / sociological view of stepfamily dynamics.

"Treating the Remarried Family," by Clifford J. Sager, Hollis Steer Brown, Helen Crohn, Tamara Engle, Evelyn Rodstein, and Libby Walker; Brunner Mazel, Publishers, New York, NY; 1983. Based on the work with hundreds of stepfamilies by the Remarried Consultation Service of the Jewish Board of Family and Children's Services of New York City.

"Understanding Stepfamilies—Their Structure and Dynamics," Edited by Craig A. Everett, Ph.D.; The Haworth Press, Binghamton, NY; 1997. A collection of 11 manuscripts from scholars in five countries. Dr. Everett has edited the Haworth Press's quarterly *Journal of Divorce and Remarriage* since 1983. Helpful for widening your perspective.

None of these books proposes assessing for or treating the five hazards in Chapter 4. I hope to publish a book on these for clinicians in 2003.

On-Line (Web) Resources

There's a growing array of informational and interactional sites to support adults and kids in stepfamilies. I've seen none

aimed explicitly at courting co-parents except http://
www.brideagain.com.

+ The non-profit educational site underlying this series of
books is http://sfhelp.org. (Stepfamily inFormation).

+ For **a free 8-module course** for groups and couples based
on this book, see http://sfhelp.org/07/bhsf/intro.htm.

+ Newsgroup: alt.support.stepparents. Once again, re/wed-
ded *bio*parents are excluded in the title.

+ Typical stepfamily and stepparent websites: http://
sfhelp.org/11/resources.htm.

Most Internet services (America Online, Microsoft Network,
Prodigy, etc.) have forums or chat groups for "stepparents"
(i.e. co-parents). Use the "search" feature: they're worth digging for. Internet sites change fast. Use search keywords like
stepfamily, *stepparent*, *stepchild*, and *remarriage*, with several
Internet search "engines" (programs). See other links below.

Organizations

Hazelden Publishing and Education, 15251 Pleasant Valley Rd., Center City, MN 55012. A rich source of multi-media
recovery (Project 1) materials, for 50 years. See their extensive
mail-order catalog for *many* resources for adults, kids, and professionals. 1-800-328-9000; Internet: http://www.hazelden.org.

Health Communications, Inc., 3201 S.W. 15th St., Deerfield
Beach, FL. 33442; 1-800-441-5569. Providing health and re-
covery-related materials and services for lay people and health
professionals since 1976. Call for a catalog, or see their online
bookstore at http://www.hci-online.com.

The Johnson Institute, 7205 Ohms Lane, Minneapolis, MN
55439. Voice 1-800-231-5165; FAX: 1-612-831-1631. The institute has a wide selection of educational recovery materials
for adults, kids, and professionals. Their materials are sold by
Hazelden (above.)

The Stepfamily Association of America (non-profit) provides
lay and professional materials by mail, supports self-help chapters, co-sponsors a bi-monthly magazine (see below), sponsors

annual professional and lay conferences, provides stepfamily advocacy; 650 J St. # 205, Lincoln, NE 68508; 1-800-735-0329, or 1-(402) 477-7837; Internet: http://saafamilies.org.

Stepfamily Foundation of New York: Directed by stepfamily pioneer and author Jeanette Lofas, C.S.W., the Foundation provides stepfamily-support materials by mail, and professional counseling by phone. Internet: http://www.stepfamily.org.

Rainbows: Materials, leader training, and consultation for organizations sponsoring divorce, death, and re/marriage grieving-support groups for children, teens, and adults; 1111 Tower Rd., Schaumburg, IL 60173; International headquarters: E-mail: rainbowshdqtrs@worldnet.att.net; 1-847-310-1880

Prepare/Enrich: Provides diagnostic questionnaires and computerized scoring service for counselors to use with clients already married, or considering first *or re/marriage* (Prepare MC). For information or referral to trained local counselors, call 1-800-331-1661, or write P.O. Box 190, Minneapolis, MN, 55440-0190. E-mail: cs@lifeinnovations.com; Internet: http://www.lifeinnovation.com

Mothers Without Custody (MWoC): a national network of self-help groups and resource people for women who give up child custody, voluntarily or not. Headquarters: PO Box 27418, Houston, TX, 77227. Call directory assistance to see if there are any local chapters.

Newsletters and Magazines

A number of stepfamily/stepparent **websites** offer electronic newsletters. These are the only ink-and-paper ones I know of:

"Bride Again—the Only Magazine for Encore Brides." See [http://www.brideagain.com].

"iStepfamily" – a new (9/02) magazine for blended families sponsored by Weyant Press [www.wyantpress.com] - $12.75/yr.

"Life's Landmines Into Landscapes" a ~10-page publication edited by stepfamily co-parent Debra S. Mogg, providing "stepfamily information, education, inspiration, and encouragement." Yearly subscriptions are $15.95. Voice / FAX: 1-(504)-443-1449; e-mail Lifestep@aol.com.

"Your Stepfamily" is a new (mid-2002) bimonthly magazine co-sponsored by the Stepfamily Association of America - $21/year. This replaces the prior quarterly newsletter "SAA Families." See [http://www.yourstepfamily.com] or call 1-800-277-2583 for subscription information.

Family Sharing / Communication Games

LifeStories: A non-competitive (win-win) board game that provides "entertaining conversation between family, friends, and people you have just met; 2 to 8 players, ages 6 to 106"; In some physical and virtual toy stores. Use your favorite Web search engine.

The Ungame: A non-competitive, fun board game to help kids and adults safely learn about each other. Optional materials for couples, families, children (5+), and teens. Available through many toy and book stores, and several on-line merchants. A nice re/wedding present!

Classes and Support Group Materials

Building A Healthy Stepfamily. The free outline of an 8-module course for courting co-parents, based on this book. This outline is based on classes I've taught since 1985 to hundreds of co-parents: http://sfhelp.org/07/bhsf/intro.htm.

Founding and Maintaining an Effective Co-parent Support Group: a series of downloadable articles based on _ my experience with 15 such groups since 1981, and _ the main topics in this and related books. Download free from http://sfhelp.org/11/sg-intro.htm. Also available as a booklet at ..site/ftp/download.htm.

Compared to these, I respectfully believe the following are of less practical (educational) value. They're of high *support* value, because they each promote co-parents focusing and talking together:

Building A Successful Stepfamily: a 13-part Christian-oriented seminar authored and presented by Ron L. Deal, M.MFT. Based on the works of Elizabeth Einstein, Patricia Papernow, and Emily and John Visher, this course is a helpful introduction to surface stepfamily issues. See http://www.betterlife.org/Stepfamily.htm, e-mail rdeal@swchurchchristjboro.org, or call 1-870-932-9254 for information.

Learning To Step Together, by Cecile Currier, LCSW. A manual for professionals leading workshops for stepfamily couples. Includes handout masters. Paperback, about $18; from the Stepfamily Association of America (above). Very simplistic.

New Beginnings: Skills for Single Parents and Stepparents, by Drs. Don Dinkmeyer, Gary McKay, and Joyce McKay. An eight session audio-visual package of materials covering parenting issues, self esteem, relationships and behavior, personality and emotional development, communication skills, decision making, discipline, and common family conflicts. From Research Press, Box 3177, Dept. 97, Champaign, IL. 61826; (217) 352-3273.

Stepfamilies Stepping Ahead: An 89-page lay leader's manual ($10) and participant texts ($10 each) for 8-session individual family or adult group programs. Order from the Stepfamily Association of America (above). A clear, readable, basic introduction.

Smart Steps for Adults and Children in Stepfamilies, developed by Francesca Adler-Baeder, Ph.D. This 12-hour research-based, educational program curriculum is for remarried or partnering couples and their children, and focuses on building couple and family strength. The program uses informational presentations, hands-on exercises, group discussions, and media. The 250+ page Curriculum includes leader lesson guides for adult and child programs, background readings, hand-out masters, resource list pre/post evaluation questionnaires, two videos and a CD with Power Point slides, hand-out files, and evaluation.

Strengthening Stepfamilies: A kit of readings, recordings, and activities for adults and children. Designed for five weekly sessions of 2-2½ hours each, with lay or professional facilitators; leader's guide included. About $90 per kit from American Guidance Service (AGS); Publishers' Bldg., PO Box 99, Circle Pines, MN 55014; 1-(800)-328-2560.

Index

A

abandonment
  defined 493
  expectation of 464
  fear of. *See* fear, of abandon-
    ment
  parental 108
abortion 52
absent parent. *See* co-parent
  defined 494
abuse
  3 requisites for 494
  child 495
  defined 494
  physical 495
  sexual 106, 430, 495
  spiritual 108, 495
  verbal 495
accepting losses 264
accountability (personal) 53, 60
ACoA. *See* Adult Child of
  Alcoholics
acting out (behavior)
  226, 346, 378, 438, 495, 513
addict, defined 305

addiction
  74, 120, 226, 252, 289, 293
  12-step recovery 13
    relapses 162
    "walk the talk" 159
  4 types of 160
    relationship
      305, 365, 544, 545
  admitting and managing 156
  and blocked grief 78, 304
  and false selves 161
  and pseudo recovery 162
  courtship red light 13
  cross (multiple)
    113, 161, 162, 305
  defined 160, 496
  denial of 161
  dry drunks 159
  implies splitting 406
  in prospective co-parents 485
  in relatives 487
  is not a "disease" 414
  is self medication 77
  predisposition to 161
  stinkin' thinkin 159
  traits of an 161

body image 464
Bolton, Robert 545
bonds (emotional) 112
  broken
    healing 58
    identifying 226
  defined 254
  difficulty forming 143, 499
  impaired infantile 255, 293
  in high-nurturance families 53
  relationship 498
  true vs. pseudo 59
Booth, Leo 537
boundaries
  family 59
  interpersonal
    53, 57, 277, 279, 458, 484
  childrens' 63, 467, 470
  co-grandparents 487
  with troubled ex mates 316
Bowlby, John 262
Bradshaw, John 73, 304

C

Campbell, David 325
caregiver. *See* co-parent
  defined 499
Catastrophizer subself 387
change
  causes losses 12, 257
  changeless 159
  fear of 527
  first order 84, 159
  in family systems 515
  positive view of 64
  second order 159
  tolerating 464
character defects 73
child. *See* also stepchild
  abuse. *See* abuse, child
  adjustment tasks

  assessing 472
  checklist 454
  from biofamily breakup 466
  stepfamily 469
conception 57, 460
  planned 52
custody 491
development tasks 457
discipline 61
financial support 491
  unpaid 319
"latch key" 454
neglect 480
of divorced parents 430
used as a weapon or spy 468
childhood
  low nurturance 433
  memory gaps about 405
childish behavior 495
chuckling about discomfort 156
Cinderella 530
clergy 25, 280, 479, 503
  choosing 390
  stepfamily unaware
    69, 80, 348, 363, 433, 445
co- (prefix) 500
co-alcoholic 413
co-dependence
  13, 86, 156, 546. *See also*
    addiction types, relationship
  enabling 421
  traits of (worksheet) 413
Co-dependents Anonymous
  (CoDA)
    158, 366, 413, 420
co-grandparents
  60, 153, 332, 338, 427, 456,
    474, 486, 487, 532
  and blocked grief 292
co-parents
  12 projects for 122
    reasons for 131

improvement goals 180
innerpersonal 179
mapping 87, 184
notebook or journal 184
outcomes
  16 possible 171
patterns 228
physical contact 61
premises about 168
R(espect) messages 170, 316
reality check 172
styles 428
tips for improving 192
compassion 229
Compassionate Friends (grief
  support group) 281, 312
compulsion
  vs. commitment 273
conflicts. *See* stepfamily,
  conflicts
  4 types of 87, 181
    innerpersonal 87, 176, 501
  avoidance of. *See* avoidances,
    of conflict
  defined 501
confusion (inner-voice battles)
  179
Connolly, Joy 41
counseling vs. therapy 535
court battles. *See* co-parent, legal
  battles
courtship
  6 questions about 126
  7 projects for suitors 135
  and chronic lying 14
  and kids' behaviors 13
  and recent losses 12
  and wounded partners 72
  danger signs 9
  illusions 78, 114, 117, 178
  is a poor guide 219, 255

metaphor for 117
motivations 238
priorities 449
rescuing 115
typical needs in 115
Covey, Stephen 174, 330
crying 294
  value of 264
cycles
  attack-react 317, 477
  diet-regain 306
  low family nurturance
    146, 369
    breaking the 80
  rage-remorse 289
  re/divorce 115, 120

D

Deal, Ron 551
death
  of a first spouse 372
  premature 71, 73
demand vs. request 337
denial (reality distortion)
  67. *See also* personality,
    splitting, 6 wounds
  defined 503
  of denial 304
  of splitting traits 410
depression 71, 120, 252, 290
  anniversary 260, 306
  chronic 304
  from others' traumas 307
  industry 252
  may be grief
    77, 85, 263, 271, 289, 304
deprivation (childhood). *See*
  neglect
  from kin absence 64
descendents, guided image of 37

nurturing your 126
pre-nuptial agreements
    429, 436, 490
preparation course 388
same gender 375
vs. first marriage 354
Reactive Attachment Disorder
    293
reality distortion. *See* personality
    splitting, wounds
recovery, defined 527
recreation 64
rejection and abandonment
    57, 209
relationship
    3 types of 87
    approach-avoid
        158, 289, 408
    cut offs 220, 290
    defined 528
    enmeshed
        160, 254, 279, 487
    failed 293
    fear-based 408
    high-nurturance factors 85
    innerpersonal 72, 193
    interdependent 55
    mission statement 127
    skills, learning 459
    toxic, defined 153, 535
    triangles
        11, 86, 127, 189, 190, 195, 292, 410
        example of 250
religion
    conflicts over 380
    vs. spirituality 537
requests vs. demands 59
rescuing 107, 367
    compulsive 155
respect 182
    among family members 57

for a partner's denials 216
    mutual 477
revenge, in a family 61
rights, personal 84
rituals, comforting 254
role strain 511
roles. *See* family, roles
rules. *See* family, rules, and
    stepfamily, rules

S

Satan 406
Satir, Virginia 304, 545
Schaef, Anne Wilson 413
Schaeffer, Brenda 365, 545
schoolphobia and blocked grief
    290
Schwartz, Richard 139, 365
Seasonal Affective Disorder
    (S.A.D.) 306
Self
    higher 267
    true
        57, 84, 109, 117, 140, 228, 461
        and re/marriage decision
            491
        defined 536
        disabled 66
        symptoms of 154
self
    abandonment (neglect)
        66, 310
        healing 464
    affirmations 311
    centered 409
    comfort 277, 465
    compassion 276
    criticism 407. *See also* Inner
        Critic
    doubt, reducing 464
    esteem, low 407

BVG